THE HANDBOOK OF
Baby Names

THE HANDBOOK OF
Baby Names

A guide to over 5000 baby names

CLARE GIBSON

For Jack and Christeen Malan,
who proved thrice equal to the baby-naming challenge.

Published by SILVERDALE BOOKS
An imprint of Bookmart Ltd
Registered number 2372865
Trading as Bookmart Ltd
Desford Road
Enderby
Leicester LE19 4AD

© 2002 D&S Books Ltd

D&S Books Ltd
Kerswell,
Parkham Ash, Bideford
Devon, England
EX39 5PR

e-mail us at:-
enquiries@dsbooks.fsnet.co.uk

This edition printed 2002

ISBN 1-856056-83-X

Creative Director: Sarah King
Editor: Yvonne Worth
Project editor: Sarah Harris
Designer: Dave Jones

Typeset in Rotis Sans Serif

Printed in China

1 3 5 7 9 10 8 6 4 2

Contents

Introduction 6

Boys' Names 12

Girls' Names 133

Bibliography 256

Credits 256

Dedication 256

Introduction

WHAT IS A NAME? Well, a dictionary would define 'name' as a word by which something or someone is known. But if you subtly change the wording of the question and ask yourself what's in a name, you suddenly find yourself leaving the realms of dry lexicality and entering a fluid world, in which a rich myriad of meanings and associations – portraits of historical personages, snatches of music, images of paintings, passages of literature and memories of faces – each tinted by personal experience, constantly shift and merge like the jewel-bright pieces of a kaleidoscope.

Apart from life itself, perhaps the most fundamentally important gift that parents can bestow upon their newborn child is its name, for a name both identifies and defines identity, a requirement that is as significant for the child as for the countless people whom it will encounter during the course of its life. Some indigenous cultures endow names with such power that their members are given two, one for everyday use and a second, secret name that is believed to contain the essence of the individual bearer and must never be divulged to strangers for fear of thus giving them the means to establish absolute control over him or her (a concept that is vividly encapsulated in the German fairytale 'Rumpelstiltskin').

But will a child's name prove a blessing or a curse? Will its name help this brand-new person to enjoy an easy passage as it sets sail on the unpredictable waters of life, or will it throw up rocky obstacles in the form of countless self-esteem-sapping, petty humiliations? Indeed, a name is so inextricably bound up with its bearer's sense of identity, and with how others see him or her, that an ill-considered choice may have life-long repercussions. (One wonders whether the Canadian communications scholar Marshall McLuhan held a long-standing grudge against his parents when he wrote, in his work *Understanding Media*, 'The name of a man is a numbing blow from which he never recovers.')

The wrong choice?

Names can, of course, be changed, be it by recourse to a nickname, a second name or even a completely new one, yet the original name will continue to live on in other people's memories. To give an example, a friend of mine (who, if you'll pardon the pun, shall remain nameless) stoically endured being called by her much-loathed first name throughout her school years, but on entering a new phase of her life, which involved moving to a different town and making new acquaintances, had no qualms about discarding it and replacing it with her second name. If that wasn't confusing enough for her childhood friends and family, on her marriage shortly thereafter, she replaced her maiden name with her husband's family name, thus completing her rebranding. Yet while those who knew her in her previous incarnation respect her decision, long-held memories cannot be erased that easily: the name that springs to mind whenever I think of her remains the one by which I originally knew her.

In my friend's case, the despised name was a traditional one with saintly connotations, but, due to notorious namesakes, others are redolent with sinister associations, notably Adolf, thanks to Herr Hitler. It is a sad truth that the actions of certain historical – or contemporary – individuals have besmirched the names of their bearers, but not necessarily forever: Guy, for example, was eschewed in England for many centuries on account of the treasonable activities of Guy Fawkes in 1603, but has now been rehabilitated.

When choosing a name for their baby, apart from avoiding names that have been tainted by infamous namesakes, there are a few other potential pitfalls that parents should be aware of. Firstly, a sequence of names whose initials would spell out a word for which their child would be mocked, such as P(atrick) I(an) G(regson). Secondly, in an era of increasing globalisation and multiculturalism, a name that may have offensive connotations in other cultures (a prime example of which can be found in Sue Browder's *The New Age Baby Name Book*, in which a certain boy's name is noted as meaning 'witness' in South African, the name in question being Paki, which, to Britons, is an overtly racist word for a person of Pakistani origin). Finally, consider how – if at all – a name could become a nickname (would Natasha become Nasty?) and if a prospective first name will partner a family name sympathetically (would little Robyn Banks grow up to become law-abiding or would Primrose Wood rejoice in her emphatically sylvan name?)

The right choice?

In the end, however, the name that is chosen for a child will be one that sounds pleasing to parental ears, although it will probably, snapshot-like, reflect the conventions, values and fashions that prevailed at the time of the baby's birth, social mores that have generally become increasingly tolerant in the twenty-first century (that is, apart from such countries as France and Brazil, where parents are still required to select a name from a legally approved list).

If a delightful-sounding name also has personal significance for the parents, then a child will be doubly blessed, and will probably be enthralled to learn the origin, or a notable bearer, of his or her name. This book differs from comparable compendiums in that it contains a wealth of notable namesakes that will not only send prospective parents on a nostalgic voyage of rediscovery through long-forgotten aspects of their past, but offers a gallery of interesting figures from history, sports and the arts to illustrate the potential of a name. Although they shouldn't be regarded as role models (and some are more notorious than notable), they will certainly act as illuminating starting points. Also included are characters drawn from fiction and legend, along with venerable figures from numerous mythological traditions and such world religions as Hinduism, Judaism, Christianity and Islam.

The natural world is yet another rich source of names, from the jewel and flower names so beloved in Victorian times, through names that evoke the sterling qualities of various birds and beasts, to sunny- or tempestuous-sounding names inspired by weather phenomena and thence to the celestial realms of the stars. Time and space can provide additional inspiration, such as a name based on the date, day or season when your baby made its world début or the place where it was conceived or born. Other potential naming possibilities include your child's appearance – and within these pages you'll find names that, for instance, echo the dark, golden or auburn hues of a person's crowning glory – as well as their behavioural characteristics, be they gentle or spirited.

Last (but not least, because there is no limit to the human imagination), the key to finding the perfect name for a baby could be an evocative name, perhaps a first name already borne by a family member or cherished friend or, if she has relinquished it, the baby's mother's maiden name, another family name that you think sounds attractive or one that celebrates your baby's cultural or national heritage. And don't let the inconvenience of a potential namesake's alternative sex put you off: a Nigel can always be commemorated in a gurgling Nigella which is also the name of a delicate flower.

The meaning of names

Whatever name you settle on, knowing its meaning will add another layer of magic to an already evocative appellation. Due to the fluid nature of language, however, meanings are not always as clear-cut as one would hope, especially when many of the names that are commonplace today originated hundreds, if not thousands, of years ago within the potent brew of a linguistic melting pot. To explain further, some historical background needs to be drawn to the fore.

Most of the languages used in the Western world evolved from Proto-Indo-European, a language that was in use before 3000 BC and that scholars speculate was derived from the tongue used by the Kurgan people of the steppes of southern Russia, nomads who eventually wandered to the Danube and Adriatic regions of Europe and beyond. A prolific progenitor, Proto-Indo-European gave life to the Indo-European family of languages, categorised in vastly simplified form below.

The Indo-European family of languages

1) Indo-Aryan, including Sanskrit, Hindi or Urdu and Romany
2) Iranian, including Persian
3) Armenian
4) Anatolian
5) Greek
6) Albanian
7) Latin (or Italic) and, through Vulgar Latin, the Romance languages, French, Italian, Spanish, Catalan, Portuguese, Rumansch or Rhaeto-Romanic, Romanian and Provençal
8) Celtic, including Celtiberian, Gaulish and Galatian; the Brythonic languages, Cumbrian, Welsh, Cornish and Breton; and the Goidelic languages, Irish Gaelic, Manx and Scots Gaelic
9) Germanic, subdivided as follows:
   a) East Germanic, including Gothic
   b) West Germanic, which today includes German, English, Frisian, Flemish, Yiddish, Dutch and Afrikaans
   c) North Germanic, including Danish, Swedish, Norwegian, Faeroese and Icelandic
10) Balto-Slavonic (or Slavic), subdivided as follows:
   a) Baltic, including Latvian and Lithuanian
   b) Slavonic, including Czech, Slovak, Bulgarian, Macedonian, Serbo-Croat, Slovene, Belorussian, Russian and Ukrainian

To clarify the attributions of many of the names in this book further, we should now home in on the evolution of the West and North German branches of Germanic, as set out below.

The evolution of West Germanic and North Germanic

1) West Germanic evolved into two languages: Low German and High German, which in turn evolved as follows:
   a) Low German evolved into three branches, Anglo-Saxon (or Old English) which was spoken from around AD 400, Old Saxon and Low Franconian
   i) Anglo-Saxon (or Old English) evolved into Middle English in around AD 1100, which in turn

contribution was Anglo-Saxon (or Old English). Next came the Norsemen, Danish (and Norwegian) Vikings, whose eventual northern English realm, the Danelaw, established in AD 886, became the province of Old Norse. Following the death of Edward the Confessor, the penultimate Anglo-Saxon king, another breed of Norsemen – the Normans, led by William, Duke of Normandy – arrived on English shores in 1066, whereafter Norman French, a dialect of Old French heavily influenced by the Old Norse spoken by the Normans' Norwegian forebears, became the prevalent language. Finally, however, the invasions ceased, and the dominant language of the British Isles gradually assimilated its Anglo-Saxon (or Old English), Old Norse and Norman French components to emerge as Middle English (which replaced French as the language of the law in England in 1362), and then Modern English.

The point of our canter through the evolution of Indo-European languages is to establish that all are to a greater or lesser extent inter-related, so that if a name's meaning is ascribed to the Old English language, it could sometimes equally have been designated as being of Germanic (given when the

gave way to Modern English in around 1550
ii) Old Saxon evolved into Middle Low German and thence into Plattdeutsch (or Low German)
iii) Low Franconian evolved into Middle Dutch and thence into Dutch and Flemish
b) High German (or Old High German, spoken from around AD 770 to 1050) evolved into Middle High German (1050–1350) and thence into Modern German
2) North Germanic evolved into Old Norse, spoken from around AD 700 to 1350, from which are derived Norwegian, Swedish, Danish, Faeroese and Icelandic

The relevance of the evolution of the Indo-European languages to this book is that many have contributed to the 'British' names that fill these pages through the successive invasions of Britain effected by their speakers. If the British Isles can be said to have an indigenous language, it is Celtic, which somehow survived both the first Roman invasion of Latin-speakers between 55 and 54 BC and the subsequent invasions of West Germanic peoples – the Jutes appropriating Kent and the Isle of Wight, the Saxons parts of the south and the Angles infiltrating the Midlands and North – from around AD 449, whose

specific Germanic source is unclear) or Old Norse origin, so similar are many of these tongues' root components. Equally, as a consequence of both the Claudian Roman conquest of Britain in AD 43 and the Norman Conquest of 1066, as well as the influence of Christianity, whose *lingua franca* was once Latin, many names identified as having an Old English source could equally be deemed to have Latin or Old French roots, while to cloud the picture further, Latin in turn borrowed many words from Greek. Yet amid this minefield of potential misattribution, the spirit of the name's meaning shines through, a far more important consideration than any etymological nitpicking or onomastic navel-gazing (which is also why, in this book, you've been spared the details of a name's original incarnation, for example, Hrodebert being the nominal ancestor of Robert).

Can the names contributed by the different peoples who, over the course of time, made up what is now the native stock of the British Isles be said to have certain characteristics? To an extent they can: Celtic names reflect personal characteristics veiled with an aura of mysticism, while Germanic and Old Norse names (which typically consist of two components, as shown in this book, which could be mixed and matched at will) convey, on the one hand, a yearning for prosperity and, on the other, a relish of savagery and a statement of noble intent.

Two other general categories were also popular among the ancestors who bequeathed us their names. Firstly, in a pious age, those drawn from the Bible, whether Hebrew, Latin or Greek in origin, along with a host of saintly names, remained perennial favourites. The more 'popish' appellations, however, were abhorred by the 17th-century Puritans, who instead preferred rugged Old Testament names – and often the more obscure, the better – or appropriated the names of qualities that they felt their children should aspire to, such as obedience, prudence and chastity. And, secondly, family names, which in turn usually owe their origin either to the first name, nickname or occupational name of a medieval ancestor – naming practices thus coming full circle – or to a place name. (Be aware, however, that, as with numerous first names, the meanings of some family names have been obscured by the many mistranslations and mispronunciations that were propagated in an age of general illiteracy.) Although usually restricted to the naming of boys, the practice of assigning first-name duties to family names was particularly prevalent during the 19th century, but today a girl is as likely to be called Taylor as a boy. Today, in fact, apart from the danger of causing a child life-long embarrassment, it seems that anything goes.

About this book

Collating all of the names that have ever existed in every culture would certainly have proved a life-long task, which would have been impractical for me, and of no use to you if you are eagerly anticipating the birth of your baby. For this reason, the names that have been included in this book are broadly traditional, but with a liberal sprinkling of imports from non-Western cultures, many of which, in our age of multiculturalism, will not sound as alien to an ear attuned to the English language as you may expect. In addition, to broaden your options even further, most names are accompanied by a generous selection of variants and diminutives: related names, alternative spellings and nicknames, which may not have separate entries (equally, the notable namesakes of similar names may have been telescoped into one entry). Finally, note that if a name is 'unisex', this is indicated after its meaning, but that the name will not usually appear in both the boys' and girls' sections.

In the days before baby-name books became the publishing phenomenon that has resulted in booksellers' shelves groaning with such tomes, my parents had to resort to borrowing a teacher's register in their search for inspiration for my first name (my second was originally my grandmother's). I doubt whether there were more than ten female names to chose from, and sometimes wonder who my young namesake was and what became of her. By contrast, today's parents are spoiled for choice, but choice can bring its own problems. Naming a child is an awesome responsibility, and I hope that you'll find this book a useful guide in your baby-naming quest. Above all, remember that 'A good name is rather to be chosen than great riches' (Proverbs, Chapter 21, verse 9).

Boys' Names

Aaron

Variants and diminutives: Aaran, Aarao, Aharon, Ahron, Aranne, Arek, Aren, Arend, Ari, Arin, Arn, Arni, Arny, Aron, Aronek, Aronne, Aronos, Arron, Haroun, Harun, Ron, Ronnie, Ronny.

Meaning: 'high mountain', 'mountaineer' or 'exalted' (Hebrew); 'messenger' (Arabic).

Notable namesakes: the brother of Moses in the Old Testament; Aaron's rod (*Verbascum thapsus*), a flowering plant; Aaron Burr (US politician); Aaron Copland (US composer); Aaron Douglas (US artist and teacher).

Abdul

Variants and diminutives: Ab, Abdal, Abdalla, Abdel, Abdullah, Del.

Meaning: 'servant of Allah [God]' (Arabic).

Notable namesakes: King Abdullah of Jordan.

Abel

Variants and diminutives: Abe, Abelard, Abeles, Abell, Abelot, Abi, Able, Hevel, Nab.

Meaning: 'breath' (Hebrew); 'son' (Assyrian).

Notable namesakes: the son of Adam and Eve, who was murdered by his brother, Cain, in the Old Testament; Abel Drugger, a character in the play *The Alchemist*, by English playwright Ben Jonson; Abel Tasman, Dutch navigator and discoverer of Tasmania, which was named for him, and New Zealand; Abel Magwitch, a character in the novel *Great Expectations*, by English writer Charles Dickens; Abel Gance (French film director).

Abner

Variants and diminutives: Ab, Abbey, Abby, Avner, Eb, Ebbie, Ebner.

Meaning: 'my father is light' or 'father of light' (Hebrew).

Notable namesakes: the commander of King Saul's army in the Old Testament; US cartoonist Al Capp's cartoon character 'Li'l Abner'.

Abraham

Variants and diminutives: Ab, Abe, Abi, Abie, Abrahamo, Abrahan, Abram, Abramo, Abran, Arram, Aubrey, Avram, Avrom, Avrum, Bram, Ham, Ibrahim.

Meaning: 'father of a multitude' (Hebrew)

Notable namesakes: an Old Testament patriarch; Abraham van Beyeren and Abraham Bloemaert (Dutch painters); Abraham Lincoln (US president); Bram Stoker, Irish novelist, author of *Dracula*.

Absolom

Variants and diminutives: Absalom, Absolon, Axel.

Meaning: 'my father is peace' or 'father of peace' (Hebrew).

Notable namesakes: the rebellious son of King David in the Old Testament; *Absolom and Achitophel*, a poem by English writer John Dryden; *Absalom, Absalom!*, a novel by US writer William Faulkner.

Ace

Variants and diminutives: Acelet, Acelin, Acey, Acie, Asce, Asselin, Azzo, Ezzelin.

Meaning: 'unity' or 'a unit' (Latin).

Adair

Meaning: 'ford made by an oak tree' (Scots Gaelic); 'happiness' or 'riches' and 'spear' (Old English) as a variant of Edgar.

Adam

Variants and diminutives: Ad, Adamec, Adamek, Adamik, Adamka, Adamko, Adamnan, Adamo, Adamok, Adams, Adamson, Adan, Adao, Adas, Addie, Addis, Addison, Addos, Addoson, Addy, Ade, Adekin, Adem, Adhamh, Adi, Adinet, Adnon, Adok, Adom, Adomas, Damek, Edie, Edom.

Meaning: 'red' or 'red earth' (Hebrew).
Notable namesakes: the first man, created by God from clay in the Old Testament, whose name is referred to in the expressions Adam's apple, part of the throat, and Adam's ale (water); Adam Smith (Scottish economist); the hero of English writer George Eliot's novel *Adam Bede*; Adam Gottlob Oehlenschlaeger (Danish writer); Adam Mickiewicz (Polish poet).

Adar

Variants and diminutives: Addar, Addi, Addie, Adin, Adino, Adir, Adna, Ard, Arda.
Meaning: 'fire', 'exalted' or 'dusky and cloudy' (Hebrew); 'prince' or 'ruler' (Syrian).
Notable namesakes: the sixth month of the Jewish calendar.

Adler

Meaning: 'eagle' (German and Old English).

Adlai

Meaning: 'my ornament' (Hebrew).
Notable namesakes: Adlai Stevenson (US politician).

Adolphus

Variants and diminutives: Ad, Adolf, Adolfo, Adolph, Adolphe, Adolpho, Aethelwulf, Dolf, Dolly, Dolph, Dolphus.
Meaning: 'noble' and 'wolf' (Germanic).
Notable namesakes: Adolf Hitler (Austrian-born dictator of Germany); Adolph Gottlieb (US painter).

Adrian

Variants and diminutives: Ade, Adi, Adie, Adorjan, Adriann, Adriano, Adrianus, Adrien, Adrik, Andreian, Andreyan, Andri, Andrian, Andriyan, Arne, Hadrian.
Meaning: 'from Adria' (a city in northern Italy) or 'dark one' (Latin).
Notable namesakes: Pope Adrian IV (the Englishman Nicholas Breakspear); Adrian Leverkühn, the hero of the novel *Doktor Faustus*, by German writer Thomas Mann; the fictional author of English writer Sue Townsend's *The Secret Diary of Adrian Mole;* Adrian Piper (US artist and political activist); Adrian Edmondson (British comedian).

Adriel

Variants and diminutives: Adri, Adrial.
Meaning: 'God's majesty' or 'of God's congregation' (Hebrew).

Adwin

Meaning: 'creativity' (Ghanaian).

Aeneas

Variants and diminutives: Angus, Aonghus, Eneas, Enne, Oenghus, Oengus.
Meaning: 'worthy of praise' (Greek).
Notable namesakes: the hero of *The Aeneid*, by Roman poet Virgil.

Ahmed

Variants and diminutives: Ahmad.
Meaning: 'greatly adored' or 'praised the most' (Arabic)
Notable namesakes: one of the names of Mohammed; Prince Ahmed, a character in the Persian collection of tales *The Arabian Nights.*

Ahren

Meaning: 'eagle' (Germanic).

Aidan

Variants and diminutives: Adan, Ade, Aden, Adie, Aedan, Aiden, Eden, Haden, Hayden, Haydon, Haydn.
Meaning: 'to help' (Middle English); 'small fiery one' (Irish Gaelic).
Notable namesakes: Saint Aidan.

Ainsley

Variants and diminutives: Ainie, Ainslee, Ainslie.
Meaning: 'my clearing' or 'my meadow' (Old English); derived from a family name, in turn derived from the Nottinghamshire place name Annesley.
Notable namesakes: Ainsley Harriott (British television cook).

Akash

Meaning: 'sky' (Hindi).

Akil

Variants and diminutives: Ahkeel, Akeel.
Meaning: 'intelligent one' (Arabic).

Akin

Variants and diminutives: Ahkeen, Akeen.
Meaning: 'courageous' (Yoruban).

Akio

Variants and diminutives: Akira.
Meaning: 'bright boy' (Japanese).
Notable namesakes: Akira Korosawa (Japanese film director).

Alan

Variants and diminutives: Ailean, Ailin, Al, Alain, Alair, Aland, Alano, Alanus, Alao, Alawn, Alein, Alen, Aleyn, Aleyne, Allain, Allan, Allayne, Allen, Alleyn, Allie, Allwyn, Ally, Allyn, Alun, Alyn.
Meaning: 'rock' (Breton); 'harmony' (Celtic); 'good-looking' or 'cheerful' (Irish Gaelic).
Notable namesakes: Allen a Dale, a character in the English folk tale of Robin Hood; Alan Turing (British mathematician and logician); Allen Ginsberg (US poet); Alan Sillitoe and Alan Bennett (British writers); Alain Resnais (French film director); Alan Ayckbourn (British playwright); Allan McCollum (US artist); Alan Alda (US actor); Alan Rickman (British actor); Alan Davies (British comedian and actor).

Alaric

Variants and diminutives: Alarick, Alarico, Alarik, Rich, Rick, Ricky, Ulric, Ulrich.
Meaning: 'noble ruler' or 'ruler of all' (Germanic).
Notable namesakes: King Alaric I of the Visigoths, conqueror of Rome.

Alastair

Variants and diminutives: Al, Alasdair, Alastair, Alastar, Alaster, Alastor, Aleister, Alisdair, Alistair, Alister, Allaster, Allister, Aly.
Meaning: 'defender of men' or 'warrior' (Greek). A Scots Gaelic variant of Alexander.
Notable namesakes: Aleister Crowley (English occultist); Alistair Maclean (Scottish thriller-writer).

Alban

Variants and diminutives: Al, Alba, Albany, Albek, Alben, Albie, Albion, Albin, Albinek, Albino, Albins, Alby, Alva, Alvah, Alvan, Alvin, Alwin, Alwyn, Aubin, Auburn, Binek, Elva, Elvin, Elvis.
Meaning: 'from Alba Longa' (a Roman city) or, as Alben and Albin, 'white' (Latin).
Notable namesakes: Saint Alban; Alban Berg (Austrian composer).

Albert

Variants and diminutives: Adalbert, Adel, Adelbert, Adell, Aethelbert, Ailbert, Al, Albe, Albek, Alberik, Alberti, Albertino, Alberto, Albertus, Albie, Albrecht, Ales, Aliberto, Alvertos, Aubert, Bechtel, Berco, Bert, Bertchen, Bertek, Bertel, Berti, Bertie, Bertik, Berto, Berty, Burt, Elbert, Elbie, Elvert, Ethelbert, Hab, Halbert, Imbert, Olbracht, Ulbricht.
Meaning: 'noble' and 'bright' or 'famous' (Germanic).
Notable namesakes: Saint Albert the Great, patron saint of scientists and medical technicians; Albrecht, Dürer (German artist); Prince Albert of Monaco; Prince Albert of Saxe-Coburg-Gotha (Queen Victoria of Britain's husband); Albert Bierstadt (US artist); Albert Camus (French writer and philosopher); Alberto Giacometti (Swiss artist); Albert Einstein (German-born US physicist); Albert Schweitzer (French theologian and missionary surgeon); Alberto Moravia (Italian writer); Albert Finney (British actor).

Aldo

Variants and diminutives: Al, Aldan, Alden, Aldin, Aldis, Aldivin, Aldon, Aldous, Aldos, Aldren, Aldus, Ealder, Eiden, Elder, Eldon, Eldor, Elton.
Meaning: 'old and wise' (Germanic).
Notable namesakes: Saint Aldo; Aldous Huxley (English writer); Aldo Rossi (Italian architect).

Aldred

Variants and diminutives: Al, Dred, Eldred.
Meaning: 'old' and 'counsel' (Old English).

Aldrich

Variants and diminutives: Al, Aldric, Aldridge, Audric,

Eldredge, Eldric, Eldridge, Elric, Rich, Richie, Richy.
Meaning: 'old' and 'powerful ruler' (Old English).

Aldwyn
Variants and diminutives: Aldan, Alden, Aidin, Aldwin, Eldwin.
Meaning: 'old' and 'friend' (Old English).

Alec
Variants and diminutives: Al.
Meaning: 'defender of men' or 'warrior'. A diminutive of Alexander.
Notable namesakes: Alec Guinness (English actor); Alec Baldwin (US actor).

Aled
Variants and diminutives: Al.
Meaning: 'offspring' or 'noble brow' (Welsh); derived from the river Aled in North Wales.
Notable namesakes: Aled Jones (Welsh chorister and singer).

Alexander
Variants and diminutives: Al, Alasdair, Alastar, Alastair, Alaster, Alec, Aleister, Alejandro, Alejo, Alek, Alekko, Aleks, Aleksander, Aleksandr, Aleksei, Alesaunder, Alessander, Alessandro, Alex, Alexandr, Alexandre, Alexandros, Alexis, Alexius, Ali, Alic, Alick, Alik, Aliks, Alisander, Alisandre, Alistair, Alister, Alix, Allesandro, Alysanyr, Alysaundre, Axel, Leks, Leksik, Lekso, Lex, Lexi, Sacha, Sande, Sander, Sanders, Sandey, Sandie, Sandor, Sandro, Sandy, Sasha, Saunder, Saunders, Sender, Xander, Zander.
Meaning: 'defender of men' or 'warrior' (Greek).
Notable namesakes: Alexander the Great, King of Macedonia; the Egyptian city of Alexandria; Saint Alexius (Alexis) of Rome, patron saint of beggars; the hero of the *Roman d'Alexandre*, a medieval French romance; Alessandro Scarlatti (Italian composer); Alexander Pope (English writer); Tsar Alexander II of Russia; Alexander von Humboldt (German naturalist); Alexandr Nikolayevich Afanasyev (Russian folklorist); Alexander Graham Bell (Scottish-born US scientist and inventor of the telephone); Alexander Calder (US artist); Aleksandr Sergeyevich Pushkin and Aleksandr

Isayevich Solzhenitsyn (Russian writers); Alexander Liberman (Russian-born US artist); Alex Haley (US writer); Alexander McQueen (British fashion designer).

Alfred
Variants and diminutives: Aelfric, Ailrid, Al Alf, Alfie, Alfredo, Alfric, Alfrick, Alfrid, Alfy, Alured, Auveray, Avere, Avery, Elfrid, Fred, Freddie, Freddy.
Meaning: 'elf' or 'good' and 'counsel' (Old English).
Notable namesakes: Alfred the Great, King of Wessex; Alfred, Lord Tennyson (English poet); Alfred Sisley (French artist); Alfred Dreyfus, a falsely accused French army officer whose predicament became a *cause célèbre*; Alfred Nobel (Swedish chemist and founder of the Nobel prize); Alfred Stieglitz (US photographer) Alfred Hitchcock (British film director).

Algar
Variants and diminutives: Aelgar, Alger, Algor, Elgar, Eylgar.
Meaning: 'elf' and 'spear' (Old English).

Algernon
Variants and diminutives: Al, Alger, Algie, Algy.
Meaning: 'moustachioed' or 'whiskered' (French).
Notable namesakes: Algernon Charles Swinburne and Algernon Blackwood (British writers); a character in Oscar Wilde's play *The Importance of Being Earnest*.

Ali
Meaning: 'Allah [God]' (Arabic).
Notable namesakes: Mohammed's cousin, son-in-law and the fourth caliph; Ali Baba, the hero of the collection of tales *The Arabian Nights*.

Alim
Variants and diminutives: Aleem, Alem.
Meaning: 'wise' (Arabic).

Alon
Variants and diminutives: Allon.
Meaning: 'oak' (Hebrew).

Aloysius
Meaning: 'famed' and 'warrior' (Germanic). A French Provençal variant of Louis.
Notable namesakes: Saint Aloysius Gonzaga, the patron saint of students and young people.

Alphonso
Variants and diminutives: Affonso, Afonso, Al, Alf, Alfie, Alfio, Alfo, Alfons, Alfonso, Alfonsus, Alfonzo, Allon, Alon, Alonso, Alonzo, Alphonse, Alphonsine, Alphonso, Alphonsus, Fons, Fonsie, Fonz, Fonzie, Fonzo, Lanzo, Lon, Lonnie, Lonny, Lonzo.
Meaning: 'noble' and 'ready' (Germanic).
Notable namesakes: Saint Alphonsus Liguori, patron saint of theologians and vocations; Alphonse Daudet (French writer); Alphonso (or Alphonse) Mucha (Czech artist and designer); Alfonso Reyes (Mexican writer); Alfonso Sastre (Spanish playwright).

Alton
Variants and diminutives: Alten, Altin, Elton.
Meaning: 'of the old town' (Old English).

Alva
Variants and diminutives: Alvah.
Meaning: 'exalted', 'brightness' or 'injustice' (Hebrew).
Notable namesakes: Thomas Alva Edison (US inventor).

Alvar
Meaning: 'elf' and 'warrior' or 'army' (Old English).
Notable namesakes: Alvar Aalto (Finnish architect and furniture designer).

Alvin
Variants and diminutives: Al, Albin, Aloin, Aluin, Aluino, Alvan, Alvi, Alvino, Alwin, Alwyn, Aylwin, Elvin, Elwyn.
Meaning: 'elf' or 'noble' and 'friend' (Old English).
Notable namesakes: Alvin Langdon Coburn (British photographer); Alvin Stardust (British singer), Elvin Jones (US jazz musician).

Alvis
Variants and diminutives: Elvis.
Meaning: 'knowing all' (Norse).
Notable namesakes: a dwarf in Norse mythology.

Amal
Meaning: 'pure' (Hindi).

Ambrose
Variants and diminutives: Ambrogio, Ambroise, Ambrosi, Ambrosio, Ambrosius, Ambrus, Emrys.
Meaning: 'divine' or 'immortal' (Greek).
Notable namesakes: Ambrosia, the immortality-bestowing 'nectar' of the Greek gods; Saint Ambrose, patron saint of bee-keepers, candlemakers, learning and bishops; Ambrosius Aurelianus (a warrior of ancient Britain sometimes associated with King Arthur); Ambrose Bierce (US writer).

Amin
Variants and diminutives: Ameen, Amen, Amitan, Ammon, Amnon, Amon.
Meaning: 'the truth' (Hebrew and Arabic); 'faithful' (East Indian).

Amir
Variants and diminutives: Ameer, Emir.
Meaning: 'prince' or 'ruler' (Arabic).

Amory
Variants and diminutives: Amati, Amery, Ames, Amias, Amice, Amiot, Amor, Amyas, Embry, Emory, Imray, Imrie.
Meaning: 'loving person' (Latin); 'renowned' and 'ruler' (Germanic).

Amos
Meaning: 'weighed down' or 'carried' (Hebrew).

Notable namesakes: the Old Testament prophet; Amos Oz (Israeli writer); Amos Tutuola (Nigerian writer).

Anatole

Variants and diminutives: Anatol, Anatolio, Anatoly, Antal.
Meaning: 'rising sun' (Greek).
Notable namesakes: Anatolia (Turkey-in-Asia), an Asian part of Turkey; Anatole France (the pseudonym of French writer Jacques Anatole Thibault).

Andrew

Variants and diminutives: Aindreas, Aindrias, Anders, Andersen, Anderson, Andi, Andie, Andor, Andras, André, Andreas, Andrei, Andrej, Andres, Andrey, Andrik, Andros, Andy, Drew.
Meaning: 'manly' (Greek).
Notable namesakes: Saint Andrew, patron saint of fishermen, Scotland and Russia; the Scottish city of St Andrews; Sir Andrew Aguecheek, a character in William Shakespeare's play *Twelfth Night*; Andrew Marvell (English poet); Andrew Jackson (US president); Andrew Carnegie (US industrialist and philanthropist); André Gide, André Malraux and André Breton (French writers); Andrew Wyeth (US artist); Andy Warhol (US artist and film-maker); Prince Andrew of the United Kingdom; Andre Agassi (US tennis player).

Aneurin

Variants and diminutives: Aneirin, Nye.
Meaning: 'man of honour' (Latin), a variant of Honorius; 'pure gold' (Welsh).
Notable namesakes: Aneurin Bevan (British politician).

Angel

Variants and diminutives: Angelico, Angelino, Angell, Angelo, Angelos.
Meaning: 'messenger' (Greek). Also a girl's name.
Notable namesakes: Fra Angelico, patron saint of artists; Angelo, characters in two of William Shakespeare's plays, *Measure for Measure* and *The Comedy of Errors*; Angel Clare, a character in English author Thomas Hardy's novel *Tess of the d'Urbervilles*

Angus

Variants and diminutives: Aeneas, Aengus, Aonghas, Aonghus.
Meaning: 'single choice' (Scots Gaelic).
Notable namesakes: Angus Og, a beneficient god in Celtic mythology; Aberdeen Angus, a Scottish breed of black cattle named for Aonghus Turimleach, the Irish invader and bringer to Scotland of the Stone of Scone; once a Scottish county in Tayside; Angus Wilson (British writer).

Anselm

Variants and diminutives: Amselmo, Ancel, Ancell, Ancelm, Ancelmo, Ansel, Anselino, Ansell, Anselmo, Ansil, Ansill, Anzelmo, Enselmo, Selmo, Semo.
Meaning: 'divine' and 'helmet' (Germanic); 'related to nobility' (Old French).
Notable namesakes: Saint Anselm; Anselm Feuerbach (German artist); Ansel Adams (US photographer); Anselm Kiefer (German artist).

Anthony

Variants and diminutives: Andonios, Andonis, Ant, Antaine, Antal, Antek, Anti, Antoin, Antoine, Anton, Antone, Antoni, Antonin, Antonio, Antonius, Antony, Antos, Toni, Tonio, Tony.
Meaning: 'flourishing' (Greek); 'without price' (Latin); derived from the Roman family name Antonius.
Notable namesakes: Mark Anthony (Marcus Antonius, Roman politician and soldier); Saint Anthony the Great; Saint Anthony of Egypt, patron saint of basket-makers; Saint Anthony of Padua, patron saint of infertile women, lost articles, the poor and starving and travellers; Antonio Vivaldi (Italian composer); Antoine Watteau (French artist); Anthony van Dyck (Flemish artist); Anton Chekhov (Russian playwright); Anthony Trollope, Anthony Burgess and Anthony Powell (English writers); Anton Bruckner (Austrian composer); Antonio Gaudí (Spanish architect and designer); Antoine de Saint-Exupéry (French writer); Anthony Quinn, (Mexican-born US actor); Anthony Caro (British sculptor); Anthony Worral Thompson (British television chef).

Apollo

Meaning: 'to push back' or 'destroy' (Greek).
Notable namesakes: the Graeco-Roman god of the sun, prophecy and the arts; a generic name used to describe an outstandingly handsome man.

Archibald

Variants and diminutives: Arch, Archaimbaud, Archambault, Archbold, Archibaldo, Archie, Archy, Arkady, Arky, Ercanbald, Erkenwald, Baldie.
Meaning: 'noble' or 'true' and 'bold' (Germanic).
Notable namesakes: Archibald MacLeish (US poet).

Arfon

Meaning: 'facing Anglesea' (Welsh).

Ari

Variants and diminutives: Aaron, Ari, Aristotle, Arri.
Meaning: 'lion' (Hebrew).

Armand

Variants and diminutives: Arek, Arman, Armande, Armando, Armen, Armin, Armine, Armino, Armon, Armond, Armonde, Armondo, Herman, Mandek, Mando, Ormond.
Meaning: 'army' and 'man' (Germanic). A variant of Herman.
Notable namesakes: Armand, Duc de Richelieu, the French statesman better known as Cardinal Richelieu; Armand Guillaumin (French artist); Armand Salacrou (French playwright).

Arnold

Variants and diminutives: Arn, Arnald, Arnaldo, Arnaud, Arnauld, Arnaut, Arnd, Arndt, Arnel, Arnell, Arne, Arnet, Arnett, Arney, Arni, Arnie, Arno, Arnoldo, Arnoll, Arnolt, Arnot, Arnott, Arny, Ernald, Ernaldus, Wado.
Meaning: 'eagle' and 'strength' or 'rule' (Germanic).
Notable namesakes: Arnold Böcklin (Swiss artist); Arnold Bennett (English writer); Arnold Toynbee (British historian); Arnold Schoenberg (Austrian composer); Arnold Wesker (English playwright); Arnold Palmer (US golfer); Arnold Schwarzenegger (Austrian-born US actor).

Arsen

Variants and diminutives: Arcenio, Arsanio, Arsemio, Arsenio, Eresenio.
Meaning: 'virile' (Greek).

Arthur

Variants and diminutives: Acur, Art, Artair, Arth, Arte, Artek, Artey, Artie, Artis, Arto, Artor, Artuir, Artur, Arturo, Artus, Arty, Atur.
Meaning: 'bear-keeper' (Greek); 'bear' (Celtic); 'stone' (Irish Gaelic); 'noble' (Welsh); 'follower of Thor' (Norse); derived from the Roman name Artorius.
Notable namesakes: King Arthur (Hero of British legend); Arthur Wellesley, Duke of Wellington; Arthur Dimmesdale, a character in the novel *The Scarlet Letter*, by US writer Nathaniel Hawthone; Arthur Rimbaud (French poet); Arthur Schopenhauer (German philosopher); Arthur Rackham (British artist); Arthur Wing Pinero (English actor and writer); Arthur Sullivan (English composer); Arthur Conan Doyle and Arthur Ransome (English writers); Arthur Koestler (Hungarian-born British writer); Arthur Schnitzler (Austrian writer); Arthur C Clarke (English science-fiction writer); Arthur Hailey (English-born Canadian writer); Arthur Miller (US playwright); Art Garfunkel (US singer).

Asa

Meaning: 'physician' or 'healer' (Hebrew); 'born in the morning' (Japanese).
Notable namesakes: a king of Judah in the Old Testament; Asa Briggs (British historian).

Asad

Variants and diminutives: Aleser, Alisid, Asid, Assid.
Meaning: 'lion' (Arabic).

Asher

Variants and diminutives: Aser, Ash, Ashur, Asser.
Meaning: 'happy' (Hebrew); as Ashur, 'martial' (eastern Semitic); 'born during Ashur [a Moslem month]' (Swahili).
Notable namesakes: a son of Jacob and Zilpah and the leader of one of the twelve tribes of Israel in the Old Testament.

Ashley

Variants and diminutives: Ash, Ashleigh, Ashlie.
Meaning: 'ash wood' (Old English). Also a girl's name.
Notable namesakes: Ashley Wilkes, a character in US writer Margaret Mitchell's novel *Gone With the Wind*; Ashley Bickerton (US artist).

Aslan

Variants and diminutives: Arslan.
Meaning: 'lion' (Turkish).
Notable namesakes: the lion in the 'Narnia' series of children's books by British author C S Lewis.

Aswad

Meaning: 'black' (Arabic).
Notable namesakes: a British reggae group.

Athelstan

Variants and diminutives: Stan.
Meaning: 'noble' and 'stone' (Old English).
Notable namesakes: an Anglo-Saxon king; a character in *Ivanhoe*, the novel by Scottish writer Sir Walter Scott.

Athol

Variants and diminutives: Atholl, Athole.
Meaning: 'new Ireland' (Scots Gaelic); derived from a Scottish family name, in turn derived from a Scottish place name.
Notable namesakes: Athol Fugard (South African actor, playwright and director).

Auberon

Variants and diminutives: Aubrey, Oberon.
Meaning: 'noble' or 'like a bear' (Germanic).
Notable namesakes: the king of the fairies in medieval belief; Auberon Waugh (British writer).

Aubrey

Variants and diminutives: Alberic, Alberich, Aubary, Aubery, Auberon, Aubri, Aubrie, Aubry.
Meaning: 'elf' and 'strength' or 'ruler' (Germanic). Also a girl's name.
Notable namesakes: Aubrey Beardsley (British illustrator); Aubrey Menen (British writer).

Augustus

Variants and diminutives: Agostin, Agostino, Agosto, Aguistin, Agustin, August, Auguste, Augustin, Augustine, Augustino, Augusto, Austen, Austin, Gus, Gussie, Gustus.
Meaning: 'venerable' or 'great' (Latin); a name assumed by Roman emperors, notably the first, Caius (or Gaius) Julius Caesar Octavianus.
Notable namesakes: the month of August; Saint Augustine of Hippo, patron saint of brewers, printers and theologians; Saint Augustine of Canterbury; Auguste Renoir (French artist); Auguste Rodin (French sculptor); Augustus John (British artist); Augustus Pugin (English architect and designer); August Strindberg (Swedish writer); August Macke (German artist); Austin Chamberlain (British politician).

Aulay

Variants and diminutives: Amhlaigh, Olaf, Olave.
Meaning: 'forebear' and 'relics' (Old Norse) as a Scots Gaelic variant of Olaf.

Avery

Meaning: 'elf' and 'ruler' (Old English).

Axel

Variants and diminutives: Aksel.
Meaning: 'oak' (Germanic); 'divine reward' (Scandinavian). Also a variant of Absolom and Alexander.
Notable namesakes: Axel Munthe (Scandinavian writer).

Aylmer

Variants and diminutives: Ailemar, Athel, Eilemar, Elmer.
Meaning: 'noble' and 'renowned' (Old English).

Azariah

Variants and diminutives: Azaria, Azriel.
Meaning: 'God is my help' (Hebrew). Also a girl's name.
Notable namesakes: a king of Judah in the Old Testament.

Bailey
Variants and diminutives: Bail, Bailie, Baillie, Baily, Bayley.
Meaning: 'to enclose' or 'bailiff' (Old French).

Baird
Variants and diminutives: Bard.
Meaning: 'poet' or 'singer of poetry' (Welsh and Scots Gaelic).

Bal
Meaning: 'hair' (Sanskrit, Tibetan, English Gypsy).

Balder
Variants and diminutives: Baldewin, Baldur, Baldwin, Ball, Baudier, Baudoin.
Meaning: 'white god' or 'god of lightness' (Old Norse); derived from the name of a benevolent god of Norse mythology, loosely equated with Jesus Christ.

Baldric
Variants and diminutives: Baldarich, Baldri, Baudrey, Baudri.
Meaning: 'bold' and 'ruler' (Germanic).
Notable namesakes: a character in the *Blackadder* British television series.

Baldwin
Variants and diminutives: Baldawin, Baudoin, Bawden, Bealdwine, Boden, Bodkin, Bowden.
Meaning: 'bold' and 'friend' (Germanic).

Balthazar
Variants and diminutives: Baltasar, Balthasar, Belshazzer.
Meaning: 'Bel [a god of Babylon] be the king's protector' (Greek).

Notable namesakes: one of the Magi who visited the newborn Jesus Christ in the New Testament; Balthasar Permoser (German sculptor); Baltasar Gracián (Spanish writer).

Barak
Meaning: 'flash of light' or 'lightning' (Hebrew).

Bardolf
Variants and diminutives: Bardell, Bardolph.
Meaning: 'bright' and 'wolf' (Germanic).
Notable namesakes: Bardolph, a character in William Shakespeare's plays *King Henry IV*, *The Life of Henry V* and *The Merry Wives of Windsor*.

Barnabas
Variants and diminutives: Bane, Barn, Barna, Barnaba, Barnabe, Barnaby, Barnebas, Barney, Barnie, Barny, Bernabe, Burnaby.
Meaning: 'son of encouragement' (Hebrew).
Notable namesakes: Saint Paul's companion in the New Testament and bringer of Christianity to Cyprus.

Baron
Variants and diminutives: Baran, Barron.
Meaning: 'warrior' or 'man' (Latin); 'free man' (Germanic); a British family name derived from the title of nobility.

Barrett
Variants and diminutives: Barret.
Meaning: 'bear' and 'strength' (Germanic); derived from an English family name.

Barry
Variants and diminutives: Bairre, Bari, Barnard, Barnett, Barra, Barre, Barret, Barrfind, Barri, Barrie, Barrie, Barrington, Barris, Barrymore, Bearach, Fionbharr.
Meaning: 'spear' or 'fair-haired boy' (Irish Gaelic); 'barrier' (Old French).
Notable namesakes: Barry Island, a holiday resort in Wales; Barry Flanagan (British sculptor); Barry White (US singer); Barry McGuigan (Irish boxer).

Bartholomew

Variants and diminutives: Bardo, Barholomee, Bart, Bartel, Bartelot, Barth, Batholomaus, Bartholomieu, Bartie, Bartle, Bartlemey, Bartlet, Bartlett, Bartley, Bartold, Bartolo, Bartolome, Bartolomé, Barton, Barty, Bat, Bate, Batkin, Batly, Batty, Bertel, Meo, Mewes, Tholy, Tolly, Tolomieu, Tolomey.
Meaning: 'son of Tolmai [or Talmai]' (Hebrew).
Notable namesakes: Saint Bartholomew, one of the twelve apostles in the New Testament and patron saint of plasterers; Bartolomé Esteban Murillo (Spanish artist).

Barton

Meaning: 'barley settlement' (Old English); derived from an English family name.

Baruch

Variants and diminutives: Barush.
Meaning: 'blessed' (Hebrew); 'good-doer' (Greek)
Notable namesakes: Barush, the companion of Jeremiah in the Old Testament; Baruch Spinoza (Dutch philosopher).

Basil

Variants and diminutives: Bale, Bas, Basie, Basile, Basilie, Basilio, Basilius, Basine, Basle, Baz, Bazek, Bazel, Bazil, Brasil, Breasal, Bresal, Vas, Vasil, Vasile, Vasilek, Vasili, Vasilis, Vasily, Vassily, Vasya, Vasyl, Vazul.
Meaning: 'kingly' or 'royal' (Greek); 'war' (Irish Gaelic).
Notable namesakes: Saint Basil the Great; Basil Bunting (British poet); Basil Spence (Scottish architect); the common name of the culinary herb *Ocimum basilicum*; Basil Fawlty, a character in the British television series *Fawlty Towers*.

Bavol

Variants and diminutives: Bevel.
Meaning: 'wind' or 'air' (English Gypsy).

Beau

Meaning: 'handsome' (French).
Notable namesakes: a name for a girl's suitor. Beau Brummell, a British dandy; the eponymous hero of the novel *Beau Geste*, by British author P C Wren; Beau Bridges (US actor).

Beck

Meaning: 'brook' or 'stream' (Old Norse).

Bede

Meaning: 'prayer' (Old English).
Notable namesakes: the Venerable Bede, the Anglo-Saxon historian, scholar and patron saint of scholars.

Beldon

Variants and diminutives: Belden, Beldin.
Meaning: 'small, beautiful place' (Old English).

Benedict

Variants and diminutives: Banet, Banko, Ben, Benayt, Bence, Benci, Bendek, Bendik, Benditto, Benedek, Benedetto, Benedick, Benedicto, Benedik, Benedikt, Benedo, Benek, Bendix, Benedetto, Benedicto, Benes, Benet, Benett, Beneyt, Bengt, Beni, Benigno, Benitin, Benito, Beniton, Benke, Bennet, Bennett, Bennie, Benny, Benoist, Benoit, Bento, Bettino, Betto, Boruch, Dick, Dix, Dixie, Venedict, Venedikt, Venka, Venya.
Meaning: 'blessed' (Latin).
Notable namesakes: Saint Benedict, founder of the Benedictine order of monks, members of which first created the liqueur called Benedictine, and patron saint of sufferers from poisoning and kidney disease; Saint Benedict Joseph Labre, patron saint of the homeless and beggars; Benito Mussolini (Italian dictator); Benedict Kiely (Irish writer).

Benjamin

Variants and diminutives: Bannerjee, Ben, Benji, Benjie, Benjy, Benmajee, Bennie, Benno, Benny, Berihert, Yemin.
Meaning: 'son of my right hand' or 'favourite son' (Hebrew).
Notable namesakes: the son of Jacob and Rachel in the Old Testament and founder of one of the twelve tribes of Israel; Ben Jonson (English playwright); Benjamin Franklin (US politician and scientist); Benjamin West (US artist);

Benjamin Disraeli (British politician); Big Ben, the clock-tower bell in the British Houses of Parliament, named for Sir Benjamin Hall; Benjamin Rowntree (British entrepreneur and philanthropist); Benjamin Britten (British composer).

Bentley
Variants and diminutives: Benm, Benny, Bently.
Meaning: 'place where there is bent grass' (Old English); derived from an English family name, in turn derived from a number of English place names.
Notable namesakes: Bentley Drummle, a character in the novel *Great Expectations*, by English writer Charles Dickens; a luxurious automobile marque.

Berenger
Meaning: 'bear' and 'spear' (Germanic).

Berg
Variants and diminutives: Bergen, Berger, Bergin, Borg, Borje, Bourke, Burke.
Meaning: 'mountain' (German); derived from a German family name, in turn derived from a number of German place names.

Berkeley
Variants and diminutives: Barclay, Barcley, Berk, Berke, Berkley, Berkly.
Meaning: 'birch wood' (Old English); derived from an English family name, in turn derived from an English place name.

Bernard
Variants and diminutives: Banet, Baretta, Barn, Barnard, Barnet, Barnett, Barney, Barnie, Barny, Barr, Barre, Barret, Barrett, Barry, Bear, Benek, Beno, Benno, Bern, Bernat, Barnadin, Bearnard, Bernado, Bernal, Bernardel, Bernardin, Bernardino, Bernardito, Bernardo, Bernardyn, Bernarr, Bernd, Berndt, Bernek, Berend, Berngards, Bernhard, Bernhardi, Bernhardt, Berni, Bernie, Bernis, Berno, Bernt, Berny, Bjarne, Björn, Bjorne, Burnard, Burnie, Burny, Levar, Nardo, Vernados.
Meaning: 'bear' and 'strength' (Germanic).
Notable namesakes: Saint Bernard of Montjoux

(Aosta or Menthon), patron saint of mountaineers and skiers, for whom the Little and Great Saint Bernard mountain passes and the Saint Bernard breed of Alpine rescue dogs were named; Saint Bernard of Clairvaux; Saint Bernardino of Siena, patron saint of weavers, preachers, advertising and public relations; George Bernard Shaw (Irish writer).

Bersh
Variants and diminutives: Besh.
Meaning: 'a year' (English Gypsy).

Berthold
Variants and diminutives: Bert, Bertell, Bertie, Bertil, Bertin, Bertol, Bertold, Bertole, Bertolt, Berton, Labert.
Meaning: 'bright' and 'power' (Germanic).
Notable namesakes: Bertolt Brecht (German dramatist).

Bertram
Variants and diminutives: Bert, Berteram, Bertie, Bertran, Bertrand, Bertrando, Bertrem, Berty.
Meaning: 'bright' and 'raven' (Germanic).
Notable namesakes: a character in William Shakespeare's play *All's Well That Ends Well;* Bertrand Russell (English philosopher and mathematician).

Berwin
Meaning: 'supportive' and 'friend' (Old English); 'harvest' and 'friend' (Middle English).

Bevan
Variants and diminutives: Bev.
Meaning: 'son of Evan' (Welsh).

Bevis
Variants and diminutives: Beavis, Bev, Bevan, Bevin, Bivian, Bix, Buell.
Meaning: 'beef' or else 'cherished' or 'handsome' and 'son' (Old French); possibly also derived from Beauvais, a French place name.
Notable namesakes: the hero of the novel *Bevis: the Story of a Boy*, by British writer and naturalist Richard Jefferies; a character in the American animated-cartoon television series *Beavis and Butthead*.

Bill

Variants and diminutives: Billy, William.
Meaning: 'will' and 'helmet' or 'protection' (Germanic).
A diminutive of William.
Notable namesakes: Bill Sikes, a character in the novel *Oliver Twist*, by English writer Charles Dickens; *Billy Budd, Foretopman*, the title of a novel by US writer Herman Melville; Wild Bill Hickok (US folk hero and marshal); Buffalo Bill Cody (US folk hero and showman); Bill Wyman, Billy Bragg and Billy Idol (British musicians); Bill Bryson (US writer); Bill Cosby (US actor); Bill Viola (US artist); Billy Joel (US musician); Bill Gates (US information-technology entrepreneur); Bill Woodrow (British sculptor).

Björn

Variants and diminutives: Bernard.
Meaning: 'bear' and 'strength' (Germanic). A Scandinavian variant of Bernard.
Notable namesakes: Björn Borg (Swedish tennis player).

Blaine

Variants and diminutives: Blain, Blane, Blayne.
Meaning: 'narrow' or 'servant of Saint Blane' (Irish Gaelic). Also a girl's name.
Notable namesakes: Saint Blane.

Blair

Variants and diminutives: Blaire.
Meaning: 'flat land' or 'plain' (Scots Gaelic); derived from a Scottish family name, in turn derived from a Scottish place name. Also a girl's name.

Blaise

Variants and diminutives: Balas, Balasz, Ballas, Biagio, Blaisot, Blas, Blase, Blasi, Blasien, Blasius, Blayze, Blaze, Blazek, Braz, Vlas.
Meaning: 'stammering' (Latin); 'taste' (Celtic); 'torch' (Old English). Also a girl's name.
Notable namesakes: Saint Blaise, patron saint of sufferers from throat ailments; Saint Blasius, patron saint of wool-combers; Blaise Pascal (French philosopher and mathematician); Blaise Cendrars (Swiss-born French writer).

Blake

Variants and diminutives: Blanchard, Blanco.
Meaning: 'pale' or 'black' (Old English).

Blythe

Variants and diminutives: Bligh, Blithe.
Meaning: 'carefree' (Old English).

Boaz

Meaning: 'strong man' or 'swiftness' (Hebrew).
Notable namesakes: the husband of Ruth in the Old Testament.

Bob

Variants and diminutives: Bobbie, Bobby, Robert.
Meaning: 'fame' and 'bright' (Germanic). A diminutive of Robert.
Notable namesakes: Sir Robert Peel, founder of the British police force, popularly known as 'bobbies' or 'peelers'; Bob Cratchit, a character in the novel *A Christmas Carol*, by English writer Charles Dickens; Bobby Fischer (US chess player); Bob Dylan (US musician); Bob Marley (Jamaican musician); Bobby Moore (British footballer); Bob Willis (British cricketer); Bob Geldof (Irish singer and philanthropist).

Bonamy

Variants and diminutives: Bonaro, Boni, Bunn.
Meaning: 'good' and 'friend' (Old French).

Bonar

Meaning: 'courteous' (Old French).
Notable namesakes: Andrew Bonar Law (British politician).

Bond

Variants and diminutives: Bonde, Bondie, Bondon, Bonds, Bondy.
Meaning: 'to bind' (Old Norse); 'earth-tiller' (Old English).

Boniface

Variants and diminutives: Boneface, Boni, Bonyface, Facio, Fazio.
Meaning: 'destined to receive blessings', 'good-doer' or 'good-looking' (Latin).
Notable namesakes: Saint Boniface.

Boris

Variants and diminutives: Borislav.
Meaning: 'battle' or 'stranger' , (Old Slavonic); 'small' (Tartar).
Notable namesakes: Saint Boris, patron saint of Moscow; Boris Godunov, Russian tsar and eponymous subject of an opera by Russian composer Modest Petrovich Mussorgsky and a drama by Russian writer Aleksandr Pushkin; Boris Karloff (British actor); Boris Pasternak (Russian author); Boris Yeltsin (Russian politician); Boris Becker (German tennis player); Boris Johnson (British journalist and politician).

Boyce

Meaning: 'wood' (Old French); derived from an English family name, in turn derived from a number of English place names.

Boyd

Variants and diminutives: Bow, Bowen, Bowie.
Meaning: 'yellow' or 'from the Island of Bute' (Scots Gaelic); derived from a Scottish family name.
Notable namesakes: Boyd Webb (New Zealand artist).

Braden

Variants and diminutives: Brad, Bradan, Bradin, Bradon, Brady, Bray, Braydan, Brayden, Braydin, Braydon, Braydun, Broadus.
Meaning: 'to broaden' (Old English); derived from an English family name.

Bradford

Variants and diminutives: Brad.
Meaning: 'broad ford' (Old English); derived from an English family name, in turn derived from a number of English place names.

Bradley

Variants and diminutives: Brad, Bradlee, Bradleigh, Bradly, Brady, Lee, Leigh.
Meaning: 'broad' and 'wood' or 'clearing' (Old English); derived from an English family name, in turn derived from a number of English place names.
Notable namesakes: Bradley Headstone, a character in the novel *Our Mutual Friend*, by English author Charles Dickens; Bradley Walker Tomlin (US artist).

Bramwell

Variants and diminutives: Bram, Branwell.
Meaning: 'raven' and 'well' (Cornish); 'brambles' and 'stream' (Old English); derived from an English family name, in turn derived from a number of English place names.
Notable namesakes: Patrick Branwell Brontë (brother of the English soriety of novelists); William Bramwell Booth (British founder of the Salvation Army).

Bran

Meaning: 'raven' (Welsh).
Notable namesakes: Bendegeit Bran, 'Brân the Blessed', god of music, poetry and immortality in Welsh mythology.

Brandon

Variants and diminutives: Bran, Brandan, Branton, Brendan.
Meaning: 'broom' and 'hill' (Old English); derived from an English family name, in turn derived from a number of English place names.

Brant

Variants and diminutives: Brand, Brandi, Brandon, Brandt, Brent.
Meaning: 'fire' or 'firebrand' (Old English).

Brendan

Variants and diminutives: Bran, Brand, Brandan, Brandon, Brannon, Branon, Brant, Breandan, Bren, Brenain, Brend, Brenden, Brendin, Brendon, Brennan,

Brenon, Brondan.
Meaning: 'prince' or 'royal' (Irish Gaelic).
Notable namesakes: Saint Brendan the Navigator, patron saint of sailors; Brendan Behan (Irish dramatist); Brendan Gill (US writer); Brendan Fraser (US actor).

Brent

Variants and diminutives: Brendt, Brenten, Brenton.
Meaning: 'high place' (Celtic); 'burned' (Old English); derived from an English family name and a number of English place names.

Brett

Variants and diminutives: Bret, Bretton, Brit, Briton, Britton.
Meaning: 'Breton' or 'Briton' (Latin); 'the ardent one's son' (Celtic).
Notable namesakes: Bret Harte (US writer); Brett Whiteley (Australian artist).

Brian

Variants and diminutives: Briano, Briant, Brianus, Briar, Brareus, Brien, Brienus, Brion, Brior, Bruinal, Bryan, Bryant, Byron.
Meaning: 'strong', 'hill' or 'elevated' (Irish Gaelic)
Notable namesakes: Brian Boru, High King of Ireland; Bryan Ferry (British musician); Bryan Adams (Canadian musician); Brian Lara (West Indian cricketer).

Brock

Variants and diminutives: Badger, Braxton.
Meaning: 'badger' or 'brook' (Old English); 'young deer' (Old French).
Notable namesakes: a traditional name for badgers.

Broderick

Variants and diminutives: Brod, Broddy.
Meaning: 'renowned' and 'ruler' (Germanic). A variant of Roderick.
Notable namesakes: Broderick Crawford (US actor).

Bruce

Variants and diminutives: Brucey, Brucie, Bruis, Brus.
Meaning: uncertain, possibly 'wood' (French); derived

from the French family name Brieuse or the Scottish family name de Brus.
Notable namesakes: Robert the Bruce, King Robert I of Scotland; Bruce Nauman (US artist); Bruce Jay Friedman (US writer); Bruce Lee (US actor and martial arts expert).

Bruno

Variants and diminutives: Brewis, Bronson, Browse, Bruin, Bruns, Labron, Lebron.
Meaning: 'brown' or 'like a bear' (Germanic).
Notable namesakes: a traditional name for bears; Saint Bruno, founder of the order of Carthusian monks; Bruno Maderna (Italian composer); Bruno Bettelheim (Austrian-born US psychologist).

Bryce

Variants and diminutives: Brice, Brick, Brycen, Brychan, Bryson, Bryston.
Meaning: 'son of the powerful ruler' (Germanic); 'dappled' (Welsh). Also a girl's name.
Notable namesakes: St Brice (Britius).

Bryn

Variants and diminutives: Brin, Brinn, Bryne, Brynmor, Brynn, Brynne.
Meaning: 'hill' (Welsh). Also a girl's name.
Notable namesakes: Bryn Terfel (Welsh opera singer).

Brynmor

Meaning: 'large hill' (Welsh).

Bud

Variants and diminutives: Budd, Buddy.
Meaning: 'friend' or 'brother' (English).
Notable namesakes: Budd Schulberg (US writer); Bud Abbott (US comedian); Buddy Holly and Bud Powerll (US musician).

Burr

Variants and diminutives: Burbank, Burrell, Burris, Burton.
Meaning: 'youth' (Scandinavian); 'roughly edged' (Middle English).

A
B
C
D
E
F
G
H
I
J
K
L
M
N
O
P
Q
R
S
T
U
V
W
X
Y
Z

Burt
Variants and diminutives: Bert, Burty.
Meaning: 'bright' (Old English).
Notable namesakes: Burt Bacharach (US composer);
Burt Lancaster and Burt Reynolds (US actors).

Byron
Variants and diminutives: Biron, Buiron, Byram,
Byrom.
Meaning: 'cowshed' or 'cattle-herder' (Old English);
'landed estate' or 'cottage' (Old French).
Notable namesakes: George Gordon, Lord Byron
(English poet).

Cadfael
Meaning: 'battle' and 'metal' (Welsh).
Notable namesakes: Brother Cadfael, the hero of a
series of novels of medieval detection by British
author Ellis Peters.

Cadwallader
Variants and diminutives: Cadwaladar, Cadwalader,
Cadwaladr, Cadwalladr.
Meaning: 'battle' and 'leader' (Welsh).

Caerwyn
Meaning: 'white castle' (Welsh).

Caesar
Variants and diminutives: Arek, Casar, Cecha, Cesar,
César, Cesare, Cesareo, Cesario, Cezar, Cezary, Cezek,
Czar, Kaiser, Kesar, Sarito, Seasar, Sezar, Tsar.
Meaning: 'to cut', 'blue-grey', 'dark hair', 'long hair' or
'head of hair' (Latin); a Roman family name and title
assumed by Roman emperors (emulated by the
German kaisers and Russian tsars).
Notable namesakes: Gaius (or Caius) Julius Caesar,

the Roman emperor, who, it was said, was born by the
Caesarian section that was subsequently named for
him and on whose love affair with Cleopatra the Irish
writer George Bernard Shaw based his play *Caesar and
Cleopatra*; Saint Caesarius of Arles, César Auguste
Frank (Belgian composer); César Moro and César
Vallejo (Peruvian poets).

Cahil
Meaning: 'young' or 'inexperienced' (Turkish).

Caius
Variants and diminutives: Cai, Kai, Kay.
Meaning: 'to rejoice' (Latin). A variant of Gaius.
Notable namesakes: Caius (or Gaius) Julius Caesar
Octavianus, the first emperor of Rome, subsequently
known as Augustus; Gonville and Caius College,
Cambridge; Caius Cibber (Danish sculptor).

Cal
Variants and diminutives: Calen, Calin, Kail, Kale,
Kalen, Kayle.
Meaning: 'thin' (Irish Gaelic).

Caleb
Variants and diminutives: Cal, Cale, Kalb, Kale, Kaleb,
Kalev.
Meaning: 'without fear' or 'bold' (Hebrew); 'brave in
victory'(Arabic).
Notable namesakes: one of the men who
reconnoitred the Promised Land (Canaan) in the Old
Testament; the leading character of the novel *The
Adventures of Caleb Williams*, by English writer
William Godwin.

Calum
Variants and diminutives: Callum, Colm, Colum,
Kallum, Kalum.
Meaning: 'dove-like' (Latin); 'servant of Saint
Columba' (Scots Gaelic). A variant of Columbus or a
diminutive of Malcolm.

Calvin
Variants and diminutives: Caiv, Cal, Calvino, Kal,
Kalvin, Vin, Vinnie, Vinny.

Meaning: 'bald' (Latin).
Notable namesakes: Jean Calvin (French-Swiss Protestant theologian and church reformer, founder of Calvinism); Calvin Coolidge (US president); Calvin Klein (US fashion designer).

Cam

Meaning: 'beloved' (English Gypsy).

Cameron

Variants and diminutives: Cam, Camaron, Camron, Kam, Kamaron, Kameron, Kamron.
Meaning: 'crooked nose' (Scots Gaelic); also the name of a Scottish clan.
Notable namesakes: Cameron Mackintosh (British theatre producer).

Camillus

Variants and diminutives: Camille, Camillo.
Meaning: 'messenger' or 'attendant at ritual' (Latin); derived from the Roman family name Camillus.
Notable namesakes: Saint Camillus de Lellis, patron saint of hospitals, nurses and sick people; Camille Pissaro (French artist); Camille Saint-Saëns (French composer); Camille Guérin, the French bacteriologist who, with Albert Calmette, developed the Bacille Calmette-Guérin (BCG) anti-tuberculosis vaccine.

Camlo

Variants and diminutives: Cam.
Meaning: 'friendly' or 'lovely' (English Gypsy); 'sweet dew' (Vietnamese).

Campbell

Variants and diminutives: Cam, Camp, Campie, Campy.
Meaning: 'beautiful plain' (Latin); 'crooked mouth' (Scots Gaelic); also the name of a Scottish clan.

Caradoc

Variants and diminutives: Caractacus, Caradawg, Caractacos, Caradog, Carthac, Carthach, Carghage, Cerdic.
Meaning: 'dear' or 'friendly' (Welsh).
Notable namesakes: also known as Caractacus, a

British chieftain captured by the Romans; Caradoc Evans (Welsh writer).

Carew

Meaning: 'dear' or 'coach' (Latin).

Carl

Variants and diminutives: Carlo, Carlos, Karl.
Meaning: 'man' or 'free man' (Germanic). A variant of Charles.
Notable namesakes: Carl von Clausewitz (Prussian military strategist); Carl Maria von Weber (German composer); Carl Spitzweg (German artist); Carl Zeiss (German manufacturer of optical instruments); Carl Larsson (Swedish artist); Carl G Jung (Swiss psychiatrist); Carl Zuckmayer (German writer); Carl Sandburg and Carl Rakosi (US poets); Carl Andre (US sculptor); Carl Lewis (US athlete).

Carr

Variants and diminutives: Karr, Kerr.
Meaning: 'marshland' (Old Norse); derived from an English family name, in turn derived from a number of place names.

Carter

Meaning: 'cart-maker' or 'cart-driver' (Old English); also an English family name and a girl's name.

Carvel

Variants and diminutives: Carvell.
Meaning: 'song' (Manx); 'from the marsh' (Old French).

Cary

Variants and diminutives: Carey.
Meaning: 'much loved' or 'costly' (Latin); 'castle-dweller' (Welsh); derived from an English family name and a number of British place names.
Notable namesakes: Cary Grant (British-born US actor).

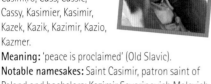

Casimir

Variants and diminutives: Cachi, Casey, Cashi, Casimer, Casimiro, Cass, Cassie, Cassy, Kasimier, Kasimir, Kazek, Kazik, Kazimir, Kazio, Kazmer.
Meaning: 'peace is proclaimed' (Old Slavic).
Notable namesakes: Saint Casimir, patron saint of Poland and bachelors; Kazimir Severinovich Malevich (Russian artist).

Caspar

Variants and diminutives: Cash, Casper, Cass, Cassie, Cassy, Gaspar, Gaspard, Gaspare, Gasparo, Gasper, Gazsi, Jaspar, Jasper, Josper, Kaspar, Kasper.
Meaning: 'jewel' (Greek); 'treasurer-keeper' (Persian); 'imperial' (Germanic). A variant of Jasper.
Notable namesakes: one of the Magi who visited the newborn Jesus Christ in the New Testament; Caspar David Friedrich (German artist); Caspar Weinberger (US politician).

Cassidy

Variants and diminutives: Caiside, Cass, Cassady, Cassie, Cassy, Kass, Kassady, Kassidy.
Meaning: 'curly' or 'intelligent' (Irish Gaelic); 'trickster' (Welsh). Also a girl's name.

Cassius

Variants and diminutives: Case, Casey, Cash, Casius, Caskey, Cass, Cassie, Cassy, Cazzie, Cazzy, Cez, Chaz, Kas.
Meaning: 'vain' (Latin).
Notable namesakes: Cassius Longinus (Greek philosopher); Cassius Clay, the former name of Muhammad Ali (US boxer).

Cathal

Variants and diminutives: Cal.
Meaning: 'strong in battle' (Irish Gaelic).

Cecil

Variants and diminutives: Caecilianus, Caecilius, Cece, Cecile, Cecilio, Cecilius, Ceese, Ces, Cis, Kilan, Seisyllt, Sissy, Sitsyllt.
Meaning: 'blind' (Latin); 'sixth' (Welsh).
Notable namesakes: Cecil Rhodes (British-born South African politician for whom Rhodesia, now Zimbabwe, was named); Cecil B de Mille (US film director); Cecil Day Lewis (Irish-born British writer); Cecil Beaton (British photographer).

Cedric

Variants and diminutives: Cad, Caddaric, Caradoc, Caradog, Ced, Cedrych, Cerdic, Ceredic, Rick, Rickie, Ricky.
Meaning: uncertain; possibly 'welcome sight' (Welsh); 'generous pattern' (Celtic); 'friendly' (Old English); possibly coined by Scottish writer Sir Walter Scott for his character Cedric Rotherwood in the novel *Ivanhoe*; possibly a misspelling of Cerdic.
Notable namesakes: Cerdic, the founder of the English kingdom of Wessex; a character in the children's novel *Little Lord Fauntleroy*, by English writer Frances Eliza Hodgson Burnett.

Cemal

Variants and diminutives: Kamal.
Meaning: 'handsome' (Arabic).

Chad

Variants and diminutives: Ceadda, Chadd, Chaddie, Chaddy.
Meaning: 'battle' (Welsh); 'martial' (Old English).
Notable namesakes: Saint Chad (Ceadda); Chad Varah (British founder of the counselling organisation The Samaritans).

Chaim

Variants and diminutives: Chaimek, Chayim, Chayyim, Chayym, Haim, Hayim, Haym, Hayyim, Hy, Hyam, Hyman, Hymie, Khaim, Mannie, Manny.
Meaning: 'life' (Hebrew).

Chand

Variants and diminutives: Chandran.
Meaning: 'the moon' (Sanskrit).

Chandler

Variants and diminutives: Chan, Chane, Chaney, Cheney, Shandler.
Meaning: 'candle-maker' or 'candle-seller' (Old French).
Notable namesakes: Joel Chandler Harris (US writer); Chandler Bing, a character in the US television series *Friends*.

Chang

Meaning: 'free' (Chinese).

Channing

Variants and diminutives: Chan, Chane, Chann, Channe, Channon.
Meaning: 'channel' (Latin); 'wolf cub' (Irish Gaelic). Also a girl's name.

Chanticleer

Meaning: 'to sing clearly' (Old French).
Notable namesakes: Chanticleer, the cock in the medieval French poem *Reynard the Fox*.

Charles

Variants and diminutives: Alcuin, Carel, Carl, Carleton, Carlie, Carling, Carlino, Carlisle, Carlo, Carlos, Carlson, Carlton, Carlus, Carly, Carlyle, Carol, Carolle, Carolo, Carolos, Carolus, Carroll, Cary, Caryl, Cathal, Cathaoir, Chad, Chaddie, Chaddy, Char, Charlet, Charley, Charlie, Charlot, Charis, Charlton, Charly, Charlys, Chas, Chay, Chaz, Chic, Chick, Chicky, Chico, Chilla, Chip, Cholly, Chuck, Corliss, Curley, Curlie, Curly, Kale, Kalle, Kalman, Karcsi, Karel, Kari, Karl, Karlen, Karlens, Karlik, Karlin, Karlis, Karol, Karole, Karolek, Karolus, Karoly, Siarl, Tearlach, Turlogh.
Meaning: 'man' or 'free man' (Germanic).
Notable namesakes: Charlemagne, the first Holy Roman emperor; Saint Charles Borromeo, patron saint of bishops, catechists and seminarians; King Charles I and II of England and Prince Charles, Prince of Wales; Bonnie Prince Charlie (Charles Edward Stuart), the Young Pretender; Charles James Fox (English politician); Dr Charles Primrose, the hero of the novel *The Vicar of Wakefield*, by Irish writer Oliver Goldsmith; Charles Darwin (English scientist); Charles Dickens and Charles Kingsley (English writers); Charles Stewart Parnell (Irish nationalist and politician); Charlie Chaplin (English actor and director); Charles Dana Gibson (US illustrator); Charles Lindbergh (US aviator); Charles De Gaulle (French statesman); Karol Wojtyla, Pope John Paul II; Carlos Santana (Mexican musician); Charlie Watts (British musician); Charlie Sheen (US actor); Charles Laughton and Charles Dance (British actors); Charlie Parker (US jazz musician); Chuck Berry (US singer); Chay Blyth (British yachtsman).

Charlton

Variants and diminutives: Carleton, Carlton, Charleton.
Meaning: 'settlement of free men' (Old English); derived from an English family name and a number of English place names.
Notable namesakes: Charlton Heston (US actor); Charlton Athletic, an English football club.

Chauncey

Variants and diminutives: Chance, Chancey, Chaunce, Chaune.
Meaning: 'to fall' (Latin); 'chance' (Old French); 'chancellor' (Old English).

Chen

Meaning: 'great' (Chinese).

Chester

Variants and diminutives: Caster, Castor, Ches, Cheslav, Chesleigh, Chesley, Chet.
Meaning: 'military camp' or 'Roman site' (Latin); derived from an English family name and a number of English place names.
Notable namesakes: Chester A Arthur (US president); Chester Himes (US writer); Chet Baker (US jazz musician).

Chevalier

Variants and diminutives: Chev, Chevi, Cheviot, Chevy.
Meaning: 'knight' (Old French); derived from the French title of nobility.
Notable namesakes: England's Cheviot Hills, subject

of the Middle English ballad *Chevy Chase*; Chevalier de Lamarck (French naturalist); Chevy Chase (US actor).

Christian

Variants and diminutives: Chrétien, Chris, Chrissie, Chrissy, Christen, Christiaan, Christiano, Christianos, Christie, Christien, Christy, Chrystian, Crispin, Cristao, Cristi, Cristian, Cristianito, Cristiano, Cristino, Crystek, Karston, Kerestel, Keresztyen, Kerstan, Kit, Kito, Kreston, Kris, Krischan, Krispin, Krist, Krista, Krister, Kristian, Kristjan, Kristo, Kristos, Krists, Krys, Krystek, Krystian, Jaan, Zan.
Meaning: 'Christian' (Latin).
Notable namesakes: Chrétien de Troyes, French medieval poet; the hero of English writer John Bunyan's Christian allegory *The Pilgrim's Progress*; Christian Dior (French fashion designer); Christian Slater (US actor).

Christopher

Variants and diminutives: Chippy, Chris, Chrissie, Chrissy, Christal, Christie, Christof, Christofer, Christoff, Christoffer, Christoforo, Christoforus, Christoph, Christophe, Christophorus, Christoval, Christovano, Christy, Chrystal, Cris, Cristi, Cristo, Cristobal, Cristoforo, Cristovao, Crystal, Gilchrist, Gillecriosd, Kester, Kit, Kris, Kriss, Kristo, Kristof, Kristofel, Kristofer, Kristoffer, Kristofor, Kristopher, Krisus, Stoffel, Tobal, Tobalito, Xit.
Meaning: 'carrier of Christ' (Greek).
Notable namesakes: Saint Christopher, the patron saint of travellers; Christopher Marlowe (British playwright); Christopher Columbus (Italian explorer); Christopher Wren (English architect); Christoph Willibald Gluck (Austrian composer); Christopher Dresser (British designer); Christopher Fry (British playwright); Christopher Robin, the son of British writer A A Milne, who was immortalised in his father's children's books; Christopher Isherwood (British writer); Christopher Lee (British actor); Christopher Okigbo (Nigerian poet); Chris Tarrant (British broadcaster).

Ciaran

Variants and diminutives: Ciaren, Keeran, Kiaran, Kieran, Kiraren, Kyran.
Meaning: 'dark' (Irish Gaelic).
Notable namesakes: Saint Ciaran of Saighir; Saint Ciaran of Clonmacnoise.

Cid

Variants and diminutives: Cyd, Sid, Syd.
Meaning: 'master' or 'lord' (Arabic).
Notable namesakes: 'El Cid', Rodrigo Diaz, Count of Bivar (Spanish soldier), whose story inspired many writers, including the French dramatist Pierre Corneille.

Clancy

Variants and diminutives: Clance, Clancey.
Meaning: 'offspring' or 'son of the red warrior' (Irish Gaelic); also an Irish family name.

Clarence

Variants and diminutives: Clair, Claire, Clancy, Claral, Clare, Claron, Sinclair.
Meaning: 'of Clare' (Latin); derived from the British title duke of Clarence, in turn derived from French and Irish place names; 'clear', 'bright' or 'famous' (Latin) as the male version of Clare.
Notable namesakes: Clarence Day (US writer); Clarence Darrow (US lawyer and writer).

Clark

Variants and diminutives: Clarke, Claxton.
Meaning: 'inheritance' (Greek); 'cleric' or 'clerk' (Old English).
Notable namesakes: Clark Gable (US actor); Clark Kent, the Superman comic-strip hero originally created by US writer Jerome Siegel and illustrator Joseph Shuster, later also of television and cinematic fame.

Claude

Variants and diminutives: Claud, Claudell, Claudian, Claudianus, Claudio, Claudius, Claus, Glade, Klaus.
Meaning: 'lame' (Latin); derived from a Roman family name.
Notable namesakes: Claudius I, the Roman emperor and subject of the novels *I Claudius* and *Claudius the*

God, by English writer Robert Graves; Saint Claude, patron saint of sculptors; Claudio, characters in two of William Shakespeare's plays, *Measure for Measure* and *Much Ado About Nothing*; Claudius, a character in William Shakespeare's play *Hamlet*; Claudio Monteverdi (Italian composer); Claude Lorrain (French artist); Claude Debussy (French composer); Claude Monet (French artist); Claude Lévi-Strauss (French anthropologist).

Clay

Variants and diminutives: Clayland, Clayten, Claytin, Clayton, Cle, Clea, Cletis, Cletus.
Meaning: 'clay' (Old English).

Clement

Variants and diminutives: Clem, Cleme, Clemen, Clemens, Clément, Clemente, Clementius, Clemento, Clemenza, Clemmie, Clemmons, Clemmy, Clemon, Clim, Kal, Kalman, Kaloymous, Kelemen, Klema, Klemens, Klement, Kelmet, Klemo, Klim, Klimek, Kliment, Klimka, Klimt, Klyment, Menz.
Meaning: 'merciful' or 'mild' (Latin).
Notable namesakes: Saint Clement, patron saint of lighthouse-keepers and marble-workers; Clemens von Metternich (Austrian statesman); Clément Marot (French poet); Clemens Maria Brentano (German poet); Clement Attlee (British politician).

Clifford

Variants and diminutives: Clif, Cliff, Cliffe, Clifton, Clyfford.
Meaning: 'ford by a cliff' (Old English); derived from an English family name and place name.
Notable namesakes: Clyfford Still (US artist); Clifford Odets (US playwright); Cliff Richard (British singer).

Clinton

Variants and diminutives: Clint, Clintin.
Meaning: 'hill settlement' (Old English); derived from an English family name, in turn derived from a place name.
Notable namesakes: Clint Eastwood (US actor).

Clive

Variants and diminutives: Cleavant, Cleavon, Cleve, Cleveland, Clevey, Clevie, Clif, Cliff, Cliffe, Clifton.
Meaning: 'cliff' (Old English); derived from an English family name, in turn derived from a place name.
Notable namesakes: 'Clive of India', the British colonial administrator Robert Clive; the hero of *The Newcomes*, a novel by English writer William Makepeace Thackeray; C(live) S(tables) Lewis (British writer); Clive Owen (British actor).

Clyde

Variants and diminutives: Cly, Clydel, Clywd.
Meaning: 'heard from a distance' (Welsh); derived from a family name, itself derived from the name of the Clyde river in Scotland.
Notable namesakes: the Clydesdale breed of horse, originating in Scotland's Clyde Valley; Clydebank, a Scottish shipyard; Clyde Barrow, the American outlaw whose partner in crime was Bonnie Parker.

Cole

Variants and diminutives: Colby, Cole, Coleman, Colier, Colin, Colis, Collayer, Colley, Collie, Collier, Collis, Collyer, Colman, Colton, Colville, Colvin, Colyer, Comghhall.
Meaning: 'swarthy' (Old English); 'hostage' or 'pledge' (Irish Gaelic); 'coal' (Middle English). Also a diminutive of Nicholas.
Notable namesakes: Colley Cibber (English playwright); 'Old King Cole', the jolly old soul of nursery-rhyme fame; Cole Porter (US composer).

Colin

Variants and diminutives: Cailean, Coilin, Colan, Cole, Colino, Collie, Collin, Collins, Colly, Colyn.
Meaning: 'victory of the people' (Greek) as a diminutive of Nicholas; 'youth' or 'puppy' (Scots Gaelic); 'young man' (Irish Gaelic); 'chieftain' (Celtic).
Notable namesakes: Colin MacInnes and Colin Wilson (British writers); Colin Cowdrey (British cricketer);

A B C D E F G H I J K L M N O P Q R S T U V W X Y Z

Colin Powell (US soldier and politician); Colin Firth (British actor).

Columba
Variants and diminutives: Callum, Calum, Colin, Colm, Colmicille, Colon, Colum, Columb, Columbus, Culva.
Meaning: 'dove-like' (Latin).
Notable namesakes: Saint Columba (Colmicille), patron saint of poets and Ireland.

Coman
Meaning: 'noble' (Arabic).

Conal
Variants and diminutives: Congal, Connall, Connell.
Meaning: 'mighty' (Celtic).

Conan
Variants and diminutives: Con, Conant, Conn, Conney, Connie, Connor, Conny, Conor, Kinan, Kynan.
Meaning: 'high' (Celtic); 'wolf' or 'hound' (Irish Gaelic); 'to be able to' (Middle English).
Notable namesakes: Sir Arthur Conan Doyle (British writer); the hero of the American film *Conan the Barbarian*.

Conor
Variants and diminutives: Con, Conchobar, Conner, Connery, Connor, Connors.
Meaning: 'high desire', 'wilful', 'lover of wolves' or 'lover of hounds' (Irish Gaelic); derived from an Irish family name.
Notable namesakes: King Conor of Ulster; Conor Cruise O'Brien (Irish writer and diplomat).

Conrad
Variants and diminutives: Con, Conn, Conni, Connie, Conny, Conrade, Conrado, Conrao, Conroy, Cort, Curt, Koenraad, Konni, Konrad, Kort, Kurt.
Meaning: 'brave' and 'advice' (Germanic).
Notable namesakes: Konrad Lorenz (Austrian ethologist and writer); Conrad Aiken (US writer); Konrad Adenauer (German statesman).

Constantine
Variants and diminutives: Con, Conney, Connie, Considine, Consta, Constans, Constant, Constantin, Constantinius, Constantino, Costa, Costain, Costane, Costin, Custance, Konstantin.
Meaning: 'constancy' (Latin).
Notable namesakes: Constantine I, 'the Great', the first Christian Roman emperor, for whom Constantinople (Istanbul), in Turkey, was named; Constantin Brancusi (Romanian sculptor).

Corbin
Variants and diminutives: Corban, Corben, Corbet, Corbett, Corby, Corbyn, Korbin, Korby, Korbyn.
Meaning: 'raven' (Old French).

Cordell
Variants and diminutives: Cord, Cordas, Cordel, Cordelle, Kord, Kordel, Kordell.
Meaning: 'instrument string' (Greek); 'cord' or 'cord-maker' (Old French).

Corin
Variants and diminutives: Caren, Carin.
Meaning: 'spear' (Sabine).
Notable namesakes: Corin Redgrave (British actor).

Cormac
Variants and diminutives: Cormack, Cormick.
Meaning: 'tree trunk' (Greek); 'charioteer' (Irish Gaelic).
Notable namesakes: a king of Irish legend.

Cornelius
Variants and diminutives: Conney, Connie, Cornall, Cornel, Cornell, Corney, Cornie, Corny, Cory, Neil, Neilus, Nelly.
Meaning: 'horn' or 'cornel tree' (Latin); derived from a Roman family name.
Notable namesakes: Cornelius Tacitus (Roman historian); Saint Cornelius; Cornelius Vanderbilt (US industrialist).

Corrigan
Variants and diminutives: Cori, Corigan, Corrie, Corry, Cory, Kori, Korigan, Korrie, Korrigan, Korry, Kory.
Meaning: 'small spear' (Irish Gaelic).

Cory
Variants and diminutives: Corey, Cori, Correy, Corry, Cory, Korey, Kori, Korrey, Korry, Kory.
Meaning: 'helmet' (Greek); 'hollow-dweller' or 'pool-dweller' (Irish and Scots Gaelic). Also a girl's name.

Cosmo
Variants and diminutives: Cosimo, Cosmas.
Meaning: 'order' (Greek).
Notable namesakes: Saint Cosmas, with Saint Damian, patron saint of physicians, surgeons, pharmacists, barbers and hairdressers; Cosimo Tura (Italian artist).

Craig
Variants and diminutives: Kraig.
Meaning: 'rock' (Scots Gaelic); derived from a Scottish family name.
Notable namesakes: Craig David (British singer).

Crispin
Variants and diminutives: Crepin, Crispian, Crispianus, Crispinian, Crispinianus, Crispino, Crispo, Crispus, Krispin.
Meaning: 'curly' (Latin).
Notable namesakes: Saint Crispin and Saint Crispinian, patron saints of shoemakers, cobblers, and leather-workers; Crispus Attucks, the first African-American to be killed in the Boston Massacre during the American War of Independence.

Crosby
Variants and diminutives: Crosbey, Crosbie.
Meaning: 'from the place of the cross' (Old Norse).

Cullen
Variants and diminutives: Cull, Cullan, Culley, Cullie, Cullin, Cully.
Meaning: 'cub' (Celtic); 'holly' (Irish Gaelic); 'from the nook' (Scots Gaelic); 'to select' (Middle English).

Curran
Variants and diminutives: Curr, Currey, Currie, Curry, Kurran, Kurrey, Kurrie, Kurry.
Meaning: 'champion' (Irish Gaelic); 'to churn' (Old English).

Curtis
Variants and diminutives: Cort, Cortie, Corty, Court, Courtenay, Courtland, Courtlandt, Courtney, Courts, Curcio, Curt, Curtell, Kurt, Kurtis.
Meaning: 'courtyard' (Latin); 'courteous' (Old French); 'short stockings' (Middle English); derived from an English family name.

Cuthbert
Variants and diminutives: Cudbert, Cudbright, Cuddie, Cuddy, Cumbert, Cuthbrid, Bert.
Meaning: 'famous' and 'bright' (Old English).
Notable namesakes: Saint Cuthbert, patron saint of shepherds.

Cyprian
Variants and diminutives: Sy.
Meaning: 'of Cyprus' (Latin).
Notable namesakes: Saint Cyprian; Cyprian Ekwensi (Nigerian writer).

Cyril
Variants and diminutives: Ciril, Cirill, Cirillo, Cirilo, Ciro, Cy, Cyriack, Cyrill, Cyrille, Cyrillo, Girioel, Kiril, Kyril, Sy, Syriack.
Meaning: 'ruler' or 'lord' (Greek).
Notable namesakes: Saint Cyril, who is credited with having devised the Glagolithic (Cyrillic) alphabet, patron saint of ecumenists; Cyril Tourneur (English playwright); Cyril M Kornbluth (US science-fiction writer); Cyril Connolly (British writer).

Cyrus
Variants and diminutives: Ciro, Cy, Cyrie, Kir, Kiril, Russ, Sy.
Meaning: 'sun', 'throne' or 'shepherd' (Persian).
Notable namesakes: King Cyrus, 'the Great', founder of the Achaemenid (Persian) Empire; Cyrus Vance (US politician).

A B C D E F G H I J K L M N O P Q R S T U V W X Y Z

Dacey
Variants and diminutives: Dace, Daci, Dacie, Dacy, Dasey, Dasi, Dasy, Daycee, Dayci, Daycie, Daycy.
Meaning: 'southerner' (Irish Gaelic). Also a girl's name.

Dalai
Meaning: 'mediator' (Sanskrit).
Notable namesakes: the Dalai Lama, the Tibetan Buddhist spiritual and temporal leader of Tibet.

Dalbert
Variants and diminutives: Bert, Bertie, Berty, Dal.
Meaning: 'valley' and 'bright' (Germanic).

Dale
Variants and diminutives: Dael, Dail, Daile, Dal, Daley, Dali, Dalibor, Dallan, Dallas, Dallin, Dalt, Dalton, Dalva, Daly, Dayle, Delles, Dillon, Dolan.
Meaning: 'valley' (Old English). Also a girl's name.
Notable namesakes: Dale Carnegie (US educator and writer); 'Daley' (Francis Morgan) Thompson (British athlete); Dale Winton (British television presenter).

Damian
Variants and diminutives: Dag, Dagan, Dagget, Dailey, Daily, Daly, Daman, Dame, Damiano, Damien, Damion, Damek, Damjan, Damlan, Damlano, Damon, Damyan, Darmon, Day, Dayman, Daymon, Daymond, Dayton, Demian, Dal, Delbert, Dema, Demyan.
Meaning: 'to tame', 'gentle' or 'fate' (Greek); 'demon' (Latin); 'bright day' (Old English).
Notable namesakes: Damon, the devoted friend of Pythias in Greek mythology; Saint Damian, with Saint Cosmas, patron saint of physicians, surgeons, pharmacists, barbers and hairdressers; Damon Runyon (US sports and crime reporter and short-story writer); Damon Hill (British racing driver); Damien Hurst (British artist); Damon Albarn (British musician).

Dane
Variants and diminutives: Dain, Daine, Dana, Daniel, Dayne, Dean.
Meaning: 'Dane' (Old Norse).

Daniel
Variants and diminutives: Dacso, Dainial, Dan, Dana, Dane, Daneal, Daneil, Danek, Dani, Daniela, Daniele, Daniels, Danil, Danila, Danilka, Danilo, Danko, Dano, Dannet, Dannie, Dannson, Danny, Danson, Danukas, Danya, Danylets, Danylo, Deiniol, Denils, Dennel, Domhnall, Donal, Donois, Dusan, Kamiela, Nelo, Taneli.
Meaning: 'judgement of God' (Hebrew).
Notable namesakes: a prophet and survivor of the lions' den in the Old Testament; Dan, a son of Jacob in the Old Testament; Saint Daniel the Stylite; Daniel Defoe (British writer); Daniel Boone (US pioneer); the eponymous leading character of the novel *Daniel Deronda*, by English writer George Eliot; 'Danny Boy', an Irish folk song; Daniel O'Connell (Irish natonalist); Danny DeVito (US actor); Daniel Day-Lewis (British actor).

Dante
Variants and diminutives: Duran, Durant, Durante, Durrant, Duryea.
Meaning: 'steadfast' (Latin); 'to endure' (Italian). A diminutive of Durante, an Italian version of Durand.
Notable namesakes: Dante Alighieri (Italian poet); Dante Gabriel Rossetti (British artist and poet).

Darby
Variants and diminutives: Dar, Darb, Darbey, Darbie, Derby, Derland, Dero, Deron, Diarmaid, Dorset, Dorsey, Dorsie, Dove, Dover, Dovey.
Meaning: 'deer park' or 'settlement by the water' (Old English); derived from an English family name and place name; 'free' (Irish Gaelic). Also a girl's name.
Notable namesakes: Darby, the husband of Joan, 'Darby and Joan' representing a contentedly married older couple.

Darius

Variants and diminutives: Daare, Dar, Dare, Dareios, Daren, Daria, Darian, Darien, Darin, Dario, Darn, Darnel, Daron, Daroosh, Darrel, Darren, Darrin, Darring, Darrius, Daryl, Derry, Dorian.
Meaning: 'rich' (Greek).
Notable namesakes: King Darius I, 'the Great', of Persia; Darius Milhaud (French composer).

Darrell

Variants and diminutives: Dar, Dare, Darel, Darell, Darlin, Darol, Darold, Darrel, Darrill, Darrol, Darroll, Darry, Darryl, Daryl, Daryle, Derel, Derial, Derland, Derral, Derrell, Derrill, Derry, Derryl, Deryl, Dorrel.
Meaning: 'dear' (Old English); 'of Airelle' (French); derived from an English family name, in turn derived from a French place name. Also a girl's name.
Notable namesakes: Darryl Zanuck (US film producer).

Darren

Variants and diminutives: Dar, Daran, Dare, Daren, Darien, Darin, Dario, Darn, Darnell, Daron, Darran, Darrin, Darring, Darron, Darun, Daryn.
Meaning: uncertain; possibly 'rich' (Greek) as a variant of Darius; possibly 'great small one' (Irish Gaelic) when derived from an Irish family name.

Darwin

Variants and diminutives: Dar, Derwin, Derwyn, Durwin.
Meaning: 'sea' or 'dear' and 'friend' (Old English).

David

Variants and diminutives: Dab, Dabbey, Dabby, Dabko, Dabney, Daffy, Dafyd, Dafydd, Dahi, Dai, Daibhead, Daibhi, Daibhidh, Daith, Daithi, Daithin, Dakin, Dako, Dathi, Daud, Daue, Dav, Dave, Daveed, Davey, Davi, Davidas, Davidde, Davide, Davidek, Davidyne, Davie, Davin, Daviot, Davis, Davit, Davito, Davy, Davyd, Daw, Dawe, Dawes, Dawid, Dawood, Dawoodji, Dawson, Dawud, Deakin, Deio, Devi, Devlin, Dew, Dewer, Dewey, Dewi, Dodya, Dowid, Dov, Dow, Dowe, Kavika, McTavish, Tab, Tafydd, Taffy, Tavi.
Meaning: 'beloved' or 'friend' (Hebrew).

Notable namesakes: King David, Israelite slayer of Goliath and harpist in the Old Testament; the Star of David, a symbol of Judaism and Israel; Saint David (Dewi), patron saint of Wales, poets and doves; Saint David I and David II, kings of Scotland; David Garrick (English actor and theatre manager); Davy Crockett (US folk hero, 'king of the wild frontier'); David Livingstone (British missionary and explorer); the eponymous hero of the novel *David Copperfield*, by English writer Charles Dickens; David Lloyd George (British politician); David Hockney (British artist); David Puttnam (British film producer); David Jason (British actor); David Blunkett (British politician); David Bowie and David Gilmour (British musicians); David Bailey (British photographer); David Gower (British cricketer); David Cassidy (US singer); David King (British publisher); David Beckham (British footballer).

Dean

Variants and diminutives: Deane, Dee, Dene, Dennit, Deno, Denton, Dino.
Meaning: 'one in charge of ten' or 'dean' (Latin); 'valley' (Old English); derived from an English family name.
Notable namesakes: the Forest of Dean in England; Dean Acheson (US politician); Dean Martin (US singer and actor).

Decimus

Meaning: 'tenth' (Latin).
Notable namesakes: Decimus Burton (British architect).

Declan

Variants and diminutives: Deaglan.
Meaning: uncertain; possibly 'good' (Irish Gaelic).
Notable namesakes: Saint Declan.

Dee

Meaning: a diminutive of any name beginning with 'D-'. Also a girl's name.

Delano

Variants and diminutives: Del, Delan, Delane, Delaine, Delainey, Delaney, Delann, Lane, Laine.
Meaning: 'dark' or 'healthy' (Irish Gaelic); 'of the night' (French).
Notable namesakes: Franklin Delano Roosevelt (US president).

Delmar

Variants and diminutives: Del, Delmer, Delmor, Delmore.
Meaning: 'of the sea' (Latin).

Delroy

Variants and diminutives: Del, Roy.
Meaning: 'of the king' (Old French).

Demetrius

Variants and diminutives: Deems, Demeter, Demetre, Demetri, Demetrio, Demitri, Demetrios, Demitrios, Demitrius, Demitry, Demmy, Dima, Dimitr, Dimitre, Dimitri, Dimitrios, Dimitry, Dimos, Dmitri, Dmitrik, Dmitry, Dometer, Domotor, Dymmek, Dymitry, Dyzek, Mimis, Mitros, Mitsos, Takis.
Meaning: 'of Demeter' (Greek), Demeter being the Greek earth goddess.
Notable namesakes: Saint Demetrius of Rostov; a character in William Shakespeare's play *A Midsummer Night's Dream*; Dmitry Dmitryevich Shostakovich (Russian composer).

Denholm

Variants and diminutives: Den, Dennie, Denny.
Meaning: 'valley' and 'island' (Old English); derived from an English family name, in turn derived from an English place name.
Notable namesakes: Denholm Elliott (British actor).

Dennis

Variants and diminutives: Deenys, Den, Denes, Denis, Denison, Denit, Denka, Denman, Dennes, Dennet, Denney, Dennie, Dennison, Dennit, Denny, Denote, Denya, Denys, Denzel, Denzell, Denzil, Deon, Diniz, Dinny, Dion, Dione, Dionigi, Dionis, Dionisio, Dionysios, Dionysius, Dionysos, Dionysus, Diot, Donnchadh, Donnet, Donoghm, Dwight, Enis, Ennis, Enzo, Nicho, Tennis.
Meaning: 'deity of the Nysa' (Greek), Nysa being the birthplace of Dionysus, the Greek god of wine, fecundity, vegetation and revelry, from whose name Dennis is derived.
Notable namesakes: Saint Dionysius the Areopagite, a Christian convert in the New Testament; Saint Dionysius of Alexandria; Saint Denys, patron saint of France; the French town, Saint-Denis, and the capital of the French island of Réunion, in the Indian Ocean; 'Dennis the Menace', British cartoon-strip character; Denis Glover (New Zealand writer, editor and typographer); Dennis Healey (British politician); Dennis Potter (British playwright); Dennis Lillee (Australian cricketer); Dennis Quaid (US actor); Dennis Waterman (British actor).

Denton

Variants and diminutives: Dennie, Denny.
Meaning: 'valley' and 'settlement' (Old English); derived from an English family name, in turn derived from a number of English place names.

Denver

Variants and diminutives: Den, Dennie, Denny.
Meaning: 'Danes' crossing' (Old English); 'little forested valley' (Middle English); 'green' (French); derived from an English family name, in turn derived from an English place name.
Notable namesakes: the American town of Denver, Colorado.

Denzil

Variants and diminutives: Dennie, Denny, Denzel, Denzell.
Meaning: uncertain; possibly 'fortress' (Celtic); 'high' (Cornish); derived from a Cornish family name, in turn derived from the Cornish place name Denzell.
Notable namesakes: the hero of the novel *The Card*, by English writer Arnold Bennett; Denzel Washington (US actor).

Derek

Variants and diminutives: Darick, Darik, Darrek, Darrick, Darrik, Dederick, Dek, Dekker, Del, Der, Derec, Dereck, Deric, Derick, Derk, Derrec, Derreck, Derrek, Derric, Derrick, Derrik, Derry, Deryck, Deryk, Diederick, Dirck, Dirk, Durk, Dyryke, Rick, Ricky, Terry, Theoderic, Thierry, Tedrick.
Meaning: 'people' and 'ruler' (Germanic). A variant of Theodoric.
Notable namesakes: derrick, a generic name for a crane (and previously also a gibbet), derived from the name of a 17th-century English hangman, Derrick; Dirk Bogarde (British actor); Derek Jarman (British film producer).

Dermot

Variants and diminutives: Darby, Der, Derby, Dermott, Diarmad, Diarmaid, Diarmait, Diarmid, Diarmit, Diarmuid, Diiarmuit, Kermit.
Meaning: 'lacking in envy' (Irish Gaelic).
Notable namesakes: Diarmaid ua Duibhne, the lover of Grainne in Irish legend; Dermot MacMurrough, an Irish king.

Deror

Variants and diminutives: Derori, Dror.
Meaning: 'free' or 'a swallow' (Hebrew).

Derry

Variants and diminutives: Dare, Darrey, Darrie, Dary.
Meaning: 'red-headed' (Irish Gaelic); 'oak trees' (Welsh). Also a diminutive of names beginning with 'Der-'.

Desiderio

Variants and diminutives: Desi, Desideratus, Desiderius, Desito, Diderot, Didi, Didier, Didon, Didot, Dizier.
Meaning: 'desiring' (Latin).
Notable namesakes: Desi Arnaz (US musician and actor).

Desmond

Variants and diminutives: Demon, Des, Desi, Dezi.
Meaning: 'of the world' (Latin); 'from south Munster' (Irish Gaelic), Munster (Deas-Mhumhan in Irish Gaelic) being an Irish province; derived from an Irish family name.
Notable namesakes: Desmond Tutu (South African religious leader); Desmond Morris (British anthropologist); Desmond O'Grady (Irish poet).

Deval

Variants and diminutives: Dev, Deven, Devmani, Devraj.
Meaning: 'divine' (Sanskrit).

Devin

Variants and diminutives: Deavon, Dev, Devan, Deven, Devlin, Devon, Devron, Devy, Devyn.
Meaning: 'poet' (Irish Gaelic). Also a girl's name.

Dexter

Variants and diminutives: Decca, Deck, Dek, Dex.
Meaning: 'right-sided' or 'right-handed' (Latin).

Dhani

Variants and diminutives: Dan, Dannie, Danny, Dhan, Dhanni, Dhannie, Dhanny.
Meaning: 'rich' (Hindi).
Notable namesakes: Dhani Harrison (son of George Harrison, British musician and former Beatle).

Dick

Variants and diminutives: Dickie, Dickon, Dicky.
Meaning: 'ruler' and 'hard' (Germanic). A diminutive of Richard.
Notable namesakes: Dick Whittington, the cat-owning mayor of London; Dick Turpin (English highwayman); Dick Swiveller, a character in the novel *The Old Curiosity Shop*, by English writer Charles Dickens; Dick Francis (British writer).

Diego

Meaning: 'supplanter' (Hebrew). A Spanish variant of James, in turn a variant of Jacob.
Notable namesakes: Saint Diego of Seville; Diego Rodriguez de Silva y Velázquez (Spanish artist); the American city of San Diego, California; Diego Rivera (Mexican artist); Diego Maradona (Argentinian footballer).

Dietrich
Variants and diminutives: Dedrick, Dedrik, Detrik, Dierck, Dierk, Dieter, Dieterich, Dietz, Dirk, Dtrik, Dytrych.
Meaning: 'powerful' and 'rich' or 'ruler of the people' (Germanic).

Digby
Meaning: 'to dig a ditch' (Old French); 'farm by a ditch' (Old English); derived from an English family name, in turn derived from an English place name.

Diggory
Variants and diminutives: Digory.
Meaning: uncertain; possibly 'gone astray' (French).
Notable namesakes: a character in the play *She Stoops to Conquer*, by Irish writer Oliver Goldsmith.

Dominic
Variants and diminutives: Chuma, Chumin, Chuminga, Deco, Dom, Domek, Domenic, Domenick, Domenico, Domenikos, Domenyk, Domi, Domicio, Domingo, Domingos, Dominick, Dominik, Dominique, Dominy, Domo, Domokos, Domonkos, Don, Donek, Dumin, Menico, Mingo, Nick, Nickie, Nicky, Niki.
Meaning: 'of the lord' (Latin).
Notable namesakes: Saint Dominic, founder of the Dominican order of friars, also known as the Blackfriars; Saint Dominic de Guzman, patron saint of astronomers; Saint Dominic Savio, patron saint of choir boys and the falsely accused; Domenikos Theotokopoulos, the real name of the Greek-born Spanish artist El Greco.

Donald
Variants and diminutives: Bogdan, Bohdan, Domhnal, Domhnall, Don, Donahue, Donal, Donaldo, Donalt, Donn, Donne, Donner, Donnie, Donny, Donahue, Donovan, Donya, MacDonald, Tauno.
Meaning: 'global might' (Scots Gaelic); also a Scottish clan name.
Notable namesakes: the name of six Scottish kings; Walt Disney's cartoon character Donald Duck; Donald Judd and Donald Sultan (US artists); Donald Bradman (Australian cricketer); Donald Dewar (Scottish politician); Donny Osmond (US singer).

Donato
Variants and diminutives: Dodek, Don, Donary, Donat, Donatello, Donati, Donato, Donatus, Donny.
Meaning: 'gift' (Latin).
Notable namesakes: Saint Donatus of Fiesole; Donato Bramante (Italian architect).

Donnel
Variants and diminutives: Donn, Donnell, Donnelly, Donny, Doon, Dun.
Meaning: 'hill' or 'hillfort' (Irish Gaelic).

Donovan
Variants and diminutives: Don, Donnie, Donny, Donovon, Dunavan, Van.
Meaning: 'dark' (Irish Gaelic); 'dark warrior' (Celtic); derived from an Irish surname.
Notable namesakes: Donovan (Irish singer).

Doran
Variants and diminutives: Darren, Dore, Dorey, Dorian, Dorie, Doron, Dorran, Dory.
Meaning: 'gift' (Greek); 'exiled' or 'estranged' (Irish Gaelic).

Dorian
Variants and diminutives: Dor, Dorrie, Dory.
Meaning: 'of the sea' or 'of Doris' (Greek), Doris being a Greek region north of the Gulf of Corinth. Also a girl's name.
Notable namesakes: the Dorians, the Hellenic invaders of Greece whose homeland was Doris; the subject of the novel *The Picture of Dorian Gray*, by Irish writer Oscar Wilde.

Dougal
Variants and diminutives: Doug, Dougie, Doyle, Dug, Dugald, Duggy, Dughall, Dubhghall.
Meaning: 'dark stranger' (Irish Gaelic).
Notable namesakes: a character in *The Magic Roundabout*, a British children's television series.

Douglas
Variants and diminutives: Doug, Dougal, Dougie, Douglass, Dougy, Dugald, Duggie.
Meaning: 'dark water' (Scots Gaelic); derived from a Scottish family name, in turn derived from a Scottish place name.
Notable namesakes: the capital of the Isle of Man; the Douglas fir, *Pseudotsuga menziesii*, named for the Scottish botanist David Douglas; Douglas Fairbanks and Douglas Fairbanks Jr (US actors); Douglas MacArthur (US general).

Dov
Variants and diminutives: Dovev.
Meaning: 'bear' (Hebrew).

Doyle
Variants and diminutives: Dougal.
Meaning: 'assembly' (Irish Gaelic); 'dark stranger' (Irish Gaelic) as a variant of Dougal.

Drake
Meaning: 'snake' or 'dragon' (Greek).

Drogo
Variants and diminutives: Drew, Drewe, Drews, Dru, Druce, Drue, Drugo.
Meaning: 'to carry' (Germanic).

Duane
Variants and diminutives: Duwayne, Dwain, Dwain, Dwane, Dwayne.
Meaning: 'dark and little' (Irish Gaelic).
Notable namesakes: Duane Hanson (US sculptor).

Dudley
Variants and diminutives: Dud, Dudd, Dudly
Meaning: 'Duddha's clearing' (Old English); derived from an English family name, in turn derived from an English place name.
Notable namesakes: Dudley Moore (British comedian, actor and musician).

Duff
Meaning: 'dark' (Scottish and Irish Gaelic); derived

from a Scottish family name; 'dough' (northern English).

Duke
Variants and diminutives: Dukey, Dukie, Duky.
Meaning: 'leader' (Latin) as a derivation of the title of nobility; 'servant of [Saint] Maedoc' (Irish Gaelic) as a variant of Marmaduke.
Notable namesakes: Duke Ellington (US musician).

Duncan
Variants and diminutives: Dun, Dunc, Dune, Dunkie, Dunn, Donncha, Donnchadh.
Meaning: 'brown warrior' (Irish and Scots Gaelic) or 'princely battle' (Scots Gaelic).
Notable namesakes: King Duncan I of Scotland, who

was murdered by Macbeth, as dramatised by William Shakespeare in his play *Macbeth*; Duncan Grant (British artist and designer); Duncan Campbell Scott (Canadian writer).

Dunstan
Variants and diminutives: Donestan, Dunn, Dunne, Dunst, Dustie, Dustin, Dusty.
Meaning: 'grey-brown', 'dark stone' or 'stony hill' (Old English).
Notable namesakes: Saint Dunstan, patron saint of blacksmiths, goldsmiths and blind people.

Durand
Variants and diminutives: Dante, Duran, Durant, Durante, Durrant, Duryea.
Meaning: 'steadfast' (Latin); 'to endure' (Italian).

Dustin
Variants and diminutives: Dust, Dustie, Dusty.
Meaning: uncertain; possibly 'Thor's stone' (Old Norse); possibly 'a warrior' (Germanic); derived from an English family name.
Notable namesakes: Dustin Hoffman (US actor).

Dwight

Variants and diminutives: Dewitt, DeWitt, Diot, Doyt, Wit, Wittie, Witty.

Meaning: uncertain; possibly 'white' (Old English and Old Dutch); possibly 'deity of the Nysa' (Greek), Nysa being the birthplace of Dionysus, the Greek god of wine, fecundity, vegetation and revelry, from which the name may be derived via a family name in turn derived from the name Diot, a variant of Dionysus.

Notable namesakes: Dwight D Eisenhower (US president); Dwight Macdonald (US writer).

Dylan

Variants and diminutives: Dill, Dillan, Dillie, Dillon, Dilly.

Meaning: 'son of the wave' or 'influence' (Welsh).

Notable namesakes: Dylan Eil Ton, a water baby and son of Aranrhod in Welsh mythology; Dylan Thomas (Welsh writer).

Eamon

Variants and diminutives: Eamonn, Edmund.

Meaning: 'happiness' or 'riches' and 'protector' (Old English) as the Irish Gaelic variant of Edmund.

Notable namesakes: Eamon de Valera (Irish politician); Eamonn Andrews (Irish television presenter).

Earl

Variants and diminutives: Earland, Earle, Earlie, Early, Erie, Erl, Erle, Errol, Erroll, Eryl, Jarl, Rollo.

Meaning: 'chieftain' (Old English); derived from the title of nobility.

Notable namesakes: Earl 'Fatha' Hines (US musician);

Erle Stanley Gardner (US crime-writer); Earl Warren (US politician and jurist).

Ebenezer

Variants and diminutives: Ben, Benezer, Eb, Eban, Ebanezer, Eben, Ebeneezer, Ebenezar Even.

Meaning: 'help-giving stone' (Hebrew).

Notable namesakes: a place (marked by a stone) where the Israelites were victorious over the Philistines in the Old Testament; Ebenezer Scrooge, the miserly character in the novel *A Christmas Carol*, by English writer Charles Dickens.

Edan

Variants and diminutives: Ed, Eddie, Eddy, Eden.

Meaning: 'fire' (Celtic).

Edgar

Variants and diminutives: Adair, Eadgar, Ed, Eddie, Eddy, Edek, Edgard, Edgardo, Edgars, Edko, Edus, Garek, Ned, Neddie, Neddy, Ted, Teddie, Teddy.

Meaning: 'happiness' or 'riches' and 'spear' (Old English).

Notable namesakes: Edgar 'the Peaceful' King of England; characters in William Shakespeare's play *King Lear* and the novel *The Bride of Lammermoor*, by Scottish writer Sir Walter Scott; Edgar Allan Poe and Edgar Rice Burroughs (US writers); Edgar Degas (French artist); Edgar Wallace (British thriller-writer).

Edmund

Variants and diminutives: Eadmond, Eamon, Eamonn, Ed, Eddie, Eddy, Edmon, Edmond, Edmondo, Edmundo, Edmunds, Esmond, Mundek, Mundo, Ned, Neddie, Neddy, Odi, Odon, Ted, Teddie, Teddy.

Meaning: 'happiness' or 'riches' and 'protector' (Old English).

Notable namesakes: Saint Edmund, King of East Anglia, for whom the English town of Bury St Edmunds was named; King Edmund I of England; Edmund Ironside, King of England; Saint Edmund of Abingdon; a character in William Shakespeare's play *King Lear*; Edmund Spenser and Edmund Waller (English poets); Edmund Halley, the English scientist for whom Halley's Comet was named; Edmund Burke (Irish-born British writer and politician); Edmund Blunden (British writer); Edmund Hillary (New Zealand mountaineer); Edmund Blackadder, the leading character in the British television series *Blackadder*.

Edom

Variants and diminutives: Adam, Idumea.
Meaning: 'red' or 'red earth' (Hebrew). A variant of Adam.
Notable namesakes: a name given to Esau, the twin brother of Jacob and son of Isaac and Rebecca in the Old Testament (see also Esau).

Edric

Variants and diminutives: Ed, Eddie, Eddy, Edred, Edrich, Edrick, Ric, Rick, Rickie, Ricky.
Meaning: 'happiness' or 'riches' and 'powerful' or 'ruler' (Old English).
Notable namesakes: Edric 'the Forester' (or 'the Wild'), an English chieftain at the time of the Norman invasion.

Edward

Variants and diminutives: Duardo, Duarte, Eadbard, Eadbhard, Eamon, Ed, Edd, Eddard, Eddie, Eddy, Ede, Edek, Edgard, Edik, Edison, Edko, Edo, Edoardo, Edouard, Edouardo, Edrardo, Edson, Eduard, Eduardo, Eduardus, Eduarelo, Eudardo, Edus, Edvard, Edwardo, Edwardus, Edzio, Eideard, Emile, Eward, Guayo, Ned, Nedd, Neddie, Neddy, Ted, Tedd, Teddie, Teddy.
Meaning: 'happiness' or 'riches' and 'guardian' (Old English).
Notable namesakes: ten kings of England, among them Saints Edward the Confessor, patron saint of difficult marriages, and Edward the Martyr; Edward Gibbon (English historian); Edward Jenner, the English physician who pioneered vaccination; Edouard Manet (French artist); Edward Bulwer-Lytton (English writer); Edward Lear (English poet and artist); Edward Burne-Jones (English artist); Edvard Munch (Norwegian artist); Edward Elgar (English composer); Edward Steichen (US photographer); Edward Hopper (US artist); Edward Heath (British politician); Edward Kennedy (US politician); Edward Woodward (British actor); Prince Edward of the United Kingdom.

Edwin

Variants and diminutives: Eaduin, Ed, Eddie, Eddy, Edred, Eduin, Eduino, Eduinus, Edwinn, Edwy, Edwyn, Ned, Neddie, Neddy, Ted, Teddie, Teddy.
Meaning: 'happiness' or 'riches' and 'friend' (Old English).
Notable namesakes: Saint Edwin, King of Northumbria, for whom, some believe, Edinburgh, the Scottish capital, was named; Edwin Landseer (British artist); the eponymous leading character of the unfinished novel *The Mystery of Edwin Drood*, by English writer Charles Dickens; Edwin Austin Abbey (US artist); Edwin Lutyens (English architect); Edwin Arlington Robinson (US poet); Edwin McMillan (US physicist).

Egan

Variants and diminutives: Aeduca, Aodhagan, Egon.
Meaning: 'small fire' (Irish Gaelic).

Egbert

Variants and diminutives: Bert, Bertie, Berty.
Meaning: 'shining' or 'famous' and 'sword' or 'blade' (Old English).
Notable namesakes: King Egbert, King of Wessex.

Elan

Variants and diminutives: Ela, Elah, Elai, Elon.
Meaning: 'tree' (Hebrew); 'spirited' (Latin); 'friendly' (Native American).

Eldon

Variants and diminutives: Edlen, Edlon, Elden, Elder, Eldor, Elton.
Meaning: 'Ella's mound' (Old English); derived from an English family name, in turn derived from a place name; 'old and wise' (Germanic) as a variant of Aldo.

Eldred

Variants and diminutives: Aldred.
Meaning: 'old' and 'counsel' (Old English).

Eleazar

Variants and diminutives: El, Elazar, Elazaro, Elie, Eliezer, Ely, Lazar, Lazarus.

Meaning: 'God is my help' (Hebrew).
Notable namesakes: a son of Aaron in the Old Testament.

Eli

Variants and diminutives: El, Eloy, Ely, Ilie.
Meaning: 'elevated' or 'Jehovah' (Hebrew).
Notable namesakes: Samuel's teacher in the Old Testament.

Elijah

Variants and diminutives: El, Eli, Elia, Elias, Elie, Eligio, Elihu, Elija, Elio, Eliot, Eliott, Elis, Elisio, Elison, Eliyahu, Elliot, Elliott, Ellis, Ellison, Elly, Elsen, Elson, Ely, Elyas, Elye, Elyot, Elys, Ilie, Ilija, Ilya.
Meaning: 'Jehovah is God' (Hebrew).
Notable namesakes: an Old Testament prophet also called Elias; Elijah Wood (US actor).

Elisha

Variants and diminutives: Elias, Eliot, Elis, Elissee, Eliseo, Elison, Elizur, Elkan, Elkanah, Ellas, Elliot, Elliott, Ellis, Ellison, Elly, Elrad, Elrod, Elsden, Elsen, Elson, Elstone, Ely, Hrod.
Meaning: 'God is my salvation' (Hebrew).
Notable namesakes: an Old Testament prophet.

Elliot

Variants and diminutives: Elias, Eliot, Elliott, Ellis.
Meaning: 'Jehovah is God' (Hebrew) as a variant of Elias (Elijah); 'noble' and 'battle' (Old English); derived from an English family name.
Notable namesakes: Elliott Gould (US actor).

Ellis

Variants and diminutives: Eelia, Eelusha, Elek, Eli, Elia, Elias, Eliasz, Elie, Elihu, Elis, Elisee, Eliseo, Elison, Ellas, Ellison, Elly, Elsden, Elsen, Elson, Elston, Ely, Elya, Ilias, Ilya.
Meaning: 'Jehovah is God' (Hebrew) as a variant of Elias (Elijah); derived from an English family name; 'benevolent' (Welsh).
Notable namesakes: Ellis Bell, the pseudonym of the English writer Emily Brontë.

Elmer

Variants and diminutives: Ailemar, Athel, Aylmar, Aylmer, Aymer, Edmar, Edmer, Eilemar, Elma, Elman, Elmo, Elmore.
Meaning: 'noble' and 'renowned' (Old English). A variant of Aylmer.
Notable namesakes: the subject of the novel *Elmer Gantry*, by US writer Sinclair Lewis; Elmer Rice (US playwright)).

Elroy

Meaning: 'the king' (Old Spanish). A variant of Leroy.

Elton

Variants and diminutives: Elden, Elsdon, Elston.
Meaning: 'Ella's settlement', 'old' or 'noble' and 'town' (Old English); derived from an English family name, in turn derived from a place name.
Notable namesakes: Elton John (British musician).

Elvis

Variants and diminutives: Alby, Alvis.
Meaning: 'knowing all' (Old Norse) as a variant of Alvis; 'white' (Latin) as a variant of Alby (Alben and Albin, see Alban).
Notable namesakes: Elvis Presley (US singer); Elvis Costello (British singer).

Elwin

Variants and diminutives: Al, Albin, Aloin, Aluin, Aluino, Alvan, Alvi, Alvin, Alvino, Alwin, Alwyn, Aylwin, El, Elva, Elvert, Elvin, Elwin, Elwyn.
Meaning: 'fair' and 'brow' (Welsh); 'old' and 'friend' (Old English); 'elf' or 'noble' and 'friend' (Old English) as a variant of Alvin.

Emery

Variants and diminutives: Almericus, Almery, Amalric, Amalrich, Amerigo, Amory, Emerick, Emericus, Emerson, Emil, Emilio, Emlin, Emlyn, Emmerich, Emmerlich, Emmery, Emmory, Emory, Imray, Imre, Imrich, Imrus.
Meaning: 'diligent' and 'ruler' (Germanic); 'powerful' and 'noble' (Old English).
Notable namesakes: a type of metamorphic rock.

Emile

Variants and diminutives: Amal, Emielo, Emil, Emilek, Emilio, Emilian, Emiliano, Emilio, Emils, Hemilio, Imelio, Melo, Milko, Milo, Miyo.

Meaning: 'eager', 'flatter' or 'rival' (Latin); derived from the Roman family name Aemilius.

Notable namesakes: the leading character of the romances *Émile, ou l'Éducation* and *Émile et Sophie*, by French writer and philosopher Jean Jacques Rousseau; Emile Zola (French writer); Emil Nolde (German artist); Emile Verhaeren (Belgian poet); the eponymous hero of the children's story *Emile and the Detectives*, by German writer Erich Kästner; Emilio Estevez (US actor).

Emlyn

Meaning: uncertain; possibly 'rival' (Latin) when derived from the Roman family name Aemilianus; possibly derived from the name of a Welsh town, Newcastle Emlyn. Also a girl's name.

Notable namesakes: Emlyn Williams (Welsh actor and playwright); Emlyn Hughes (British footballer).

Emmanuel

Variants and diminutives: Emanuel, Emanuele, Imanuel, Immanuel, Mani, Manny, Mannye, Mano, Manoel, Manuel.

Meaning: 'God is with us' (Hebrew).

Notable namesakes: a name for the messiah in the Old Testament; Emanuel Swedenborg (Swedish scientist, theologian and philosopher); Immanuel Kant (German philosopher); Emmanuel Roblès (French writer); Emanuel Ungaro (French fashion designer).

Emmet

Variants and diminutives: Emmett, Emmit, Emmitt.
Meaning: 'truth' (Hebrew); 'ant' (Old English).

Emrys

Meaning: 'divine' or 'immortal' (Greek) as a Welsh variant of Ambrose.

Engelbert

Variants and diminutives: Bert, Bertie, Berty, Englebert, Ingelbert, Inglebert.
Meaning: 'angel' and 'bright' (Germanic).

Notable namesakes: Engelbert Humperdinck (German composer), a stage name also assumed by a US singer.

Enoch

Meaning: 'dedicated', 'sacred to God', 'educated' or 'teacher' (Hebrew).

Notable namesakes: the son of Cain and father of Methuselah in the Old Testament; the subject of the poem *Enoch Arden*, by English poet Alfred, Lord Tennyson; Enoch Powell (British politician).

Enos

Variants and diminutives: Enosh.
Meaning: 'man' (Hebrew).
Notable namesakes: a son of Seth and a grandson of Adam and Eve in the Old Testament.

Ephraim

Variants and diminutives: Efim, Efraim, Efrain, Efrasha, Efrat, Efrayim, Efrem, Efren, Efron, Ephrayim, Ephrem, Ephrim, Rema.
Meaning: 'fruitful' (Hebrew).
Notable namesakes: a son of Joseph and Asenath in the Old Testament; Saint Ephraim.

Erasmus

Variants and diminutives: Elmo, Erasme, Erasmo, Eraste, Erastus, Ras, Rastus.
Meaning: 'beloved' or 'desired' (Greek).
Notable namesakes: Saint Erasmus (Elmo), patron saint of sailors and sufferers of intestinal diseases, for whom St Elmo's fire, a form of electrical discharge seen above ships' masts, was named; Desiderius Erasmus of Rotterdam (Dutch humanist scholar); Erasmus Darwin (English writer and physician).

Eric

Variants and diminutives: Erek, Erich, Erick, Erico, Erik, Eriks, Ric, Rick, Ricki, Rickie, Ricky.
Meaning: 'eternal', 'honourable' or 'island' and 'ruler' (Old Norse).
Notable namesakes: Eric

A B C D E F G H I J K L M N O P Q R S T U V W X Y Z

the Red, the Norwegian discoverer of Greenland; the subject of the romance *Eric Brighteyes*, by English writer Rider Haggard; Erik Satie (French composer); Eric Gill (British sculptor, engraver and typographer); Eric Linklater (British writer); Erich Maria Remarque and Erich Kästner (German writers); Erik Erikson and Erich Fromm (German-born US psychoanalysts); Eric Rohmer (French writer and film-maker); Erich von Stroheim (Austrian-born US film director); Eric Burdon and Eric Clapton (British musicians); Eric Idle (British comic actor); Eric Fischl (US artist); Eric Cantona (French footballer and actor).

Ernest

Variants and diminutives: Earnan, Earnest, Ern, Erneis, Erneste, Ernestino, Ernesto, Ernestus, Ernie, Ernis, Erno, Ernst, Erny, Neto.
Meaning: 'earnest' (Old English).
Notable namesakes: Ernst Gombrich (Austrian-born British art historian); Ernst Ludwig Kirchner (German artist); Ernst Lubitsch (German-born US film director); Ernst Toller (German writer); Ernest Hemingway and Ernest J Gaines (US writers).

Eros

Meaning: 'erotic love' (Greek).
Notable namesakes: the god of love, son of Aphrodite, the goddess of love, in Greek mythology.

Errol

Variants and diminutives: Earl, Erroll, Eryl, Harold, Rollo, Rolly.
Meaning: uncertain; possibly 'chieftain' (Old English) as a variant of Earl; possibly derived from a Scottish family name, in turn derived from a Scottish place name; possibly 'watcher' (Welsh) when the spelling Eryl is used.
Notable namesakes: Errol Flynn (Australian actor).

Esau

Meaning: 'hairy' (Hebrew).

Notable namesakes: the twin brother of Jacob and son of Isaac and Rebecca in the Old Testament (see also Edom).

Esmond

Variants and diminutives: Esmund.
Meaning: 'grace' and 'defence' (Old English).

Ethan

Variants and diminutives: Etan, Ethe.
Meaning: 'constancy' or 'strength' (Hebrew).
Notable namesakes: Ethan Allen, the American Revolutionary soldier whose story is told in the novel *Green Mountain Boys*, by US writer Daniel Pierce Thompson; the eponymous leading character of the novel *Ethan Frome*, by US writer Edith Wharton.

Ethelbert

Variants and diminutives: Adalbert, Adelbert, Elbert, Elbie.
Meaning: 'noble' and 'bright' (Old English).
Notable namesakes: Saint Ethelbert, King of Kent, who was converted to Christianity by Saint Augustine; Saint Ethelbert, King of the East Angles.

Ethelred

Variants and diminutives: Aethelraed, Aillred, Alret, Edred.
Meaning: 'noble' and 'counsel' (Old English).
Notable namesakes: Kings Ethelred I and Ethelred II, 'the Unready', of England.

Eugene

Variants and diminutives: Egen, Eoghan, Eugen, Eugène, Eugenio, Eugenios, Eugenius, Evgeni, Evgenios, Ewan, Ewen, Geka, Gencho, Gene, Genek, Genie, Genio, Genya, Jano, Jenci, Jeno, Jensi, Owain, Owen, Yevgeniy, Yevgeny, Zenda, Zheka, Zhenka.
Meaning: 'well-born' (Greek).
Notable namesakes: Saint Eugenius; the eponymous subject of the novel *Eugene Onegin*, by Russian writer Aleksandr Pushkin; Eugène Delacroix (French artist and writer); Eugene O'Neill (US playwright); Eugène Ionesco (Romanian-French playwright); Gene Kelly (US actor and dancer); Eugene Gant, the leading character

of the novels *Look Homeward, Angel* and *Of Time and the River*, by US writer Tom Wolfe; Gene Hackman and Gene Wilder (US actors).

Eustace
Variants and diminutives: Eustache, Eustachius, Eustasius, Eustathius, Estatius, Eustazio, Eustis, Stace, Stacey, Stacy.
Meaning: 'fruitful', 'good' or 'ear of corn' (Greek).
Notable namesakes: Saint Eustace (Eustachius), patron saint of hunters; Eustace, Duke of Cambenet in Arthurian legend.

Evan
Variants and diminutives: Ev, Evin, Ewan, Owen, Eoin.
Meaning: 'God has favoured', 'God is gracious' or 'God is merciful' (Hebrew) as a variant of Ieuan, in turn a Welsh variant of John; 'young warrior' or 'young archer' (Old Welsh).
Notable namesakes: Evan Hunter (US writer).

Evander
Meaning: 'good man' (Greek).
Notable namesakes: a name of Pan, the pipe-playing god of flocks and herds in Greek mythology; Evander Holyfield (US boxer).

Evelyn
Variants and diminutives: Evel, Evelio, Evelle.
Meaning: 'hazelnut' (Germanic); 'bird' (Latin). Also a girl's name.
Notable namesakes: Evelyn Waugh (British writer, whose first wife bore the same first name).

Everard
Variants and diminutives: Averitt, Devereux, Eberhard, Eberhart, Eberle, Ebert, Everart, Everet, Everett, Everette, Everhard, Everley, Evert, Eward, Ewart.
Meaning: 'boar' and 'tough' (Old English).

Ewan
Variants and diminutives: Eaven, Eoghan, Eugene, Ev, Evan, Evander, Evans, Evin, Evo, Ewen, Euan, Owain, Owen.
Meaning: 'youth' (Scots Gaelic); 'well-born' (Greek) as a variant of Eugene; 'God has favoured', 'God is gracious' or 'God is merciful' (Hebrew) as a variant of Ieuan, in turn a Welsh variant of John.
Notable namesakes: Ewan McGregor (Scottish actor).

Ewart
Variants and diminutives: Euel, Ewell.
Meaning: 'settlement by the river' (Old English); derived from an English family name, in turn derived from a place name; 'ewer' (Old French).
Notable namesakes: William Ewart Gladstone (British politician).

Ezekiel
Variants and diminutives: Ezechial, Ezell, Eziechiele, Haskel, Haskell, Hehezkel, Yehezekel, Zeke.
Meaning: 'God give strength' (Hebrew).
Notable namesakes: an Old Testament prophet.

Ezra
Variants and diminutives: Azariah, Azrikam, Azur, Esdras, Esra, Ezar, Ezer, Ezera, Ezri, Ezzard, Ezzret.
Meaning: 'help' (Hebrew).
Notable namesakes: a Jewish scribe and prophet who established Mosaic law in Jerusalem in the Old Testament; Ezra Pound (US poet).

Fabian
Variants and diminutives: Fabe, Fabek, Faber, Fabert, Fabi, Fabiano, Fabianus, Fabien, Fabio, Fabius, Fabiyan, Fabyan.
Meaning: uncertain; possibly 'bean' or 'skilful' (Latin); derived from the Roman family name Fabius.
Notable namesakes: the Roman general Quintus Fabius Maximus (*Cunctator*, 'Delayer'), the opposer of

Hannibal, after whom the British socialist organisation the Fabian Society was named; Saint Fabianus.

Faisal

Variants and diminutives: Faisel, Faisil, Faisl, Faizal, Fasil, Faysal, Faysul, Fayzal, Fayzel.
Meaning: 'a fair judge' (Arabic).
Notable namesakes: King Faisal of Saudi Arabia.

Farid

Meaning: 'unique' (Arabic).

Farouk

Variants and diminutives: Farook, Farooq, Faruq.
Meaning: 'detector of lies' (Arabic).
Notable namesakes: Farouk, King of Egypt.

Farquhar

Variants and diminutives: Fearchar.
Meaning: 'dear' or 'amiable' and 'man' (Scots Gaelic).
Notable namesakes: King Farquhar of Scotland.

Farrell

Variants and diminutives: Farell, Farr, Farrall, Farril, Ferrel, Ferrell.
Meaning: 'superior' or 'valiant' (Irish Gaelic).

Felix

Variants and diminutives: Bodog, Fee, Fela, Felex, Felic, Felice, Felicio, Felike, Feliks, Felis, Felixiano, Felizano, Feliziano, Felizio, Phelim.
Meaning: 'happy' or 'fortunate' (Latin).
Notable namesakes: Felix, King of Cornwall, grandfather of Tristan in Arthurian legend; Saint Felix of Dunwich, for whom the English town Felixstowe was named; the eponymous hero of the novel *Felix Holt the Radical*, by English writer George Eliot; Felix Mendelssohn (German composer); Felix Adler (German-born US educator); 'Felix the Cat', a cartoon character.

Ferdinand

Variants and diminutives: Fardie, Fardy, Faron, Farran, Farren, Fearn, Ferando, Ferd, Ferde, Ferdenando, Ferdi, Ferdie, Ferdinando, Ferdino, Ferdy, Fern, Fernand, Fernandas, Fernandeo, Fernando, Fernandus, Ferni, Ferrand, Ferrando, Ferrant, Ferrante, Ferren, Ferrentus, Hernán, Hernándo, Nando, Nano.
Meaning: 'spirited' (Latin); 'journey' or 'peace' and 'prepare' or 'venture' (Germanic).
Notable namesakes: Saint Ferdinand III, King of Castile and Leon, patron saint of engineers and governors; King Ferdinand II of Aragon, the first king of Spain following his marriage to Queen Isabella of Castile; characters in William Shakespeare's plays *Love's Labour's Lost* and *The Tempest*; Ferdinand Magellan, the Portuguese navigator for whom the Strait of Magellan, linking the south Pacific and south Atlantic, was named; Ferdinand Porsche (German founder of the Porsche automobile factory); Fernand Léger (French artist); Fernando Arrabal (Spanish writer).

Fergal

Variants and diminutives: Fearghal.
Meaning: 'brave' (Irish Gaelic).

Fergus

Variants and diminutives: Fearghas, Feargus, Fergie, Ferguson, Fergy.
Meaning: 'strong and brave' or 'supreme choice' (Irish and Scots Gaelic).
Notable namesakes: Fergus Mac Roigh, King of Ulster, in Celtic legend.

Fidel

Variants and diminutives: Fedele, Fidelio.
Meaning: 'trust' or 'faithful' (Latin).
Notable namesakes: the name assumed by the heroine of the opera *Fidelio*, by German composer Ludwig van Beethoven; Fidel Castro (Cuban president).

Finbar

Variants and diminutives: Fin, Finbarr, Finn, Fionnbharr.
Meaning: 'fair-haired' (Irish Gaelic).
Notable namesakes: Saint Finbarr.

Finlay

Variants and diminutives: Fin, Findlay, Findley,

Findlaech, Finley, Finn, Fionnlagh.
Meaning: 'fair-haired' and 'warrior' or 'hero' (Scots Gaelic).
Notable namesakes: Findlaech, the father of the Scottish king, Macbeth; Finley Peter Dunne (US journalist and humorist).

Finn

Variants and diminutives: Eifion, Finan, Finian, Finnegan, Finnian, Fion, Fionn.
Meaning: 'fair' (Irish Gaelic); also a citizen of Finland.
Notable namesakes: Finn mac Cumhail, a hero of Irish legend, chief of the Fianna and father of the poet Ossian; Saint Finnian of Clonard; Saint Finan.

Fisk

Variants and diminutives: Fish, Fiske.
Meaning: 'fish' or 'to fish' (Germanic).

Fitz

Variants and diminutives: Fitzgerald, Fitzpatrick, Fitzroy.
Meaning: 'son' (Old English).

Flavius

Variants and diminutives: Flavian, Flavio.
Meaning: 'yellow' (Latin).

Fletcher

Variants and diminutives: Fletch.
Meaning: 'arrow-maker' (Old English); derived from an English family name.
Notable namesakes: Fletcher Christian, leader of the sailors' mutiny on *The Bounty*.

Florian

Variants and diminutives: Ferenc, Fiorello, Florence, Florentino, Florents, Florentz, Florenz, Florus, Flory.
Meaning: 'flowering' or 'blossoming' (Latin). A male version of Florence.
Notable namesakes: Saint Florian (Florus), twin brother of Saint Laurus and patron saint of firefighters, floods and Poland.

Floyd

Variants and diminutives: Lloyd.
Meaning: 'grey' (Welsh) as a variant of Lloyd.
Notable namesakes: Floyd Dell (US writer).

Flynn

Variants and diminutives: Flin, Flinn, Flyn.
Meaning: 'son of the red-headed man' (Irish Gaelic).

Forbes

Meaning: 'fodder' (Greek); 'field-owner' or 'prosperous' (Irish Gaelic).

Ford

Meaning: 'river crossing' (Old English).
Notable namesakes: Ford Madox Ford (English writer).

Fortunatus

Variants and diminutives: Fortunato, Fortune, Fortunio.
Meaning: 'luck' (Latin). A male version of Fortuna.

Foster

Variants and diminutives: Forest, Forester, Forrest, Forrester, Forster, Foss.
Meaning: 'forester' (Old English), when derived from an English family name; 'foster child' (Old English).
Notable namesakes: John Foster Dulles (US politician).

Francis

Variants and diminutives: Chicho, Chico, Chilo, Chito, Cisco, Currito, Curro, Farruco, Fenenc, Fra, Fran, Franc, Franca, Francesco, Franchot, Francie, Francisco, Franciscus, Franciskus, Franck, Franco, François, Farnio, Frank, Frankie, Franky, Frannie, Frans, Frants, Franus, Franz, Franzen, Franzi, Frasco, Frascuelo, Frenz, Firso, Paco, Pacorro, Palani, Panchito, Pancho, Paquito, Proinnsias, Quico.
Meaning: 'French' (Latin).
Notable namesakes: Saint Francis of Assisi, founder of the Franciscan order of monks and patron saint of

conservationists, ecology, animals and birds; Saint Francis of Paola, patron saint of sailors; François Rabelais (French scholar and writer); Sir Francis Drake (English buccaneer and explorer); Sir Francis Walsingham (English politician); Saint Francis of Sales, patron saint of deaf people, writers, authors and journalists; Frans Hals (Dutch artist); Francisco Pizzaro (Spanish conquistador); Francisco de Zurbarán and Francisco José de Goya y Lucientes (Spanish artists); Francis Bacon (English politician and philosopher); Saint Francis Xavier, patron saint of missionaries; François Boucher (French artist); Francis Poulenc (French composer); the eponymous leading character of the short story *The Short Happy Life of Francis Macomber*, by US writer Ernest Hemingway; Francis Bacon (British artist); François Mitterand (French politician); François Truffaut (French film director); Francis Chichester (British sailor); Francis Ford Coppola (US film director).

Frank

Variants and diminutives: Cisco, Fenenc, Ferenc, Feri, Fran, Franc, Franca, Franck, Franco, Franek, Franio, Franki, Frankie, Franky, Frannie, Frans, Frants, Franus, Franz, Franzl, Frenz, Paco.

Meaning: 'free' (Latin); derived from the name of the Franks, a Germanic tribe whose western kingdom is now France, while their eastern kingdom is Germany. Also a diminutive of Francis and Franklin.

Notable namesakes: Frank Wedekind (German actor and playwright); Frank Winfield Woolworth (US businessman); Frank Lloyd Wright (US architect); Frank Capra (US film director); Frank Sinatra (US singer); Frank McCourt (Irish-born US writer); Frank Stella (US artist); Frank Bruno (British boxer).

Franklin

Variants and diminutives: Francklyn, Frank, Franki, Frankie, Franklyn.

Meaning: 'free man' (Middle English); derived from an English family name.

Notable namesakes: a class of English medieval landowners; Franklin D Roosevelt (US president).

Fraser

Variants and diminutives: Frase, Frasier, Fraze, Frazer, Frazier.

Meaning: uncertain; possibly 'curly' (Old English); possibly 'charcoal-burner' or 'strawberry' (Old French); possibly derived from a Scottish family name, in turn derived from the French place name La Fraselière.

Notable namesakes: a river in south-western Canada; Frazer Hines (British actor); Frasier Crane, the eponymous leading character of the US television sitcom *Frasier*.

Frederick

Variants and diminutives: Bedrich, Eric, Erich, Erick, Erik, Federico, Federigo, Federoquito, Fred, Freddie, Freddy, Fredek, Frédéric, Frederic, Frederich, Frederico, Frederigo, Frederik, Fredi, Fredric, Fredrick, Fredrik, Freed, Freeman, Frides, Fridrich, Friedel, Friedrich, Frits, Fritz, Fritzchen, Fritzi, Lico, Ric, Rich, Rick, Rickey, Rickie, Ricky, Rico, Riki.

Meaning: 'peace' and 'ruler' (Germanic).

Notable namesakes: the Holy Roman emperors Frederick I (*Barbarossa*, 'Red Beard') and Frederick II (*Stupor mundi*, 'Wonder of the World'); Friedrich von Schiller (German writer); King Frederick II, 'the Great', of Prussia; Fredericton, the capital of New Brunswick, Canada, named for Prince Frederick, son of King George III of Britain; Frederic, Lord Leighton (English artist); Frédéric Chopin (Franco-Polish composer and pianist); Frederick Douglass (US anti-slavery campaigner); Frederic Remington (US artist); Friedrich Engels (German socialist); Friedrich Hölderlin (German poet); Friedrich Nietzsche (German philosopher); Frederic Henry, a leading character in the novel *A Farewell to Arms*, by US writer Ernest Hemingway; Freddie Eynsford Hill, a character in Irish writer George Bernard Shaw's play *Pygmalion*, and in the subsequent musical and film *My Fair Lady*; Friedrich Murnau (German film director); Fred Astaire (US dancer and actor); Federico García Lorca (Spanish writer); Federico Fellini (Italian film director); Friedrich Dürrenmatt

(Swiss playwright); Frederick Forsyth (British thriller-writer); Frederick Brown (US artist); Freddie Mercury (British singer).

Fulbert

Variants and diminutives: Bert, Berty, Filbert, Filberte, Filibert, Fulbright, Phil, Philbert, Philibert.
Meaning: 'very' and 'bright' (Germanic).

Gabriel

Variants and diminutives: Gab, Gabby, Gabe, Gabi, Gabian, Gabie, Gabiel, Gabirel, Gabko, Gabo, Gabor, Gabrial, Gabriele, Gabrielli, Gabriello, Gabris, Gaby, Gabys, Gavril, Gay, Riel.
Meaning: 'man of God' or 'my strength is God' (Hebrew).
Notable namesakes: the archangel Gabriel in the Old and New Testaments, patron saint of diplomats, messengers, communication, radio, broadcasters and postal workers; Gabriel Dante Fahrenheit, German physicist and inventer of the Fahrenheit temperature scale; Dante Gabriel Rossetti (British painter and poet); Gabriel Oak, a character in the novel *Far From the Madding Crowd*, by English writer Thomas Hardy; Saint Gabriel Possenti (Gabriel of Our Lady of Sorrows), patron saint of clerics and young people; Gabriel Fauré (French composer); Gabriele D'Annunzio (Italian writer and soldier); Gabriel Marcel (French philosopher and writer); Gabriel García Márquez (Colombian writer).

Gaius

Variants and diminutives: Caius, Kay.
Meaning: 'to rejoice' (Latin).
Notable namesakes: Gaius Cilnius Maecenas (Roman statesman); Gaius (or Caius) Julius Caesar Octavianus, the first Roman emperor, subsequently called Augustus; Gaius Valerius Catullus (Roman poet).

Galahad

Variants and diminutives: Gwalchafed.
Meaning: 'battle hawk' or 'falcon of summer' (Welsh).
Notable namesakes: Sir Galahad, 'the perfect knight', the son of Sir Lancelot and Elaine in Arthurian legend.

Gale

Variants and diminutives: Gael, Gail, Gaile, Gallard, Gay, Gayle.
Meaning: 'gallant' (Old French); 'lively' (Old English); 'stranger' (Irish Gaelic). Also a male version of Gail.

Galen

Variants and diminutives: Gaelan, Gail, Gailen, Gale, Galeno, Gay, Gayle, Gaylen.
Meaning: 'calm' (Greek).
Notable namesakes: a Greek physician and inventor of the theory of the four humours.

Galvin

Variants and diminutives: Gal, Galvan, Galven.
Meaning: 'sparrow' or 'brilliant white' (Irish Gaelic).

Gamaliel

Variants and diminutives: Gamliel.
Meaning: 'God's recompense' (Hebrew).
Notable namesakes: Warren Gamaliel Harding (US president); Gamaliel Bradford (US biographer).

Gandalf

Meaning: 'the elf of the wand' in the fictional language of the Men of the North in Middle Earth; coined by British writer J R R Tolkien for a leading character – a wizard – in his epic fantasies *The Hobbit* and *The Lord of the Rings*.

Gareth

Variants and diminutives: Gary, Garry, Garth.
Meaning: 'gentle' (Welsh).
Notable namesakes: Sir Gareth, a knight of the Round Table in the romance *Le Morte d'Arthur*, by English writer Thomas Malory, and in 'Gareth and Lynette', part of the poetic series of poems *The Idyll of the King*, by English poet Alfred, Lord Tennyson.

A B C D E F G H I J K L M N O P Q R S T U V W X Y Z

Garfield

Variants and diminutives: Gar, Field.
Meaning: 'triangle' and 'field', 'promontory' or 'spears' and 'field' (Old English); derived from an English family name, in turn derived from a place name.
Notable namesakes: Gary (Garfield) Sobers (West Indian cricketer); a cartoon cat.

Garrick

Variants and diminutives: Garek, Garick, Garik, Garreck, Garrek, Garrik, Garry, Gary, Gerek, Gerick, Gerreck, Gerrek, Gerrick, Gerrik, Rick, Rickie, Ricky, Rik, Rikky.
Meaning: 'spear' and 'ruler' (Old English).

Garth

Variants and diminutives: Gareth, Garret, Garton, Garvie, Garvin, Garry, Gary.
Meaning: 'enclosure' (Old Norse); 'garden' (Old English); derived from an English family name, in turn derived from a place name. Also a variant of Gareth.
Notable namesakes: Garth Brooks (US country musician).

Gary

Variants and diminutives: Gareth, Gareym Garfield, Gari, Garret, Garrett, Garri, Garry, Garth, Gerold.
Meaning: dependent on the meaning of the name of which it is a diminutive, for example: 'gentle' (Welsh) as a diminutive of Gareth; also derived from a British family name.
Notable namesakes: Gary Cooper (US actor); Garry Kasparov (Azerbaijani chess player); Gary Snyder (US writer); Gary Hill (US artist); Gary Oldman (British actor and film director); Gary Lineker (British footballer).

Gavin

Variants and diminutives: Gauen, Gauvain, Gauvin, Gav, Gavan, Gaven, Gavino, Gavvy, Gawain, Gawaine, Gawen, Gawin, Gwalchmai, Gwalchmei, Walwain, Walwyn.
Meaning: 'falcon of May' or 'hawk of the plain' (Welsh); 'district' (Germanic).
Notable namesakes: Sir Gawain (Gwalchmei), a knight of the Round Table in Arthurian legend and hero of the medieval poem *Sir Gawayne and the Greene Knight*; Gavin Stevens, a character who appears in several novels by the US writer William Faulkner.

Gaylord

Variants and diminutives: Gae, Gail, Gaile, Gallard, Gay, Gayelord, Gayle, Gayler, Gaylor.
Meaning: 'merry' (Old French); derived from an English family name. Recently rendered unfashionable by its homosexual connotations.

Geoffrey

Variants and diminutives: Geof, Geoff, Giotto, Gisfrid, Godfrey, Godofredo, Gottfried, Gotz, Govert, Jef, Jeff, Jefferies, Jefferson, Jeffery, Jeffie, Jeffrey, Jeffries, Jeffry, Jeffy.
Meaning: uncertain; possibly 'God', 'good', 'district', 'traveller' or 'pledge' and 'peace' (Germanic) as a variant of Godfrey.
Notable namesakes: Geoffrey Plantagenet, Count of Anjou, father of King Henry II of England; Geoffrey of Monmouth (Welsh chronicler); Geoffrey Chaucer (English poet); Geoffrey Boycott (British cricketer).

George

Variants and diminutives: Deòrsa, Dod, Durko, Egor, Geo, Geordie, Georg, Georges, Georgi, Georgie, Georgio, Georgios, Georgius, Georgiy, Georgy, Giorgis, Giorgos, Gogos, Goran, Gyorgy, Gyuri, Gyurka, Igor, Jarge, Jeorg, Jerzy, Jiri, Jörgen, Jorgen, Jorge, Jorgen, Jorje, Jorn, Jur, Juraz, Jurek, Jurg, Jürgen, Jurgen, Jurgi, Jurgis, Juri, Jurik, Jurko, Juro, McGeorge, Seoirse, Seòras, Sior, Siors, Siorys, Xorge, Yegor, Yorick, York, Yura, Yurchik, Yuri, Yurik, Yurko, Yusha, Zhorka.
Meaning: 'farmer' (Greek).
Notable namesakes: Saint George, patron saint of England, Germany and Portugal, as well as of soldiers, archers, knights, armourers, husbandmen, boy scouts and sufferers of syphilis; six British kings; George Washington (first US president); George Frideric Handel (German composer); George Cruikshank (British caricaturist); George Stubbs (English artist); George, Lord Byron (English poet); Georgetown, capital of

Guyana; Georgia, a Russian republic; George Armstong Custer (US general of last-stand fame); Georg Friedrich Wilhelm Hegel (German philosopher); George Meredith and George Orwell (English writers); George Bernard Shaw (Irish writer); Georg Grosz (German artist); Georges Seurat and Georges Braque (French artists); Giorgio Morandi (Italian artist); George Gershwin (US composer); Georges Duhamel and Georges Simenon (French writers); George Santayana (Spanish-born US writer and philosopher); George Bush and George W Bush (US presidents); George Passmore (British artist of 'Gilbert and George' fame); George Lucas (US film director); George Best (Northern Irish footballer); George Harrison and George Michael (British musicians); George Clooney (US actor).

Geraint

Variants and diminutives: Gerontius.
Meaning: 'old man' (Greek); a Welsh variant of the Latin name Gerontius.
Notable namesakes: an Arthurian character whose story is told in 'Geraint and Enid', part of English poet Alfred, Lord Tennyson's, series of poems *The Idylls of the King*; Geraint Evans (Welsh opera singer).

Gerald

Variants and diminutives: Erhard, Garald, Garet, Garett, Garey, Garo, Garold, Garolds, Garret, Garrett, Garritt, Garry, Gary, Geaóid, Gearóid, Ged, Gerallt, Ger, Gerado, Geralde, Geraldo, Gerardo, Geraud, Gerek, Gerold, Gerret, Gerrie, Gerrit, Gerritt, Gerry, Gerwald, Cherardo, Giraldo, Girald, Girard, Giraud, Girauld, Girault, Giraut, Herrardo, Jarett, Jarrett, Jed, Jerald, Jeraldo, Jerrald, Jerral, Jerre, Jerrel, Jerrell, Jerrie, Jerrold, Jerry.
Meaning: 'spear' and 'rule' (Germanic).
Notable namesakes: Gerald of Wales (Giraldus Cambrensis, Welsh historian); Gerald Durrell (British zoologist and writer); Gerald Ford (US president); Gerald Murphy (US artist); Garret FitzGerald (Irish politician).

Gerard

Variants and diminutives: Erhard, Garald, Garey, Garo, Garold, Garolds, Garrard, Garret, Garrett, Garry, Gary, Gearard, Ged, Gellart, Gellert, Ger, Gerado, Geraud, Gerek, Gerhard, Gerharde, Gerhart, Gerrard, Gerret, Gerrie, Gerrit, Gerry, Gerwald, Gherardo, Giralt, Girard, Giraud, Girauld, Girault, Giraut, Herrado, Jarett, Jarrett, Jed, Jerald, Jeraldo, Jerrald, Jerral, Jerrard, Jerre, Jerrel, Jerrell, Jerrie, Jerrold, Jerry.
Meaning: 'spear' and 'hard' (Germanic).
Notable namesakes: Saint Gerard Majella, patron saint of lay-brothers, pregnant women and childbirth; Gerard Ter Borch (Dutch artist); Gerard Manley Hopkins (British poet); Gerhart Hauptmann (German playwright); Gérard Dépardieu (French actor).

Gervaise

Variants and diminutives: Gervais, Gervase, Gervasius, Gervis, Jarvis.
Meaning: uncertain; possibly 'spear' (Germanic) and 'servant' (Celtic).
Notable namesakes: Saint Gervasius; a leading character in the '*Les Rougon-Macquart*' series of novels, by French writer Émile Zola.

Gerwin

Variants and diminutives: Gerwyn.
Meaning: 'fair' and 'love' (Welsh).

Gibor

Meaning: 'strong' (Hebrew).

Gibson

Variants and diminutives: Gib, Gibb, Gibbie, Gibby.
Meaning: 'son of Gilbert' (Old English), Gilbert meaning 'pledge' or 'hostage' and 'bright' (Germanic), 'servant', 'servant of Saint Bridget' or 'servant of Saint Gilbert' (Scots Gaelic); derived from a British family name.
Notable namesakes: the Gibson Desert in Western Australia; John Gibson (English sculptor); a type of US cocktail.

Gideon

Variants and diminutives: Gedeon, Gid, Gideone, Hedeon.

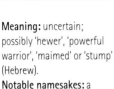

Meaning: uncertain; possibly 'hewer', 'powerful warrior', 'maimed' or 'stump' (Hebrew).

Notable namesakes: a judge in the Old Testament; the Gideons, a Christian society known for its editions of the Bible.

Gilbert

Variants and diminutives: Bert, Bertie, Berty, Burt, Burtie, Birty, Gib, Gibb, Gibbie, Gibbon, Gibby, Gibson, Gil, Gilberto, Gilbride, Gilburt, Gilibeirt, Gill, Gilleabart, Gilli, Gillie, Giselbert, Guilbert, Wilbert, Wilbur, Wilburt, Will.

Meaning: 'pledge' or 'hostage' and 'bright' (Germanic); 'servant', 'servant of Saint Bridget' or 'servant of Saint Gilbert' (Scots Gaelic).

Notable namesakes: Saint Gilbert of Sempringham, founder of the religious order the Gilbertines and patron saint of mobility-impaired people; Gilbert of the White Hand, one of Robin Hood's band of merry men in English lore; Gilbert Osmond, a character in the novel *The Portrait of a Lady*, by US writer Henry James; Gilbert O'Sullivan (British singer); Gilbert Proesch (Italian artist of 'Gilbert and George' fame).

Giles

Variants and diminutives: Egide, Egidio, Egidius, Gide, Gidie, Gil, Gile, Gilean, Gileon, Gill, Gilles, Gillette, Gillian, Gyles.

Meaning: 'kid' or 'goatskin' (Greek); derived from the Roman name Aegidius; 'servant' (Scots Gaelic).

Notable namesakes: Saint Giles, patron saint of hermits, beggars, lepers, nursing mothers and mobility-impaired people; Giles Fletcher, the Younger (English poet); the subject of the poem *The Farmer's Boy*, by English poet Robert Bloomfield; Gyles Brandreth (British writer and broadcaster).

Gillespie

Variants and diminutives: Gill.

Meaning: 'bishop's servant' (Scots Gaelic); derived from a Scottish family name.

Gilroy

Variants and diminutives: Gill, Gilly, Roy.

Meaning: 'servant of the red-headed man' or 'servant of the king' (Scots Gaelic).

Glen

Variants and diminutives: Glenard, Glenn, Glennard, Glennon, Glyn, Glynn.

Meaning: 'valley' (Scots Gaelic); derived from a Scottish family name, in turn derived from a geographical feature. As Glenn, also a girl's name.

Notable namesakes: Glenn Miller (US musician and band leader); Glenn Ford (Canadian-born US actor); Glen Campbell (US singer); Glen Hoddle (British footballer and football manager).

Glyndwr

Variants and diminutives: Glendower.

Meaning: 'valley' and 'water' (Welsh).

Notable namesakes: Owain Glyndwr (Owen Glyndower), an anti-English Welsh revolutionary leader after whom the Welsh nationalist group Meibion Glyndwr (Sons of Glendower) was named.

Godfrey

Variants and diminutives: Goraidh.

Meaning: 'God', 'good', 'district, 'traveller' or 'pledge' and 'peace' (Germanic).

Notable namesakes: Godfrey de Bouillon (French crusader); Godfrey Kneller (German-born English artist).

Godwin

Variants and diminutives: Godewyn, Godwyn, Goodwin, Win, Winny, Wyn.

Meaning: 'God' or 'good' and 'friend' (Old English).

Notable namesakes: Godwin, Earl of Wessex, father-in-law of the Edward the Confessor, King of England.

Gordon

Variants and diminutives: Goran, Gordan, Gorden, Gordey, Gordie, Gordy, Gore, Gorham, Gorrell, Gorton.

Meaning: uncertain; possibly 'large' and 'fort' or 'marsh' and 'wooded dell' (Scots Gaelic); derived from a Scottish family name, in turn derived from a Scottish or Norman place name.

Notable namesakes: the title character of the novella *The Narrative of A Gordon Pym*, by US writer Edgar Allan Poe; Gordon Brown (British politician); Gordon Ramsey (British chef).

Grady

Variants and diminutives: Gradey.
Meaning: 'step' (Latin); 'bright one' or 'exalted one' (Irish Gaelic).

Graham

Variants and diminutives: Graeham, Graeme, Graemer, Graenem, Graenum, Grahame, Gram, Gramm.
Meaning: 'Granta's', 'gravelly', 'grey' or 'grant' and 'homestead' (Old English); derived from Grantham, an English town; also a Scottish family name.
Notable namesakes: Graham Sutherland (British artist); Graham Greene (British writer); Graham Chapman (British comedian); Graham Hill (British racing driver); Graham Norton (Irish comedian); Graham Thorpe (British cricketer).

Grant

Variants and diminutives: Grantland, Grantley.
Meaning: 'large', 'tall' or 'to bestow' (French); derived from a Scottish family name.
Notable namesakes: Grant Wood (US artist).

Granville

Variants and diminutives: Grenville.
Meaning: 'large' and 'town' (French); derived from an English family name, in turn derived from a Norman place name.
Notable namesakes: Granville Hicks (US writer).

Gray

Variants and diminutives: Graydon, Grey, Greyson.
Meaning: 'grey' or 'bailiff' (Old English).
Notable namesakes: Gray Jolliffe (British cartoonist).

Gregory

Variants and diminutives: Gero, Greg, Gregg, Greggory, Gregoire, Gregor, Gregorio, Gregorios, Gregorius, Gregors, Gregos, Gregour, Gregus, Greig, Greis, Gries, Grigoi, Grigor, Grigorios, Grigory, Griogair, Grischa.
Meaning: 'watchful' (Greek).
Notable namesakes: sixteen popes, including Saint Gregory I, 'the Great', for whom the form of plainsong called Gregorian chant was named, patron saint of popes, musicians, singers, students and teachers; and Gregory XIII, who introduced the Gregorian calendar to the Western world; Saint Gregory of Tours; Grigory Aleksandrovich Potemkin (Russian solder); Gregor Mendel (Austrian botanist); Grigory Yefimovich Rasputin (Russian monk); Gregor Samsa, the subject of the short story *The Metamorphosis*, by Czech writer Franz Kafka; Gregory Corso (US poet); Gregory Peck (US actor); Greg Rusedski (Canadian-born British tennis player).

Griffith

Variants and diminutives: Griff, Griffin, Gruffudd, Gruffydd, Gryphon.
Meaning: uncertain; possibly 'strong warrior' or 'lord' (Welsh) as a variant of Gruffydd; also a British family name.
Notable namesakes: Griff Rhys Jones (British comedian).

Gustave

Variants and diminutives: Gus, Gussie, Gustaf, Gustaff, Gustav, Gustavo, Gustavs, Gustavus, Gusti, Gustik, Gusty, Gustus, Kosti, Tabo, Tavo.
Meaning: 'staff' and 'of the gods' or 'of the Goths' (Swedish).
Notable namesakes: six Swedish kings, including Gustavus II, 'the Lion of the North' or 'the Snow King'; Gustave Flaubert (French writer); Gustave Doré, Gustave Courbet and Gustave Moreau (French artists); Gustav Holst (English composer); Gustav Klimt (Austrian artist); Gustav Mahler (Austrian composer).

Guy

Variants and diminutives: Gui, Guido, Guyon, Gye, Vitus, Viti, Wido, Wyatt.
Meaning: 'wood', 'wide', 'warrior' or 'guide' (Germanic).

Notable namesakes: Saint Guy, also called Saint Vitus (for whom St Vitus' dance, the disease chorea, was named), patron saint of dancers, comedians and epileptics; the eponymous hero of the Middle English romance *Guy of Warwick*; Guy Fawkes, an English Gunpowder Plot conspiritor whose effigy ('guy') is traditionally burned on 5 November, Bonfire Night, in England; the eponymous subject of the novel *Guy Mannering*, by Scottish writer Sir Walter Scott; Guy de Maupassant (French writer); Guy Pène DuBois (US artist); Guy Ritchie (British film producer).

Gwyn

Variants and diminutives: Gwynne, Wyn, Wynne.
Meaning: 'fair' (Welsh). A male version of Gwen.

Gwynfor

Meaning: 'fair' and 'lord' or 'place' (Welsh).

Gyan

Meaning: 'erudite' (Sanskrit).

Habib

Meaning: 'lover' or 'beloved' (Arabic).

Hadar

Meaning: 'glory' (Hebrew).

Hadrian

Variants and diminutives: Ade, Adi, Adie, Adorjan, Adriann, Adriano, Adrianus, Adrien, Adrik, Andreian, Andreyan, Andri, Andrian, Andriyan, Arne, Hadrian.
Meaning: 'from Adria' (a city in northern Italy) or 'dark one' (Latin) as a variant of Adrian.
Notable namesakes: Hadrian (Publius Aelius Hadrianus), the Roman emperor for whom Hadrian's Wall, in the north of England, was named.

Hadyn

Variants and diminutives: Aidan, Hayden, Haydon.
Meaning: uncertain; possibly 'to help' (Middle English) or 'small fiery one' (Irish Gaelic) as a variant of Aidan; possibly 'hay' and 'hill' (Old English) when derived from an English family name, in turn derived from a number of English place names.

Haidar

Meaning: 'lion' (Arabic).

Hakan

Meaning: 'fiery' (Native American).

Hakeem

Variants and diminutives: Hakim.
Meaning: 'wise' (Arabic).

Hakon

Variants and diminutives: Haakon, Hacon, Hak, Hako.
Meaning: 'useful' or 'exalted race' (Old Norse).
Notable namesakes: as Haakon, seven kings of Norway.

Hale

Variants and diminutives: Hal, Haley, Halford, Halley, Hallie, Halsey, Halsy, Hollis, Holly.
Meaning: 'safe', 'healthy' or 'whole' (Old English).
Notable namesakes: Hale Woodruff (US artist).

Halil

Variants and diminutives: Hallil.
Meaning: 'flute' (Hebrew); 'close friend' (Turkish).

Hallam

Variants and diminutives: Halam, Hallum.
Meaning: 'nook', 'stone' or 'far-off valley' (Old English); derived from an English family name, in turn derived from an English place name.

Ham

Variants and diminutives: Abraham.
Meaning: 'hot' or 'swarthy' (Hebrew); 'home' or 'village' (Old English); also a name for cured pork.
Notable namesakes: a son of Noah in the Old

Testament; Ham Peggotty, a character in the novel *David Copperfield*, by British writer Charles Dickens; Ham Steinbach (Israeli-born US artist).

Hamal

Meaning: 'lamb' (Arabic).

Hamilton

Variants and diminutives: Hamel, Hamil, Hamill, Tony. **Meaning:** 'home' and 'lover' or 'place' (Old English); derived from a Scottish family name, in turn derived from a number of British place names.

Hamish

Variants and diminutives: Seamus, Shamus, Shemais. **Meaning:** 'supplanter' (Hebrew) as an anglicised Scots Gaelic version of James (Jacob).

Hamlet

Variants and diminutives: Amleth, Amlothi, Haimes, Ham, Hamelin, Hames, Hamil, Hamilton, Hamlin, Hamlyn, Hammond, Hamnet, Hamo, Hamon, Hamond, Hampden, Hampton, Haymund, Haymo, Tony. **Meaning:** 'home' (Germanic); 'small village' (Old English). **Notable namesakes:** Prince Amleth of Denmark, the eponymous hero of William Shakespeare's play *Hamlet, Prince of Denmark*; Hamnet Shakespeare, son of William Shakespeare and Anne Hathaway; *The Hamlet*, the title of a novel by US writer William Faulkner.

Hamza

Meaning: 'powerful' or 'strong' (Arabic). **Notable namesakes:** Prophet Mohammed's warrior uncle.

Hannibal

Variants and diminutives: Annibal, Annibale, Hanniball, Honeyball. **Meaning:** 'grace' (Punic) and 'Baal' [the chief god of the Phoenicians and Canaanites] or 'lord' (Semitic). **Notable namesakes:** the Carthaginian general whose army crossed the Alps with elephants; Hannibal Lecter, the cannibalistic character in the thrillers the *The*

Silence of the Lambs and *Hannibal*, by US writer Thomas Harris, as well as in the subsequent films.

Hans

Variants and diminutives: Hanan, Handley, Hanes, Hanley, Hanns, Hansel, Hansen, Hanson, Haynes, Heinz, Henlee, Honus, Johannes. **Meaning:** 'God has favoured', 'God is gracious' or 'God is merciful' (Hebrew) as a northern European version of John. **Notable namesakes:** Hans Memling (German-born Flemish artist); Hans Holbein (two German artists); the young hero of the fairy tale 'Hansel and Gretel', popularised by the German folklorists the Brothers Grimm; Hans Christian Andersen (Danish fairy-tale writer); the young hero of the children's story *Hans Brinker or The Silver Skates*, by English writer Mary Mapes Dodge.

Hanuman

Meaning: 'leader of the monkeys' (Hindi). **Notable namesakes:** the monkey god of Hinduism, whose alliance with Rama is told in the *Ramayana*.

Hardy

Variants and diminutives: Eberhard, Hardee, Harden, Hardey, Hardie, Hardin, Harding. **Meaning:** 'bold' or 'tough' (Germanic); derived from an English family name. **Notable namesakes:** Hardy Amies (British courturier); Hardy Kruger (German actor).

Harley

Variants and diminutives: Harl, Harlan. **Meaning:** 'archer' or 'deer hunter' (Teutonic); 'flax' and 'field' (Middle Low German); 'hare' and 'clearing' (Old English); derived from an English family name, in turn derived from a number of English place names. **Notable namesakes:** Harley Granville-Barker (British theatre director and writer); the Harley Davidson motorbike marque.

Harold

Variants and diminutives: Arailt, Araldo, Aralt, Arold, Aroldo, Arrigo, Enric, Eral, Errol, Garald, Garold, Gerahd, Giraldo, Hal, Haldon, Hale, Halford, Harailt, Harald, Haraldr, Haralds, Haroldas, Haroldo, Hardoldus, Harivlad, Hariwald, Harlow, Haroldus, Harolt, Harry, Heral, Hereweald, Heronim, Hieronim, Hiraldo, Jindra, Kharald, Parry, Rigo.
Meaning: 'army' and 'ruler' or 'power' (Old English).
Notable namesakes: two kings of England, including King Harold II, who died at the battle of Hastings; the subject of the poem *Childe Harold,* by English poet George, Lord Byron; Harold J Laski (British political scientist); Harold Nicolson (English writer and diplomat); Harold MacMillan and Harold Wilson (British politicians); Harold Pinter (British playwright); Harry Potter, the leading character of the eponymous series of children's books by British writer J K Rowling.

Harper

Meaning: 'sickle' (Latin); 'harp-player' (Old English). Also a girl's name.
Notable namesakes: Harper Lee (US writer).

Harrison

Variants and diminutives: Harris, Harrisen.
Meaning: 'son of Harry' or 'son of', 'home' and 'ruler' as a variant of Henry.
Notable namesakes: Harrison Ford (US actor).

Harte

Variants and diminutives: Hart, Hartley, Hartman, Hartwell, Hartwig, Heartley, Hersch, Herschel, Hersh, Hershel, Hertz, Hertzl, Heschel, Heshel, Hirsch, Hirsh.
Meaning: 'hart' or 'stag' (Old English); a diminutive of Hartley, 'hart' and 'clearing' (Old English), derived from an English family name, in turn derived from a number of English place names.
Notable namesakes: Hartley Coleridge (British poet); Hart Crane (US writer).

Harvey

Variants and diminutives: Ervé, Harv, Harve, Harveson, Harvie, Hervé, Hervey, Hervi.
Meaning: 'battle' and 'worthy' (Breton); derived from an English family name.
Notable namesakes: Saint Harvey; Hervey Allen (US writer); Harvey Cushing (US pioneer of neurosurgery); Harvey Keitel (US actor); Harvey Smith (British equestrian).

Hassan

Meaning: 'nice' or 'handsome' (Arabic).
Notable namesakes: two kings of Morocco.

Heath

Meaning: 'heath' or 'place where wild plants grow' (Old English); derived from an English family name, in turn derived from a number of English place names.
Notable namesakes: William Heath Robinson (British cartoonist).

Hector

Variants and diminutives: Eachann, Eachdonn, Ector, Ettore, Heck, Heckie, Hecky.
Meaning: 'holding firm' (Greek).
Notable namesakes: the son of King Priam, husband of Andromache and a Trojan hero who was killed by Achilles in Greek mythology; Hector Berlioz (French composer); Hector Hugh Munro (the British writer whose pseudonym was Saki).

Hedley

Variants and diminutives: Headley, Hedly.
Meaning: 'heather' or 'male sheep' and 'clearing' (Old English); derived from an English family name, in turn derived from a number of English place names.

Helios

Variants and diminutives: Heller, Heli.
Meaning: 'sun' (Greek).
Notable namesakes: the god of the sun in Greek mythology.

Helmut

Variants and diminutives: Hellmut, Helm, Helmuth.

Meaning: 'spirited' and 'brave' (Teutonic); 'helmet' (Germanic).
Notable namesakes: Helmut Kohl (German politician).

Henry

Variants and diminutives: Anraoi, Anrique, Arrigo, Bambis, Eanraig, Enri, Enric, Enrico, Enrikos, Enrique, Enriquillo, Enzio, Erizio, Erizo, Guccio, Hagan, Haimirich, Hal, Halkin, Hank, Hanraoi, Haralpos, Harris, Harrison, Harry, Hawkin, Hedric, Hecrich, Hedrick, Heimadall, Heiman, Heindrick, Heine, Heinemann, Heinie, Heinrich, Heinrick, Heinrik, Heinz, Hen, Hendri, Hendric, Hendrick, Hendrik, Heneli, Heniek, Henier, Henke, Henning, Henny, Henri, Henric, Henrico, Henricus, Henrik, Henrim, Henriot, Henrique, Henryk, Henty, Heriot, Herriot, Herry, Hersz, Hinrich, Honok, Inriques, Jindra, Jindrich, Khambis, Kharlambos, Kiko, Lambos, Quico, Quinto, Quique, Rico, Rik, Riki, Rogberto.
Meaning: 'home' and 'ruler' (Germanic).
Notable namesakes: eight kings of England, four kings of France (Henri) and seven Holy Roman emperors (Heinrich); Henry the Navigator, a prince of Portugal; Henry Hudson, the English navigator for whom the Hudson River, Hudson Strait and Hudson Bay, on the east coast of North America, were named; Henry Purcell (English composer); Henry Fielding (British writer); Heinrich Heine, Heinrich von Kleist and Heinrich Mann (German writers); Henry Wadsworth Longfellow, Henry Miller and Henry James (US writers); the eponymous narrator of the novel *The History of Henry Esmond, Esquire*, by English writer William Makepeace Thackeray; Henry Palmerston (British politician); Henri Toulouse Lautrec and Henri Matisse (French artists); Henrik Johan Ibsen (Norwegian playwright); Henry Moore (British sculptor); Henri Cartier-Bresson (French photographer); Henry Kissinger (German-born US politician); Henry Fonda (US actor); Prince Harry of the United Kingdom.

Herbert

Variants and diminutives: Bert, Bertie, Berty, Eberto, Harbert, Heber, Hebert, Herb, Herbertus, Herbie, Herby, Heriberto.
Meaning: 'army' and 'bright' (Germanic).

Notable namesakes: Saint Herbert of Cologne; Herbert Beerbohm Tree (British actor); Herbert Hoover (US president); Herbert von Karajan (German conductor); Herbert Marcuse (German-born US political philosopher); H(erbert) E Bates (British writer); Herbert Read (British writer); Herbert Gold (US writer); Herbie Hancock (US musician).

Hercules

Variants and diminutives: Hacon, Heracles, Herakles, Herc, Hercule, Herk, Herkie, Herky.
Meaning: 'glory of Hera' (Greek), Hera being the wife of Zeus and goddess of marriage in Greek mythology.
Notable namesakes: the heroic son of Zeus and Alkmene in Greek mythology, for whom the Pillars of Hercules, rocks that stand at the entrance to the Mediterranean Sea at Gibraltar and Ceuta, were named; the fictional Belgian detective Hercule Poirot, who features in British writer Agatha Christie's detective novels.

Hereward

Meaning: 'army' and 'protection' (Old English).
Notable namesakes: Hereward the Wake, English leader of an anti-Norman revolt and subject of the eponymous novel by English writer Charles Kingsley.

Herman

Variants and diminutives: Armand, Armando, Armant, Armin, Armino, Ermanno, Ermin, Harman, Harmen, Harmon, Herenan, Herm, Hermann, Hermanze, Hermie, Herminio, Hermon, Hermy.
Meaning: 'army' and 'man' (Germanic).
Notable namesakes: the hero of the epic poem *Hermann und Dorothea*, by German writer Johann Wolfgang von Goethe; Hermann Hesse and Hermann Sudermann (German writer); Herman Melville (US writer).

Hermes

Variants and diminutives: Hermus.
Meaning: 'support' or 'stone' (Greek).
Notable namesakes: the messenger of the gods in Greek mythology; Hermes Trismegistus ('Thrice-greatest Hermes'), another name for the Egyptian god

Thoth and the reputed author of the *Hermetica*, an alchemical work.

Hesketh

Variants and diminutives: Hezeki, Hezekiah.
Meaning: 'God's strength' (Hebrew) as a variant of Hezekiah.
Notable namesakes: Hezekiah, a king of Judah in the Old Testament.

Hippolytus

Variants and diminutives: Hippolyte, Ipppolitus, Ypolit, Ypolitus.
Meaning: 'horse' and 'release' (Greek).
Notable namesakes: the son of Theseus and Hippolyta in Greek mythology; Saint Hippolytus of Rome, patron saint of horses; Hippolyte Taine (French philosopher, historian and writer).

Hiram

Variants and diminutives: Ahiram.
Meaning: 'brother' and 'elevated' (Hebrew).
Notable namesakes: a king of Tyre in the Old Testament; Hiram Powers (US sculptor); Hiram Stevens Maxim, the US inventor of the Maxim machine gun.

Hiroshi

Meaning: 'generous' (Japanese).

Ho

Meaning: 'good' (Chinese).

Holden

Variants and diminutives: Holbrook.
Meaning: 'hollow' and 'valley' or 'watcher' (Old English); derived from an English family name, in turn derived from a number of English place names.
Notable namesakes: Holden Caulfield, the hero of the novel *The Catcher in the Rye*, by US writer J D Salinger.

Homer

Variants and diminutives: Homero, Omero.
Meaning: uncertain; possibly 'hostage' (Greek); 'helmet-maker' (Old French); 'pool in a hollow' (Old English) when derived from an English family name, in turn derived from a number of English place names.
Notable namesakes: a Greek epic poet; Homer Dodge Martin (US artist); Homer Simpson, a character in the US animated television series *The Simpsons*.

Horace

Variants and diminutives: Horacio, Horatio, Horatius, Horry, Orazio.
Meaning: uncertain; possibly 'time' or 'hour' (Latin); derived from the Roman family name Horatius.
Notable namesakes: Quintus Horatius Flaccus, the Roman poet known as Horace; Horatio, a character in William Shakespeare's play *Hamlet*; the eponymous hero of the play *Horace*, by French playwright Pierre Corneille; Horatio, Viscount Nelson (English admiral); Horatio Greenough (US sculptor); Horace Walpole (British writer); Horace Greeley (US journalist); Horatio Hornblower, the hero of the 'Hornblower' series of novels by British writer C S Forester.

Howard

Variants and diminutives: Haoa, Hogg, Howey, Howie, Ward.
Meaning: uncertain; possibly 'heart' and 'protector' or 'bold' (Germanic); possibly 'hogwarden' or 'swineherd', 'eweherd' or 'fence-keeper' (Old English); derived from the family name of the ducal house of Norfolk.
Notable namesakes: Howard Robard Hughes (US tycoon); Howard Hawks (US film director); Howard Fast (US writer); Howard Keel (US actor); Howard Hodgkin (British artist); Howard Jones (British musician).

Howi

Meaning: 'dove' (Native American).

Hubert

Variants and diminutives: Berdy, Bert, Bertie, Berto, Berty, Bart, Bartie, Barty, Hobard, Hobart, Hub, Hubbard, Hubbell, Hube, Huber, Huberd, Hubertek, Huberto, Hubi, Hubie, Huet, Huey, Hugh, Hughie, Hugi, Hugibert, Hutchin, Huw, Uberto.
Meaning: 'spirit', 'heart' or 'mind' and 'bright' (Germanic).
Notable namesakes: Saint Hubert, patron saint of

hunters and dogs; Hubert van Eyck (Flemish artist); Hubert Humphrey (US politician); Hubert de Givenchy (French fashion designer).

Hugh

Variants and diminutives: Aodh, Hew, Hewe, Huet, Huey, Hughie, Hugi, Hugin, Hugo, Hugolino, Hugon, Hugues, Huguito, Huw, Shug, Shuggie, Shuggy, Ugo, Ugolino, Ugone, Uisdean.

Meaning: 'spirit', 'heart' or 'mind' (Germanic); 'inspiration' or 'flame' (Celtic).

Notable namesakes: Saint Hugh of Liège; Saint Hugh of Cluny; Saint Hugh of Lincoln; the subject of the poem *Hugh Selwyn Mauberley*, by US poet Ezra Pound; Hugh Gaitskell (British politician); Hugh Trevor-Roper (British historian); Hugh MacLennan (Canadian writer); Hugh MacDiarmid (Scottish writer); Hugh Grant and Hugh Laurie (British actors).

Humbert

Variants and diminutives: Bert, Bertie, Berty, Hum, Humbaldo, Humberto, Hunfredo, Hunfrido, Umberto.

Meaning: 'home', 'warrior' or 'giant' and 'bright' (Germanic).

Notable namesakes: Humbert Humbert, the protagonist of the novel *Lolita*, by Russian-born US writer Vladimir Nabokov.

Humphrey

Variants and diminutives: Amhlaoibh, Dumpty, Hum, Humfrey, Humfrid, Humfried, Hump, Humph, Humphry, Humpty, Humpo, Hundredo, Hunfredo, Hunfrey, Onfre, Onfroi, Onofre, Onofredo, Umphrey.

Meaning: 'home', 'warrior', 'giant' or 'strength' and 'peace' (Germanic).

Notable namesakes: Humphrey, Duke of Gloucester, son of King Henry IV of England; Humphrey Gilbert (English navigator); the eponymous hero of the novel *The Expedition of Humphrey Clinker*, by Scottish writer Tobias Smollett; the nursery-rhyme character Humpty Dumpty; Humphry Davy (English chemist and inventor of the Davy lamp); Humphrey Chimpden Earwicker, the leading character in the novel *Finnegans Wake*, by Irish writer James Joyce; Humphrey Bogart (US actor).

Hunter

Variants and diminutives: Hunt, Huntington, Huntley, Lee, Leigh.

Meaning: 'to grasp' (Old Norse); 'hunter' (Middle English). Also a girl's name.

Notable namesakes: Hunter S Thomson (US writer).

Hussain

Variants and diminutives: Hosein, Hossein, Husain, Hussein.

Meaning: 'good' or 'handsome' (Arabic).

Notable namesakes: Hussein ibn Ali, leader of the Arab revolt against the Turks; Hussein ibn Talal, King of Jordan.

Hyman

Variants and diminutives: Chaim, Hy, Hyam, Hymie.

Meaning: 'life' (Hebrew).

Hywel

Variants and diminutives: Hoel, Hough, Houghton, Howe, Howel, Howell, Howey, Howland, Hulett, Hywell, Powell.

Meaning: 'conspicuous' or 'eminent' (Welsh); 'swine' and 'hill' (Old English).

Notable namesakes: Hywel Dda (Howel the Good), King of Wales; Hywel Bennett (British actor).

Iago

Variants and diminutives: James.

Meaning: 'supplanter' (Hebrew) as a Spanish and Welsh version of James (Jacob).

Notable namesakes: a character in William Shakespeare's play *Othello*.

A B C D E F G H I J K L M N O P Q R S T U V W X Y Z

Ian

Variants and diminutives: Ean, Iain, Ieuan, Iwan.
Meaning: 'God has favoured', 'God is gracious' or 'God is merciful' (Hebrew) as a Scottish version of John.
Notable namesakes: Ian Fleming (British writer); Ian Drury (British musician); Ian Botham (British cricketer); Ian Woosnam (British golfer); Iain Duncan Smith (British politician); Ian Rankin (Scottish crime writer).

Idris

Meaning: 'lord' and 'ardent' (Welsh).
Notable namesakes: Cader Idris, a mountain in Wales that was said to have been the observatory of Idris the Giant, a poet and astronomer in Welsh mythology.

Idwal

Meaning: 'master' and 'wall' (Welsh).

Ignatius

Variants and diminutives: Egnacio, Eneco, Hignacio, Iggie, Iggy, Ignace, Ignacio, Ignacius, Ignasio, Ignatio, Ignatius, Ignatz, Ignaz, Ignazio, Ignocio, Inigo, Inigue, Nacho, Nacio, Nas, Ygnasio, Ygnocio.
Meaning: uncertain; possibly 'fiery' (Latin); derived from a Roman family name.
Notable namesakes: Saint Ignatius of Antioch, patron saint of sufferers from throat ailments; Saint Ignatius of Loyola, the Spanish founder of the Society of Jesus, or the Jesuits, a Roman Catholic religious order, and patron saint of retreatants; Ignace Paderewski (Polish pianist, composer and statesman).

Igor

Variants and diminutives: Inge, Ingmar, Ingvar.
Meaning: 'Ing's warrior' (Old Norse), Ing being a Norse fertility god, as a Slavic variant of Ingvar; 'farmer' (Greek) as a variant of George.
Notable namesakes: a Russian prince whose anti-Polovtsy campaign is described in the Russian heroic poem *The Song of Igor's Campaign*; Igor Stravinsky (Russian composer).

Ingram

Variants and diminutives: Ingamar, Ingemar, Inglis, Ingmar, Ingo, Ingra, Ingrim.
Meaning: 'Ing's raven' (Germanic), Ing being a Norse fertility god; derived from an English family name.

Inigo

Variants and diminutives: Eneco, Ignatius, Inigue.
Meaning: uncertain; possibly 'fiery' (Latin) as a variant of Ignatius.
Notable namesakes: Inigo Jones (English architect).

Iorwerth

Variants and diminutives: Iolo, Yorath.
Meaning: 'lord' and 'value' (Welsh).

Ira

Meaning: 'stallion' (Aramaic); 'watchful' (Hebrew).
Notable namesakes: a captain in King David's army in the Old Testament; Ira Gershwin (US song-writer); Ira Levin (US writer).

Irvin

Variants and diminutives: Earvin, Eireambon, Erv, Erve, Ervin, Erwin, Irv, Irvine, Irving, Irwin, Irwyn.
Meaning: uncertain; possibly 'handsome' (Irish Gaelic); possibly 'white river' (Welsh); possibly 'sea' or 'boar' and 'friend' (Old English); possibly 'green water' (Scots Gaelic); derived from a Scottish family name, in turn derived from a number of British place names.
Notable namesakes: Irving Stone and Irwin Shaw (US writers); Irvine Welsh (British writer).

Isaac

Variants and diminutives: Aizik, Eisig, Ike, Ikey, Ikie, Isaacus, Isaak, Isac, Isacco, Isak, Itzhak, Itzik, Izaak, Izak, Izik, Yitzhak, Yithak, Yitzchak, Zack, Zak.
Meaning: 'laughter' (Hebrew).
Notable namesakes: the son of Abraham and Sarah in the New Testament; Izaak Walton (English writer); Isaac Oliver (British artist); Isaac Newton (British physicist and mathematician); Isaac Pitman, the English inventor of the Pitman system of shorthand; Isaac Rosenberg (English poet and artist); Izaak

Babel (Russian writer); Isaac Azimov (Russian-born US writer and scientist); Itzhak Rabin (Israeli politician).

Isaiah

Variants and diminutives: Esaias, Ikaia, Is, Isa, Isaias, Issa, Yeshaya, Yeshayahu.
Meaning: 'God is salvation' or 'God is generous' (Hebrew).
Notable namesakes: an Old Testament prophet Isaiah Berlin (British philosopher).

Ishmael

Variants and diminutives: Esmael, Isamel, Ishmael, Ismael, Ismail, Ismeal, Ismeil, Ysmael.
Meaning: 'God hears' or 'outcast' (Hebrew).
Notable namesakes: Abraham and Hagar's son in the Old Testament; the narrator of the novel *Moby Dick*, by US writer Herman Melville; Ishmael Read (US writer).

Isidore

Variants and diminutives: Dore, Dory, Isador, Isadore, Isidor, Isidoro, Isidro, Izzy.
Meaning: 'gift of Isis' (Greek), Isis being the supreme goddess of Egyptian mythology whose cult was subsequently adopted by the Greeks and Romans.
Notable namesakes: Saint Isidore of Seville, patron saint of computer users and the Internet; Saint Isidore the Farmer, patron saint of agricultural workers; Isidore Opsomer (Belgian artist).

Israel

Variants and diminutives: Irving, Issy, Izzy, Srully.
Meaning: 'struggle with God' or 'God prevail' (Hebrew).
Notable namesakes: the name bestowed on Jacob following his struggle with the angel in the Old Testament, his descendents subsequently being called the Israelites; the Jewish nation of Israel; the eponymous leading character of the novel *Israel Potter, or, Fifty Years of Exile*, by US writer Herman Melville; Israel Baline, the Russian-born US composer who is better known as Irving Berlin; Israel Horovitz (US playwright).

Ithel

Meaning: 'munificent lord' (Welsh).

Ivan

Variants and diminutives: Evo, Evon, Ivo, Vanya, Yvan, Yvon.
Meaning: 'God has favoured', 'God is gracious' or 'God is merciful' (Hebrew) as a Slavic version of John.
Notable namesakes: six Russian rulers, including the tsars Ivan III, 'the Great', and Ivan IV, 'the Terrible'; Ivan Aleksandrovich Goncharov, Ivan Sergeyevich Turgenev and Ivan Alekseyevich Bunin (Russian writers); the eponymous leading character of the story *The Death of Ivan Ilyich*, by Russian writer Leo Tolstoy; Ivan Pavlovich Shatov, a character in the novel *The Possessed*, by Russian writer Fyodor Mikhailovich Dostoyevsky; Ivan Petrovich Pavlov (Russian neurophysiologist); Ivan Mestrovic (Yugoslavian sculptor); the title character of the novel *One Day in the Life of Ivan Denisovich*, by Russian writer Aleksandr Solzhenitsyn; Ivan Lendl (Czech tennis player).

Ivo

Variants and diminutives: Ives, Ivon, Ivor, Yves.
Meaning: 'yew' or 'small archer' (Germanic).
Notable namesakes: Saint Ivo of Brittany, patron saint of lawyers and judges; Saint Ives, for whom St Ives, a town in Cambridgeshire, was named; St Ives, a town in Cornwall (named for the female Saint Ia); Ivo Andric (Yugoslav writer).

Ivor

Variants and diminutives: Ifor, Iomhar, Ivair, Ivar, Ivarr, Ive, Iver, Ivon, Yvon, Yvor.
Meaning: uncertain; possibly 'bow made of yew' and 'warrior' (Old Norse); possibly, as Ifor, 'lord' or 'archer' (Welsh).
Notable namesakes: Ivor Novello (Welsh composer and actor).

Jabez

Meaning: 'born in pain' or 'born in sorrow' (Hebrew).
Notable namesakes: an Old Testament character whose birth was difficult.

Jack

Variants and diminutives: Jackey, Jackie, Jackson, Jacky, Jake, Jakson, Jan, Jankin, Jock, John.
Meaning: 'God has favoured', 'God is gracious' or 'God is merciful' (Hebrew) as a diminutive of John.
Notable namesakes: Jack Frost, an English personification of winter; a playing card; jack bean, the common name of the flowering plant *Canavalia ensiformis;* jack-in-the-pulpit, the common name of the flowering plants *Arisaema triphyllum* and *Arum maculatum*; jack-o'lantern, a will-o'-the-wisp or Hallowe'en pumpkin; jack pine, the common name of the *Pinus banksiana* tree; a device for jacking up heavy weights; the young hero of the fairy tale 'Jack and the Beanstalk'; Jack Sprat and Jack (and Jill), nursery-rhyme characters; Jack Ketch, the generic name for hangmen inspired by the English executioner John Ketch; Jack the Ripper, an anonymous London serial murderer; Jack Kerouac and Jack London (US writers); Jack Lemmon and Jack Nicholson (US actors); Jack Nicklaus (US golfer); Jackie Stewart (British racing driver); Jackson Browne (US singer); Jack Straw (British politician).

Jacob

Variants and diminutives: Akevy, Akiba, Akiva, Akkoobjee, Akkub, Cob, Cobb, Cobbie, Cobby, Como, Coppo, Cub, Diego, Gemmes, Giacobbe, Giacobo, Giacomo, Giacopo, Hamish, Iago, Iakabos, Iakov, Iakovos, Ikov, Jaap, Jacinto, Jaco, Jacobo, Jacobos, Jacobs, Jacobson, Jacobus, Jacoby, Jacopo, Jacomus, Jacque, Jacques, Jacquet, Jago, Jaime, Jakab, Jake, Jakie, Jakiv, Jakob, Jakon, Jakov, Jakub, Jakubek, Jalu, James, Jamie, Jaques, Jaquot, Jasha, Jascha, Jaschenka, Jasha, Jayme, Jeb, Jecis, Jekebs, Jeks, Jem, Jemmy, Jeska, Jockel, Jokubas, Kivi, Kobi, Kub, Kuba, Kubaa, Kubes, Kubik, Kubo, Kubus, Lapo, Santiago, Seumuis, Yaagov, Yaakov, Yago, Yakov, Yanka, Yashko, Yuki.
Meaning: 'supplanter' (Hebrew).
Notable namesakes: the son of Isaac and Rebecca and twin brother of Esau, who dreamt of a ladder rising to heaven in the Old Testament and for whom the Jacob's ladder, the common name of the *Polemonium caeruleum* flowering plant, is named; Jacob sheep, an ancient breed of ovines; Jacob van Maerlant (Flemish poet); Jakob Böhme (German mystic); the Jacobean artistic style popularised during the reign of King James I of England; Jacobins, left-wing revolutionaries or French Dominican friars; Jacobites, supporters of the house of Stuart following the deposition of King James II of England; Jacob Flanders, the leading character of the novel *Jacob's Room*, by English writer Virginia Woolf; Jacob Epstein (British sculptor); Jacob Bronowski (British scientist and philosopher); Jacob Lawrence (US artist).

Jahan

Meaning: 'the world' (Sanskrit).

Jake

Variants and diminutives: Jack, Jacob, Jakey, Jakie.
Meaning: 'supplanter' (Hebrew) as a diminutive of Jacob; 'God has favoured', 'God is gracious' or 'God is merciful' (Hebrew) as a variant of Jack (John).
Notable namesakes: Jake Barnes, a leading character in the novel *The Sun Also Rises*, by US writer Ernest Hemingway; Jake, one of the eponymous siblings in the US film *The Blues Brothers*.

Jamal

Variants and diminutives: Cemal, Gamal, Jahmal, Jamaal, Jamael, Jamahl, Jamall, Jameel, Jamel, Jamiel, Jamil, Jamile.
Meaning: 'handsome' (Arabic).
Notable namesakes: Jamal Abd-al Nasir (Egyptian politician).

James

Variants and diminutives: Chago, Chango, Chanti, Dago, Diago, Diego, Giacomo, Giamo, Hamish, Jaco, Jacob, Jacobus, Jacomus, Jacques, Jaime, Jaimie, Jaimito, Jam, Jamesy, Jamey, Jamie, Jas, Jay, Jayme, Jaymie, Jem, Jim, Jimbo, Jimmie, Jimmy, Santiago, Séamas, Seamus, Seumas, Seumus, Shamus, Shay, Sheumais, Tiago, Zebedee.
Meaning: 'supplanter' (Hebrew) as a variant of Jacob.
Notable namesakes: Saint James the Great (or Greater), son of Zebedee, brother of Saint John and one of Christ's apostles in the New Testament, patron saint of soldiers, Spain, Chile, milliners, labourers, and people suffering from arthritis and rheumatism; Saint James the Just, brother of Christ and author of the Epistle of James in the New Testament; Saint James the Little (or Less), a disciple of Christ in the New Testament; seven kings of Scotland; James I, 'the Conqueror', King of Aragon; two kings of England, including James I (also King James VI of Scotland), for whom the Anglican King James Bible and Jamestown, a colonial settlement in the US state of Virginia, were named; James Edward Stuart, the 'Old Pretender' (to the British throne); James Boswell (Scottish writer); James Gillray (British caricaturist); James Tissot (French artist); James Fenimore Cooper and James A Michener (US writers); James Abbott McNeill Whistler (US artist); James Joyce (Irish writer); James Dean (US actor); James Clavell (English-born US writer); James Bond, also known as '007', the fictional spy popularised by British writer Ian Fleming; James Herriot (English vet and writer); James Brown (US singer); Jamie Oliver (British chef and television presenter).

Janus

Variants and diminutives: Januarius, Jarek.
Meaning: 'archway' (Latin).
Notable namesakes: the double-headed god of gateways and beginnings in Roman mythology, for whom January is named; Saint Januarius, patron saint of Naples and blood banks and protector against volcanoes; Januarius Johann Rasso Zick (German artist).

Japheth

Variants and diminutives: Japhet, Yafet, Yaphet.
Meaning: 'enlargement' or 'handsome' (Hebrew).
Notable namesakes: a son of Noah in the Old Testament.

Jared

Variants and diminutives: Gerard, Jareth, Jarod, Jarred, Jarret, Jarrod, Jed, Jerrod.
Meaning: 'rose' or 'heir' (Hebrew); 'spear' and 'hard' (Germanic) as a variant of Gerard.
Notable namesakes: the father of Enoch in the Old Testament; Jared Sparks (US historian).

Jaron

Variants and diminutives: Yartron.
Meaning: 'to sing' or 'to call out' (Hebrew).

Jarvis

Variants and diminutives: Gary, Gervais, Gervaise, Gervase, Gervise, Jary, Jarry, Jerve, Jervis.
Meaning: uncertain; possibly 'spear' (Germanic) and 'servant' (Celtic) as a variant of Gervaise.
Notable namesakes: Jarvis Cocker (British singer).

Jason

Variants and diminutives: Jace, Jaeson, Jaison, Jase, Jasen, Jay, Jayce, Jaycen, Jaysen, Jayson, Joshua.
Meaning: uncertain; possibly 'to heal' (Greek); possibly 'God saves' (Hebrew) as a variant of Joshua.
Notable namesakes: the heroic leader of the Argonauts in Greek mythology; a relative of Saint Paul in the New Testament; an author of the Book of Ecclesiasticus in the New Testament; Jason Robards and Jason Robards Jr (US actors).

Jasper

Variants and diminutives: Cash, Casper, Cass, Cassie, Cassy, Gaspar, Gaspard, Gaspare, Gasparo, Gasper, Gazsi, Jaspar, Jasper, Josper, Kaspar, Kasper.

Meaning: 'jewel' (Greek); 'treasurer-keeper' (Persian); 'imperial' (Germanic).
Notable namesakes: one of the Magi who visited the newborn Jesus Christ in the New Testament; a quartz gemstone; jasperware, a type of stoneware invented by the English potter Josiah Wedgwood; Jasper Johns (US artist); Jasper Conran (British designer).

Jay

Variants and diminutives: Jaye, Jey, Jeye.
Meaning: 'supplanter' (Hebrew) as a diminutive of James (Jacob); 'victory' (Sanskrit). Also a diminutive of any other name beginning with 'J' and a girl's name.
Notable namesakes: birds of the *Corvidae* family; Jay Gatsby, the leading character of the novel *The Great Gatsby*, by US writer F Scott Fitzgerald; Jay MacPherson (Canadian poet); Jay Kay (British musician).

Jed

Variants and diminutives: Jedd.
Meaning: 'hand' (Arabic).

Jedidiah

Variants and diminutives: Didi, Jed, Jedadiah, Jedd, Jeddy, Jedediah, Jediah, Yehiel.
Meaning: 'loved by the Lord' (Hebrew).
Notable namesakes: another name of King Solomon in the Old Testament.

Jeffrey

Variants and diminutives: Fred, Fredo, Frici, Friedl, Geof, Geoff, Geoffrey, Geoffroi, Geoffroy, Geofredo, Geofri, Giotto, Gisfrid, Godfrey, Godofredo, Godfrids, Godofredo, Godoired, Gofredo, Gotfrid, Gotfryd, Gottfrid, Gottfried, Gotz, Govert, Jef, Jeff, Jefferey, Jefferies, Jefferson, Jeffery, Jeffie, Jeffrey, Jeffries, Jeffry, Jeffy, Jeoffroi, Sheary, Sheron, Sieffre.
Meaning: uncertain; possibly 'God', 'district', 'traveller' or 'pledge' and 'peace' (Germanic) as a variant of Godfrey.

Jem

Variants and diminutives: James, Jemmie, Jemmy, Jeremy, Jeremiah.
Meaning: 'supplanter' (Hebrew) as a diminutive of James (Jacob); 'appointed by God' or 'exalted by God' (Hebrew) as a diminutive of Jeremy (Jeremiah).

Jephthah

Variants and diminutives: Jephtah, Yiftach, Yiftah.
Meaning: 'to open' (Hebrew).
Notable namesakes: a leader, 'the Gileadite', of the Israelites in the Old Testament.

Jeremiah

Variants and diminutives: Diarmaid, Geremia, Gerome, Gerrie, Gerry, Jem, Jere, Jereme, Jeremia, Jeremias, Jeremija, Jeremy, Jerre, Jerrie, Jerrome, Jerry, Yirmeehayu.
Meaning: 'appointed by God' or 'exalted by God' (Hebrew).
Notable namesakes: an Old Testament prophet, author of the Book of Lamentations, from whom the generic name for prophesiers of doom and gloom is derived; Jeremiah Clarke (English composer).

Jeremy

Variants and diminutives: Ember, Geremia, Gerome, Gerrie, Gerry, Jem, Jemmie, Jemmy, Jemy, Jer, Jereme, Jeremiah, Jeremie, Jeremija, Jerr, Jerre, Jerrie, Jerrome, Jerry, Katone, Nemet, Yeremey, Yerik, Yirmeeyahu.
Meaning: 'appointed by God' or 'exalted by God' (Hebrew) as an English version of Jeremiah.
Notable namesakes: Jeremy Bentham (English philosopher and social and legal reformer); Jeremy Thorpe (British politician); Jeremy Paxman and Jeremy Vine (British broadcasters).

Jermaine

Variants and diminutives: Germain, Germane, Germayne, Jamaine, Jermain, Jermaine, Jermane, Jermayn, Jermayne, Jerr, Jerrie, Jerry.
Meaning: 'brother' (Latin) or 'German' (French).
Notable namesakes: Jermaine Jackson (US singer)

Jerome

Variants and diminutives: Gerome, Geronima, Gerrie, Gerry, Hieremas, Hieronymus, Jere, Jereme, Jérôme, Jeromo, Jeronim, Jerram, Jerre, Jerrie, Jerrome, Jerry.
Meaning: 'holy' and 'name' (Greek) as a French variant of Hieronymus (Hyeronimos).
Notable namesakes: Saint Jerome (Sophronius Eusebius Hieronymus), patron saint of archaeologists, librarians and students; Saint Jerome Emiliani, patron saint of orphans and abandoned children; Jerome K Jerome (English writer); Jerome Weidman and J(erome) D(avid) Salinger (US writers).

Jerry

Variants and diminutives:
Meaning: 'spear' and 'rule' (Germanic) as a diminutive of Gerald; 'spear' and 'hard' (Germanic) as a diminutive of Gerard; 'appointed by God' or 'exalted by God' (Hebrew) as a diminutive of Jeremy; 'holy' and 'name' (Greek) as a diminutive of Jerome.
Notable namesakes: a pejorative name for Germans, particularly German soldiers; Jerry Lewis (US comic actor); Jerry Lee Lewis (US musician).

Jesse

Variants and diminutives: Jess, Jessie, Jessy.
Meaning: 'gift' or 'God exists' (Hebrew).
Notable namesakes: the father of King David in the Old Testament, for whom the ecclesiastical Jesse window, or tree of Jesse, delineating Christ's descent from Jesse, is named; Jesse James (US outlaw); Jesse Owens (US athlete); Jesse Jackson (US politician).

Jesus

Variants and diminutives: Hesus, Jesous, Jesu, Jesuso, Jezus, Joshua.
Meaning: 'God saves' (Hebrew) as a variant of Joshua.
Notable namesakes: Jesus Christ, the Christian messiah of the New Testament;

Jethro

Variants and diminutives: Jeth, Jett.
Meaning: 'excellence' or 'abundance' (Hebrew).
Notable namesakes: the father of Zipporah and father-in-law of Moses in the Old Testament; Jethro

Tull, the English agriculturalist and inventor of the seed drill after whom a British rock group was named.

Jim

Variants and diminutives: James, Jimbo, Jimi, Jimmie, Jimmy.
Meaning: 'supplanter' (Hebrew) as a diminutive of James (Jacob).
Notable namesakes: the hero of the novel *Lord Jim*, by Polish-born English writer Joseph Conrad; Jim Dixon, the subject of the novel *Lucky Jim*, by British writer Kingsley Amis; Jimmy Carter (US president); Jimi Hendrix (US musician); Jim Morrison (US singer-songwriter); Jim Broadbent (British actor).

Joab

Meaning: 'God the father' or 'praise the Lord' (Hebrew).
Notable namesakes: a nephew of King David in the Old Testament.

Joachim

Variants and diminutives: Akim, Giachimo, Jehoiachin, Jehoiakim, Joa, Jochim, Joaquin, Yehoiakim.
Meaning: 'God exalts', 'God establishes' or 'God judges' (Hebrew).
Notable namesakes: a king of Judah in the Old Testament; Saint Joachim, the apocryphal father of the Virgin Mary; Joachim Beuckelaer (Flemish artist); Joachim du Bellay (French poet).

Job

Meaning: 'persecuted' (Hebrew).
Notable namesakes: an Old Testament patriarch whose patience was sorely tested by God as described in the Book of Job, hence the generic name for someone who patiently endures suffering.

Jock

Variants and diminutives: Jack, Jocko, John.
Meaning: 'God has favoured', 'God is gracious' or 'God is merciful' (Hebrew) as a Scottish diminutive of John.
Notable namesakes: a slang name for Scots people.

Joe

Variants and diminutives: Joey, Jojo.
Meaning: 'God will increase' (Hebrew) as a diminutive of Joseph.
Notable namesakes: Joe Christmas, the leading character of the novel *Light in August*, by US writer William Faulkner; Joe Frazier (US boxer); Joe Orton (British playwright); Joe Walsh (US musician).

Joel

Variants and diminutives: Yoel.
Meaning: 'Jehovah is God' or 'God is willing' (Hebrew).
Notable namesakes: a prophet and book of the Old Testament; Joel Chandler Harris (US writer); Joel Barlow (US poet and diplomat); Joel Shapiro (US sculptor); Joel Garner (West Indian cricketer).

John

Variants and diminutives: Ansis, Eoin, Evan, Ewan, Gehan, Gennaro, Geno, Gian, Gianetto, Gianni, Giannini, Giannis, Giannos, Gioannes, Giovanni, Haines, Hanan, Hannes, Hannu, Hans, Hansel, Hansl, Hanus, Hasse, Hazze, Honza, Hovhannes, Iain, Ian, Iancu, Ianos, Iban, Ieuan, Ifan, Ignac, Ioan, Ioann, Ioannes, Ioannis, Ion, Ionel, Ivan, Ivanchik, Ivano, Ivas, Iwan, Jack, Jackie, Jackman, Jakon, Jan, Janco, Jancsi, Janek, Janes, Jani, Janika, Jankiel, Janko, Janne, Jano, Janos, Jas, Jasio, Jean, Jeanno, Jeannot, Jehan, Jenda, Jenkin, Jenner, Jennings, Jens, Joanico, Joannes, Joao, Joba, Jochanan, Jock, Jocko, Jofan, Johan, Johanan, Johann, Johannes, Johnie, Johnnie, Johnny, Jon, Jonam, Jonas, Jone, Jonelis, Jonni, Jonnie, Jonny, Jonukas, Jonutis, Jovan, Juan, Juanch, Juancho, Juanito, Juhana, Juho, Jukka, Jussi, Ohannes, Owen, St John, Sean, Seann, Seonaidh, Shane, Shaughn, Shaun, Shawn, Sion, Sionym, Vanek, Vanka, Vanko, Vanya, Vanni, Yan, Yana, Yancy, Yank, Yanka, Yankee, Yanni, Yannis, Yochanan, Yohanan, Yves, Zan, Zane, Zebedee.
Meaning: 'God has favoured', 'God is gracious' or 'God is merciful' (Hebrew).
Notable namesakes: Saint John the Baptist, the cousin of Christ in the New Testament, patron saint of monks, baptism and lambs; Saint John the Evangelist (Apostle, Divine or Theologian), one of Christ's apostles, the author of the Gospel of St John, three epistles and the Book of Revelation in the New Testament, patron saint of theologians, writers and publishers; Saint John Chrysostom, patron saint of orators, preachers and epileptics; Saint John of Damascus; Saint John of Capistrano, patron saint of judges and jurists; Saint John of God, patron saint of fire-fighters, hospitals, nurses, sick people, heart patients, booksellers and printers; Saint John of Kanti, patron saint of university lecturers; Saint John of Nepomuk, patron saint of bridge-builders, discretion, slandered people and floods; John Dory, the common name of the *Zeus faber* fish; John o'Groats, a Scottish town and reputedly Britain's most northerly point, named for the Dutch settler Jan de Groot; John of Salisbury (English ecclesiastical historian and philsopher); King John, 'Lackland', of England; John of Gaunt (English politician); as Jean, two kings of France; twenty-three popes, plus two more as John Paul; as Jan, three kings of Poland; as Joao, six kings of Portugal; Saint John of the Cross, patron saint of poets, mystics and contemplatives; Saint John Bosco, patron saint of editors, boys, students and young people; Saint Jean-Baptist de la Salle, patron saint of teachers; Saint Jean-Baptiste Vianney, patron saint of parish priests; John Donne (English poet); John Dee (English astrologer and mathematician); John Milton and John Gay (English writers); John Bull, the personification of England as popularised by *The History of John Bull*, by the Scottish physician and pamphleteer John Arbuthnot; John Barleycorn, the personification of alcohol; Johnny Canuck, the personification of Canada; John Hancock, the US statesman whose handwriting inspired the US and Canadian slang term for a signature; John Keats (English poet); John Constable (English painter); John Galsworthy, John Osborne and John le Carré (British writers); John Singer Sargent (US artist); John Fitzgerald Kennedy (US president); John Huston (US film director); John Updike (US writer); John Cleese (British comic actor); John Lennon (British musician); John Major (British politician); John Hop, an Australian slang term for a policeman; John Doe, the generic US name for an unidentified man; John Travolta (US actor).

Jolyon

Variants and diminutives: Jolly, Joly, Julian.
Meaning: uncertain; possibly 'fair-skinned' (Latin) as a variant of Julian.
Notable namesakes: Jolyon Forsyte, a character in *The Forsyte Saga*, a collection of novels by the British writer John Galsworthy.

Jonah

Variants and diminutives: Giona, Guisepe, Iona, Jonas, Yona, Yonah, Yunus.
Meaning: 'dove' (Hebrew).
Notable namesakes: the prophet who survived being swallowed by a whale in the Old Testament; Jonah Lomu (New Zealand rugby player).

Jonathan

Variants and diminutives: Johnathan, Johnathon, Jon, Jonathon, Jonnie, Jonny, Jonty, Yonatan.
Meaning: 'God's gift' (Hebrew).
Notable namesakes: a son of King Saul and friend of David in the Old Testament; Jonathan Swift (Irish writer); Jonathan Wild (English highwayman); Jonathan Wild, the eponymous leading character of the novel *The Life of Jonathan Wild, the Great*, by English writer Henry Fielding; Jonathan Ross (British television presenter).

Jordan

Variants and diminutives: Giordano, Ira, Jared, Jarrod, Jerad, Jordain, Jordane, Jordann, Jordie, Jordy, Jordyn, Jorey, Jori, Jorie, Jorrie, Jorry, Jory, Jourdain, Judd, Yarden.
Meaning: 'to flow down' (Hebrew); derived from the Middle Eastern river Jordan. Also a girl's name.
Notable namesakes: the Hashemite Kingdom of Jordan; the Jordan almond, a variety of almond used in confectionary.

Joseph

Variants and diminutives: Beppe, Beppi, Beppo, Che, Cheche, Chepe, Chepito, Guiseppe, Jazeps, Iosep, Ioseph, Iosif, Jaska, Jo, Jobo, Joce, Jodi, Jodie, Jody, Joe, Joey, Joie, Jojo, Joosef, Jooseppi, Jos, Josce, José, Josecoto, Josef, Joseito, Joselito, Josep, Josephe, Josephus, Joses, Josip, Joska, Josko, Joszef, Joza, Joze, Jozef, Jozhe, Jozhef, Jozio, Jozka, Jozsef, Jozsi, Jupp, Juzef, Juziu, Osip, Osya, Pepa, Pepe, Pepik, Pepillo, Pepin, Pepito, Peppi, Peppo, Pino, Pipo, Seosamh, Seosap, Seosaph, Sepp, Yazid, Yeska, Yesya, Yosayf, Yosef, Yosel, Yoseph, Yosi, Yosif, Yossel, Yossele, Yousef, Yusef, Yusif, Yussuf, Yusuf, Yusup, Yuzef, Zeusef.
Meaning: 'God will increase' (Hebrew).
Notable namesakes: the youngest son of Jacob and Rachel in the Old Testament, whose story is told in the *Joseph and His Brothers* series of novels by German writer Thomas Mann and in a musical by Andrew Lloyd-Webber and Tim Rice; Saint Joseph, the husband of the Virgin Mary in the New Testament, patron saint of Canada, Peru, carpenters, fathers, bursars, people who are dying, social justice and the universal church; Saint Joseph of Arimathea in the New Testiment, patron saint of funeral directors and undertakers; Saint Joseph of Copertino, patron saint of astronauts, pilots and air passengers; the eponymous hero of the novel *Joseph Andrews*, by English writer Henry Fielding; Joseph Mallord William Turner (English artist); Joseph Paxton (English architect); Joseph Conrad (Polish-born British writer); Joseph K, the hero of the novel *The Castle*, by Czech writer Franz Kafka; Joseph Stalin (Soviet dictator); Josef Albers (German artist and designer); Joseph Kennedy, father of the Kennedy US political dynasty; Joseph Kosuth (US artist); Josip Tito (Yugoslavian politician); Joe Louis (US boxer); Joe DiMaggio (US baseball player); Joseph Beuys (German artist); Joseph Heller and Joseph Roth (US writers); José Carreras (Spanish opera singer).

Joshua

Variants and diminutives: Giosia, Hosea, Hoshayah, Iosua, Jason, Jesous, Jesus, Joaquim, Joaquin, Jos, Josh, Joss, Josua, Josue, Jozsua, Mosha, Yehoshua, Yeshua.
Meaning: 'God saves' (Hebrew).
Notable namesakes: the successor of Moses who led the Israelites into Canaan; the Joshua tree, *Yucca brevifolia;* Joshua Reynolds (English artist).

Josiah

Variants and diminutives: Josh, Josias, Josie, Josy.
Meaning: 'God heals' or 'God supports' (Hebrew).
Notable namesakes: a king of Judah in the Old Testament; Josiah Wedgwood (English potter); Josiah Bounderby, a chracter in the novel *Hard Times*, by English writer Charles Dickens.

Jotham

Meaning: 'God is perfect' (Hebrew).
Notable namesakes: a son of Gideon and also a king of Judah in the Old Testament.

Judd

Variants and diminutives: Jordan, Judah.
Meaning: 'to flow down' (Hebrew), derived from the Middle Eastern river Jordan, as a diminutive of Jordan; 'praise' (Hebrew) as a diminutive of Judah.

Jude

Variants and diminutives: Jud, Juda, Judah, Judas, Judd, Judson, Yehuda, Yehudah, Yehudi.
Meaning: 'praise' (Hebrew) as a diminutive of Judah. Also a girl's name as a diminutive of Judith.
Notable namesakes: Judah, a son of Jacob and Leah in the Old Testament, for whom the kingdom of Judah was named; Judas Iscariot, Christ's betrayer in the New Testament, for whom the Judas tree, *Cercis siliquastrum*, is named; Saint Jude (also known as Judas or Thaddaeus), an apostle of Christ and author of the New Testament book the Epistle of Jude, patron saint of lost causes and desperate situations; Judas Maccabaeus, the leader of the Jews in the revolt against the Seleucids; Judah ha-Levi (Jewish poet and philosopher); Jude Fawley, the eponymous hero of the novel *Jude the Obscure*, by English writer Thomas Hardy; 'Hey Jude', a song by the British band The Beatles; Jude Law (British actor).

Jules

Variants and diminutives: Julian, Julius.
Meaning: uncertain; possibly 'fair-skinned' (Latin) as a French variant of Julian. Also a girl's name as a diminutive of Julia, Julie and Juliana.
Notable namesakes: Jules Mazarin (French statesman); Jules Laforgue (French poet); Jules Verne (French writer); Jules Romains (French writer); Jules Olitski (Russian-born US artist).

Julian

Variants and diminutives: Giuliano, Giulio, Guliano, Halian, Iola, Iolo, Jellon, Jolin, Jolian, Jollanus, Jolyon, Jule, Jules, Julianus, Julien, Julio, Julius, Julot, Julyan.
Meaning: uncertain; possibly 'fair-skinned' (Latin); derived from the Roman family name Julianus.
Notable namesakes: the Julian Alps in Slovenia; Gaius Julius Caesar, the Roman emperor for whom the month of July and the Julian calendar were named, and on the circumstances surrounding whose death William Shakespeare based his eponymous play; the Roman emperor Julian the Apostate (Flavius Claudius Julianus); Saint Julian the Hospitaller, patron saint of hoteliers, travellers and ferrymen; as Julius, the name of two popes; Julian Huxley (British scientist); Julien Green (French writer); Julian Schnabel (US artist); the eponymous leading character of the novel *Count Julian*, by Spanish writer Juan Goytisolo; Julien Macdonald (British fashion designer).

Junior

Variants and diminutives: Junius.
Meaning: 'younger' (Latin); derived from the US practice of adding 'Junior' (Jr) to a boy's name when he shares it with his father.

Justin

Variants and diminutives: Giustino, Giusto, Inek, Iustin, Jusa, Just, Justas, Justek, Justen, Justinian, Justinas, Justino, Justins, Justinus, Justis, Justo, Justs, Justukas, Justus, Justyn, Jut, Jute, Tuto, Ustin, Yestin, Yusts, Yustyn.
Meaning: 'just' (Latin); derived from the Roman family name Justinus.
Notable namesakes: Saint Justin Martyr, patron saint of philosophers, lecturers, apologists and travellers; as Justinian, two Byzantine emperors.

Kahil

Variants and diminutives: Kahlil, Kalil.
Meaning: 'beloved' (Arabic).

Kai

Variants and diminutives: Cai, Caius, Kay.
Meaning: 'rejoice' (Latin) as a Welsh variant of Caius (Gaius); 'sea' (Hawaiian).
Notable namesakes: as Kay, a knight of the Round Table in Arthurian legend; Kay, a character in 'The Snow Queen', a fairytale by the Danish writer Hans Christian Andersen.

Kalil

Variants and diminutives: Kahil, Kahlil, Kailil, Kal, Kallie, Kalton, Khaleel, Khalil.
Meaning: 'good friend' (Arabic); 'beautiful' (Greek); 'wealth' or 'crown' (Hebrew).
Notable namesakes: Kahlil Gibran (Syrian-born US writer and artist).

Kalman

Variants and diminutives: Kal.
Meaning: 'man' or 'free man' (Germanic) as a variant of Charles; 'merciful' or 'mild' (Latin) as a variant of Clement.

Kamil

Variants and diminutives: Kameel.
Meaning: 'perfection' (Arabic).

Kane

Variants and diminutives: Cathair, Kain, Kaine, Kayne.
Meaning: uncertain; possibly 'warrior' (Irish Gaelic); possibly 'lovely' (Welsh); possibly 'battlefield' (Old French) when derived from Caen, a French town; possibly 'tribute', 'battler' or 'dark' (Celtic); 'golden' (Japanese); 'man' (Hawaiian).

Kaniel

Variants and diminutives: Kan, Kani, Kanny.
Meaning: 'reed' or 'stalk' (Hebrew); 'spear' (Arabic).

Karim

Variants and diminutives: Kareem, Kario.
Meaning: 'noble' or 'generous' (Arabic).
Notable namesakes: Kareem Abdul-Jabbar (US basketball player).

Karl

Variants and diminutives: Carl, Carlo, Carlos, Charles.
Meaning: 'man' or 'free man' (Germanic) as a German variant of Charles.
Notable namesakes: Karl Baedeker (German printer and founder of the Baedeker series of guidebooks); Karl Marx (German social philosopher, political theorist and founder of communism); Karl Liebknecht (German founder of the German Communist Party, or Spartacus League); Karl Popper (Austrian-born British philosopher); Karl Gjellerup (Danish writer); Karl Shapiro (US writer); Karl Lagerfeld (German fashion designer).

Kavi

Meaning: 'poetic' (Sanskrit).

Keane

Variants and diminutives: Kane, Kani, Kayne, Kean, Keen, Keenan, Keene, Kene, Kian, Kienan.
Meaning: 'warrior's son' (Irish Gaelic); 'clever' or 'sharp' (Old English).

Kedem

Meaning: 'eastern' or 'ancient' (Hebrew).

Keefe

Variants and diminutives: Keeffe, Keever, Kief, Kiefer, Kif.
Meaning: 'euphoria' (Arabic); 'the handsome one's grandson' (Irish Gaelic) when derived from an Irish family name.

A B C D E F G H I J K L M N O P Q R S T U V W X Y Z

Keir
Variants and diminutives: Kerr.
Meaning: 'dark-skinned' or 'spear' (Irish Gaelic); 'marshland containing brushwood' (Old Norse); derived from a Scottish family name, in turn a variant of Kerr.

Keith
Meaning: 'battlefield' (Irish Gaelic); 'wood' (Scots Gaelic); derived from a Scottish family name.
Notable namesakes: Keith Richard (British musician); Keith Haring (US artist).

Kelsey
Variants and diminutives: Kelcey, Kelci, Kelcie, Kelley, Kellog, Kellow, Kelo, Kelsi, Kelsie, Kelson, Kelsy, Kelton.
Meaning: 'warrior' (Irish Gaelic); 'ship's keel' (Old English). Also a girl's name.
Notable namesakes: Kelsey Grammer (US actor).

Kelvin
Variants and diminutives: Kelvan, Kelven, Kelwin.
Meaning: uncertain; possibly 'ship's keel' and 'friend' (Old English); possibly 'narrow stream' (Scots Gaelic) when derived from a British family name, itself derived from the name of a Scottish river.
Notable namesakes: the kelvin thermodynamic temperature scale.

Kendal
Variants and diminutives: Ken, Kendahl, Kendale, Kendall, Kendel, Kendell, Kendyl, Kenn, Kennie, Kenny, Kyndal.
Meaning: 'ruler' and 'valley' (Old English); 'valley of the Kent river' (Old English) when derived from an English family name, in turn derived from a Cumbrian place name; 'spring' and 'valley' (Old English) when derived from an English family name, in turn derived from Kendale, a place in Humberside. Also a girl's name.

Kenelm
Variants and diminutives: Ken, Kennie, Kenny.
Meaning: 'brave' and 'helmet' (Old English).
Notable namesakes: Saint Kenelm.

Kennedy
Variants and diminutives: Cinneidid, Kemp, Ken, Kenman, Kenn, Kennard, Kennie, Kenny.
Meaning: 'head' and 'ugly' (Irish Gaelic) when derived from an Irish family name; 'ruler' (Old English). Also a girl's name.

Kenneth
Variants and diminutives: Cainnech, Caioneach, Canice, Cennydd, Cenydd, Cinaed, Cynnedd, Ken, Kene, Kenney, Kennie, Kenny, Kenya, Kesha.
Meaning: 'born of fire' or 'handsome' (Scottish and Irish Gaelic); 'royal oath' (Old English).
Notable namesakes: Saint Caioneach; two kings of Scotland, including Kenneth I (Cinaed mac Alpin or Kenneth MacAlpin), who defeated the Picts, Angles and Britons and founded the kingdom of Scotland; a character in the novel *The Talisman*, by Scottish writer Sir Walter Scott; Kenneth Grahame (British writer); Kenneth Tynan (British drama critic); Kenneth Noland (US artist); Kenneth Clark (British politician); Kenneth Brannagh, Kenneth Williams and Kenneth More (British actors).

Kenrick
Variants and diminutives: Cynric, Ken, Kendig, Kendric, Kendrick, Kendrik, Kendrix, Kenerick, Kenn, Kennie, Kenny, Kenric, Kenrik, Kenward, Kerrick, Kerrik, Ric, Rick, Rickie, Ricky.
Meaning: 'hero' and 'chief' (Welsh); 'royal' and 'ruler' (Old English).

Kent
Variants and diminutives: Ken, Kenton, Kenyon.
Meaning: 'white' or 'border' (Celtic); derived from an English family name, in turn derived from the name of the English county of Kent.

Kentigern
Variants and diminutives: Ceanntigher, Kent.
Meaning: 'chief lord' or 'not condemned' (Celtic).
Notable namesakes: Saint Kentigern.

Kenton
Variants and diminutives: Ken, Kent, Kenyon.

Meaning: uncertain; possibly 'royal manor' (Old English).

Kenward

Variants and diminutives: Cenweard, Ken, Kennie, Kenny.
Meaning: 'brave' and 'protector' (Old English).

Kermit

Variants and diminutives: Dermott, Diarmad, Diarmaid, Diarmait, Diarmid, Diarmit, Diarmuid, Diiarmuit, Ker, Kerm, Kermie, Kermode, Kermy, Kerr.
Meaning: 'church' (Dutch); 'lacking in envy' (Irish Gaelic) as a variant of Diarmaid (Dermot).
Notable namesakes: 'Kermit the Frog', the leading puppet character in the US children's television series *The Muppet Show*.

Kerr

Variants and diminutives: Keir.
Meaning: 'dark-skinned' or 'spear' (Irish Gaelic); 'marshland containing brushwood' (Old Norse); derived from a British family name, itself derived from a British place name.

Kevin

Variants and diminutives: Caoimhinn, Caomhghin, Coemgen, Kev, Kevan, Keven, Kevvie, Kevvy.
Meaning: 'handsome' or 'loved' and 'at birth' (Irish Gaelic).
Notable namesakes: Saint Kevin; Kevin Spacey and Kevin Costner (US actors); Kevin Keagan (British footballer and football manager).

Kiefer

Variants and diminutives: Kief.
Meaning: uncertain; possibly 'pine tree' or 'jaw' (German).
Notable namesakes: Kiefer Sutherland (US actor).

Kieran

Variants and diminutives: Cianon, Ciaran, Kearn, Kearne, Keeran, Keiran, Keiren, Keiron, Kern, Kerne, Kiaran, Kieren, Kieron.
Meaning: 'dark' (Irish Gaelic).

Killian

Variants and diminutives: Cilian, Cillian, Cillin, Kilian, Killie, Killy, Kilmer.
Meaning: 'church' or 'little warrior' (Irish Gaelic).
Notable namesakes: a number of Irish saints.

Kimball

Variants and diminutives: Cymbeline, Kim, Kimbell, Kimble, Kimmie, Kimmy.
Meaning: uncertain; possibly 'empty vessel' (Greek); possibly 'kin' or 'royal' and 'bold' (Old English); possibly 'chief' and 'war' (Welsh); derived from a British family name.

Notable namesakes: Kimball O'Hara, the hero of the novel *Kim*, by the British writer Rudyard Kipling.

King

Variants and diminutives: Kingsley.
Meaning: 'king' (Germanic); derived from an English family name.
Notable namesakes: Nat 'King' Cole (US musician); King Vidor (US film director).

Kingsley

Variants and diminutives: King, Kingsleigh, Kingsly, Kingston, Kinnaird, Kinsey, Kinsley.
Meaning: 'king's clearing' or 'king's wood' (Old English); derived from an English family name, in turn derived from a number of English place names.
Notable namesakes: Kingsley Amis (British writer).

Kipp

Variants and diminutives: Kip, Kipper, Kippie, Kippy.
Meaning: 'pointed hill' (Old English).

Kiral

Meaning: 'king' (Turkish).

Kiran

Meaning: 'ray of light' (Sanskrit).

Kirk
Variants and diminutives: Kerby, Kerk, Kirby, Kirklan, Kirkland, Kirklen, Kirklin, Kirtland, Kirtley, Kirtly, Kyrk, Kyrksen.
Meaning: 'church' (Old Norse); derived from a British family name.
Notable namesakes: Kirk Douglas (US actor).

Kit
Variants and diminutives: Kitt.
Meaning: 'carrier of Christ' (Greek) as a diminutive of Christopher. Also a girl's name.
Notable namesakes: Kit Carson (US folk hero, a guide and a trapper).

Knut
Variants and diminutives: Canute, Canutus, Knud, Knute, Note, Nute, Nutkin, Nutt.
Meaning: 'knot' (Old Norse); 'type' or 'race' (Old Danish).
Notable namesakes: King Knut (Canute) of England, Denmark and Norway, for whom the sea famously refused to retreat; Saint Knut; Knut Hamsun (Norwegian writer).

Koji
Meaning: 'child' (Japanese).

Kumar
Meaning: 'son' (Sanskrit).

Kurt
Variants and diminutives: Curt, Curtis, Kurtis.
Meaning: 'brave' and 'advice' (Germanic) as a diminutive of Konrad (Conrad).
Notable namesakes: Kurt Weill (German composer); Kurt Schwitters (German artist); Kurt Vonnegut (US writer); Kurt Cobain (US musician).

Kyle
Variants and diminutives: Kiel, Kile, Kiley, Ky, Kylie.
Meaning: 'crowned with laurel' (Hebrew); 'narrow' or 'narrow strait' (Scots Gaelic); derived from a Scottish family name, in turn derived from a Scottish place

name. Also a girl's name.
Notable namesakes: Kyle MacLachlan (US actor).

Laban
Meaning: 'white' (Hebrew).
Notable namesakes: the brother of Rebecca, brother-in-law of Isaac, father of Leah and Rachel and father-in-law of Jacob in the Old Testament.

Lachlan
Variants and diminutives: Lachann, Lachie, Lachlann.
Meaning: 'from the land of the lakes [Norway]' or 'martial' (Scots Gaelic); derived from a Scottish family name.

Lal
Meaning: 'beloved' (Hindi).

Lambert
Variants and diminutives: Bert, Bertie, Berty, Lamberto, Lammie, Landbert.
Meaning: 'land' and 'bright' (Germanic).
Notable namesakes: Saint Lambert of Maastricht, patron saint of children; Lambert Simnel, an imposter involved in a plot to overthrow King Henry VII of England; a unit of luminance.

Lamont
Variants and diminutives: Lammond, Lamond, LaMont, Lamonte, Lemont, Monty.
Meaning: 'the mountain' (Old French); 'lawgiver' (Scots Gaelic).

Lance
Variants and diminutives: Lancelot, Lancing, Lansing, Launce, Launcelot.
Meaning: 'lance' (Latin); 'spear' (Old French); 'land'

(Germanic). Both the origin and diminutive of Lancelot.

Lancelot

Variants and diminutives: Lance, Lancing, Lansing, Launce, Launcelot.
Meaning: 'lance' (Latin); 'spear' (Old French); 'land' (Germanic).
Notable namesakes: a knight of the Round Table and lover of Queen Guinevere in Arthurian legend; Lancelot Hogben (British scientist).

Lang

Variants and diminutives: Laing, Langdon, Langer, Langford, Langhorne, Langley, Langly, Langsdon, Langston, Langtry, Lanny, Largo, Longfellow.
Meaning: 'long' (Old English).

Larry

Variants and diminutives: Labhrainn, Lary, Laurence, Laurie, Lawrence, Lawrie, Lorrie, Lorry.
Meaning: 'from Laurentum' (Latin), Laurentum being the Roman name of an Italian town, as a diminutive of Laurence.
Notable namesakes: Larry McMurtry (US writer); Larry Rivers (US artist).

Lars

Variants and diminutives: Larse, Laurans, Laurence, Lawrence, Lorens.
Meaning: 'from Laurentum' (Latin), Laurentum being the Roman name of an Italian town, as a Scandinavian version of Laurence.

Laurence

Variants and diminutives: Brencis, Chencho, Inek, Labhrainn, Labhras, Labhruinn, Labrencis, Labrentsis, Lanty, Larikin, Larka, Larkin, Larns, Larrance, Larrence, Larry, Larya, Lars, Larse, Larson, Lary, Laudalino, Laurans, Laurel, Lauren, Laurencho, Laurencio, Laurens, Laurent, Lauri, Laurie, Lauriston, Lauritz, Lauro, Lavr, Lavrik, Lavro, Lawrance, Lawrence, Lawrey, Lawrie, Lawry, Lencho, Lenci, Lochlainn, Lon, Lonnie, Lonny, Loran, Lorant, Lorcan, Loren, Lorence, Lorenco, Lorens, Lorentz, Lorenz, Lorenzo, Loretto, Lorin, Loring, Lorn,

Lorne, Lornic, Lorrie, Lorry, Lourenco, Lowrence, Rance, Raulas, Raulo, Renzo.
Meaning: 'from Laurentum' (Latin), Laurentum being the Roman name of an Italian town.
Notable namesakes: Saint Laurence (Lawrence), patron saint of deacons, cooks, fire prevention, comedians, the poor and France, for whom North America's St Lawrence river is named; Saint Lawrence of Canterbury; Saint Lawrence O'Toole (Lorcan ua Tuathail); Lorenzo, characters in William Shakespeare's plays *Romeo and Juliet* and *The Merchant of Venice*; Laurence Sterne (British writer); Lawrence Alma-Tadema (British artist); L(aurence) S(tephen) Lowry (British artist); Laurence Olivier (British actor); Lawrence Durrell and Laurie Lee (British writers); Lorin Maazel (US conductor).

Lazarus

Variants and diminutives: Eleazar, Lazar, Lazare, Lazaro, Lazer, Lazlo, Lesser.
Meaning: 'God is my help' (Hebrew) as a Greek variant of Eleazar.
Notable namesakes: a beggar in a parable in the New Testament; the brother of Mary and Martha whom Christ caused to rise from the dead in the New Testament; the eponymous leading character of the play *Lazarus Laughed*, by US playwright Eugene O'Neill.

Leander

Variants and diminutives: Ander, Andor, Lea, Leandre, Leandro, Leanther, Lee, Leo, Leon, Maclean.
Meaning: 'lion' and 'man' (Greek).
Notable namesakes: the lover of Hero in Greek mythology, whose tragic story is told in the plays *Hero and Leander*, by English playwright Christopher Marlowe, and *Des Meeres und der Liebe Wellen* (*The Waves of Sea and Love*), by Austrian playwright Franz Grillparzer; Saint Leander.

Leben

Meaning: 'life' (Yiddish and German).

Lee

Variants and diminutives: Leigh.

Meaning: 'meadow', 'clearing' or 'wood' (Old English); derived from an English family name, in turn derived from a number of English place names. Also a girl's name.
Notable namesakes: Leigh Hunt (English writer); Lee Marvin (US actor).

Leif

Variants and diminutives: Lief.
Meaning: 'beloved' (Old Norse).
Notable namesakes: Leif Ericsson (Norse explorer).

Leighton

Variants and diminutives: Latton, Lay, Layton, Leigh.
Meaning: 'herb garden' (Old English).

Lemuel

Variants and diminutives: Lem, Lemmie, Lemmy.
Meaning: 'dedicated to God' (Hebrew).
Notable namesakes: an Old Testament king; Lemuel Gulliver, the hero of the allegorical novel *Gulliver's Travels*, by Irish writer Jonathan Swift.

Len

Variants and diminutives: Lendal, Lendall, Lendon, Lennie, Lennon, Lennnox, Lenvil, Lenny, Lenwood Leonard.
Meaning: 'tenant house' (Old English); 'flute' (Hopi); 'lion' and 'hard' (Germanic) as a diminutive of Leonard; 'elms' and 'water' (Scots Gaelic) as a diminutive of Lennox.
Notable namesakes: Lenny Kravitz (US musician); Lenny Henry (British comedian).

Lennox

Variants and diminutives: Len, Lenn, Lenox.
Meaning: 'elms' and 'water' (Scots Gaelic); derived from a Scottish family name, in turn derived from a Scottish place name.
Notable namesakes: Lennox Berkeley (British composer); Lennox Lewis (Canadian-born British boxer).

Leo

Variants and diminutives: Label, Leander, Leao, Lee, Leib, Leibel, Len, Leni, Lenn, Lennie, Leodis, Leofric, Léon, Leon, Leonard, Leonardo, Leonas, Leondaus, Leone, Leonid, Leonida, Leonidas, Leonis, Leopold, Leos, Leosko, Lev, Leva, Levka, Levko, Levnek, Levya, Lio, Lion, Lionel, Lionello, Liutas, Llewellyn, Llywellyn, Loeb, Loew, Loewy, Lon, Lonnie, Lowe, Lyon, Lyonel, Lyons, Lyron.
Meaning: 'lion' (Latin).
Notable namesakes: the name of a constellation and zodiacal sign; six Byzantine emperors; a number of saints and thirteen popes, including Saint Leo the Great (Pope Leo I); Leo Nikolaievich Tolstoy (Russian writer); Leo Naphta, a character in the novel *The Magic Mountain*, by German writer Thomas Mann.

Leofric

Variants and diminutives: Leo.
Meaning: 'dear' and 'ruler' (Old English).
Notable namesakes: Leofric, Earl of Mercia, the husband of Lady Godiva.

Leonard

Variants and diminutives: Laya, Lee, Len, Lenard, Lennard, Lenn, Lennard, Lennart, Lenne, Lennie, Lenny, Leo, Leon, Leonala, Leonardo, Leonards, Leonek, Leonerd, Leongard, Leonhard, Leonhards, Leonid, Leons, Lewenhart, Lienard, Linek, Lionardo, Lon, Lonnard, Lonnie, Lonny, Nardek, Nenne.
Meaning: 'lion' and 'hard' (Germanic).
Notable namesakes: Saint Leonard, patron saint of prisoners; Leonardo da Vinci (Italian artist and scientist); Saint Leonard of Port Maurice, patron saint of parish missions; Leonid Ilyich Brezhnev (Soviet politician); Leonard Bernstein (US composer and conductor); Leonard Rossiter (British comic actor); Leonard Cohen (US singer-songwriter); Leonardo DiCaprio (US actor).

Leopold

Variants and diminutives: Leo, Leopoldo, Leupold, Poldi, Poldie, Poldo.
Meaning: 'people' and 'bold' (Germanic).
Notable namesakes: Saint Leopard of Austria; two Holy Roman emperors; three kings of the Belgians; Leopold von Sacher-Masoch, the Austrian novelist from whose name the word masochism is derived; Leopold Bloom, the leading character of the novel

Ulysses, by Irish writer James Joyce; Leopoldo Lugones (Argentinian poet).

Leor
Meaning: 'light' (Hebrew).

Leron
Variants and diminutives: Lerond, Lerone, Lerin, Lerrin, Liron, Lirone.
Meaning: 'my song' (Hebrew); 'the circle' (Old French).

Leroy
Variants and diminutives: Elroy, Lee, Lee Roy, Leroi, Roy.
Meaning: 'the king' (Old French); derived from a French family name.

Leslie
Variants and diminutives: Lee, Les, Lesley, Lesly.
Meaning: 'garden' and 'pool' or 'hollies' (Scots Gaelic); derived from a Scottish family name, in turn derived from a number of Scottish place names. Also a girl's name (generally Lesley).
Notable namesakes: Leslie Stephen (British critic and editor and father of the writer Virginia Woolf); Leslie A Fiedler (US writer); Leslie Howard (US actor); Les Murray (Australian poet).

Lester
Variants and diminutives: Leicester, Les, Letcher, Leycester.
Meaning: 'Roman clearing' (Old English); derived from an English family name, in turn derived from the English town of Leicester.
Notable namesakes: Lester Pearson (Canadian politician); Lester Piggott (British jockey); Lester Young (US jazz musician).

Levi
Variants and diminutives: Lavey, Lavi, Lavy, Leavitt, Lev, Levic, Lever, Levey, Levy, Lewi.
Meaning: 'attached' or 'pledged' (Hebrew).
Notable namesakes: a son of Jacob and Leah in the Old Testament, whose descendents were the Levites; Levi Strauss, a US brand of jeans.

Lewis
Variants and diminutives: Laoiseach, Lew, Llewellyn, Lothar, Lothair, Louis, Ludovicus, Lughaidh, Lutwidge, Ludwig.
Meaning: 'famed' and 'warrior' (Germanic) as a variant of Ludwig.
Notable namesakes: the Isle of Lewis in the Scottish Hebrides; Lewis Carroll, the pseudonym of the English writer Charles Lutwidge Dodgson.

Lex
Variants and diminutives: Alexander, Laxton, Lexton.
Meaning: 'word' (Greek). 'defender of men' or 'warrior' (Greek) as a diminutive of Alexander.

Liam
Variants and diminutives: Uilliam, William.
Meaning: 'will' and 'helmet' or 'protection' (Germanic) as a diminutive of Uilliam, in turn an Irish Gaelic variant of William.
Notable namesakes: Liam O'Flaherty (Irish writer); Liam Neeson (British actor); Liam Gallagher (British singer).

Liang
Meaning: 'excellent' (Chinese).

Lincoln
Variants and diminutives: Linc, Link.
Meaning: 'Roman colony by the pool' (Old English); derived from an English family name, in turn derived from the English town of Lincoln.

Linfred
Variants and diminutives: Lin, Linnie, Linny, Fred, Freddie, Freddy.
Meaning: 'gentle' and 'peace' (Germanic).

Linus
Variants and diminutives: Linos.
Meaning: uncertain; possibly 'flax' (Latin).
Notable namesakes: Linus Van Pelt, a character in the

Peanuts series of cartoons, by US animator Charles Schulz; Linus Roache (British actor).

Lionel
Variants and diminutives: Len, Lennie, Lenny, Leo, Léon, Leon, Leonel, Lionell, Lonnell, Lonnell.
Meaning: 'little lion' (Latin) as a variant of Leon (Leo).
Notable namesakes: a knight of the Round Table in Arthurian legend; Lionel Johnson (English writer); Lional Barrymore (British actor); Lionel Bart (British composer); Lionel Richie (US singer).

Llewellyn
Variants and diminutives: Fluellen, Leoline, Lew, Lewlin, Lleelo, Llew, Llewelyn, Llywellwyn, Llywelyn, Lyn.
Meaning: 'leader' or 'lion' and 'resemblance' (Welsh).
Notable namesakes: two Welsh princes.

Lloyd
Variants and diminutives: Floyd, Llwyd, Loy, Loyd.
Meaning: 'grey' (Welsh).
Notable namesakes: Lloyd Bridges (US actor); Loyd Grossman (UK television presenter).

Logan
Variants and diminutives: Login.
Meaning: 'little hollow' (Scots Gaelic); derived from a Scottish family name, in turn derived from a Scottish place name; 'record' (Old English).
Notable namesakes: Mount Logan, in northwestern Canada.

Lorcan
Variants and diminutives: Laurence.
Meaning: 'silent' or 'fierce' (Irish Gaelic); 'from Laurentum' (Latin), Laurentum being the Roman name of an Italian town, as an Irish variant of Laurence.
Notable namesakes: Saint Lorcan ua Tuathail (Lawrence O'Toole).

Lorne
Variants and diminutives: Lorn.
Meaning: uncertain; derived from a Scottish place name; possibly 'from Laurentum' (Latin), Laurentum being the Roman name of an Italian town, as a diminutive of Laurence; possibly 'forlorn' (Old English) as a male version of Lorna.
Notable namesakes: Lorne Greene (Canadian actor).

Louis
Variants and diminutives: Aloys, Aloysius, Chlodovech, Clovis, Elois, Hluodowig, Lew, Lewellen, Lewes, Lewi, Lewie, Lewis, Llewelyn, Llwellyn, Loeis, Lon, Lothar, Lothair, Lou, Louie, Lowes, Lude, Ludeg, Ludek, Ludirk, Ludis, Ludko, Ludovic, Ludovici, Ludovicus, Ludvig, Ludvik, Ludwig, Ludwik, Lui, Luigi, Luis, Lutek, Lutwidge.
Meaning: 'famed' and 'warrior' (Germanic) as a variant of Ludwig.
Notable namesakes: eighteen kings of France, including King Louis IX, Saint Louis of France, patron saint of royalty and barbers; Louis Pasteur, the French chemist who invented the process of pasteurisation; Louis Braille, the French inventor of the Braille reading codes for the visually impaired; Robert Louis Stevenson (Scottish writer); Louis Comfort Tiffany (US glass designer); Louis Armstrong (US musician); Luis Buñuel (Spanish film director); Louis Fischer and Louis Auchincloss (US writers); Louis Sullivan (US architect); Louis Malle (French film director); Louis MacNeice (Northern Irish poet); Louis Theroux (British television documentary maker).

Lovell
Variants and diminutives: Lovel, Lowell, Loyal, Loyte.
Meaning: 'wolf cub' (Old French); derived from a British family name.

Lucas
Variants and diminutives: Luc, Lucais, Lucan, Luka, Lukas, Luke.
Meaning: 'from Lucania' (Greek), Lucania being a southern Italian region, as a variant of Luke.
Notable namesakes: Lucas Cranach (German painter).

Lucian

Variants and diminutives: Luc, Luciano, Lucien, Lucio.
Meaning: uncertain; derived from the Roman family name Lucianus.
Notable namesakes: a Greek satirist and writer; Saint Lucian of Antioch; Luciano Fabro (Italian artist); Lucian Freud (British artist).

Lucius

Variants and diminutives: Lu, Luc, Lucais, Luce, Lucian, Luciano, Lucien, Lucio, Lusio.
Meaning: 'light' (Latin).
Notable namesakes: Lucius Junius Brutus, one of the first two Roman consuls; Lucius Apuleius (Roman writer); Lucius Cornelius Sulla (Roman soldier and dictator); three popes, including Saint Lucius I.

Ludovic

Variants and diminutives: Lewis, Lodowick, Louis, Ludo, Ludovick, Ludovico, Ludovicus, Ludwig, Vic.
Meaning: 'famed' and 'warrior' (Germanic) as a diminutive of Ludovicus (Ludwig).

Ludwig

Variants and diminutives: Chlodevech, Clovis, Hluodowig, Lewis, Lothar, Lothair, Louis, Ludeg, Ludek, Ludirk, Ludis, Ludko, Ludvic, Ludovic, Ludovici, Ludovicus, Ludvig, Ludwik, Lutek.
Meaning: 'famed' and 'warrior' (Germanic).
Notable namesakes: Ludwig van Beethoven (German composer); three kings of Bavaria, including King Ludwig II, also known as the 'mad king of Bavaria'; Ludwigshafen, a German port; Ludwig Feuerbach (German philosopher); Ludwig Tieck (German writer); Ludwig Wittgenstein (Austrian philosopher); Ludwig Mies van der Rohe (German architect).

Luke

Variants and diminutives: Loukas, Lucan, Lucas, Luce, Luchok, Luck, Lucky, Luka, Lukacs, Lukas, Lukash, Lukasha, Lukass, Lukasz, Lukyan.
Meaning: 'from Lucania' (Greek), Lucania being a southern Italian region.
Notable namesakes: Saint Luke, author of the eponymous gospel and the Acts of Apostles in the New Testament and patron saint of doctors, surgeons, artists, brewers, butchers and glassworkers; Luke Perry (US actor); Luke Skywalker, hero of the *Star Wars* series of films.

Luther

Variants and diminutives: Lotario, Lothaire, Lothar, Lothario, Lother, Lothur, Lutero.
Meaning: 'famous' and 'people' or 'army' (Germanic); derived from the family name of the protestant German religious reformer Martin Luther.
Notable namesakes: Martin Luther King, Jr (US civil-rights leader); Luther Vandross (US singer).

Lyle

Variants and diminutives: Lille, Lisle, Ly, Lyall, Lyell.
Meaning: 'the island' (Old French); derived from a British family name, in turn derived from English and French place names.

Lyndon

Variants and diminutives: Lin, Lindon, Lindy, Lyn, Lynn.
Meaning: 'lime tree' and 'hill' (Old English); derived from an English family name, in turn derived from an English place name.
Notable namesakes: Lyndon B Johnson (US president).

Lysander

Variants and diminutives: Sandie, Sandy.
Meaning: 'freer of men' (Greek).
Notable namesakes: a Spartan leader during the Peloponnesian War; a character in William Shakespeare's play *A Midsummer Night's Dream*.

Lyulf

Variants and diminutives: Ligulf, Liul, Lyolf, Lyulph.
Meaning: 'flame' and 'wolf' (Old English).

Mac

Variants and diminutives: Macaulay, Mack.
Meaning: 'son of' (Scots Gaelic). Also a diminutive of any name beginning with 'Mac-', such as Macaulay.
Notable namesakes: Mack Sennett (Canadian-born US film producer).

Macauley

Variants and diminutives: Mac, Macalay, MacAulay, Macaulay, MacAuley, MacAuliffe, Macauliffe, Mack, McAulay, McAuley, McAuliffe, Maccauley, Macawlay.
Meaning: 'son of Olaf' (Irish and Scots Gaelic); derived from a British family name.
Notable namesakes: Macauley Culkin (US actor)

Mackenzie

Variants and diminutives: Mac, Mack, MacKensie, Mackensie, MacKenzie, McKensie, McKenzie, Kensie, Kenzie.
Meaning: 'son of Comely [the handsome one]' (Scots Gaelic); derived from a Scottish family name. Also a girl's name.

Maddison

Variants and diminutives: Maddi, Maddie, Maddy, Madison.
Meaning: 'son of Maud', 'son of Matthew' or 'son of Magdalene' (Old English); derived from an English family name. Also a girl's name.
Notable namesakes: Madison, the capital of the US state of Wisconsin.

Madoc

Variants and diminutives: Maddoc, Madoch, Maedoc, Marmaduke.
Meaning: 'lucky' or 'generous' (Welsh).

Notable namesakes: Saint Madoc; King Arthur's brother-in-law in Arthurian legend.

Magnus

Variants and diminutives: Manas, Manus.
Meaning: 'great' (Latin).
Notable namesakes: a number of Scandinavian kings; Saint Magnus, patron saint of fishermen; Magnus Magnusson (Scottish broadcaster).

Maitland

Variants and diminutives: Mait, Maitie, Maity, Mate, Matey.
Meaning: uncertain; possibly 'inhospitable' (Old French); derived from a British family name, in turn derived from the French place name Mautalant.

Majid

Variants and diminutives: Magid, Maj, Majdi, Majeed.
Meaning: 'glorious' (Arabic).

Malachy

Variants and diminutives: Mal, Malachai, Malachi, Malachias.
Meaning: 'my messenger' (Hebrew).
Notable namesakes: a prophet whose oracles are contained in the Book of Malachi in the Old Testament; Saint Malachy (Mael Maedoc ua Morgair).

Malcolm

Variants and diminutives: Callum, Calum, Colm, Colum, Columba, Kallum, Kalum, Mal, Malcom, Maolcolm.
Meaning: 'servant of Saint Columba' (Scots Gaelic).
Notable namesakes: four Scottish kings, including Malcolm III, who features in William Shakespeare's play *Macbeth*; Malcolm Sargent (British conductor); Malcolm X (Malcolm Little, US civil-rights leader); Malcolm Forbes (US publisher and philanthropist); Malcolm Morley (British artist); Malcolm Muggeridge and Malcolm Bradbury (British writers); Malcolm McDowell (British actor); Malcolm Marshall (West Indian cricketer).

Malik
Variants and diminutives: Mal, Mali.
Meaning: 'master' (Arabic).

Malise
Variants and diminutives: Mal, Mali.
Meaning: 'servant of Jesus' (Scots Gaelic).

Mallory
Variants and diminutives: Lory, Mal, Mallorey, Mallori, Mallorie, Malori, Malorie, Malory.
Meaning: 'unlucky' (Latin); derived from a British family name. Also a girl's name.

Manasseh
Variants and diminutives: Manasses.
Meaning: 'to forget' (Hebrew).
Notable namesakes: a son of Joseph in the Old Testament.

Manchu
Meaning: 'pure' (Chinese).
Notable namesakes: the Chinese region of Manchuria, homeland of the Manchu people and of the Manchu dynasty that once ruled China.

Manfred
Variants and diminutives: Fred, Freddie, Freddy, Manifred, Mannie, Manny, Mannye.
Meaning: 'man' and 'peace' (Germanic).
Notable namesakes: the title of a poem by English poet George, Lord Byron; Manfred Mann's Earth Band, a British rock group.

Manley
Variants and diminutives: Manly.
Meaning: 'manly' (Middle English); derived from an English family name.
Notable namesakes: Gerard Manley Hopkins (English poet).

Mansa
Meaning: 'king' (African).

Mansel
Variants and diminutives: Mansell.
Meaning: 'from Le Mans', 'from Maine' or 'dweller in a manse' (Old French); derived from an English family name, in turn derived from a number of French place names.

Mansur
Meaning: 'divinely helped' (Arabic).

Manuel
Variants and diminutives: Eman, Emanuel, Emanuele, Emek, Emmanuel, Emmanuil, Immanuel, Maco, Mango, Mannie, Manny, Mano, Manoel, Manolo, Manue, Manuelito, Manuil, Manuyil, Mel, Minel, Nelo.
Meaning: 'God is with us' (Hebrew) as a Spanish diminutive of Emmanuel.
Notable namesakes: Manuel Gálvez (Argentinian writer); Manuel Altolaquirre (Spanish poet); Manuel de Falla (Spanish composer); the hapless waiter in the British television comedy series *Fawlty Towers*.

Marcel
Variants and diminutives: Marc, Marceau, Marcelino, Marcellino, Marcello, Marcellus, Marcelo, Marcelo, Marci, Marco, Marcus.
Meaning: uncertain; possibly 'martial' (Latin) through association with Mars, the god of war in Roman mythology, as a French diminutive of Marcellus (Marcus).
Notable namesakes: Marcel Proust (French writer); Marcel Duchamp (French artist); Marcel Breuer (Hungarian-born US architect and industrial designer); Marcel Broodthaers (Belgian artist); Marcel Pagnol (French playwright and film director); Marcel Marceau (French mime artist).

Marcellus
Variants and diminutives: Marc, Marcel, Marcelino, Marcellin, Marcellino, Marcello, Marcelo, Marco, Marcus.

Meaning: uncertain; possibly 'martial' (Latin) through association with Mars, the god of war in Roman mythology, as a Latin variant of Marcus.

Notable namesakes: two popes and a number of saints; Marcellus Laroon the Elder and Marcellus Laroon the Younger (respectively Dutch and British artists); Marcellus Wallace, a character in the US film *Pulp Fiction*.

Marco

Variants and diminutives: Marc, Marceau, Marcos, Marcus, Mark, Markos.

Meaning: uncertain; possibly 'martial' (Latin) through association with Mars, the god of war in Roman mythology, as an Italian variant of Marcus.

Notable namesakes: Marco Polo, the Venetian traveller and writer who appears in the play *Marco Millions*, by US playwright Eugene O'Neill; Marco Pierre White (British chef and restaurateur).

Marcus

Variants and diminutives: Marc, Marcel, Marcellin, Marcellus, Marco, Marcos, Mark, Markos, Markus.

Meaning: uncertain; possibly 'martial' (Latin) through association with Mars, the god of war in Roman mythology; derived from the Roman family name Marcius.

Notable namesakes: Marcus Junius Brutus (Roman politician, soldier and instigator of the murder of Julius Caesar); Marcus Antonius (Mark Anthony, Roman politician and soldier); Marcus Aurelius (Roman emperor and philosopher); Marcus Tullius Cicero (Roman consul and writer); Marcus G(h)eeraerts the Elder and Marcus G(h)eeraerts the Younger (Flemish artists); Markus Lüpertz (German artist).

Mario

Variants and diminutives: Marcus, Mark, Mari, Marilo, Marion, Marius.

Meaning: uncertain; possibly 'martial' (Latin) through association with Mars, the god of war in Roman mythology, as an Italian version of Marius; possibly 'longed-for child' or 'rebellion' (Hebrew) as a male Italian and Spanish version of Maria (Miriam via Mary).

Notable namesakes: the title character of the story *Mario and the Magician*, by German writer Thomas Mann; Mario Lanza (US singer); Mario Vargas Llosa (Peruvian writer); Mario Merz (Italian artist); Mario Puzo (US writer); Mario Testino (Peruvian photographer).

Marius

Variants and diminutives: Marcus, Mari, Mario, Marion, Mark.

Meaning: uncertain; possibly 'martial' (Latin) through association with Mars, the god of war in Roman mythology; derived from a Roman family name.

Notable namesakes: a Roman general and political leader; the eponymous hero of the novel *Marius the Epicurian*, by English writer Walter Pater; Marius Petipa (Russian dancer and choreographer); Marius Goring (British actor).

Mark

Variants and diminutives: Marc, Marceau, Marcel, Marcelino, Marcellin, Marcellino, Marcello, Marcellus, Marcelo, March, Marci, Marcilka, Marco, Marcos, Marcus, Marcy, Marek, Mari, Marilo, Marinos, Mario, Marion, Marius, Marka, Marko, Markos, Markus, Markusha, Marques, Marquis, Mars, Marsh, Marshe, Martin, Marts.

Meaning: uncertain; possibly 'martial' (Latin) through association with Mars, the god of war in Roman mythology. A variant of Marcus.

Notable namesakes: Saint Mark, author of the second gospel of the New Testament, patron saint of lions, prisoners, lawyers and notaries; King Mark of Cornwall in medieval romantic legend; Mark Twain, the pseudonym of US writer Samuel Langhorne Clemens; Marc Chagall (Russian-born French artist); Mark Rothko (Russian-born US artist); Marc Bolan (British musician); Mark Wahlberg (US actor).

Marlon

Variants and diminutives: Mar, Mario, Marle, Marlen, Marlin, Marlis, Marlo, Marlow, Marlowe, Marne, Marnin, Merlin.
Meaning: uncertain; possibly 'pond' and 'remnant' (Old English) as a variant of Marlow; possibly 'sea' and 'hill' or 'fort' (Welsh) as a variant of Merlin.
Notable namesakes: Marlon Brando (US actor).

Marlow

Variants and diminutives: Marlon, Marlowe.
Meaning: 'pond' and 'remnant' (Old English); derived from an English family name, in turn derived from an English place name.
Notable namesakes: the narrator of a number of literary works by Polish-born English writer Joseph Conrad.

Marmaduke

Variants and diminutives: Duke, Dukie, Madoc.
Meaning: 'servant of [Saint] Madoc' (Irish Gaelic).
Notable namesakes: Marmaduke Hussey (former chairman of the BBC).

Marnin

Meaning: 'rejoicer' or 'singer' (Hebrew).

Marquis

Variants and diminutives: Mark, Marq, Marques, Marquess, Marquette.
Meaning: 'count of the march [border]' (Old French) when derived from a European rank of nobility; 'son of Mark' (Latin) when derived from Marques, a Spanish family name.

Marshall

Variants and diminutives: Marsh, Marshal, Marshe, Marshel, Marshell.
Meaning: 'servant of the horse' (Germanic).
Notable namesakes: a military rank and judicial officer in Britain; a court, police or fire officer in the USA; Marshall McLuhan (Canadian communications theorist).

Martin

Variants and diminutives: Maarten, Mairtin, Marci, Marcilki, Marcin, Mart, Martainn, Martan, Martel, Marten, Martey, Marti, Martie, Martijn, Martinas, Martine, Martinet, Martinho, Martiniano, Martinka, Martino, Martinos, Martins, Martlet, Marto, Marton, Martoni, Marty, Martyn, Mertil, Mertin, Tino, Tynek, Tynko.
Meaning: uncertain; possibly 'martial' (Latin) through association with Mars, the god of war in Roman mythology; derived from the Roman family name Martinus.
Notable namesakes: Saint Martin of Tours, patron saint of France, soldiers, equestrians and beggars, whose feast day, on 11 November, is known as Martinmas; Saint Martin (Sint Maarten), an island in the Caribbean Sea; Saint Martin de Porres, patron saint of barbers, hairdressers, poor people and racial harmony; a number of popes; Martin Luther (German Protestant religious reformer); Martin Frobisher (English navigator and explorer); the title character of the novel *Martin Chuzzlewit*, by English writer Charles Dickens; the eponymous hero of the poem *Martín Fierro*, by Argentinian poet José Hernández; Martin Heidegger (German philosopher); Martin Luther King, Jr (US civil-rights leader); the common name of various genera of swallows, such as the house martin, *Delichon urbica*; Martin Scorsese (US film director); Martin Amis (British writer); Martin Crane, a character in the US television sitcom *Frasier*.

Marvin

Variants and diminutives: Marv, Marve, Marven, Marvine, Marvyn, Marwin, Mervin, Mervyn, Merwin, Merwyn, Myrwyn.
Meaning: 'famous' or 'sea' and 'friend' (Old English).
Notable namesakes: Marvin Gay (US singer).

Mason

Meaning: 'mason' or 'stone-worker' (Old French).

Masud

Meaning: 'lucky' (Arabic).

Matthew

Variants and diminutives: Macey, Mack, Maitiu, Mat, Mata, Mate, Matei, Matek, Mateo, Mateus, Matfei, Matfey, Matha, Mathe, Matheiu, Mathern, Mathew, Mathia, Mathias, Mathieu, Mati, Matia, Matiah, Matias, Matok, Matomon, Matt, Mattaeus, Mattathias, Matteo, Matteus, Matthaios, Matthaus, Mattheo, Matthia, Matthias, Matthieu, Matti, Mattie, Mattieu, Mattmias, Matty, Matus, Matvey, Matyas, Matyi, Matyo, Mayo, Motka, Motya, Teo.
Meaning: 'gift of God' (Hebrew).
Notable namesakes: Saint Matthew, author of the first gospel of the Old Testament and patron saint of tax collectors, bankers, accountants and book-keepers; Matthew Paris (English chronicler); Matthew Bramble, the leading character in the novel *Humphrey Clinker*, by Scottish writer Tobias Smollett; Mathew Brady (US photographer); Matthew Walker, a type of knot; Matthew Arnold (British writer); Matt Monro (British singer); Matthew Perry (one a US naval officer and one a US actor); Matthew Pinsent (British oarsman).

Matthias

Variants and diminutives: Macey, Mack, Mat, Mata, Mateo, Mateus, Matheiu, Mathern, Mathew, Mathia, Mathias, Mathieu, Mati, Matia, Matiah, Matias, Matok, Matomon, Matt, Mattaeus, Mattathias, Matteo, Matteus, Matthaios, Matthaus, Matthia, Matthias, Matthieu, Matti, Mattie, Mattieu, Mattmias, Matty, Matus, Matyas, Mayo.
Meaning: 'gift of God' (Hebrew) as a Greek variant of Matthew.
Notable namesakes: Saint Matthias, an apostle of Christ and substitute for Judas Iscariot in the New Testament, patron saint of carpenters and protector against alcoholism; King Matthias I Corvinus of Hungary; Mathias Grünewald (German artist).

Maurice

Variants and diminutives: Maolmuire, Maryse, Maur, Maurey, Mauricio, Maurie, Mauris, Maurise, Maurits, Mauritius, Maurizio, Mauro, Maury, Merrick, Meuric, Meuriz, Meyrick, Mo, Morets, Morey, Morie, Moris, Moritz, Moriz, Morrey, Morrice, Morrie, Morris, Morriss, Morry, Morys, Morus, Moss, Muirgheas.
Meaning: 'Moorish' or 'African' (Latin).
Notable namesakes: Saint Maurice (Moritz), for whom the Swiss ski resort of St Moritz is named, patron saint of Piedmont, Savoy, Sardinia, soldiers, infantrymen, swordsmiths, weavers, dyers and sufferers from gout; Maurice, Duke of Saxony; Maurice of Nassau, Prince of Orange; Maurice Maeterlinck (Belgian writer); Maurice Ravel (French composer); Maurice Utrillo (French artist); Maurice Prendergast (Canadian-born US artist); Maurice Chevalier (French actor and singer).

Max

Variants and diminutives: Mac, Mack, Maks, Maxey, Maxie, Maxim, Maxime, Maximilian, Maximilianus, Maximilien, Maximino, Maxwell, Maxy.
Meaning: generally 'great' (Latin) as a diminutive of both boys' and girls' names beginning with 'Max-', but 'the spring' or 'the well' and 'of Magnus' (Scots Gaelic) as a dimunitive of Maxwell.
Notable namesakes: Max Beerbohm (British writer and caricaturist); Max Planck (German physicist); Max Beckmann, Max Liebermann and Max Ernst (German artists); Max Frisch (Swiss writer); Max Bygraves (British entertainer); Max Hastings (British writer and journalist).

Maximilian

Variants and diminutives: Mac, Mack, Makimus, Maks, Maksim, Maksimka, Maksym, Maksymilian, Makszi, Massimiliano, Massimo, Max, Maxey, Maxi, Maxie, Maxim, Maximalian, Maxime, Maximilianus, Maximiliao, Maximilien, Maximillian, Maximino, Maximo, Maximus, Maxwell, Maxy, Miksa, Sima.
Meaning: 'greatest' (Latin).
Notable namesakes: Saint Maximilian; Maximilian I, King of Germany and Holy Roman Emperor; Maximilien François Marie Isidore de Robespierre (French revolutionary); an archduke of Austria and emperor of Mexico; Saint Maximilian Kolbe, patron saint of political prisoners; Maxim, a character in the novel *Rebecca*, by British writer Daphne du Maurier; Maximus, the hero of the US film *Gladiator*.

Maxwell

Variants and diminutives: Mac, Mack, Maks, Max, Maxey, Maxie, Maxim, Maxime, Maximilian, Maxy.
Meaning: 'the spring' or 'the well' and 'of Magnus' (Scots Gaelic); derived from a Scottish family name, in turn derived from a Scottish place name.
Notable namesakes: Maxwell Bodenheim and Maxwell Anderson (US writers).

Maynard

Variants and diminutives: May, Mayne, Menard.
Meaning: 'strength' and 'hard' (Germanic); derived from an English family name.
Notable namesakes: John Maynard Keynes (British economist).

Mehmet

Variants and diminutives: Mahomet, Mohamma, Mohammed, Muhammad, Muhammed.
Meaning: 'deserving praise' or 'deserving glory' (Arabic) as a variant of Mohammed.

Meical

Variants and diminutives: Meic, Michael.
Meaning: 'who is like God?' (Hebrew) as a Welsh variant of Michael.

Melchior

Variants and diminutives: Melchi, Melchie, Melchisadek, Melchizedek, Melchs, Melchy.
Meaning: uncertain; possibly 'king' or 'king of the city' (Hebrew).
Notable namesakes: one of the Magi who visited the newborn Jesus Christ in the New Testament; Melchior Broederlam (Flemish artist); Melchior D'Hondecoeter (Dutch artist).

Melville

Variants and diminutives: Mel, Melbourne, Melburn, Meldon, Melford, Mell, Melton, Melwood, Melvin, Melvyn.
Meaning: uncertain; possibly 'Amalo's settlement' (Germanic); possibly 'bad' and town' (Old French); derived from a Scottish family name, in turn derived from a Scottish place name.

Melvin

Variants and diminutives: Malvin, Mel, Mell, Melville, Melvyn, Vinny, Vynnie.
Meaning: uncertain; possibly 'council' and 'friend' (Old English); possibly 'Amalo's settlement' (Germanic) or 'bad' and 'town' (Old French) as a variant of Melville.
Notable namesakes: Melvyn Douglas (US actor); Melvyn Bragg (British writer and broadcaster).

Menachem

Variants and diminutives: Manasseh, Mann, Mannes, Menasseh, Menahem, Mendel, Mendeley.
Meaning: 'comforter' (Hebrew).
Notable namesakes: Menachem Begin (Israeli politician).

Mercury

Variants and diminutives: Mercurius.
Meaning: 'messenger of Jupiter' (Latin); derived from the name of the messenger of the gods and god of trade in Roman mythology.
Notable namesakes: a planet; a liquid metallic element also known as quicksilver; the common name of the *Mercurialis* genus of plants.

Merlin

Variants and diminutives: Marlin, Marlon, Merle, Merlo, Merlon, Merlyn, Myrddin.
Meaning: 'sea' and 'hill' or 'fort' (Welsh); possibly derived from the Welsh town Carmarthen. Also a girl's name (generally Merlyn).
Notable namesakes: Merlin Ambrosius (Myrddin Emrys), the magician and adviser of King Arthur in Arthurian legend; the title of a poem by US writer and philosopher Ralph Waldo Emerson; the common name of the *Falco columbarius* species of falcon.

Merrick

Variants and diminutives: Maurice, Merick, Merik, Meril, Merle, Merrik, Merrill, Meryl, Meuric, Meyrick, Myril, Myrl.
Meaning: 'Moorish' or 'African' (Latin) as a Welsh variant of Maurice.

Merton

Variants and diminutives: Mert, Mertie, Merty.
Meaning: 'lake' and 'place' (Old English); derived from an English family name, in turn derived from a number of English place names.
Notable namesakes: Merton Densher, a character in the novel *The Wings of the Dove*, by US writer Henry James.

Mervyn

Variants and diminutives: Marvin, Marvyn, Merfyn, Merv, Merven, Mervin.
Meaning: 'famous' or 'sea' and 'friend' (Old English) as a variant of Marvin.
Notable namesakes: Mervyn Peake (British writer).

Micah

Variants and diminutives: Mica, Micha, Michael, Misha, Mishka, Miska.
Meaning: 'who is like God?' (Hebrew) as a variant of Michael.
Notable namesakes: an Old Testament prophet.

Michael

Variants and diminutives: Dumichel, Machas, Maguel, Makis, Meic, Meical, Mica, Micah, Micha, Michail, Michak, Michal, Michalek, Michau, Micheal, Micheil, Michel, Michelangelo, Michele, Michiel, Micho, Michon, Mick, Mickel, Mickey, Micki, Mickie, Micky, Mietek, Miguel, Migui, Mihail, Mihailo, Mihal, Mihalje, Mihaly, Mihangel, Mihas, Mihel, Mihkel, Mika, Mikael, Mikas, Mike, Mikel, Mikelis, Mikey, Mikhail, Mikhalis, Mikhalka, Mikhos, Miki, Mikk, Mikkel, Mikko, Miks, Mikus, Miles, Milkins, Min, Minka, Mique, Misa, Mischa, Misha, Mishca, Misi, Miska, Misko, Miso, Mitch, Mitchel, Mitchell, Mitchele, Mitchell, Mitchiel, Myall, Mychal, Myles.
Meaning: 'who is like God?' (Hebrew).
Notable namesakes: Saint Michael, an archangel and guardian angel of Israel in the Old and New Testaments, patron saint of radiologists, sick people, grocers, paratroopers, airborne people and police officers, for whose feast day, Michaelmas (29 September), the Michaelmas daisy (from the *Aster* genus of flowering plants) was named; Michelangelo Buonarroti (Italian painter, sculptor, architect and poet); Mont-Saint-Michel, the Benedictine abbey in the Bay of St Michel off the coast of northwestern France; nine Byzantine emperors; Tsar Michael of Russia (Mikhail Fyodorovich Romanov), founder of the Romanov dynasty of Russian rulers; five kings of Romania; Miguel de Cervantes (Spanish writer); the eponymous hero of the novella *Michael Kohlhaas*, by German writer Heinrich von Kleist; Mikhail Gorbachev (Russian politician); Michael Douglas (US actor); Michael Caine (British actor); Mike Leigh (British film director); Michael Palin (British comic actor), Mike Oldfield (British musician); Michael Hutchence (Australian musician); Michael Jackson (US musician); Mike Atherton (British cricketer); Michael Owen (British footballer).

Mick

Variants and diminutives: Michael, Mickey, Micky.
Meaning: 'who is like God?' (Hebrew) as a diminutive of Michael.
Notable namesakes: a derogatory slang word used to describe Irish people or Roman Catholics; Mickey Spillane (US crime-writer); Mickey Finn, the generic term for a spiked alcoholic drink; Mickey Mouse, an animated cartoon character popularised by US film producer Walt Disney, whose name is also used to describe something trivial or spiritless; Mick Jagger (British musician).

Miles

Variants and diminutives: Michael, Mihel, Milan, Mills, Milo, Myles.
Meaning: uncertain; possibly 'soldier' (Latin); possibly 'grace' (Old Slavic) or 'merciful' (Germanic) as a variant of Milo; possibly 'gentle' or 'of Michael' (Old English); possibly 'beloved servant of Mary' (Irish Gaelic).
Notable namesakes: Miles Coverdale, the English translator of the first English version of the Bible; Miles Standish, a leader of the *Mayflower* pilgrims to America and the subject of the poem *The Courtship of Miles Standish*, by US poet Henry Wadsworth

Longfellow; Miles Franklin (Australian writer); Miles Davis (US jazz trumpeter and composer).

Milo
Variants and diminutives: Miles, Myles.
Meaning: 'grace' (Old Slavic); 'merciful' (Germanic).

Milton
Variants and diminutives: Millard, Miller, Mills, Milt, Miltie, Milty, Mull, Muller.
Meaning: 'middle' or 'mill' and 'settlement' or 'farm' (Old English); derived from an English family name, in turn derived from a number of English place names.
Notable namesakes: Milton Friedman (US economist); Milton Avery (US artist).

Mitchell
Variants and diminutives: Michael, Mitch, Mitchel.
Meaning: 'who is like God?' (Hebrew) as a variant of Michael; 'big' (Old English); derived from a British family name.

Mohammed
Variants and diminutives: Ahmad, Ahmed, Amad, Amed, Hamdrem, Hamdun, Hamid, Hammad, Hammed, Humayd, Mahmud, Mahmoud, Mahomet, Mehemet, Mehmet, Mohamad, Mohamet, Mohammad, Muhammad, Muhammed.
Meaning: 'deserving praise' or 'deserving glory' (Arabic).
Notable namesakes: the founder and prophet of Islam; Muhammad Ali (US boxer).

Mohan
Variants and diminutives: Mohandas.
Meaning: 'delightful' (Sanskrit).
Notable namesakes: a name of Krishna, the Hindu god of creation and preservation; Mohandas Karamchand Gandhi, the Indian spiritual and political leader better known as Mahatma ('great' and 'soul' in Sanskrit) Gandhi.

Monroe
Variants and diminutives: Monro, Munro, Munroe.
Meaning: 'mouth of the Roe', the Roe being a river in Ireland (Irish Gaelic); derived from a British family name.
Notable namesakes: the Monroe Doctrine of non-intervention proclaimed by US President James Monroe.

Montague
Variants and diminutives: Mante, Montacute, Montagu, Monte, Monty.
Meaning: 'hill' and 'pointed' (Old French); derived from a French and British family name, in turn derived from a French place name.
Notable namesakes: Montague grammar, a theory of logic and linguistics named for US logician Richard Merett Montague; Montagu's harrier, the common name of the *Circus pygargus* bird of prey.

Montgomery
Variants and diminutives: Monte, Montgomerie, Monty.
Meaning: 'hill' and of 'the powerful man' (Old French); derived from a British family name, in turn derived from two French place names.
Notable namesakes: the former Welsh county of Montgomeryshire; a city in the US state of Alabama; Montgomery Clift (US actor).

Monty
Variants and diminutives: Monte, Montague, Montgomery.
Meaning: 'hill' and 'pointed' (Old French) as a diminutive of Montague; 'hill' and 'of the powerful man' (Old French) as a diminutive of Montgomery.
Notable namesakes: the nickname of the British World War II general Bernard Law Montgomery; 'the full monty', a term used to describe something in its entirety, popularised by a British film of the same name.

Mordecai
Variants and diminutives: Marduk, Mord, Mordechai, Mordkhe, Mordy, Mort, Mortie, Morty.
Meaning: 'follower of Marduk' (Hebrew), Marduk being the supreme god of Babylonian mythology.
Notable namesakes: the guardian of Esther in the Old Testament; Mordecai Richler (Canadian writer).

A B C D E F G H I J K L M N O P Q R S T U V W X Y Z

Mordred

Variants and diminutives: Modred, Modris.
Meaning: uncertain; possibly 'to bite' (Latin); possibly 'host' or 'own' and 'course' (Welsh).
Notable namesakes: a knight of the Round Table and nephew or son of King Arthur in Arthurian legend.

Morley

Variants and diminutives: Morle, Morlie, Morley.
Meaning: 'moor' or 'fen' and 'clearing' (Old English); derived from an English family name, in turn derived from a number of English place names.
Notable namesakes: Morley Callaghan (Canadian writer).

Morris

Variants and diminutives: Maurey, Maurie, Maury, Mo, Moor, Moreton, Morey, Morgan, Morie, Morrey, Morrie, Morrissey, Morrison, Morry, Morse, Mort, Mortimer, Morton, Morty, Myrton.
Meaning: 'Moorish' or 'African' (Latin) as a variant of Maurice.
Notable namesakes: morris dancing ('Moorish dancing'), a genre of English folk-dancing; Morris West (Australian writer).

Mortimer

Variants and diminutives: Mort, Mortie, Morty.
Meaning: 'dead' and 'sea' (Old French); derived from an English family name, in turn derived from a French place name.
Notable namesakes: Mortimer Wheeler (British archaeologist).

Morton

Variants and diminutives: Mort, Mortie, Morty.
Meaning: 'moor' or 'fen' and 'settlement' or 'farm' (Old English); derived from an English family name, in turn derived from a number of English place names.

Moses

Variants and diminutives: Moe, Moise, Moisei, Moises, Moisey, Moishe, Moisis, Moke, Mose, Moshe, Mosheh, Moss, Mosya, Mosze, Moszek, Moy, Moyes, Moys, Moyse, Moze, Mozes.
Meaning: uncertain; possibly 'son' (Egyptian); possibly 'drawn out' or 'saved [from the water]' (Hebrew).
Notable namesakes: an Old Testament prophet who led the Israelites to the Promised Land and received the Ten Commandments (the Mosaic Law) from God; Moses Mendelssohn (German philosopher); *Go Down, Moses*, the title of a collection of short stories by US writer William Faulkner; Moshe Dayan (Israeli soldier and politician).

Mostyn

Variants and diminutives: Moss, Mostie, Mosty.
Meaning: 'field of the fortress' (Welsh); 'moss' and 'settlement' (Old English); derived from a British family name, in turn derived from a Welsh place name.

Mungo

Variants and diminutives: Kentigern.
Meaning: uncertain; possibly 'beloved' or 'friendly' (Scots Gaelic).
Notable namesakes: the nickname of Saint Kentigern; Mungo Park (Scottish explorer); a type of felt fabric.

Muraco

Meaning: 'white moon' (Native American).

Murdoch

Variants and diminutives: Muireadhach, Murdo, Murdock, Murtagh, Murtaug, Murtaugh.
Meaning: 'mariner' (Scottish and Irish Gaelic).

Murphy

Variants and diminutives: Meriadoc, Morty, Murph, Murphey, Murphie.
Meaning: 'descendent of the sea warrior' (Irish and Scots Gaelic); derived from a British family name. Also a girl's name.
Notable namesakes: a slang word for a potato; Murphy's Law, the maxim that anything that can go wrong will.

Murray

Variants and diminutives: Moray, Muirioch, Murrey, Murry.
Meaning: 'seaboard' and 'settlement' (Scots Gaelic);

derived from a British family name, in turn derived from the Scottish area and former county of Moray.
Notable namesakes: a river in Australia; Murray Walker (British sports commentator).

Myron

Variants and diminutives: Miron, My, Ron, Ronnie, Ronny.
Meaning: 'myrrh' (Aramaic and Arabic). A male version of Myrna.
Notable namesakes: a Greek sculptor.

Nabil

Variants and diminutives: Nadiv, Nagid.
Meaning: 'noble' (Arabic).

Nagid

Meaning: 'noble', 'wealthy' or 'ruler' (Hebrew).

Nahum

Meaning: 'comforting' (Hebrew).
Notable namesakes: an Old Testament prophet; Nahum Tate (English writer).

Namid

Meaning: 'star dancer' (Native American).

Namir

Meaning: 'leopard' (Arabic).

Napier

Variants and diminutives: Nape, Napper, Neper.
Meaning: 'naperer [a keeper of table linen]' (Old French); derived from an English family name.
Notable namesakes: a New Zealand port; the Napierian logarithm, or natural logarithm, a mathematical reckoning system named for its inventor, the Scottish mathematician John Napier, who also devised a calculation aid called Napier's bones.

Napoleon

Variants and diminutives: Leon, Nap, Nappie, Nappy.
Meaning: 'new town' (Greek); derived from Ne'apolis, the ancient Greek name of the Italian town of Naples (Napoli).
Notable namesakes: Napoleon Bonaparte, Emperor Napoleon I of France, who gave his name to the adjective Napoleonic, the Napoleonic Wars and the Napoleonic Code; Emperor Napoleon II of France, the title given by Bonapartists to Napoleon Bonaparte's son, the king of Rome and duke of Reichstadt; Emperor Napoleon III, or Louis-Napoleon, of France; the napoleon, a former French unit of currency; the napoleon cake, a US name for a millefeuille.

Narcissus

Variants and diminutives: Cissus, Narcie, Narcisse, Narcy.
Meaning: 'numbness' (Greek); derived from the name of the self-absorbed youth of Greek mythology who pined away to become the narcissus flower.
Notable namesakes: the *Narcissus* genus of flowering plants, which are said to have narcotic properties; narcissism, a word used to describe extreme self-absorption; Narcisse Diaz (French artist).

Naren

Meaning: 'manly' (Sanskrit).

Naresh

Meaning: 'lord' or 'king' (Sanskrit).

Nasser

Variants and diminutives: Nassor.
Meaning: 'victorious' (Arabic).

Notable namesakes: Nasser Hussain (British cricketer).

Nathan

Variants and diminutives: Nata, Natan, Nat, Nate, Nathon, Natt, Natty.
Meaning: 'gift' (Hebrew).
Notable namesakes: an Old Testament prophet; the subject of the play *Nathan der Weise (Nathan the Wise Man)*, by German playwright Gotthold Ephraim Lessing; Nathan Hale (American hero of the American War of Revolution); Nathan Weinstein, the real name of US writer Nathanael West.

Nathaniel

Variants and diminutives: Nat, Nata, Natan, Natanael, Natale, Nataniel, Nataniele, Nate, Nathan, Nathanael, Nathon, Natt, Natty, Neal, Niel, Noel, Nowell.
Meaning: 'gift of God' (Hebrew).
Notable namesakes: Nathanael, an apostle (probably Bartholomew) of Christ in the New Testament; Nathaniel Hawthorne and Nathanael West (US writers); Nathaniel Hone (Irish painter).

Ned

Variants and diminutives: Edmund, Edward, Neddie, Neddy, Ted, Teddie, Teddy.
Meaning: 'happiness' or 'riches' and 'guardian' (Old English) as a diminutive of Edward; 'happiness' or 'riches' and 'friend' (Old English) as a diminutive of Edmund. Also a diminutive of other names beginning with 'Ed-'.
Notable namesakes: neddy, the slang name for a donkey or horse, as well as for a foolish person.

Neil

Variants and diminutives: Neal, Neale, Neall, Nealson, Neaton, Neely, Neill, Neils, Neilson, Neilus, Nellie, Nels, Nelsi, Nelson, Nial, Niall, Niel, Niels, Nigel, Nil, Niles, Nilo, Nils, Nilson, Nilya, Niul, Nyles.
Meaning: 'champion', 'cloud' or 'vehement' (Irish Gaelic).
Notable namesakes: Niall of the Nine Hostages, an Irish king; Neil Simon (US playwright); Neil Armstrong (US astronaut); Neil Diamond (US musician).

Nelson

Variants and diminutives: Nealson, Neaton, Neil, Nels, Nelsen, Nils, Nilsen, Nilson.
Meaning: 'son of Nell' or 'son of Neil' (Old English); derived from an English family name.
Notable namesakes: Nelson Rockefeller (US politician); Nelson Algren (US writer); Nelson Mandela (South African political activist and statesman); a wrestling hold; an English town; a New Zealand port; a Canadian river.

Nestor

Variants and diminutives: Nest, Nesty, Tory.
Meaning: 'journey' or 'safe return' (Greek).
Notable namesakes: in Greek mythology, the king of Pylos and oldest and wisest of the Greek participants in the Trojan War, whose name is now used to describe a sage or wise old man.

Neville

Variants and diminutives: Nev, Nevil, Nevile, Nevill, Newton.
Meaning: 'new' and 'place' or 'town' (Old French); derived from an English family name, in turn derived from a number of French place names.
Notable namesakes: Neville Chamberlain (British politician); Nevil Shute (British-born Australian writer).

Nevin

Variants and diminutives: Nefen, Nev, Nevan, Neven, Nevins, Niven.
Meaning: 'little saint' or 'worshipper of the saint' (Irish Gaelic); 'nephew' (Germanic).

Newton

Variants and diminutives: Neville, Newgate, Newland, Newman, Newt, Niland.
Meaning: 'new' and 'place' or 'settlement' (Old English); derived from an English family name, in turn

derived from a number of English place names.
Notable namesakes: a crater on the moon; a unit of
force named for English scientist Isaac Newton;
Newton's cradle, an ornamental demonstration of Isaac
Newton's laws of motion; Newt Gingrich (US politician).

Nicholas

Variants and diminutives: Claus, Col, Cola, Colas,
Cole, Colet, Colin, Collet, Collett, Colley, Collis, Colly,
Kalya. Klaas, Klaus, Kola, Kolya, Micu, Miki, Miklos,
Mikolai, Milek, Nic, Nicanor, Niccolo, Nichol, Nick,
Nickie, Nickolas, Nickolaus, Nicky, Nico, Nicodemus,
Nicol, Nicola, Nicolaas, Nicolai, Nicolaio, Nicolas,
Nicolau, Nicolaus, Nicole, Nicoll, Nicolo, Nicy, Niel, Nik,
Nike, Niki, Nikita, Nikki, Nikkie, Nikky, Niklas, Niklavs,
Niklos, Nikola, Nikolai, Nikolais, Nikolaos, Nikolas,
Nikolaus, Nikolos, Nikos, Nikula, Nikulas, Nilo, Nils.
Meaning: 'victory of the people' (Greek).
Notable namesakes: Saint Nicholas (Santa Claus) of
Myra, patron saint of Greece, Russia, sailors,
merchants, pawnbrokers, apothecaries, perfumiers,
bakers, brewers, would-be brides, travellers and
children; Saint Nicholas of Tolentino, patron saint of
mariners, infants and souls in purgatory; Saint
Nicholas of Flue, patron saint of Switzerland; five
popes, including Saint Nicholas I, 'the Great'; Nicolas
of Cusa (German philosopher and mathematician);
Niccolò Machiavelli (Florentine statesman and political
theorist); Old Nick, an irreverent name for Satan;
Nicolaus Copernicus (Polish astronomer); Nicholas
Culpeper (English herbalist); Bailie Nicol Jarvie, a
character in the novel *Rob Roy*, by Scottish writer Sir
Walter Scott; Nicolas Poussin (French artist); Nikolay
Vasilyevich Gogol (Russian writer); the eponymous
hero of the novel *Nicholas Nickleby*, by English writer
Charles Dickens; Nicolo Paganini (Italian violinist and
composer); two tsars of Russia, including Nicholas II,
who was overthrown and murdered during the
Russian Revolution; Nicolas Cage (US actor); Nicol
Williamson and Nicholas Lyndhurst (British actors).

Nicodemus

Variants and diminutives: Demus, Nico, Nicholas.
Meaning: 'victory of the people' (Greek).
Notable namesakes: the assistant of Joseph of
Arimathea in the burial of Christ in the New Testament.

Nigel

Variants and diminutives: Neil, Nidge, Nig, Nige,
Niguel, Nye.
Meaning: 'champion', 'cloud' or 'vehement' (Irish
Gaelic) as a Latinised form of Neil.
Notable namesakes: the eponymous leading
character of the novel *The Fortunes of Nigel*, by
Scottish author Sir Walter Scott; Nigel Lawson (British
politician); Nigel Mansell (British racing driver); Nigel
Slater (British chef and cookery writer).

Ninian

Variants and diminutives: Nennus, Ninidh.
Meaning: uncertain; derived from the name of a
Christian saint.

Noah

Variants and diminutives: Noach, Noak, Noe, Noel,
Noi, Noy.
Meaning: 'comfort', 'respite' or 'long-lived' (Hebrew).
Notable namesakes: an ark-building patriarch in the
Old Testament; Noah Webster (US lexicographer).

Noam

Meaning: 'pleasant' or 'my delight' (Hebrew). A male
version of Naomi.
Notable namesakes: Noam Chomsky (US linguist and
social and political theorist).

Noël

Variants and diminutives: Natal, Natale, Noel,
Nowell.
Meaning: 'birthday' (Latin); 'Christ's birthday' or
'Christmas' (French).
Notable namesakes: Noël Coward (British playwright
and composer); Noel Edmonds (British broadcaster);
Noel Gallagher (British musician).

Nolan

Variants and diminutives: Noland.
Meaning: 'son of the noble one' (Irish Gaelic); derived
from an Irish family name.

Norbert
Variants and diminutives: Bert, Bertie, Berty, Norrie, Norry.
Meaning: 'north' and 'bright' or 'famous' (Germanic).
Notable namesakes: Saint Norbert, founder of the religious order the Premonstratensian Order of Canons; Norbert Goeneutte (French artist).

Norman
Variants and diminutives: Norm, Normand, Normann, Normie, Norrie, Norris, Norry, Tormod.
Meaning: 'north' and 'man' [Norseman or Viking] (Germanic).
Notable namesakes: the French former province of Normandy, which was settled by the Vikings, their Norman descendents bestowing their name on an architectural style and invading England in the Norman Conquest; Norman Rockwell (US artist); Norman Shaw (British architect); Norman Mailer (US writer); Norman Hartnell (British couturier); Norman Schwarzkopf (US soldier); Norman Foster (British architect); Norman Fowler and Norman Lamont (British politicans); Norman Cook (British disc jockey).

Norris
Variants and diminutives: Norice, Noris, Norman, Norreys, Norrie, Norriss, Norry.
Meaning: 'northerner' or 'nurse' (Old French).
Notable namesakes: Norris McWhirter, British editor and, with his twin brother Ross, compiler of *The Guinness Book of Records*.

Norton
Variants and diminutives: Nort, Nortie, Norty.
Meaning: 'northern' and 'place' or 'settlement' (Old English); derived from an English family name, in turn derived from a number of English place names.

Noy
Meaning: 'bejewelled by nature' (Hebrew). A male version of Noya.

Nuncio
Variants and diminutives: Nunzio.
Meaning: 'messenger' (Latin).
Notable namesakes: papal nuncio, a diplomatic representative of the pope.

Nye
Variants and diminutives: Aneirin, Aneurin, Ny, Nyle.
Meaning: 'man of honour' (Latin) or 'pure gold' (Welsh) as a diminutive of Aneurin.
Notable namesakes: Nye (Aneurin) Bevan (British politician).

Odo
Variants and diminutives: Aodh, Audo, Oates, Oddie, Oddo, Oddy, Odey, Odinal, Ody, Otes, Othes. Otho, Otis, Ottes, Otto.
Meaning: 'riches' (Germanic).
Notable namesakes: Saint Odo of Cluny.

Ogden
Variants and diminutives: Oak, Oakden, Oakes, Oakie, Oakleigh, Oakley, Oaks, Ogdan, Ogdon.
Meaning: 'oak' and 'valley' (Old English); derived from an English family name, in turn derived from a number of English place names.
Notable namesakes: Ogden Nash (US humorous poet).

Olaf
Variants and diminutives: Amhlaigh, Anleifr, Aulay, Olafur, Olav, Olave, Olay, Ole, Olen, Olif, Olin, Oliver.
Meaning: 'forebear' and 'relics' (Old Norse).
Notable namesakes: five kings of Norway, including Saint Olaf II, patron saint of Norway; Olaf Stapledon (British writer and philosopher); Olav Duun (Norwegian writer).

Oliver

Variants and diminutives: Alvar, Noll, Nollie, Nolly, Oli, Olivero, Olivier, Oliviero, Olley, Olli, Ollie, Olly, Olvan.
Meaning: uncertain; possibly 'olive' (Old French); possibly 'elf' and 'army' (Germanic); possibly 'forebear' and 'relics' (Old Norse) as a variant of Olave (Olaf); derived from a French and English family name.
Notable namesakes: Olivier, a paladin of Charlemagne and friend of Roland in the French romance *Chanson de Roland (Song of Roland)*; Oliver Cromwell (English soldier and statesman); Saint Oliver Plunket; Oliver Goldsmith (Irish writer); the eponymous hero of the novel *Oliver Twist*, by English writer Charles Dickens; Oliver Wendell Holmes (US writer); Oliver Hardy, the US comic actor of Laurel and Hardy fame; Oliver Reed (British actor); Oliver Stone (US film director); Bath Oliver, a type of biscuit named for Dr William Oliver, a resident of Bath.

Omar

Variants and diminutives: Oner, Omri.
Meaning: 'eloquent' (Hebrew); 'long-lived', 'first son', 'follower of the Prophet' or 'highest' (Arabic).
Notable namesakes: a grandson of Esau in the Old Testament; Omar Khayyám (Persian poet, astronomer and mathematician); Omar Sharif (Egyptian actor).

Oran

Variants and diminutives: Odhran, Oren, Orin, Orren.
Meaning: 'sallow' or 'greenish' (Irish Gaelic).
Notable namesakes: the brother of Saint Columba.

Orde

Variants and diminutives: Ordell.
Meaning: 'order' (Latin).
Notable namesakes: Orde Wingate (British soldier).

Orestes

Variants and diminutives: Orest, Oreste, Orin.
Meaning: 'mountain' (Greek).
Notable namesakes: the son of Agamemnon and Clytemnestra and brother of Electra in Greek mythology, who features in the plays *Orestes*, by Greek playwright Euripides, and *Mourning Becomes Electra*, by US playwright Eugene O'Neill.

Orlando

Variants and diminutives: Arland, Arlando, Land, Lando, Lannie, Lanny, Ordando, Orlan, Orland, Orleans, Orley, Orlin, Orio, Orval, Orville, Roland.
Meaning: 'fame' and 'land' (Germanic) as an Italian variant of Roland.
Notable namesakes: the lover of Melora, daughter of King Arthur, in Arthurian legend; a character in William Shakespeare's play *As You Like It*; the leading character of the poems *Orlando Innamorato*, by Italian poet Matteo Maria Boiardo, and *Orlando Furioso*, by Italian poet Lodovico Ariosto; Orlando Gibbons (English organist and composer); the title of a novel by British writer Virginia Woolf; the US town in Florida, home of Disney World, which was named for the US soldier Orlando Reeves.

Ormerod

Variants and diminutives: Ormie, Ormy, Rod, Roddie, Roddy.
Meaning: 'Orm's clearing' (Old Norse and Old English); derived from an English family name, in turn derived from an English place name.

Ormonde

Variants and diminutives: Orma, Orman, Ormand, Ormond.
Meaning: 'snake' (Old Norse); 'elm' (French); 'from east Munster' (Irish Gaelic), Munster being an Irish province, when derived from an Irish family name.

Orson

Variants and diminutives: Sonnie, Sonny, Urson.
Meaning: 'bear cub' (Old French).
Notable namesakes: the twin brother of Valentine, who was raised by a bear, in a medieval story; Orson Welles (US actor and director).

Ortho

Variants and diminutives: Orth, Othie, Orthy.
Meaning: 'straight' (Greek).

Orville

Variants and diminutives: Orval.
Meaning: uncertain; possibly 'gold' and 'town' (Old French); coined by the English writer Fanny Burney for her character Lord Orville, the hero of the novel *Evelina*.
Notable namesakes: Orville Wright (US aviation pioneer).

Osbert

Variants and diminutives: Osgood, Osborne, Osric, Ossie, Ossy, Oz, Ozzie, Ozzy.
Meaning: 'god' and 'bright' (Old English).
Notable namesakes: Osbert Sitwell (British writer); Osbert Lancaster (British cartoonist).

Osborne

Variants and diminutives: Osborn, Osbourn, Osbourne, Osburn, Oz, Ozzie, Ozzy.
Meaning: 'god' and 'bear' or 'man' (Old English); derived from an English family name.
Notable namesakes: Osborne House, Queen Victoria's residence on the Isle of White.

Oscar

Variants and diminutives: Oke, Oskar, Ossie, Ossy, Ozzie, Ozzy.
Meaning: 'god' and 'spear' (Old English); 'deer' or 'dear' and 'friend' or 'love' (Irish Gaelic).
Notable namesakes: the son of the poet Ossian in Irish legend (according to the Scottish poet James Macpherson); two kings of Sweden and Norway; Oscar Wilde (Irish writer); Oskar Kokoschka (Austrian artist and writer); Oscar Hammerstein (US lyricist and librettist); Oscar Lewis (US anthropologist); the common name for an Academy Award awarded for outstanding cinematic achievements by the US Academy of Motion Picture Arts and Sciences; the code for the letter 'O' in verbal communications; Oscar de la Renta (US fashion designer).

Osmond

Variants and diminutives: Esmand, Esme, Osman, Osmand, Osmanek, Osmant, Osmen, Osmon, Osmont, Osmund, Osmundo, Oswin, Oz, Ozzi, Ozzie, Ozzy.
Meaning: 'god' and 'protector' (Old English and Old Norse); derived from an English family name.
Notable namesakes: Saint Osmond (or Osmund), protector against paralysis, rupture, toothache and madness.

Ossian

Variants and diminutives: Oisin, Ossin.
Meaning: 'little deer' or 'fawn' (Irish Gaelic).
Notable namesakes: the legendary Irish poet, the son of Finn Mac Cumhall (or Finn MacCool) and Sadb (whom a druid transformed into a deer), whose works the Scottish poet James Macpherson falsely claimed to have translated.

Oswald

Variants and diminutives: Ossie, Osvald, Oswal, Oswaldo, Oswall, Oswold, Oz, Ozzie, Ozzy, Waldo, Waldy.
Meaning: 'god' and 'ruler', 'power' or 'wood' (Old English and Old Norse).
Notable namesakes: Saint Oswald, King of Northumbria, patron saint of soldiers; Saint Oswald of Worcester; Oswald Mosley (British fascist politician).

Oswin

Variants and diminutives: Oz, Ozzie, Ozzy.
Meaning: 'god' and 'friend' (Old English).

Otis

Variants and diminutives: Otes, Otto.
Meaning: 'riches' (Germanic) as a variant of Otto (Odo); derived from an English family name.
Notable namesakes: Otis Redding (US singer).

Otto

Variants and diminutives: Audr, Odo, Odon, Onek, Osman, Otek, Otello, Otfried, Othello, Othman, Othmar, Otho, Othon, Otik, Otilio, Otis, Otman, Oto, Oton, Ottmar, Ottomar, Otton, Ottone, Tilo, Tonek.
Meaning: 'riches' (Germanic) as a variant of Odo.

Notable namesakes: another name for an attar, an essential oil extracted from flowers; four Holy Roman emperors; Otto von Bismarck (German statesman); the Otto cycle, the four-stroke engine cycle devised by the German engineer Nikolaus Otto; Otto Dix (German artist); Otto Ludwig (German writer).

Owen

Variants and diminutives: Bowen, Bowie, Eoghan, Eugene, Euan, Evan, Ewan, Ewen, Owain, Owayne, Ovin, Uwen, Ywain.
Meaning: 'well-born' (Greek) as a Welsh variant of Eugene.
Notable namesakes: Owain, the son of Urien and Morgan Le Fay in Arthurian legend; Prince Owen Gwynedd of Wales; Owain Glyndwr (Owen Glyndower), an anti-English Welsh revolutionary leader (see also Glyndwr).

Pablo

Variants and diminutives: Paolo, Paul.
Meaning: 'small' (Latin) as a Spanish variant of Paul.
Notable namesakes: Pablo Picasso (Spanish artist); Pablo Neruda (Chilean poet); Pablo Casals (Catalan cellist, conductor and composer).

Paco

Variants and diminutives: Francis, Frank.
Meaning: 'bald eagle' (Native American); 'French' (Latin) as a Spanish version of Francis; 'free' (Latin) as a Spanish version of Frank.
Notable namesakes: Paco Rabanne (Spanish fashion designer).

Paddy

Variants and diminutives: Patrick.
Meaning: 'noble' or 'patrician' (Latin) as a diminutive

of Patrick (and of Patricia).
Notable namesakes: a slang name for Irish people and for a fit of pique; Paddy Chayefsky (US writer).

Palmer

Meaning: 'palm' or 'hand' (Latin); 'pilgrim' (Old French); derived from an English family name.
Notable namesakes: a medieval name for a pilgrim, derived from the practice of bringing back palm branches from pilgrimages to the Holy Land; types of angling flies; the Palmer Archipelago (Antarctic Archipelago), an island group between South America and Antarctica; Palmer Land, the southern region of the Antarctic Peninsula (formerly called the Palmer Peninsula); Palmer Hayden (US artist).

Pan

Meaning: 'all' (Greek).
Notable namesakes: the goat-like, panpipe-playing god of woods, fields, shepherds and their flocks in Greek mythology.

Pancho

Variants and diminutives: Panchito.
Meaning: 'French' (Latin) as a Spanish diminutive of Francisco (Francis).

Paolo

Variants and diminutives: Pablo, Paul.
Meaning: 'small' (Latin) as an Italian variant of Paul.
Notable namesakes: the lover of Francesca in Italian poet Dante's *Inferno*, the first part of the epic poem *The Divine Comedy*; Paolo Uccello (Florentine artist); Paolo Veronese (Italian artist).

Paris

Variants and diminutives: Parris.
Meaning: uncertain; possibly 'marshes of the Parisii' (Latin), the Parisii being a Gaulish Celtic tribe; possibly 'pouch' (Greek) when derived from the name of the Trojan prince.
Notable namesakes: the son of King Priam of Troy, whose abduction of Helen precipitated the Trojan War; a character in William Shakespeare's play *Romeo and Juliet*; the capital city of France.

Parish

Variants and diminutives: Parrie, Parrish, Parry.
Meaning: 'neighbour' (Greek); derived from an English family name.
Notable namesakes: a subdivision of a diocese.

Parker

Variants and diminutives: Park, Parke.
Meaning: 'park-keeper' (Old French); derived from an English family name.

Parnell

Variants and diminutives: Parnall, Parnel, Parrnell, Pernel, Pernell.
Meaning: uncertain; possibly 'rock' (Greek) as a diminutive of Petronella, in turn derived from the Roman family name Petronius; derived from an English family name. Also a girl's name.

Parry

Variants and diminutives: Harry.
Meaning: 'son of Harry' (Welsh); derived from a Welsh family name.

Pascal

Variants and diminutives: Pace, Paco, Pascalo, Paschal, Pasco, Pascoe, Pascual, Pascualo, Pashell, Pasqual, Pasquel, Pasqul, Pesach.
Meaning: 'to pass over' (Hebrew); 'of Easter' (Old French).
Notable namesakes: a unit of pressure named for the French mathematician, physicist and philosopher Blaise Pascal, for whom the Pascal's triangle is also named; Pascal's wager, a philosophical argument; a computer-programming language.

Pascoe

Variants and diminutives: Pascal, Pasco.
Meaning: 'to pass over' (Hebrew) or 'of Easter' (Old French) as a variant of Pascal.

Patrick

Variants and diminutives: Pad, Paddie, Paddy, Padhra, Padhraic, Padi, Padraic, Padraig, Padriac, Padrig, Padruig, Paidin, Pat, Patek, Paton, Patraic, Patric, Patrice, Patricio, Patricius, Patrizio, Patrizius, Patsy, Patten, Patti, Pattie, Pattison, Patty, Paxton, Payton, Peter, Peyton, Ticho.
Meaning: 'noble' or 'patrician' (Latin).
Notable namesakes: Saint Patrick, patron saint of Ireland, engineers and people who fear snakes; the title character of the Scottish ballad *Sir Patrick Spens*; Patrick Heron (British artist); Patrick Swayze (US actor); Pat Cash (Australian tennis player).

Paul

Variants and diminutives: Oalo, Pablo, Pail, Pal, Paley, Pali, Palika, Pall, Paolo, Pasha, Pashka, Paulie, Paulin, Paulino, Paulinus, Paulis, Paullus, Paulo, Paulos, Paulot, Pauls, Paulus, Pauly, Pavel, Pavils, Pavlik, Pavlo, Pawel, Pawl, Pawley, Pewlin, Pol, Poul, Powel, Powle.
Meaning: 'small' (Latin).
Notable namesakes: Saint Paul, author of epistles in the New Testament, patron saint of snake-bite victims and missionary bishops; Saint Paul Aurelian (Saint Pol de Léon); Saint Paulinus of York; six popes; Paul Revere, an American patriot and the subject of the poem *Paul Revere's Ride*, by US poet Henry Wadsworth Longfellow; Paul Verlaine and Paul Éluard (French poets); Paul Gauguin and Paul Cézanne (French artists); Paul Hindemith (German-born US composer); Paul Klee (Swiss artist); Paul Nash (British artist); Paul Robeson and Paul Simon (US musicians); Paul Newman (US actor); Paul Scott (British writer); Paul Scofield (British actor); Paul Theroux (US writer); Paul McCartney, Paul Weller and Paul Young (British musicians); Paul Gascoigne (British footballer); Paul Merton (British comedian).

Paxton

Variants and diminutives: Pax, Paxon.
Meaning: a composite name comprising 'peace' (Latin) and 'place' or 'settlement' (Old English); derived from an English family name.

Pedro

Variants and diminutives: Peter.
Meaning: 'rock' (Greek) as an Italian, Portuguese and Spanish variant of Peter.
Notable namesakes: two emperors of Brazil; Pedro

Calderón de la Barca (Spanish playwright); Pedro Salinas (Spanish writer).

Pelham
Variants and diminutives: Pel, Pellie, Pelly, Plum.
Meaning: 'Peola's' or 'hide' and 'place' (Old English); derived from an English family name, in turn derived from an English place name.
Notable namesakes: P (Pelham) G (Grenville) Wodehouse (British-born US writer).

Pepin
Variants and diminutives: Pep, Pepi, Peppie, Peppy, Pipi, Pippi.
Meaning: 'petitioner' or 'perseverant' (Germanic).
Notable namesakes: Pepin 'the Short', King of the Franks, the son of Charles Martel and father of Charlemagne, the first Holy Roman emperor.

Percival
Variants and diminutives: Parsifal, Parzival, Perce, Perceval, Perciful, Percival, Percy, Peredur.
Meaning: uncertain; possibly 'pierce' and 'valley' (Old French); coined by the French poet Chrétien de Troyes for a knight of Arthurian legend in his romance *Perceval, ou le conte du Graal (Percival, or the Story of the Grail)*.
Notable namesakes: building on Chrétien de Troyes' legacy, Percival features in English writer Thomas Malory's collection of Arthurian romances; *Le Morte d'Arthur*, and in English poet Alfred, Lord Tennyson's series of Arthurian poems; *The Idylls of the King*, along with the verse epic *Parzival*, by German lyric poet Wolfram von Eschenbach, on which German composer Richard Wagner based his opera *Parsifal*; a character in the novel *The Waves*, by British writer Virginia Woolf.

Percy
Variants and diminutives: Perce, Perceval, Percival, Perseus.
Meaning: uncertain; derived from the Roman first name Percius as a British family name, in turn derived from a number of French place names; possibly 'pierce' and 'valley' (Old French) as a diminutive of Percival.

Notable namesakes: Percy Bysshe Shelley (English poet); Sir Percy Blakeney, also known as the Scarlet Pimpernel in the novel of the same name by the Hungarian-born British writer Baroness Emmusca Orczy; Percy MacKaye (US writer).

Peregrine
Variants and diminutives: Perry.
Meaning: 'pilgrim', 'foreigner' or 'traveller' (Latin).
Notable namesakes: Saint Peregrine Laziosi, patron saint of people suffering from cancer, skin disease and AIDS; the peregrine falcon, *Falco peregrinus*; the eponymous hero of the novel *The Adventures of Peregrine Pickle*, by Scottish writer Tobias Smollet; Peregrine Worsthorne (British journalist).

Perry
Variants and diminutives: Peregrine, Peter.
Meaning: 'pear tree' (Old English) when derived from a British family name; 'pilgrim', 'foreigner' or 'traveller' (Latin) as a diminutive of Peregrine; 'rock' (Greek) as a diminutive of Peter.
Notable namesakes: a wine made from pears; Perry Mason, a fictional detective created by US writer Erle Stanley Gardner; Perry Como (US singer).

Peter
Variants and diminutives: Farris, Ferris, Padraig, Panos, Parlett, Parnell, Parren, Parry, Peadair, Peadar, Peader, Pearce, Peder, Pedrin, Pedro, Peet, Peeter, Peirce, Pequin, Per, Perequin, Perico, Perka, Perkin, Pernell, Pero, Perren, Perry, Petar, Pete, Peterus, Petey, Petie, Petinka, Petko, Petr, Petras, Petrelis, Petro, Petronio, Petros, Petru, Petrukas, Petruno, Petrus, Petrusha, Petter, Petur, Peyo, Pictrus, Pier, Pierce, Piero, Pierre, Pierrot, Piers, Piet, Pieter, Pietr, Pietrek, Pietro, Piotr, Piotrek, Piti, Petits, Pettis, Pettus, Piran, Pyatr, Pyotr, Rock, Rockey, Rockie, Rocky, Takis.
Meaning: 'rock' (Greek).

Notable namesakes: Saint Peter, the leader of Christ's apostles, author of two epistles in the New Testament, the first bishop of Rome, or pope, who traditionally holds the keys to heaven, and patron saint of fishermen, popes, Rome and longevity; Saint Peter Damian (Pietro Damianai); Peter Lombard (Italian theologian); Saint Peter Celestine, patron saint of bookbinders; Peter the Hermit, a French preacher during the First Crusade; Saint Peter Claver, patron saint of African-Americans, Colombia, missions and slaves; Peter Paul Rubens (Flemish artist); three tsars of Russia, including Peter I, 'the Great'; Saint Petersburg, towns in Russia and the US state of Florida; Petersburg, a city in the US state of Virginia and an American Civil War battle site; two kings of Yugoslavia; Peter Lely (Dutch-born English painter); the leading character of the children's book *The Tale of Peter Rabbit*, by English writer and illustrator Beatrix Potter; the eponymous leading character of the children's play *Peter Pan*, by Scottish writer J M Barrie, whose name now describes a type of collar and an immature man; Piet Mondrian (Dutch artist); Peter Ustinov, Peter Cushing and Peter Sellers (British actors); Peter Shaffer (British playwright); Peter Gabriel (British musician); Peter Osgood (British footballer); Pete Sampras (US tennis player).

Peyton

Variants and diminutives: Pate, Payton.
Meaning: 'Paega's' and 'place' or settlement' (Old English); derived from an English family name, in turn derived from a number of English place names.

Phelan

Variants and diminutives: Phel, Phele.
Meaning: 'wolf' (Irish Gaelic).

Philander

Variants and diminutives: Phil.
Meaning: 'lover' and 'men' (Greek).

Notable namesakes: a poetic name for a lover; philanderer, a man who flirts with women; a character in the poem *Orlando Furioso*, by Italian poet Ludovico Ariosto.

Philbert

Variants and diminutives: Bert, Berty, Filbert, Filberte, Filibert, Fulbert, Fulbright, Phil, Philbert, Philibert.
Meaning: 'very' and 'bright' (Germanic) as a variant of Filibert (Fulbert).
Notable namesakes: Saint Philibert.

Philemon

Variants and diminutives: Phil, Philo.
Meaning: 'kiss' (Greek).
Notable namesakes: the husband of Baucis in *Metamorphoses*, a poetic collection of mythology by the Roman poet Ovid, as well as in the play *Faust*, by German writer Johann Wolfgang von Goethe; an addressee of one of Saint Paul's epistles in the New Testament.

Philip

Variants and diminutives: Feeleep, Felip, Felipe, Felipino, Felippe, Fil, Filip, Filipek, Filipo, Filipp, Filippo, Filips, Filya, Fischel, Fulop, Hippolytos, Lipp, Lippo, Pepe, Phelps, Phil, Philipot, Philipp, Philippe, Philippus, Phill, Phillip, Phillipos, Phillipp, Phip, Pilib, Pip, Pippo.
Meaning: 'horse-lover' (Greek).
Notable namesakes: Saint Philip, one of Christ's apostles in the New Testament; King Philip II, the father of Alexander the Great, King of Macedonia; Philip the Bold, Duke of Burgundy; Philip the Good, Duke of Burgundy; six kings of France; Saint Philip Neri, patron saint of Rome; five kings of Spain, including King Phillip II, husband of Queen Mary I of England, for whom the Philippines were named; Fra Filippo Lippi (Florentine artist); Philip the Magnanimous, Landgrave of Hesse; Philipp Melanchthon (German religious reformer); Philip Freneau (US poet); Philip Larkin (British poet); Prince Philip, Duke of Edinburgh, husband of Queen Elizabeth II of the United Kingdom; Philip Roth (US writer); Phil Lynott (Irish musician); Philippe Starck (French designer); Philip Kerr (British writer).

Phineas

Variants and diminutives: Phinehas, Phinhas, Pinchas, Pinchos, Pincus, Pini, Pink, Pinkus, Pinky.
Meaning: uncertain; possibly 'black' (Egyptian); possibly 'oracle' (Hebrew).
Notable namesakes: a grandson of Aaron and son of Eli in the Old Testament; Phineas Fletcher (English poet); Phineas T Barnum (US showman); Phineas Fogg, main character in French Writer Jules Verne's novel *Around the World in Eighty Days*.

Pierce

Variants and diminutives: Pearce, Peter, Piers, Pierse.
Meaning: 'rock' (Greek) as a variant of Peter.
Notable namesakes: Pierce Brosnan (Irish actor).

Pierre

Variants and diminutives: Peter, Piers.
Meaning: 'rock' (Greek) as a French variant of Peter.
Notable namesakes: Pierre Abélard (French theologian); Pierre Corneille (French playwright); Pierre Bonnard (French artist and designer); Pierre Joseph Proudhon (French socialist and anarchist); Pierre Glendinning, the leading character of the novel Pierre, or the Ambiguities, by the US writer Herman Melville; Pierre Reverdy (French writer); Pierre Boulez (French composer); Pierre Teilhard de Chardin (French theologian and palaeontologist); Pierre Trudeau (Canadian politician).

Pierro

Variants and diminutives: Piero, Pierrot, Pirro.
Meaning: 'flame-haired' (Greek); 'little Peter' (Old French).
Notable namesakes: Piero della Francesca (Italian artist); Pierrot, the lover of Pierrette or Columbine in the Italian dramatic tradition and *commedia dell'arte*.

Piers

Variants and diminutives: Pearce, Peers, Peter, Piaras, Pierce, Pierre, Pierse.
Meaning: 'rock' (Greek) as a variant of Peter.
Notable namesakes: the eponymous hero of the poem *Piers Plowman*, by English poet William Langland.

Pip

Variants and diminutives: Philip.
Meaning: 'horse-lover' (Greek) as a diminutive of Philip.
Notable namesakes: the nickname of Philip Pirrip, the leading character in the novel *Great Expectations*, by English writer Charles Dickens.

Piran

Variants and diminutives: Perran, Peter.
Meaning: uncertain; possibly 'rock' (Greek) as a variant of Peter.
Notable namesakes: Saint Piran, patron saint of Cornish miners.

Pius

Variants and diminutives: Pitkin.
Meaning: 'pious' or 'dutiful' (Latin).
Notable namesakes: twelve popes.

Placido

Variants and diminutives: Placedo, Placid, Placijo, Plasido, Plasio.
Meaning: 'peaceful' (Latin).
Notable namesakes: Placido Domingo (Spanish opera singer).

Porter

Variants and diminutives: Port.
Meaning: 'door-keeper' or 'gate-keeper' (Latin); 'to carry' (Old French); derived from an English family name.
Notable namesakes: a type of ale.

Pravin

Meaning: 'skilful' or 'able' (Hindi).

Prem

Meaning: 'endearing' or 'affectionate' (Sanskrit).

Prentice

Variants and diminutives: Prent, Prentis, Prentise, Prentiss.
Meaning: 'apprentice' (Old French); derived from an English family name.

Preston

Variants and diminutives: Prescott.
Meaning: 'priest's' and 'place' or 'farm' (Old English); derived from an English family name, in turn derived from a number of English place names.

Price

Meaning: 'son of Rhys' (Old Welsh); derived from a Welsh family name.

Prior

Variants and diminutives: Pry, Pryor.
Meaning: 'before' (Latin); 'prior [the deputy head of a monastery]' (Old French and Old English); derived from an English family name.

Prince

Meaning: 'first', 'leader' or 'chief' (Latin); derived from a British family name, in turn derived from a title of nobility.
Notable namesakes: *The Prince*, the title of a political treatise by Florentine statesman and political theorist Niccolò Machiavelli; Prince Rogers Nelson (US musician).

Prosper

Variants and diminutives: Prospero.
Meaning: 'successful' (Latin).
Notable namesakes: Prospero, the rightful duke of Milan in William Shakespeare's play *The Tempest*; Prosper Mérimée (French writer).

Putnam

Meaning: 'Putta's homestead' (Old English); derived from an English family name, in turn derived from a number of English place names.

Quentin

Variants and diminutives: Quent, Quentin, Quenton, Quincy, Quinn, Quint, Quintin, Quintus, Quito.
Meaning: 'fifth' (Latin) as a variant of the Roman family name Quintus.
Notable namesakes: Saint Quentin (Quintus or Quintinus), for whom the French town of Saint-Quentin was named; Quentin (or Quinten) Massys (Flemish artist); the eponymous hero of the novel *Quentin Durward*, by Scottish writer Sir Walter Scott; Quintin Hogg, Lord Hailsham (British lawyer and politician); Quentin Crisp (British writer and self-styled 'stately homo'); Quentin Tarantino (US film producer).

Quillan

Variants and diminutives: Quill, Quillie, Quilly.
Meaning: 'cub' (Irish Gaelic).

Quincy

Variants and diminutives: Quentin, Quincey, Quintus.
Meaning: 'fifth' (Latin) as a variant of the Roman family name Quintus; derived from a French family name, in turn derived from a number of French place names.
Notable namesakes: John Quincy Adams (US president); Quincy Jones (US jazz musician).

Quinlin

Variants and diminutives: Quinley, Quinn.
Meaning: 'strong' (Irish Gaelic).

Quinn

Variants and diminutives: Quin, Quine, Quinney.
Meaning: 'son of' and 'counsel' (Irish Gaelic); derived from an Irish family name.

Quirinal
Variants and diminutives: Quirino, Quirinus.
Meaning: 'of Romulus' (Latin), Romulus being a son of Mars and Rhea Silvia and a founder of Rome, who was deified as Quirinus after his death.
Notable namesakes: one of the seven hills on which ancient Rome was built.

Rab
Variants and diminutives: Rabbie, Rabby, Robert.
Meaning: 'fame' and 'bright' (Germanic) as a Scottish diminutive of Robert.
Notable namesakes: Rabbie (Robert) Burns (Scottish poet).

Rabi
Meaning: 'breeze' (Arabic). A male version of Rabia.

Radburn
Variants and diminutives: Burnie, Burny, Rad, Radborn, Radborne, Radbourne, Radburne, Radd, Raddie, Raddy, Radley.
Meaning: 'reed' or 'red' and 'stream' (Old English); derived from an English family name, in turn derived from a number of English place names.

Radcliff
Variants and diminutives: Cliff, Cliffe, Clyffe, Racliff, Racliffe, Rad, Radcliffe, Radclyffe, Radd, Raddie, Raddy, Redcliff, Redcliffe.
Meaning: 'red' and 'cliff' (Old English); derived from an English family name, in turn derived from a number of English place names.

Radomil
Variants and diminutives: Rad, Rado.
Meaning: 'peace-loving' (Slavic).

Rafe
Variants and diminutives: Rafer, Ralf, Ralph.
Meaning: 'advice' or 'might' and 'wolf' (Germanic) as a variant of Ralph.

Rafferty
Variants and diminutives: Rafe, Rafer, Raff, Raffer.
Meaning: uncertain; possibly 'descendent of' and 'prosperity', 'wielder' or 'floodtide' (Irish Gaelic); derived from an Irish family name.

Rahim
Variants and diminutives: Rahman.
Meaning: 'compassionate' (Arabic).

Rahman
Variants and diminutives: Rahim, Rahmet.
Meaning: 'compassionate' or 'merciful' (Arabic).

Raja
Variants and diminutives: Raj.
Meaning: 'king' (Sanskrit); 'anticipated' or 'hoped for' (Arabic). Also a male version of Rani.
Notable namesakes: Raja Rao (Indian writer).

Raleigh
Variants and diminutives: Lee, Leigh, Rally, Rawleigh, Rawley.
Meaning: 'red', 'roe deer' or 'rye' and 'clearing' (Old English); derived from an English family name, in turn derived from a number of English place names.

Ralph
Variants and diminutives: Raaf, Rafe, Raff, Raffy, Ralf, Ralston, Randolph, Ranulf, Raol, Raoul, Raoulin, Rauf, Rauffe, Raul, Raulio, Rawley, Relman, Rolf, Rolph, Rulo.
Meaning: 'advice' or 'might' and 'wolf' (Germanic).
Notable namesakes: the hero of the comic play *Ralph Roister Doister*, by English school teacher and playwright Nicholas Udall;

Ralph Earle (US artist); Ralph Waldo Emerson (US philosopher and writer); Ralph Blakelock (US artist); Ralph Gustafson (Canadian poet); Ralph Richardson (British actor); Ralph Lauren (US fashion designer).

Rama

Variants and diminutives: Ramah.
Meaning: 'black', 'dark' or 'pleasing' (Sanskrit); 'exalted' (Hebrew). Also a girl's name.
Notable namesakes: a name of Vishnu, the god of preservation, in his incarnation as Balarama, Parashurama or Ramachandra in Hindu mythology.

Ramón

Variants and diminutives: Raymond.
Meaning: 'advice' or 'might' and 'protector' (Germanic) as a Spanish version of Raymond.
Notable namesakes: Ramón Perez de Ayala, Ramón Gómez de la Serna, Ramón José Sender and Ramón María del Valle-Inclán (Spanish writers).

Ramsay

Variants and diminutives: Ram, Ramsey, Ramsy.
Meaning: 'wild garlic', 'ram' or 'raven' and 'island' (Old English); derived from a British family name, in turn derived from a number of English place names.
Notable namesakes: Ramsay MacDonald (British politician).

Randall

Variants and diminutives: Rand, Randal, Randel, Randell, Randi, Randie, Randl, Randle, Randolph, Randy, Rankin, Ranulf.
Meaning: 'shield' or 'raven' and 'wolf' (Old English).
Notable namesakes: Randall Jarrell (US writer).

Randolph

Variants and diminutives: Dolf, Rand, Randal, Randall, Randel, Randell, Randi, Randie, Randl, Randle, Randolf, Randulf, Randulfus, Randy, Rankin, Ranulf, Raoul.

Meaning: 'shield' or 'raven' and 'wolf' (Germanic) as a variant of Randall.
Notable namesakes: Randolph Churchill (British politicians, a son and father of Winston Churchill); Randolph Scott (US actor); Randolph Stow (Australian writer).

Ransom

Variants and diminutives: Rance, Rand, Ransome, Ranson.
Meaning: 'son of Rand' (Old English), Rand meaning 'shield' or 'raven' and 'wolf' (Old English and Old German) as a diminutive of Randall or Randolph; derived from an English family name.
Notable namesakes: a payment made to redeem a captive.

Ranulf

Variants and diminutives: Ralph, Ranulph.
Meaning: 'advice' or 'might' and 'wolf' (Germanic) as a variant of Ralph.
Notable namesakes: Ranulph Fiennes (British explorer).

Raoul

Variants and diminutives: Ralph, Raolin, Raul.
Meaning: 'advice' or 'might' and 'wolf' (Germanic) as a French variant of Ralph.
Notable namesakes: Raoul Hausmann (Austrian artist); Raoul Dufy (French artist).

Raphael

Variants and diminutives: Felio, Raf, Rafael, Rafaelle, Rafaello, Rafaelo, Rafe, Rafeal, Rafel, Raffael, Raffaello, Rafi, Rafito, Raphel, Refael, Refi, Rephael.
Meaning: 'healed by God' (Hebrew).
Notable namesakes: an archangel in the Apocrypha, patron saint of blind people, love and travellers; the Italian artist whose full name was Raffaello Sanzio (or Santi); Raphael Holinshed (English historian); Raphael Delorme (French artist); Rafael Alberti (Spanish writer).

Rashid

Variants and diminutives: Rasheed.
Meaning: 'follower of the correct path' (Sanskrit and

Arabic); 'righteous' (Swahili).

Notable namesakes: an Egyptian town, once called Rosetta, where the Rosetta Stone was discovered.

Ravi

Meaning: 'conferring' (Hindi).

Notable namesakes: an alternative name for the sun god Surya in Hindu mythology; the Ravi river in India; Ravi Shankar (Indian musician).

Raviv

Meaning: 'dew' or 'rain' (Hebrew).

Ray

Variants and diminutives: Raymond, Rayner, Reigh, Reo, Rey, Rio, Riordan, Roy.

Meaning: 'king' (Old French); 'roe deer', 'stream' or 'rye' (Old English); 'advice' or 'might' and 'protector' (Germanic) as a diminutive of Raymond; 'advice' or 'might' and 'army' (Germanic) as a diminutive of Rayner.

Notable namesakes: Ray Charles (US musician); Ray Bradbury (US science-fiction writer); Ray Davies (British musician).

Raymond

Variants and diminutives: Monchi, Mondo, Mundo, Raimon, Raimond, Raimondo, Raimund, Raimundo, Rajmund, Ramon, Ramond, Ramone, Ramundo, Ray, Raymon, Raymondo, Raymund, Raymundo, Raynard, Rayner, Reamonn, Redmond, Reimond.

Meaning: 'advice' or 'might' and 'protector' (Germanic).

Notable namesakes: Saint Raymond of Toulouse; Saint Raymund of Pennaforte, patron saint of lawyers and canonists; Saint Raymond Nonnatus, patron saint of mothers-to-be, midwives, childbirth and people who have been falsely accused; Raymond Poincaré (French politician); Raymond Chandler (US crime writer).

Rayner

Variants and diminutives: Ragnar, Ragnor, Rain, Raine, Rainer, Raines, Rainier, Rains, Ranier, Ray, Raynor, Reiner.

Meaning: 'advice' or 'might' and 'army' (Germanic).

Notable namesakes: Rainer Maria Rilke (Austrian writer); Prince Rainier III of Monaco; Rainer Werner Fassbinder (German film and theatre director).

Redford

Variants and diminutives: Ford, Red, Redd.

Meaning: 'red' or 'reedy' and 'ford' (Old English); derived from an English family name, in turn derived from an English place name.

Reeve

Variants and diminutives: Reave, Reeves.

Meaning: 'bailiff', 'overseer' or 'chief magistrate' (Old English); derived from an English family name.

Reginald

Variants and diminutives: Naldo, Raghnall, Ranald, Reg, Reggie, Reggy, Reginauld, Regnauld, Regnault, Reinald, Reinaldo, Reinaldos, Reinhold, Reinold, Reinwald, Renaldo, Renato, Renaud, Renault, René, Rex, Reynaldo, Reynaldos, Reynold, Reynolds, Rinaldo, Rinold, Ronald.

Meaning: 'advice' or 'might' and 'power' (Germanic) as a variant of Reynold.

Notable namesakes: Reginald Marsh (US artist); the eponymous hero of the British television series *The Rise and Fall of Reginald Perrin*.

Remus

Variants and diminutives: Remer, Rémi, Remy.

Meaning: 'oar' (Latin).

Notable namesakes: the brother of Romulus and co-founder of Rome in Roman mythology; Saint Rémi (or Remigius); the title character of *Uncle Remus, His Songs and His Sayings*, a collection of folk tales by US writer Joel Chandler Harris.

René

Variants and diminutives: Renato, Renatus, Reni.

Meaning: 'reborn' (French).

Notable namesakes: Saint Reni (or Renatus); Saint René Goupil, patron saint of anaethethists; René Descartes (French philosopher and mathematician); the leading character of the novel *René*, by French

writer François René de Chateaubriand; *René* Lalique (French glass designer); René Magritte (Belgian artist); the leading character of the British television sitcom 'Allo, 'Allo.

Reuben

Variants and diminutives: Reuven, Revie, Ribbans, Rouvin, Rube, Ruben, Rubens, Rubin, Ruby, Ruvane, Ruvim.
Meaning: 'behold, a son' (Hebrew).
Notable namesakes: a son of Jacob and founder of a tribe of Israel in the Old Testament.

Rex

Variants and diminutives: Ray, Rayner, Regino, Regis, Rexer, Rexford, Rey, Reynaud, Reyner, Roy.
Meaning: 'king' (Latin) and, as such, a male version of Regina; 'advice' or 'might' and 'power' (Germanic) as a diminutive of Reginald (Reynold).
Notable namesakes: Rex Stout (US crime-writer); Rex Ingamells (Australian poet); Rex Harrison (British actor); Rex Mottram, a character in the novel *Brideshead Revisited*, by British writer Evelyn Waugh.

Reynard

Variants and diminutives: Rainardo, Ray, Raynard, Regnard, Reinhard, Reinhart, Renard, Renart, Renaud, Renke, Rey, Reynaud, Raynauld, Reyner.
Meaning: 'advice' or 'might' and 'hard' (Germanic).
Notable namesakes: Reynard the Fox, a character in many medieval tales, as a result of which Reynard has become a generic name for foxes.

Reynold

Variants and diminutives: Ranald, Reginald, Reinald, Reinaldo, Reinaldos, Reinhold, Reinwald, Renaldo, Renaud, Renault, Rene, Reynaldos, Reynolds, Rinaldo, Rinold, Ronald.
Meaning: 'advice' or 'might' and 'power' (Germanic).

Rhett

Variants and diminutives: Rhet, Rhys.
Meaning: 'advice' (Germanic) when derived from a Dutch family name; 'the ardent one' (Old Welsh) as a variant of Rhys.

Notable namesakes: Rhett Butler, hero of the novel *Gone with the Wind*, by US writer Margaret Mitchell.

Rhys

Variants and diminutives: Price, Race, Rase, Ray, Reece, Rees, Reese, Rey, Rhett, Rhyence, Rice, Royce.
Meaning: 'the ardent one' (Old Welsh).
Notable namesakes: Rhys ap Tewdwr and Rhys ap Gruffudd, medieval Welsh princes.

Richard

Variants and diminutives: Aric, Arick, Arri, Dic, Diccon, Dick, Dickie, Dickon, Dicky, Dix, Dixey, Dixie, Dixy, Dizzy, Hicks, Hickson, Hudd, Hudde, Hudi, Hudson, Juku, Rab, Reku, Ric, Ricard, Ricardo, Riccardo, Ricciardo, Ricoo, Rice, Rich, Richardo, Richardon, Richards, Richart, Richerd, Richi, Richie, Richy, Rici, Ricci, Ricco, Rick, Rickard, Rickert, Rickey, Ricki, Rickie, Ricky, Rico, Riczi, Rico, Rihardos, Rihards, Riik, Rik, Rikard, Riki, Riks, Riocard, Riqui, Risa, Risardas, Ritch, Ritchie, Ritchy, Rocco, Rolli, Rostik, Rostislav, Rostya, Rye, Rysio, Slava, Slavik, Slavka.
Meaning: 'ruler' and 'hard' (Germanic).
Notable namesakes: three kings of England, including Richard I, 'the Lionheart'; Saint Richard of Wyche; Saint Richard of Chichester, patron saint of coachmen; Richard of Wallingford (English mathematician); Richard Lovelace (English poet); Richard Brinsley Sheridan (Irish-born English writer); Richard Wagner and Richard Strauss (German composers); the eponymous leading character of the novel The Ordeal of Richard Feverel, by English writer George Meredith, of the trilogy The Fortunes of Richard Mahony, by Australian writer Henry Handel Richardson, and of the novel Richard Carvel, by British writer and politician Winston Churchill; Richard Rodgers (US composer); Richard Nixon (US president); Richard Hamilton (British artist); Richard Burton and Richard Briars (British actors); Richard Attenborough (British actor and director); Richard Branson (British entrepreneur); Richard Serra (US sculptor); Richard Deacon (British sculptor); Richard Gere (US actor); Richard E Grant (British actor); Rik Mayall (British comedian and comic actor).

Rider

Variants and diminutives: Rid, Riddle, Ridgeley, Ridley, Ryder, Ryerson.
Meaning: 'rider', 'knight' or 'cavalryman' (Old English).
Notable namesakes: (Henry) Rider Haggard (English writer).

Ridley

Variants and diminutives: Rid, Riddle, Rigeley.
Meaning: 'wood-cleared' or 'reedy' and 'clearing' (Old English); derived from an English family name, in turn derived from a number of English place names.
Notable namesakes: Ridley Scott (British film director).

Riley

Variants and diminutives: Reilly, Reyly, Ryley.
Meaning: 'descendant of the valiant one' (Irish Gaelic); 'rye' and 'clearing' (Old English); derived from a British family name.
Notable namesakes: the life of Riley, an expression denoting a carefree existence; Riley B King, the real name of US blues musician B B King.

Riordan

Variants and diminutives: Rearden, Riorden.
Meaning: 'descendent of the royal bard' (Irish Gaelic); derived from an Irish family name.

Ripley

Variants and diminutives: Lee, Leigh, Rip, Ripp.
Meaning: 'strip-like' and 'wood' or 'clearing' (Old English); derived from an English family name, in turn derived from a number of English place names.

River

Variants and diminutives: Rivers, Riverton, Rivington.
Meaning: 'river bank' (Latin). Also a girl's name.
Notable namesakes: River Phoenix (US actor).

Roald

Variants and diminutives: Roderick.
Meaning: 'renowned' and 'ruler' (Germanic) as a Norwegian variant of Roderick.
Notable namesakes: Roald Amundsen (Norwegian explorer); Roald Dahl (British writer).

Robert

Variants and diminutives: Bert, Bertie, Berto, Berty, Bob, Bobbi, Bobbie, Bobby, Bobek, Dob, Dobb, Dobbs, Dobs, Dobson, Hab, Hob, Hobs, Hobson, Hodge, Hodges, Hopkins, Hopson, Hutchins, Nob, Nobbie, Nobby, Rab, Rabbie, Rabby, Raibeart, Ralf, Riobard, Rip, Rob, Roban, Robard, Robart, Robb, Robben, Robbi, Robbie, Robby, Rober, Robers, Roberto, Roberts, Robertson, Robers, Robi, Robin, Robinet, Robinson, Robson, Robyn, Roibeard, Rolf, Rori, Rosertas, Roy, Rubert, Ruberto, Rudbert, Rupert, Ruperto, Ruprecht, Tito.
Meaning: 'fame' and 'bright' (Germanic).
Notable namesakes: Robert I, 'the Devil', and Robert II, dukes of Normandy; three kings of Scotland, including Robert I, 'the Bruce'; Saint Robert

Bellarmine, patron saint of catechists and canonists; Robert MacGregor, a Scottish Jacobite outlaw whose story is told in the novel *Rob Roy*, by Scottish writer Sir Walter Scott; Robert Burns (Scottish poet); Robert Browning (English poet); Robert Schumann (German composer); Robert E Lee (US soldier); Sir Robert Peel, British politician and founder of the British police force; Robert Louis Stevenson (Scottish writer); Robert Falcon Scott (British explorer); Robert Musil (Austrian writer); Robert Frost (US poet); Robert Delaunay (French artist); Robert Graves (British writer); Robert Heinlein (US science-fiction writer); Robert Kennedy (US politician); Robert Rauschenberg (US artist); Roberto Rossellini (Italian film director); Robert Redford and Robert De Niro (US actors); Robert Venturi (US architect); Robert Plant, Robert Palmer and Robbie Williams (British musicians).

Robin

Variants and diminutives: Hob, Rob, Robbie, Robby, Robert, Robinet, Robinson, Robyn.
Meaning: 'fame' and 'bright' (Germanic) as a diminutive of Robert. Also a girl's name.
Notable namesakes: Robin Goodfellow, also known as

Puck, a mischievous spirit of English folklore; Robin Hood (legendary English outlaw and folk hero); robin redbreast, the common name of the *Erithacus rubecula* species of songbird; Robin Day (British broadcaster); the partner of the US comic-book and movie hero Batman; Robin Knox-Johnston (British yachtsman).

Rocco

Variants and diminutives: Rocky.
Meaning: 'rock' (Italian).
Notable namesakes: Rocco Forte (British hotelier); Rocco Ritchie, son of the US singer Madonna and the British film director Guy Ritchie.

Rocky

Variants and diminutives: Rocco.
Meaning: 'rocky' (English). Also an anglicised version of Rocco.
Notable namesakes: Rocky Marciano (US boxer).

Roderick

Variants and diminutives: Broderick, Drigo, Eric, Erick, Gigo, Rhodric, Rhydderch, Rick, Rickie, Ricky, Roald, Rod, Rodd, Roddie, Roddy, Roden, Roderic, Roderich, Roderigo, Rodi, Rodito, Rodrego, Rodrich, Rodrick, Rodrigo, Rodrique, Rori, Roric, Rory, Ruaraidh, Rurich, Rurik, Ruy.
Meaning: 'renowned' and 'ruler' (Germanic).

Notable namesakes: the eponymous heroes of the novels *The Adventures of Roderick Random*, by Scottish writer Tobias Smollett, *The Vision of Don Roderick*, by Scottish writer Sir Walter Scott, and *Roderick Hudson*, by US writer Henry James; Rod (Roderick) Stewart (British singer).

Rodney

Variants and diminutives: Rod, Rodd, Roddie, Roddy.
Meaning: 'Hroda's' or 'reed' and 'island' (Old English); derived from an English family name, in turn derived from a number of English place names.

Notable namesakes: the eponymous hero of the novel *Rodney Stone*, by British writer Arthur Conan Doyle; Rodney Trotter, a character in the British television sitcom *Only Fools and Horses*.

Rodrigo

Variants and diminutives: Drigo, Rod, Roddie, Roddy, Roderick, Roderigo, Rodito, Rodrego.
Meaning: 'renowned' and 'ruler' (Germanic) as a Spanish variant of Roderick.
Notable namesakes: a Visigoth king and hero of Spanish legend; Rodrigo Diaz, Count of Bivar, a Spanish soldier better known as 'El Cid'.

Rogan

Meaning: 'red-haired' (Irish and Scots Gaelic).

Roger

Variants and diminutives: Dodge, Gerek, Hodge, Rod, Rodge, Rodger, Rodgers, Rog, Roge, Rogelio, Rogerio, Rogerios, Rogers, Rogier, Roj, Rozer, Rudiger, Rüdiger, Rugero, Ruggerio, Ruggero, Rutger, Ruttger.
Meaning: 'fame' and 'spear' (Germanic).
Notable namesakes: Roger Bacon (English philosopher and scientist); Rogier van der Weyden (Flemish artist); the code for 'message received and understood' in verbal communications; a slang verb for copulation; Jolly Roger, the name for the 'skull-and-crossbones' pirate flag; Roger Fry (British artist and critic); Roger Sessions (US composer); Roger Moore (British actor); Roger Daltry and Roger Waters (British musicians); Roger Black (British athlete).

Rohan

Variants and diminutives: Rowan.
Meaning: 'sandalwood' (Hindi); 'mountain ash' (Old Norse) or 'red' (Irish Gaelic) as a variant of Rowan.

Roland

Variants and diminutives: Lando, Lorand, Lorant, Olo, Orland, Orlando, Orlo, Rolando, Roldan, Rolek, Rolla, Rollan, Rolland, Rollen, Rollin, Rollins, Rollo, Rollon, Rolly, Rolon, Roly, Rowe, Rowland, Rudland, Ruland.
Meaning: 'fame' and 'land' (Germanic).
Notable namesakes: a paladin of Charlemagne,

whose story is told in the French epic poem *Chanson de Roland (Song of Roland)* and in the poem *Orlando Furioso,* by Italian poet Ludovico Ariosto; Rowland, a son of King Arthur in Arthurian legend; Rowland Hill (reformer of the British postal system and deviser of the first postage stamp); Roland Barthes (French literary theorist and critic); Roland Giguère (Canadian poet, typographer and artist).

Rolf

Variants and diminutives: Ralf, Rolfe, Rollo, Rolph, Rolphe, Roul, Roulf, Rudolf, Rudolph.
Meaning: 'fame' and 'wolf' (Germanic) as a German and Scandinavian variant of Rudolf (Rudolph).
Notable namesakes: Rolf Hochhuth (German playwright); Rolf Harris (Australian-born British television entertainer).

Rollo

Variants and diminutives: Rolf, Rolly, Rolon, Roul, Rudolf, Rudolph.
Meaning: 'fame' and 'wolf' (Germanic) as a variant of Rolf (Rudolph).
Notable namesakes: the Viking founder of the duchy of Normandy and its first duke.

Romain

Variants and diminutives: Roman, Romano, Romeo, Romulus.
Meaning: 'of Rome' (French).
Notable namesakes: Romain Rolland (French writer); Romain Gary (Russian-born French writer and diplomat).

Roman

Variants and diminutives: Mancho, Romain, Romano, Romao, Romarico.
Meaning: 'of Rome' (Latin). A male version of Roma.
Notable namesakes: Roman Polanski (Polish film director).

Romeo

Variants and diminutives: Romain, Romallus, Roman, Romanus, Romao, Rommie, Romney, Romolo, Romulus.
Meaning: 'of Rome' (French). A male version of Roma.
Notable namesakes: the hero of William Shakespeare's play *Romeo and Juliet;* a name for a wooer of women; the code for the letter 'R' in verbal communications.

Romulus

Variants and diminutives: Quirinus, Romain, Romeo, Romolo, Romulo, Rómulo.
Meaning: uncertain; possibly 'strength' (Latin); derived from the name of the co-founder of Rome in Roman mythology.
Notable namesakes: Rómulo Gallegos (Venezuelan writer, politician and educator).

Ronald

Variants and diminutives: Naldo, Raghnall, Rainald, Ranald, Ranaldo, Raynaldo, Reginald, Reinaldo, Renaldo, Rey, Reynaldo, Reynold, Rinhaldo, Roald, Ron, Ronel, Ronello, Roni, Ronnie, Ronny, Roone.
Meaning: 'advice' or 'might' and 'power' (Germanic) as a Scottish variant of Reynold.
Notable namesakes: Ronald August Fangen (Norwegian writer); Ronald Firbank (English writer); Ronald Colman (British actor); Ronald Reagan (US actor and politician); Ron Weasley, a character in the 'Harry Potter' series of children's books by British writer J K Rowling.

Ronan

Variants and diminutives: Rónán.
Meaning: 'little seal' (Irish Gaelic).
Notable namesakes: a number of saints; Ronan Keating (Irish singer).

Rory

Variants and diminutives: Roderick, Ruadidhri, Ruairi, Ruari, Ruaridh, Rurik.
Meaning: 'red' (Scottish and Irish Gaelic) as an anglicised form of Ruaridh (Scots Gaelic) and Ruairi (Irish Gaelic).
Notable namesakes: Rory O'Connor, an Irish king; Rory O'More, three anti-English Irish chiefs; Rory Bremner (British comedian).

Ross

Variants and diminutives: Roosevelt, Roscoe, Rosey, Rosie, Rosano, Rosse, Rossie, Rossy, Roswald, Royce.
Meaning: 'cape' or 'promontory' (Scots Gaelic); 'wood' (Scottish and Irish Gaelic); 'moor' (Cornish and Welsh); 'horse' or 'fame' (Germanic) or 'rose' (Latin) as a male version of Rose.
Notable namesakes: Ross Island, two islands in Antarctica; Ross Sea, an Antarctic inlet of the South Pacific; Ross Macdonald (US crime-writer); Ross Bleckner (US artist); Ross Geller, a character in the US television series *Friends*.

Rowan

Variants and diminutives: Rohan, Rooney, Rowen, Rowney.
Meaning: 'mountain ash' (Old Norse); 'red' (Irish Gaelic). Also a girl's name.
Notable namesakes: Rowan Atkinson (British comedian).

Roy

Variants and diminutives: Deroy, Elroy, Leroy, Loe, Ray, Rey, Roi, Royal, Royce, Roye, Royle, Royston.
Meaning: 'red' (Scots Gaelic); 'king' (Old French).
Notable namesakes: Roy Fuller (British writer); Roy Campbell (South African poet); Roy Rogers (US actor and singer); Roy Lichtenstein (US artist); Roy Hattersley and Roy Jenkins (British politicians).

Rudolph

Variants and diminutives: Dodek, Dolf, Dolfe, Dolfi, Dolph, Ralph, Raoul, Raul, Rezso, Rodolfo, Rodolph, Rodolphe, Rodolpho, Rodulfo, Rolf, Rolfe, Rollo, Rolo, Rolph, Roul, Ruda, Rude, Rudek, Rudi, Rudie, Rudolf, Rudolfo, Rudolfs, Rudy, Rufo, Rutz.
Meaning: 'fame' and 'wolf' (Germanic).
Notable namesakes: Rudolf I, King of Habsburg and Holy Roman emperor; the hero of the novel *The Prisoner of Zenda*, by English writer Anthony Hope; Rudolph Valentino (Italian-born US actor); Rudolf Nureyev (Russian-born Austrian ballet dancer); 'Rudolph, the red-nosed reindeer', a reindeer that pulls Santa Claus' sleigh, according to a children's Christmas song; Rudolph Giuliani (US politician).

Rudyard

Variants and diminutives: Rudd, Ruddie, Ruddy, Rudel, Rudi, Rudy, Rutledge, Rutter.
Meaning: 'red' and 'pole' (Germanic).
Notable namesakes: Rudyard Kipling (British writer).

Rufus

Variants and diminutives: Rufe, Rush, Rushkin, Russ, Rusty.
Meaning: 'red' (Latin).
Notable namesakes: William Rufus, also known as King William II of England; Rufus Thomas (US singer); Rufus Sewell (British actor).

Rupert

Variants and diminutives: Robert, Rubert, Ruberto, Rudbert, Rupe, Ruperto, Ruprecht.
Meaning: 'fame' and 'bright' (Germanic) as a German variant of Robert.
Notable namesakes: Prince Rupert of the Rhine (German-born Royalist soldier), for whom Rupert's Land, an area of northern Canada, was named; the eponymous hero of the novel *Rupert of Hentzau*, by English writer Anthony Hope; Rupert Brooke (English poet); Rupert Bear, a British children's cartoon character; Rupert Everett (British actor).

Russell

Variants and diminutives: Rosario, Rus, Russ, Russel, Rustie, Rustin, Rusty.
Meaning: 'red-haired' or 'red-faced' (Old French).
Notable namesakes: Russell Drysdale (British-born Australian artist); Russell Crowe (Australian actor).

Ryan

Variants and diminutives: Rian, Ryen, Ryon.
Meaning: uncertain; possibly 'little king' or 'descendant of a worshipper of Riaghan' (Irish Gaelic), Riaghan referring to a water deity; derived from an Irish family name.
Notable namesakes: Ryan O'Neal (US actor); Ryan Giggs (British footballer).

Sacha

Variants and diminutives: Alexander, Sasha.
Meaning: 'defender of men' or 'warrior' (Greek) as a Russian diminutive of Alexander. Also a girl's name (generally Sasha).
Notable namesakes: Sacha Guitry (French actor and film director); Sacha Distel (French singer).

Sacheverell

Variants and diminutives: Sach, Sacheverall.
Meaning: 'kid's' and 'leap' (Old French); derived from an English family name, in turn derived from the French place name Sault-Chevreuil.
Notable namesakes: Sacheverell Sitwell (British writer).

Sakima

Meaning: 'king' (Native American).

Salim

Variants and diminutives: Saleem.
Meaning: 'peace' or 'safe' (Arabic).

Salvador

Variants and diminutives: Sal, Sallie, Sally, Salvator, Salvatore, Sauveur.
Meaning: 'saviour' (Latin).
Notable namesakes: a Spanish appellation for Christ; San Salvador Island (Watling Island), an island in the Bahamas; El Salvador, a republic in Central America, whose capital is San Salvador; Salvador, a port in eastern Brazil; Salvator(e) Rosa (Italian artist, poet, musician and actor); Salvador Dali (Spanish artist); Salvatore Quasimodo (Italian writer).

Samir

Variants and diminutives: Zamir.
Meaning: 'entertainment' (Arabic).

Samson

Variants and diminutives: Sam, Sami, Samm, Sammie, Sammy, Sampson, Sams, Samy, Sansao, Sansom, Sanson, Sansone, Sansum, Shem, Simson.
Meaning: 'sun' (Hebrew).
Notable namesakes: an Israelite strongman in the Old Testament whose strength was bound up in his hair and whose name is now used to describe any outstandingly strong man; Saint Samson.

Samuel

Variants and diminutives: Sahm, Sam, Samaru, Sami, Samko, Samm, Sammel, Sammie, Sammy, Samo, Samouel, Samu, Samuele, Samuelis, Samuil, Samvel, Samy, Sawyl, Schmuel, Sem, Shem, Shemuel, Somhairle, Uel, Zamiel.
Meaning: 'asked of God', 'heard by God' or 'name of God' (Hebrew).
Notable namesakes: a judge and prophet for whom two books in the Old Testament are named; Samuel van Hoogstraten (Dutch artist); Samuel Pepys (English diarist); Samuel Cooper (English artist); Samuel Johnson (English writer and lexicographer); Samuel Taylor Coleridge (English poet); Samuel Pickwick, the leading character of the novel *Pickwick Papers*, by English writer Charles Dickens; Samuel Morse, the US inventor of the telegraph; Samuel Beckett (Irish writer); two Samuel Butlers, one an English poet, the other an English novelist and satirist; Samuel Tayor (US playwright); Sammy Davis Jr (US singer); Samuel L Jackson (US actor).

Sandy

Variants and diminutives: Alexander, Sandee, Sandi, Sandie.
Meaning: 'defender of men' or 'warrior' (Greek) as a diminutive of Alexander (and, as a girl's name, also of Alexandra).

Notable namesakes: Sandy Lyle (Scottish golfer).

Santiago
Variants and diminutives: Antiago, Chago, Chano, Sandiago, Sandiego, Saniago, Tago, Vego.
Meaning: 'Saint James' (Spanish), James (Jacob) meaning 'supplanter' (Hebrew).
Notable namesakes: Santiago de Compostela, the Spanish city where Saint James is buried and consequently a place of pilgrimage; the capital of Chile; Santiago de Cuba, a Cuban port on Santiago Bay; Santiago del Estero, a city in Argentina; San Diego, a port in the US state of California.

Santo
Variants and diminutives: Santos.
Meaning: 'holy' (Latin); 'saint' (Portuguese and Spanish). A male version of Santa.

Saul
Variants and diminutives: Paul, Saulo, Shaul, Sol, Sollie, Solly, Zollie, Zolly.
Meaning: 'prayed for' or 'asked for' (Hebrew).
Notable namesakes: the first king of the Israelites in the Old Testament; Saul of Tarsus, the name of the apostle Paul before his conversion to Christianity in the New Testament; Saul Steinberg (Romanian-born US artist); Saul Bellow (US writer).

Saxon
Variants and diminutives: Sasanach, Sass, Sasunn, Sax, Saxe.
Meaning: 'of the sea', 'of the dagger' or 'of the short sword' (Germanic); derived from the name of the western Germanic tribe. Also a girl's name.
Notable namesakes: a member of the Saxon tribe; a native of the former German duchy and state of Saxony; Saxon blue, a blue dye.

Scott
Variants and diminutives: Scot, Scoti, Scotti, Scottie, Scotty.
Meaning: 'a Scot', 'Scots' or 'Scottish' (English).
Notable namesakes: Scott Joplin (US musician); F Scott Fitzgerald (US writer); Scott Burton (US sculptor).

Seamus
Variants and diminutives: Hamish, Séamas, Seumas, Seumus, Seusmas, Shamus, Shay, Shaymus.
Meaning: 'supplanter' (Hebrew) as an Irish Gaelic variant of James (Jacob).
Notable namesakes: Seamus Heaney (Irish poet).

Sean
Variants and diminutives: Eoin, Séan, Shane, Shanen, Shannon, Shanon, Shaughn, Shaun, Shawn, Shoon.
Meaning: 'God has favoured', 'God is gracious' or 'God is merciful' (Hebrew) as an Irish Gaelic variant of John.
Notable namesakes: Sean O'Casey and Sean O'Faolain (Irish writers); Sean Connery (Scottish actor); Sean Scully (Irish artist); Sean Penn (US actor); Sean Bean (British actor).

Sebastian
Variants and diminutives: Basti, Bastian, Bastiano, Bastiao, Bastien, Bastion, Seb, Sebastiao, Sebastiano, Sebastien, Sebo, Steb.
Meaning: 'venerable' or 'from Sebastia' (Greek), Sebastia being a city in the ancient kingdom of Pontus, in Asia Minor.
Notable namesakes: Saint Sebastian, patron saint of athletes and archers; Sebastian Brant (German poet and satirist); Sebastiano del Plombo (Italian artist); characters in William Shakespeare's plays *Twelfth Night* and *The Tempest*; Johann Sebastian Bach (German composer); Sebastian Coe (British athlete and politician); Sebastian Faulks (British writer).

Segel
Meaning: 'treasure' (Hebrew).

Selwyn
Variants and diminutives: Selwin, Silas, Silvanus, Silvester, Win, Winnie, Winny, Wyn, Wynn.
Meaning: uncertain; possibly 'sylvan' or 'of the woods' (Latin) as an Old English variant of Silvanus; possibly

'wild' or 'savage' (Old French); possibly 'hall' or 'house' and 'friend' (Old English); possibly 'ardour' and 'fair' (Old Welsh); derived from a British family name.
Notable namesakes: the subject of the poem *Hugh Selwyn Mauberley*, by US poet Ezra Pound; John Selwyn Gummer (British politician).

Sepp
Variants and diminutives: Joseph.
Meaning: 'God will increase' (Hebrew) as a German diminutive of Joseph.
Notable namesakes: Sepp Dietrich (German Nazi soldier).

Septimus
Variants and diminutives: Sep.
Meaning: 'seventh' (Latin). A male version of Septima.
Notable namesakes: Lucius Septimus Severus (Roman soldier).

Serge
Variants and diminutives: Cergio, Checho, Checo, Serg, Sergai, Sergei, Sergeo, Sergey, Sergeyka, Sergi, Sergie, Sergio, Sergiu, Sergius, Sergiusz, Sergo, Sergunya, Serhiy, Serhiyko, Serjio, Serzh, Sewek, Syarhey, Zergio.
Meaning: uncertain; possibly 'silk' (Greek).
Notable namesakes: a woollen or worsted fabric; Saint Sergius; four popes; Serge Poliakoff (Russian artist); Serge Gainsbourg (French musician, actor and writer).

Seth
Variants and diminutives:
Meaning: uncertain; possibly 'to appoint', 'to settle' or 'compensation' (Hebrew).
Notable namesakes: a son of Adam and Eve in the Old Testament; Seth Pecksniff, a character in the novel *Martin Chuzzlewit*, by English writer Charles Dickens; a character in the novel *Cold Comfort Farm*, by British writer Stella Gibbons.

Sextus
Meaning: 'sixth' (Latin).
Notable namesakes: Sextus Propertius (Roman poet).

Seymour
Variants and diminutives: Seymor, Seymore.
Meaning: 'Saint-Maur' (Old French); derived from an English family name, in turn derived from a number of French place names named for Saint Maur (or Maurus), Maur meaning 'Moorish' or 'African' (Latin) as a diminutive of Maurice.
Notable namesakes: Saint Maur (or Maurus).

Shane
Variants and diminutives: Sean, Shaine, Shanen, Shannon, Shanon, Shaughn, Shaun, Shawn, Shayn, Shayne, Shoon.
Meaning: 'God has favoured', 'God is gracious' or 'God is merciful' (Hebrew) as an anglicised version of Sean, in turn an Irish Gaelic variant of John.
Notable namesakes: the title of a US Western film and television series; Shane Warne (Australian cricketer).

Sharif
Meaning: 'honest' or 'noble' (Arabic).

Shaun
Variants and diminutives: Sean, Shane, Shaughn, Shawn, Shonn, Shoon.
Meaning: 'God has favoured', 'God is gracious' or 'God is merciful' (Hebrew) as an anglicised version of Sean, in turn an Irish Gaelic variant of John.
Notable namesakes: Shaun the Postman, a character in the novel *Finnegans Wake*, by Irish writer James Joyce.

Shaw
Meaning: 'small wood', 'thicket' or 'copse' (Old English); derived from an English family name, in turn derived from a number of English place names.

Sheldon
Variants and diminutives: Shel, Shelden, Shelley, Shelly, Shelton.
Meaning: 'steep' and 'valley' or 'flat-topped' and 'hill' (Old English); derived from an English family name, in turn derived from a number of English place names.
Notable namesakes: Sheldon Glashow (US physicist).

Shem

Variants and diminutives: Shammai, Shemuel.
Meaning: 'fame' or 'name' (Hebrew and Yiddish).
Notable namesakes: a son of Noah in the Old
Testament; Shem the Penman, a character in the novel
Finnegans Wake, by Irish writer James Joyce.

Sheridan

Variants and diminutives: Sheridon.
Meaning: uncertain; possibly 'descendent of Siridean',
'eternal' and 'treasure', 'peaceful' or 'wild' (Irish Gaelic);
derived from an Irish family name. Also a girl's name.
Notable namesakes: Sheridan Morley (British theatre
critic).

Sherman

Variants and diminutives: Sharman, Shearman, Sher,
Shermann.
Meaning: 'shears' and 'man' (Old English); derived
from an English family name.

Shing

Meaning: 'victorious' (Chinese).

Shiva

Variants and diminutives: Siv, Siva.
Meaning: 'the auspicious [one]' (Sanskrit); derived
from the name of the god of destruction and personal
destiny, one of the three leading gods in Hindu
mythology.

Sholto

Variants and diminutives: Sioltaich
Meaning: 'sower' (Scots Gaelic).

Sidney

Variants and diminutives: Cid, Cyd, Cydney, Si, Sid,
Sidon, Sidonio, Syd, Sydney, Sydny.
Meaning: 'wide' and 'island' or 'well-irrigated land' or
'south of the water' (Old English) when derived from
an English family name, in turn derived from a number
of English place names; 'Saint-Denis' (Old French),
when derived from the name of the French town, in
turn named for Saint Denys, Denys (Dennis) meaning
'deity of the Nysa' (Greek). Also a girl's name as a

diminutive of Sidony.
Notable namesakes: Sydney, Australia's largest city
and the capital of New South Wales, which was named
for Thomas Townshend, Viscount Sydney; Sydney silky,
an Australian breed of terrier; Sidney Lanier (US poet);
Sydney Carton, the hero of the novel *A Tale of Two
Cities*, by English writer Charles Dickens; Sidney
Howard (US playwright); Sidney Nolan (Australian
artist); Sidney Poitier (US actor); Syd Barrett (British
musician).

Siegfried

Variants and diminutives: Fredo, Friedl, Seifert,
Seifried, Siffre, Sig, Sigefriedo, Sigfrid, Sigfrido,
Sigfried, Sigfroi, Siggi, Siggy, Sigifredo, Siguefredo,
Sigurd, Sigvard, Singefrid, Siurt, Szigfrid, Zigfrid,
Zigfrids, Zygfryd, Zygi.
Meaning: 'victory' and 'peace' (Germanic).
Notable namesakes: a hero, also known as Sigurd, of
German legend, who appears in the epic German poem
the *Nibelungenlied (Song of the Nibelungs)* and is also
the eponymous hero of the opera *Siegfried*, as well as
of *Götterdämmerung (Twilight of the Gods)*, by
German composer Richard Wagner; the Siegfried Line,
a German defensive line established in France during
World War I and the Allied name for the West Wall, a
German defensive line along Germany's western
frontier, in World War II; Siegfried Sassoon (British
poet); Siegfried Lenz (German writer).

Sigmund

Variants and diminutives: Siegmond, Siegmund, Sig,
Siggi, Siggy, Sigismondo, Sigismund, Sigsmond.
Meaning: 'victory' and 'protection' (Germanic).
Notable namesakes: as Sigismund, a Holy Roman
emperor and three Polish kings; Siegmund, the father
of Siegfried in the operas of Richard Wagner; Sigmund
Freud (Austrian psychoanalyst).

Sigurd

Variants and diminutives: Siegfried.
Meaning: 'victory' and 'guardian' (Old Norse).
Notable namesakes: a hero (equated with Siegfried)
of Norse mythology.

Silas

Variants and diminutives: Selwyn, Silo, Silus, Silvanus, Silvester.
Meaning: 'sylvan' or 'of the woods' (Latin) as a Greek variant of Silvanus; 'to borrow' (Aramaic); 'snub-nosed' (Latin).
Notable namesakes: Saint Silas (or Silvanus), a companion of Paul in the New Testament; the eponymous heroes of the novels *Silas Marner*, by English writer George Eliot, and *The Rise of Silas Lapham*, by US writer William Dean Howells.

Silvanus

Variants and diminutives: Selwyn, Silas, Silvain, Silvan, Silvano, Silvanus, Silvester, Silvio, Sly, Sy, Sylvan, Sylvanus, Sylveanus, Sylvester.
Meaning: 'sylvan' or 'of the woods' (Latin).
Notable namesakes: the god of woods, fields and flocks in Roman mythology.

Silvester

Variants and diminutives: Selwyn, Silas, Silvain, Silvan, Silvano, Silvestio, Silvestre, Silvestro, Silvio, Sly, Sy, Sylvan, Sylvanus, Sylveanus, Sylvester, Sylvestre, Vesta, Vester.
Meaning: 'sylvan' or 'of the woods' (Latin) as a variant of Silvanus.
Notable namesakes: Saint Silvester I, a pope whose feast day is celebrated in Europe on New Year's Eve, hence its alternative name, 'Silvester', along with two other popes; the leading character of the novel *The Crime of Sylvestre Bonnard*, by French writer Anatole France; Sylvester Stallone (US actor); Sylvester, a cartoon cat; Sly Stone (US musician).

Simeon

Variants and diminutives: Imon, Shimeon, Shimone, Si, Sim, Simen, Simion, Simmy, Simon.
Meaning: 'God has heard', 'listening' or 'little hyena' (Hebrew).
Notable namesakes: a son of Jacob and Leah in the Old Testament; the priest who blessed the infant Jesus in the Temple in the New Testament; Saint Simeon the Stylite.

Simon

Variants and diminutives: Cimon, Imon, Samein, Semon, Shimon, Shimone, Si, Silas, Sim, Simao, Simen, Simeon, Simi, Simie, Simion, Simkin, Simmie, Simmy, Simone, Simp, Simpson, Sims, Sy, Symon, Ximenes, Ximenez.
Meaning: 'God has heard', 'listening' or 'little hyena' (Hebrew) as a variant of Simeon; 'snub-nosed' (Greek).
Notable namesakes: the original name of Saint Peter (also called Simon Peter) in the New Testament; Saint Simon Zelotes (Simon the Zealot), one of Christ's apostles in the New Testament; Simon the Tanner, a host of Saint Peter in the New Testament; Simon Magus, a Samaritan sorcerer in the New Testament and founder of the Gnostic sect, from whose name the word 'simony', the

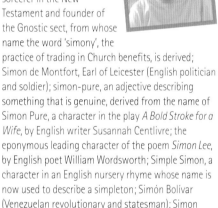

practice of trading in Church benefits, is derived; Simon de Montfort, Earl of Leicester (English politician and soldier); simon-pure, an adjective describing something that is genuine, derived from the name of Simon Pure, a character in the play *A Bold Stroke for a Wife*, by English writer Susannah Centlivre; the eponymous leading character of the poem *Simon Lee*, by English poet William Wordsworth; Simple Simon, a character in an English nursery rhyme whose name is now used to describe a simpleton; Simón Bolívar (Venezuelan revolutionary and statesman); Simon Gray (British writer); Simon Templar, a fictional character, also known as 'The Saint', created by British-born US writer Leslie Charteris.

Sinclair

Variants and diminutives: Clarence, Sinclaire, Sinclar.
Meaning: 'Saint-Clair' (Old English), Clair (Clare) meaning 'clear', 'bright' or 'famous' (Latin); derived from a Scottish family name, in turn derived from a French place name named for a Norman martyr.
Notable namesakes: Sinclair Ross (Canadian writer); Sinclair Lewis (US writer).

Skelly

Variants and diminutives: Skelley, Skellie.
Meaning: 'story-teller' (Irish Gaelic).

Solomon

Variants and diminutives: Lasimonne, Salaman, Salamen, Salamon, Salamun, Salaun, Salman, Salmen, Salmon, Salo, Saloman, Salome, Salomo, Salomon, Salomonas, Salomone, Selim, Selman, Shelomo, Shelomoh, Shlomo, Sol, Solaman, Sollie, Solly, Solmon, Solom Soloman, Suleiman, Zalman, Zalmon, Zelmen, Zelmo, Zollie, Zolly.
Meaning: 'peace' (Hebrew).
Notable namesakes: King Solomon, the wise, Temple-building son of David and Bathsheba, to whom the Song of Solomon is attributed in the Old Testament; the Solomon Islands in the Pacific Ocean; Solomon's seal, another name for the star of David, a symbol of Judaism, and the common name of the *Polygonatum* genus of plants.

Spencer

Variants and diminutives: Spence, Spens, Spense, Spenser.
Meaning: 'butler', 'house steward' or 'controller of the spence [larder or buttery]' (Old French); derived from an English family name.
Notable namesakes: Spencer Perceval (British politician); a short coat or knitted vest; a nautical word for a type of gaffsail; Spencer Gulf, an Australian inlet of the Indian Ocean; Spencer Tracy (US actor).

Spike

Meaning: 'sharp point', 'ear' or 'tuft' (Latin).
Notable namesakes: Spike Milligan (British comedian); Spike Lee and Spike Jonze (US film director).

Spiro

Meaning: 'I breathe', 'I exist' or 'I am inspired' (Latin).

Stafford

Variants and diminutives: Ford, Staff, Stanford.
Meaning: 'landing place' or 'staithe', 'stony' or 'steers' and 'ford' (Old English); derived from an English family name, in turn derived from a number of English place names.
Notable namesakes: Stafford Cripps (British politician); Stafford Johns (British actor).

Stanford

Variants and diminutives: Ford, Stafford, Stan, Stamford, Standford.
Meaning: 'stony' and 'ford' (Old English); derived from an English family name, in turn derived from a number of English place names.

Stanislas

Variants and diminutives: Estanislao, Estanislau, Lao, Slava, Slavik, Slavka, Stan, Stana, Stando, Stane, Stanislao, Stanislau, Stanislaus, Stanislav, Stanislaw, Stanislus, Stanni, Stanny, Stano, Stas, Stashko, Stasiek, Stasio, Staska, Tano, Tanix, Tilo.
Meaning: 'camp' and 'glory' (Old Slavic).
Notable namesakes: Saint Stanislaus of Cracow, patron saint of Poland; Saint Stanislaus Kostka, patron saint of young people and people suffering from broken bones; two kings of Poland; Stanislaw Lem (Polish science-fiction writer).

Stanley

Variants and diminutives: Stan, Stanfield, Stanleigh, Stanly, Stanton.
Meaning: 'stony' and 'clearing' or 'field' (Old English); derived from an English family name, in turn derived from a number of English place names.
Notable namesakes: the capital of the Falkland Islands; Mount Stanley (Ngaliema Mountain), a mountain in central Africa; Stanley Pool, a lake formed by the river Congo in Africa; Stanley Spencer (British artist); Stanley Baldwin (British politician); Stan Laurel, the British-born US comic actor of Laurel and Hardy fame; Stanley Matthews (British footballer); Stanley Kubrick (US film director); Stanley knife, a type of knife first manufactured by the US Stanley Rule and Level Company.

Stephen

Variants and diminutives: Astevan, Este, Esteban, Esteben, Estefan, Estefon, Estes, Estevan, Estevao, Estiban, Estien, Estienne, Estiennes, Estifa, Estovan, Estvan, Etienne, Etiennes, Istevan, Isti, Istvan, Stamos, Stavros, Steenie, Stef, Stefan, Stefano, Stefanos, Stefans, Steffan, Steffel, Steffen, Stefos, Stepan, Stenya, Stepan, Stepanya, Steph, Stephan, Stéphane, Stephanos, Stephanus, Stepka, Stevan, Steve, Steven, Stevie, Stevy, Stiofan, Tapani, Teb, Teppo, Tiennot.
Meaning: 'crown' (Greek).
Notable namesakes: Saint Stephen, the first Christian martyr, patron saint of bricklayers, stone masons and headache-sufferers; Saint Stephen I, King of Hungary, patron saint of Hungary; King Stephen of England; ten popes; Stefan Lochner (German artist); Saint Stephen Harding; Stéphane Mallarmé (French poet); Stefan George (German poet); Stefan Zweig (Austrian writer); Stephen Dedalus, the leading character of the novel *A Portrait of the Artist as a Young Man*, by Irish writer James Joyce; Stephen Spender (British poet); Steven Runciman (British historian); Stephen Sondheim (US lyricist and composer); Stephen King (US writer); Steve Redgrave (British oarsman); Steve Tyler (US musician); Steve Harley (British musician); Stephen Fry (British actor and writer); Steve Coogan (British comic actor).

Stirling

Variants and diminutives: Sterling.
Meaning: uncertain; possibly 'dwelling of Melyn' (Old Welsh); possibly 'little star' (Middle English); derived from a Scottish family name, in turn derived from the name of a Scottish town.
Notable namesakes: Stirling engine, an engine that operates in accordance with the Stirling cycle, both named for their inventor, the Scottish minister Robert Stirling; Stirling's formula, a mathematical formula named for its inventor, the Scottish mathematician James Stirling; Stirling Moss (British motor-racing driver).

Stuart

Variants and diminutives: Steuart, Stew, Steward, Stewart, Stu.
Meaning: 'steward' or 'seneshal' (Old English); derived from a Scottish family name.
Notable namesakes: the Stuart, or Stewart, dynasty of Scottish, and later also English, monarchs; Stewart Granger (British actor); Stuart Cloete (South African writer).

Sullivan

Variants and diminutives: Sullavan, Sullevan, Sullie, Sully.
Meaning: 'descendant of' and 'the black person' or 'the hawk-eyed person' (Irish Gaelic); derived from an Irish family name.

Sven

Variants and diminutives: Svarne, Svend, Swen.
Meaning: 'boy' (Old Norse).
Notable namesakes: Sven-Göran Eriksson (Swedish football manager).

Swithin

Variants and diminutives: Swithun.
Meaning: 'strong' (Old English).
Notable namesakes: Saint Swithin, English tradition holding that the weather prevailing on his feast day, 15 July, will endure for forty days.

Tabbai

Variants and diminutives: Tab, Tabb, Tabbie, Tabby, Tavi.
Meaning: 'good' (Aramaic).

Tabib

Meaning: 'doctor' (Turkish).

Tabor

Variants and diminutives: Tab, Tabb, Tabbie, Tabby, Tabor.

Meaning: 'drum' (Persian).
Notable namesakes: a small type of drum; Mount Tabor in Israel, where Christ's transfiguration is said to have occurred.

Taffy

Variants and diminutives: Daffy, Dafyd, Daffyd, David, Taafe, Tab, Tafydd, Taffy, Tavi.
Meaning: 'beloved' or 'friend' (Hebrew) as a Welsh diminutive of David.
Notable namesakes: a slang term for Welsh people.

Tahir

Variants and diminutives: Taher.
Meaning: 'pure' (Arabic).

Taj

Variants and diminutives: Tahj.
Meaning: 'crown' (Urdu and Arabic). A male version of Taja.
Notable namesakes: the Taj Mahal ('crown of buildings'), a white marble mausoleum erected at Agra, India, for his wife, Mumtaz Mahal, by the Mogul emperor Shah Jaran; a type of conical cap worn by Muslims.

Tal

Variants and diminutives: Talor.
Meaning: 'dew' (Hebrew). Also a girl's name.

Talbot

Variants and diminutives: Tal, Talbert, Tallie, Tally.
Meaning: uncertain; possibly 'dale' or 'valley' and 'command' or 'offer' (Germanic); possibly 'cut' and 'bundle' or 'faggot' (Old French); derived from an English family name, in turn derived from a number of English place names.
Notable namesakes: a breed of large hound.

Talib

Meaning: 'seeker' (Arabic).
Notable namesakes: the Taliban, the fundamentalist Islamic regime that ruled Afghanistan until ousted during the US-led War on Terror in 2001.

Taliesin

Meaning: 'shining' or 'radiant' and 'brow' (Welsh).
Notable namesakes: a poet of Welsh legend, the son of Ceriddwen and reputedly the author of *The Book of Taliesin*, for whom Taliesin, Dyfed, where he is said to have died, is named.

Talman

Variants and diminutives: Tal, Tallie, Tally, Talmon.
Meaning: 'to oppress' or 'to injure' (Aramaic).

Talor

Variants and diminutives: Tal.
Meaning: 'morning dew' (Hebrew). Also a girl's name.

Tam

Variants and diminutives: Tammie, Tammy, Thomas.
Meaning: 'twin' (Aramaic) as a Scottish diminutive of Thomas; 'eighth child' (Vietnamese).
Notable namesakes: the eponymous hero of the poem *Tam o'Shanter*, by Scottish poet Robert Burns, from which the name of a Scottish type of bobble hat is derived.

Tamir

Variants and diminutives: Timur.
Meaning: 'date palm' or 'palm tree' (Hebrew) as a male version of Tamar.

Tancred

Meaning: 'think' and 'advice' (Germanic).
Notable namesakes: a Norman who featured prominently in the First Crusade, as told in the opera *Tancredi*, by Italian composer Gioachino Rossini, and the novel *Tancred, or the New Crusade*, by British writer and politician Benjamin Disraeli.

Tanner

Variants and diminutives: Tan, Tann, Tanney, Tannie, Tanny.
Meaning: 'tanner [a tanner of hides or skins]' (Old English); derived from an English family name.
Notable namesakes: a slang name for a sixpence, a former unit of British currency.

Tariq
Variants and diminutives: Tareek, Tarick, Tarik.
Meaning: 'knocker at the door' (Arabic).

Taro
Meaning: 'first son' or 'big boy' (Japanese).

Tarquin
Variants and diminutives: Quin, Tarq.
Meaning: uncertain; possibly 'of Tarquinni' (Latin), Tarquinni being an ancient Etruscan town; derived from the Roman family name Tarquinius.
Notable namesakes: Lucius Tarquinius Priscus and Lucius Tarquinius Superbus, two kings of ancient Rome.

Tate
Variants and diminutives: Tait, Taite, Tatum, Tayte.
Meaning: uncertain; possibly 'windy' or 'garrulous' (Native American); possibly 'cheerful' (Old Norse), 'dear', 'happy', 'dice', 'hilltop', 'tress of hair', 'father' or 'teat' (Old English) when derived from an English family name.
Notable namesakes: Tate Britain and Tate Modern, art galleries in London named for the original Tate Gallery's founder, the British sugar refiner and philanthropist Sir Henry Tate.

Tavi
Variants and diminutives: David, Tabbai, Tov, Tovi, Tuvia.
Meaning: 'good' (Aramaic); 'beloved' or 'friend' (Hebrew) as an Israeli diminutive of David.

Tavish
Variants and diminutives: Tammas, Tav, Tavis, Tevis, Thomas.
Meaning: 'twin' (Aramaic) as a Scottish variant of Thomas.

Tayib
Meaning: 'delicate' or 'good' (Arabic).

Taylor
Variants and diminutives: Tailer, Tailor, Tayler, Taylour.
Meaning: 'tailor' or 'cutter' (Old French); derived from an English family name. Also a girl's name.
Notable namesakes: Samuel Taylor Coleridge (English poet).

Teague
Variants and diminutives: Tadhg, Taig, Taogh, Teagan, Tegan, Teige, Teigue, Thady.
Meaning: 'poet' or 'philosopher' (Irish Gaelic); 'lovely' (Welsh) as a male version of Tegan.

Ted
Variants and diminutives: Edmund, Edward, Tedd, Teddie, Teddy, Theobald, Theodore, Theodoric.
Meaning: 'happiness' or 'riches' and 'guardian' (Old English) as a diminutive of Edward; 'happiness' or 'riches' and 'protector' (Old English) as a diminutive of Edmund; 'God's gift' (Greek) as a diminutive of Theodore. Also a diminutive of other names beginning with 'Ed-' or 'Theo-'.
Notable namesakes: Ted (Edward) Kennedy (US politician); teddy bear, a toy bear named for the US president Theodore Roosevelt; teddy, a woman's piece of underwear; Ted Hughes (British poet); teddy boy, a member of a youth cult of the 1950s who wore pseudo-Edwardian clothes.

Teman
Variants and diminutives: Temani.
Meaning: 'right side' or 'south' (Hebrew).

Terence
Variants and diminutives: Tel, Telly, Terencio, Terrance, Terrel, Terrence, Terris, Terry, Terryal, Toirdhealbhach, Torn, Torrance, Torrence, Torrey, Tory, Turlough.
Meaning: uncertain; possibly 'to wear out' or 'to polish' (Latin) when derived from the Roman family name Terentius; 'initiator of an idea' (Irish Gaelic).
Notable namesakes: a Roman playwright whose full name was Publius

Terentius Afer; Terence Rattigan (British writer); Terence Conran (British designer, retailer and restaurateur); Terence Trent D'Arby (US singer).

Terry

Variants and diminutives: Tel, Telly, Terence, Terrel, Terris, Terryal, Theodoric, Torry, Tory.
Meaning: 'people' and 'ruler' (Germanic) as a diminutive of Theodoric; possibly 'to wear out' or 'to polish' (Latin) or 'initiator of an idea' (Irish Gaelic) as a diminutive of Terence. Also a girl's name as a diminutive of Theresa.
Notable namesakes: Terry Jones (British comic actor); Terry Venables (British football manager).

Tertius

Variants and diminutives: Tert, Tertie, Terty.
Meaning: 'third' (Latin). A male version of Tertia.

Tex

Variants and diminutives: Texan.
Meaning: 'Texan' (English), referring to the US state of Texas.
Notable namesakes: a slang word for someone from the US state of Texas; Tex Ritter (US actor).

Thaddeus

Variants and diminutives: Faddei, Fadey, Jude, Tad, Tadd, Taddeo, Taddeus, Taddeusz, Taddy, Tade, Tadeas, Tadek, Tadeo, Tades, Tadey, Tadzio, Thad, Thadd, Thaddaeus, Thaddaus, Thaddeo, Thaddy, Thadee, Thadeus, Thady, Theodore.
Meaning: 'valiant' (Hebrew); 'God's gift' (Greek) as a variant of Theodore.
Notable namesakes: Saint Jude (also known as Judas or Thaddaeus), an apostle of Christ and author of the New Testament book the Epistle of Jude, patron saint of lost causes and desperate situations; Thad Jones (US jazz musician).

Thane

Variants and diminutives: Thain, Thaine, Thayne.

Meaning: 'thane' or 'tenant by military service', 'chieftain of a Scottish clan' or 'monarch's baron' (Old English); derived from a British family name, in turn derived from various ranks of lesser nobility.

Theo

Variants and diminutives: Theobald, Theodore, Theodoric, Theophilus.
Meaning: 'God' (Greek); 'God's gift' (Greek) as a diminutive of Theodore; 'people' and 'bold' (Germanic) as a diminutive of Theobald; 'people' and 'ruler' (Germanic) as a diminutive of Theodoric; 'God-loving' (Greek) as as diminutive of Theophilus. Also a male version of Thea.
Notable namesakes: Theo van Doesburg (Dutch artist and writer).

Theobald

Variants and diminutives: Tebald, Ted, Tedd, Teddie, Teddy, Thebault, Theo, Theodore, Theophilus, Thibaud, Thibault, Thibaut, Tibald, Tibbald, Tibold, Tiebout, Toiboid, Tybalt.
Meaning: 'people' and 'bold' (Germanic).
Notable namesakes: an archbishop of Canterbury; Tybalt, a character in William Shakespeare's play *Romeo and Juliet*.

Theodore

Variants and diminutives: Bohdan, Dorek, Fedar, Fedinka, Fedir, Fedor, Fedya, Feodor, Feodore, Fyoder, Tad, Tadd, Taddeo, Taddeus, Taddeusz, Tadeo, Ted, Tedd, Teddie, Teddy, Tedik, Telly, Teodomiro, Teodor, Teodorek, Teodoro, Teodus, Teos, Tewdor, Tewdwr, Thad, Thaddaus, Thadeus, Thaddeus, Thaddy, Thady, Theo, Theobald, Theodor, Theodoric, Theodoro, Theodosiuus, Theophilus, Tivadar, Tod, Todd, Todor, Todos, Tolek, Tudor.
Meaning: 'God's gift' (Greek).
Notable namesakes: Theodore I, ruler of a Byzantine state in exile; a number of saints; Théodore Géricault (French artist); Theodor Fontane and Theodor Storm (German writers); Theodor Mommsen (German historian); Theodore Roosevelt (US president); Theodore Dreiser (US writer); Theodor Seuss Geisel, the US writer and illustrator of children's books who is better known as Dr Seuss.

Theodoric

Variants and diminutives: Derek, Derk, Derrick, Deryck, Deryk, Dieter, Dietrich, Dirk, Ric, Rick, Rickie, Ricky, Ted, Tedd, Teddie, Teddy, Teodorico, Terrie, Terry, Theo, Theobald, Theodore, Theophilus, Thierry.
Meaning: 'people' and 'ruler' (Germanic).
Notable namesakes: Theodoric (or Theoderic), 'the Great', King of the Ostrogoths; Theodoric of Freiburg (German scientist); Theodoric of Prague (Bohemian artist).

Theophilus

Variants and diminutives: Theo, Theobald, Theodore, Theodoric, Théophile, Theophillus.
Meaning: 'God-loving' (Greek).
Notable namesakes: the addressee of the Gospel of Saint Luke and the Acts of the Apostles in the New Testament; Théophile Gautier (French writer); Théophile-Alexandre Steinlen (Swiss-born French artist).

Theron

Variants and diminutives: Tharon.
Meaning: 'hunter' or 'wild beast' (Greek).

Thomas

Variants and diminutives: Chumo, Foma, Fomka, Formo, Masaccio, Maso, Massey, Slawek, Tam, Tamas, Tameas, Tamlane, Tammany, Tammen, Tammie, Tammy, Tamsen, Tamson, Tavis, Tavish, Tevis, Tevish, Thom, Thoma, Thompson, Thurmas, Tip, Tom, Tomas, Tomás, Tomaso, Tomasso, Tomcio, Tome, Tomek, Tomelis, Tomi, Tomie, Tomislaw, Tomm, Tommie, Tommy, Tomos, Toomas, Tuomas, Tuomo.
Meaning: 'twin' (Aramaic).
Notable namesakes: one of Christ's apostles ('doubting Thomas', now a name for a sceptical person) in the New Testament, patron saint of architects and blind people; Saint Thomas Aquinas, Italian theologian and philosopher, whose philosophical system is known as Thomism, patron saint of theologians, university lecturers, schools and students; Thomas of Erceldoune, or 'Thomas the Rhymer' (Scottish poet and seer); Thomas of Woodstock, a son of King Edward III of England; Saint Thomas Becket; Thomas à Kempis (German Augustinian monk); Saint Thomas of Hereford; Thomas Malory (English writer of Arthurian legends); Saint Thomas More, patron saint of lawyers, court clerks and civil servants; Thomas Hobbes (English philosopher); Thomas Jefferson (US president); Thomas 'Stonewall' Jackson (US soldier); Thomas Hughes and Thomas Hardy (English writers); Thomas Gainsborough and Thomas Lawrence (English artists); Thomas Chatterton (English poet); Thomas Eakins (US artist); Thomas Edison (US inventor); T(homas) E(dward) Lawrence (English soldier and writer); Thomas Mann (German writer); Thomas Kinsella (Irish poet); Thomas Keneally (Australian writer); the 'Thomas the Tank Engine' series of children's books, and subsequent animated British television series, by British writer the Reverend W Awdry.

Thor

Variants and diminutives: Thurston, Tor, Torquil.
Meaning: 'the thunderer' (Old Norse); derived from the name from the god of thunder in Norse mythology.

Thorley

Variants and diminutives: Thornton.
Meaning: 'thorn' and 'wood' or 'clearing' (Old English); derived from an English family name, in turn derived from a number of English place names.

Thornton

Variants and diminutives: Thorley, Thorn, Thorndike, Thorne, Thornie, Thorny.
Meaning: 'thorn' and 'place' or 'settlement' (Old English); derived from an English family name, in turn derived from a number of English place names.
Notable namesakes: Thornton Wilder (US writer).

Thorpe

Variants and diminutives: Thorp.
Meaning: 'farm' or 'village' (Old Norse and Old English); derived from an English family name, in turn derived from a number of English place names.

Thurston

Variants and diminutives: Stan, Thor, Thurstan, Thursting, Torquil.

Meaning: 'Thor's', Thor referring to the thunder god of Norse mythology, and 'stone' or 'farm' (Old English); derived from an English family name, in turn derived from an English place name.

Tiernan

Variants and diminutives: Tiarnan, Tierney.

Meaning: 'son of the lord' (Irish Gaelic); derived from an Irish family name.

Tiger

Variants and diminutives: Tige, Tigger.

Meaning: 'tiger' (Greek); derived from the common name of the *Panthera tigris* genus of striped big cat.

Notable namesakes: *The Tiger*, the title of a poem by English poet, artist and mystic William Blake; the tiger beetle, *Cicindelidae*; the tiger cat, *Felis tigrina*; the tiger lily; *Lilium tigrinum*; the tiger moth, *Arctia Parasemia*; tiger's-eye, a variety of crocidolite and a semi-precious stone; the tiger shark, *Galeocerdo cuvieri*; the tiger snake, *Notechis scutatus*; Tiger balm, a oriental brand of ointment; *Tiger at the Gates*, the title of a play by French writer Jean Giraudoux; Tiger Woods (US golfer).

Tilden

Variants and diminutives: Tilford, Tilton.

Meaning: 'convenient' and 'valley' (Old English); derived from an English family name, in turn derived from an English place name.

Timothy

Variants and diminutives: Tim, Tima, Timka, Timkin, Timmie, Timmy, Timo, Timofei, Timofey, Timok, Timon, Timot, Timotei, Timoteo, Timoteus, Timothe, Timothee, Timotheos, Timotheus, Tiomoid, Tisha, Tishka, Tymek, Tymon.

Meaning: 'in honour of God' (Greek).

Notable namesakes: Timotheus, a Greek poet and musician; Saint Timothy, a companion of Saint Paul, to whom two epistles were addressed in the New Testament, patron saint of people who suffer from

stomach problems; Tiny Tim Cratchit, a character in the novel *A Christmas Carol*, by English writer Charles Dickens; Timothy Mofolorunso Aluko (Nigerian writer); Tim Head (British artist); Tim Henman (British tennis player).

Tirion

Variants and diminutives: Tyrion.

Meaning: 'gentle' and 'kind' (Welsh).

Titus

Variants and diminutives: Titan, Tite, Titek, Tito, Titos, Toto, Totos, Tytus.

Meaning: uncertain; possibly 'giant', 'day' or 'sun' (Greek); derived from a Roman name.

Notable namesakes: Titus (Flavius Sabinus Vespasianus), son of Vespasian and emperor of Rome; Titus Maccius Plautus (Roman playwright); Saint Titus; the subject of William Shakespeare's tragic play *Titus Andronicus*; Titus Oates, an English conspirator in the 'Popish Plot' to murder King Charles II of Great Britain and Ireland; the leading character of the 'Gormenghast' trilogy of novels, by British writer and illustrator Mervyn Peake.

Tivon

Variants and diminutives: Tibon, Tiv, Tivvie, Tivvy.

Meaning: 'nature-lover' (Hebrew). A male version of Tivona.

Tobias

Variants and diminutives: Tavi, Tivon, Tobe, Tobey, Tobiah, Tobie, Tobin, Tobit, Toby, Tobye, Tobyn.

Meaning: 'God is good' (Hebrew).

Notable namesakes: the son of Tobit who was guided by an angel in the Apocryphal Book of Tobit; Tobias Smollett (Scottish writer).

Toby

Variants and diminutives: Tobe, Tobey, Tobiah, Tobias, Tobie, Tobin, Tobit, Tobye, Tobyn.

Meaning: 'God is good' (Hebrew) as a diminutive of Tobias.

Notable namesakes: Sir Toby Belch, a character in William Shakespeare's play *Twelfth Night*; the dog that features in the English children's puppet show 'Punch and Judy'; toby jug, an English type of mug fashioned in the form of a man; Uncle Toby, a character in the novel *The Life and Opinions of Tristram Shandy, Gent*, by Irish writer Laurence Sterne.

Todd
Variants and diminutives: Reynard, Tad, Tod, Toddie, Toddy.
Meaning: 'fox' (Middle English); derived from an English family name.

Tom
Variants and diminutives: Thomas, Tomas, Tomás, Tomlin, Tommie, Tommy.
Meaning: 'twin' (Aramaic) as a diminutive of Thomas.
Notable namesakes: a name used for male animals, especially cats; tommy, or Tommy Atkins, slang for a private in the British Army; the feline protaganist of the US cartoon series *Tom and Jerry*, a name also given to a type of cocktail in the USA; the title character of the novel *Uncle Tom's Cabin, or, Life Among the Lowly*, by US writer Harriet Beecher Stowe; Tom Collins, a type of cocktail; tommy bar, a type of lever; Tom Thumb, a tiny hero of English folk legend and also the stage name of the US entertainer Charles Stratton, who exhibited himself in P T Barnum's circus; tom-tom, types of drum; the eponymous hero of the novel *The History of Tom Jones, a Foundling*, by English writer Henry Fielding; the eponymous hero of the novel *The Adventures of Tom Sawyer*, by US writer Mark Twain; the eponymous hero of the novel *Tom Brown's Schooldays*, by English writer Thomas Hughes; the Tommy gun, a popular name for the Thompson sub-machine gun named for its US co-inventor John T Thompson; Tom Stoppard (British playwright); Tom Jones (Welsh singer); Tom Berenger, Tom Hanks and Tom Cruise (US actors); Tommy Hilfiger (US fashion designer).

Tony
Variants and diminutives: Antony, Toni, Tonio.
Meaning: 'flourishing' (Greek) or 'without price' (Latin) as a diminutive of Anthony.
Notable namesakes: the title character of the novel *Tonio Kröger*, by German writer Thomas Mann; Tony Curtis (US actor); Tony Bennett (US musician); Tony Hancock (British comedian); Tony Benn and Tony Blair (British politicians); Tony Cragg (British sculptor).

Torquil
Variants and diminutives: Thor, Thurston, Torcal, Torcul.
Meaning: 'Thor [the Norse god of thunder]' and 'cauldron' (Old Norse).

Townsend
Variants and diminutives: Town, Townend, Townie, Townshend.
Meaning: 'town' and 'end' (Old English); derived from an English family name.

Trahern
Variants and diminutives: Traherne, Tray.
Meaning: 'excellent' and 'iron' (Welsh).
Notable namesakes: a prince of North Wales.

Travis
Variants and diminutives: Traver, Travers, Travus.
Meaning: 'tollgate', 'tollbridge' or 'crossing' (Old French); derived from an English family name.
Notable namesakes: the name of a British rock group.

Tremaine
Variants and diminutives: Tremain, Tremayne, Trey.
Meaning: 'farm' or 'place' and 'of the stone' (Cornish); derived from a Cornish family name, in turn derived from a Cornish place name.

Trevor
Variants and diminutives: Tref, Trefor, Trev, Trevar, Trever.
Meaning: 'village' and 'big' (Welsh); derived from a Welsh family name, in turn derived from two Welsh place names.
Notable namesakes: Trevor Howard (British actor); Trevor MacDonald (British broadcaster); Trevor Baylis (British inventor).

Trey

Variants and diminutives: Tremaine.
Meaning: 'third' (Middle English); 'farm' or 'place' and 'of the stone' (Cornish) as a diminutive of Tremaine.

Tristan

Variants and diminutives: Drest, Driscoll, Durst, Drystan, Tris, Trist, Tristram, Tristrem, Trys, Tryst, Trystan, Trystram.
Meaning: 'noise' or 'tumult' (Celtic) or 'sad' (Old French) as a French, German and Welsh variant of Tristram.
Notable namesakes: the nephew of King Mark of Cornwall and lover of Iseult (or Isolde), an Irish princess in Celtic legend and medieval Arthurian romance, on whose story the German composer Richard Wagner based his opera *Tristan and Isolde*; Tristan da Cunha, an island group in the southern Atlantic Ocean; Tristan Tzara (Romanian poet).

Tristram

Variants and diminutives: Drest, Driscoll, Drust, Drystan, Tris, Trist, Tristan, Tristrem, Tryst, Tryst, Trystan, Trystram.
Meaning: 'noise' or 'tumult' (Celtic) or 'sad' (Old French) as an English variant of Tristan.
Notable namesakes: Sir Tristram of Lyoness, a knight of the Round Table in English writer Sir Thomas Malory's collection of Arthurian romances, *Le Morte d'Arthur*, and in the poems *Tristram of Lyonesse*, by English poet Algernon Swinburne, and *Tristram*, by US poet Edwin Arlington Robinson; the eponymous hero of the novel *The Life and Opinions of Tristram Shandy, Gent*, by Irish writer Laurence Sterne.

Troy

Variants and diminutives: Troilus.
Meaning: 'Troyes' (Old French) when derived from an English and French family name, in turn derived from a French place name; 'son of the footsoldier' (Irish Gaelic). Also a girl's name.
Notable namesakes: an ancient city in Asia Minor that was besieged during the Trojan War; the troy system of units for measuring precious gems and metals.

Tudor

Variants and diminutives: Tewdwr, Theodore, Theodoric, Tudur, Tudyr.
Meaning: 'people' and 'ruler' (Germanic) as a Welsh variant of Theodoric; 'God's gift' (Greek) as a Welsh variant of Theodore; derived from a Welsh family name.
Notable namesakes: the English royal dynasty founded by the Welsh squire Owen Tudor.

Tyler

Variants and diminutives: Tiler, Ty, Tye.
Meaning: 'tiler' or 'tile-maker' (Old English); derived from an English family name.

Tyrone

Variants and diminutives: Ty, Tye, Tyron.
Meaning: 'Eoghan's [or Euen, Eugene, Ewan or Owen's] country' (Irish Gaelic); derived from the name of a county in Northern Ireland.
Notable namesakes: Tyrone Power (two US actors).

Tyson

Variants and diminutives: Tie, Ty, Tye, Tysen, Tysone.
Meaning: 'firebrand' (Old French); derived from an English family name. Also a girl's name.

Udell

Variants and diminutives: Del, Dell, Udale, Udall.
Meaning: 'yew' and 'valley' (Old English); derived from an English family name, in turn derived from an English place name.

Ulim

Variants and diminutives: Ulem.
Meaning: 'wise' or 'learned' (Arabic). A male version of Ulima.

Ulric

Variants and diminutives: Alaric, Ric, Rich, Richie, Richy, Rick, Ricki, Rickie, Ricky, Ulf, Ulfa, Ull, Ulrich, Ulrick, Ulu, Wolfrid, Wolfrich, Wulfric, Wulfrich.
Meaning: 'wolf' and 'ruler' (Germanic).
Notable namesakes: a number of saints, including Saint Ulric (or Ulrich) of Augsburg; Ulrich Zwingli (Swiss religious reformer); Ulrich Rückriem (German sculptor).

Ultimus

Variants and diminutives: Ult, Ulti, Ultimo, Ulty.
Meaning: 'furthest' or 'last ' (Latin). A male version of Ultima.

Ulysses

Variants and diminutives: Odysseus, Uileos, Ulick, Ulises, Uluxe.
Meaning: uncertain; possibly 'hater' (Greek) as a Latin version of Odysseus.
Notable namesakes: Odysseus, the hero of the epic poem the *Odyssey*, by the Greek poet Homer; Ulysses S Grant (US soldier and president); the title of a novel by Irish writer James Joyce.

Umberto

Variants and diminutives: Bert, Berto, Humbert, Humberto, Umber.
Meaning: 'shade' (Latin); 'earth shadow' (Italian); 'home', 'warrior' or 'giant' and 'bright' (Germanic) as an Italian diminutive of Humberto (Humbert).
Notable namesakes: umber, a type of brown earth that yields a brownish pigment; umber moth, the common name of various genera of moths, such as *Menophra abruptaria*; two kings of Italy; Umberto Boccioni (Italian artist and writer); Umberto Eco (Italian writer and semiologist).

Upton

Meaning: 'upper' and 'farm' or 'place' (Old English); derived from an English family name, in turn derived from a number of English place names.
Notable namesakes: Upton Sinclair (US writer); Upton Park, the home ground of the English football club West Ham United.

Uranus

Variants and diminutives: Ouranos.
Meaning: 'heaven' (Greek); derived from the name of the primeval sky god of Greek mythology. Also a male version of Urania.
Notable namesakes: a planet.

Urban

Variants and diminutives: Orban, Urbain, Urbaine, Urbane, Urbano, Urbanus, Urvan.
Meaning: 'of the city' or 'citizen', 'polite', 'witty' or 'refined' (Latin).
Notable namesakes: seven popes, including Saint Urban (or Urbanus) I.

Uri

Variants and diminutives: Uriah, Urias, Urie, Uriel, Uriano, Yuri.
Meaning: 'light of God' (Hebrew) as a diminutive of Uriah.
Notable namesakes: Uri Geller (Israeli proponent of the paranormal).

Uriah

Variants and diminutives: Uri, Uriano, Urias, Urie, Uriel, Yuri.
Meaning: 'light of God' (Hebrew).
Notable namesakes: Uriah the Hittite, the first husband of Bathsheba in the Old Testament; Uriah Heep, a character in the novel *David Copperfield*, by English writer Charles Dickens, as well as the name of a British rock group.

Urien

Variants and diminutives: Urian, Uren, Uryan, Yurvan.
Meaning: 'town-born' or 'born into privilege' (Old Welsh); derived from a British family name.
Notable namesakes: a Welsh king of Rheged who was reputedly the father of Owain by Morgan Le Fay in Arthurian mythology.

Ursell

Variants and diminutives: Ursel, Urshell.
Meaning: 'little bear' (Latin). Also a male version of
Ursula.

Uzi

Variants and diminutives: Uziel.
Meaning: 'my strength' (Hebrew).
Notable namesakes: a type of sub-machine gun
named for its designer, the Israeli soldier Uziel Gal.

Valentine

Variants and diminutives: Val, Vale, Valentijn,
Valentin, Valentinian, Valentino, Valentinus, Valerius,
Vallie.
Meaning: 'healthy' or 'vigorous' (Latin). Also a girl's
name.
Notable namesakes: Saint Valentine, patron saint of
lovers and greetings, whose feast day, 14 February, is
celebrated by lovers with Valentine cards, hearts and
roses; Valentinian, three Roman emperors; the twin
brother of Orson, who was raised by a bear, in a
medieval story; Valentin Serov (Russian painter);
Valentin Petrovich Katayev (Russian writer); Valentine
Dyall (British actor).

Valerius

Variants and diminutives: Valentine, Valerian, Valerio,
Valery, Vallie.
Meaning: 'to be healthy' or 'to be vigorous' (Latin).
Notable namesakes: 'herb of Valerius', the Latin root
of the name of the *Valeriana* genus of medicinal herbs,
whose common names include valerian and all-heal.

Van

Variants and diminutives: Vander, Vann.
Meaning: 'God has favoured', 'God is gracious' or 'God
is merciful' (Hebrew) as a diminutive of Ivan (John); 'of'
or 'from' (Dutch).
Notable namesakes: Van (George Ivan) Morrison
(Northern Irish musician).

Vance

Variants and diminutives: Fance.
Meaning: 'of the fen' (Old English); derived from an
English family name.
Notable namesakes: Vance Palmer (Australian writer);
Vance Bourjaily (US writer).

Vane

Variants and diminutives: Fane, Van, Vanne, Von.
Meaning: 'sanctuary temple' or 'cloth' (Latin); 'eager'
or 'glad' (Old English) when derived from an English
family name.
Notable namesakes: a flat blade that is a component
of such structures as weather vanes and windmills.

Varden

Variants and diminutives: Vardon, Verdon, Verdin,
Verduin, Verdon, Verdun, Verdyn.
Meaning: 'green' and 'hill' or 'fort' (Old French);
derived from an English family name, in turn derived
from a number of French place names.

Vassily

Variants and diminutives: Basil, Vas, Vasil, Vasile,
Vasilek, Vasili, Vasilis, Vasily, Vassily, Vasya, Vasyl, Vazul,
William.
Meaning: 'kingly' or 'royal' (Greek) or 'war' (Irish
Gaelic) as a Russian variant of Basil; 'will' and 'helmet'
or 'protection' (Germanic) as a Russian variant of
William.
Notable namesakes: Vasily Vereshchagin, Vassily
Surikov and Vasili Kandinsky (Russian artists); Vasily
Aksyonov (Russian writer).

Vaughan

Variants and diminutives: Vaughn, Vaune, Vawn,
Vawne, Von, Vonn, Vonne.
Meaning: 'little' (Old Welsh).

Vere

Meaning: uncertain; possibly 'truthful' (Latin) or 'faith' (Russian) as a male version of Vera; possibly 'a slave born in his [or her] master's house' or 'of spring' (Latin) as a male version of Verna; possibly 'alder tree' (Old French) as a variant of Vernon; derived from a French and English family name.

Vered

Meaning: 'rose' (Hebrew).

Vernon

Variants and diminutives: Lavern, Laverne, Laverno, Varney, Vern, Verne, Vernen, Vernice, Vernin, Vernn, Verrier.
Meaning: 'alder tree' (Old French); derived from an English family name, in turn derived from a number of French place names.
Notable namesakes: Mount Vernon, Virginia, the home of US President George Washington; Vernon Watkins (Welsh poet).

Victor

Variants and diminutives: Vic, Vick, Victoir, Victorino, Victorio, Victuriano, Vika, Viktor, Vince, Vincent, Vitenka, Vitin, Vitka, Vito, Vitor, Vittore, Vittorio, Vitya, Wiktor, Witek.
Meaning: 'victor' (Latin). Also male version of Victoria.
Notable namesakes: three popes; a number of saints; Victor Hugo (French writer); Victor Borissov-Mussatov (Russian artist); Victor Emmanuel, three kings of Italy; Victor de Vasarély (Hungarian artist); Victor Pasmore (British artist); Victor Mature (US actor); Victor Borge (Danish entertainer); Victor Meldrew, the leading character in the British television sitcom *One Foot in the Grave*.

Vince

Variants and diminutives: Victor, Vin, Vincent.
Meaning: 'conqueror' (Latin) as a diminutive of Vincent.

Vincent

Variants and diminutives: Bink, Binkentios, Chenche, Enzo, Kesha, Victor, Vika, Vikent, Vikenti, Vikesha, Vin, Vince, Vincenc, Vincente, Vincenz, Vicenso, Vinci, Vinco, Vine, Vinicent, Vinn, Vinnie, Vinny, Vinsent, Vinson, Vint, Wicek, Wicent, Wicus.
Meaning: 'conqueror' (Latin).
Notable namesakes: a number of saints, including Saint Vincent of Saragossa, patron saint of vintners and vineyards, Saint Vincent Ferrer, patron saint of builders, and Saint Vincent de Paul, patron saint of charitable societies; Vincent of Beauvais (French encyclopaedist); Vincent van Gogh (Dutch artist); Vincent Price (US actor); Vinnie Jones (British footballer and actor).

Virgil

Variants and diminutives: Verge, Vergil, Vergit, Virge, Virgie, Virgilio.
Meaning: uncertain; derived from the Roman family name Vergilius, perhaps in turn derived from the collective name of the Roman goddesses of the Pleiades constellation, the Vergiliae.
Notable namesakes: a Roman poet whose full name was Publius Vergilius Maro; Saint Virgil of Salzburg; Virgil Thomson (US composer).

Vitas

Variants and diminutives: Vida, Vidal, Viel, Vitalis, Vito, Vitus.
Meaning: 'life' (Latin). A male version of Vita.
Notable namesakes: Saint Vitus (or Guy), patron saint of dancers, epileptics and comedians, for whom St Vitus' dance, the disease chorea, was named; Vitas Gerulaitis (US tennis player).

Vivian

Variants and diminutives: Bibiana, Fithian, Phythian, Vivien, Vyvyan.
Meaning: 'living' (Latin); derived fom the Roman family name Vivianus. Also a girl's name (generally Vivien).
Notable namesakes: the eponymous hero of the novel *Vivian Grey*, by British writer and politician Benjamin Disraeli; Vivian Fuchs (British explorer).

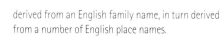

Vladimir

Variants and diminutives: Ladimir, Ladislas, Ladislaw, Laidslaw, Landislaus, Vladi, Vladko, Vladmir, Vlady, Walter.

Meaning: 'prince of the world', 'mighty warrior' or 'army ruler' (Old Slavonic).

Notable namesakes: Saint Vladimir the Great, a prince of Kiev and the first Christian ruler of Russia; a city in central Russia, once the capital of the principality of Vladimir; Vladimir Ilyich Lenin (Soviet leader), after whom the Russian city of Leningrad, formerly – and latterly – St Petersburg (Petrograd), was named; Vladimir Vladimirovich Mayakovsky (Russian writer); Vladimir Vladimirovich Nabokov (Russian-born US writer); Vladimir Tatlin (Russian artist); Vladimir Ashkenazy (Russian-born Icelandic pianist and conductor); Vladimir Putin (Russian president).

Wade

Variants and diminutives: Wadell, Wadsworth.

Meaning: uncertain; possibly derived from the name of a hero of English legend, Wada or Wade; possibly 'at the ford' (Old English); derived from an English family name, in turn derived from an English place name.

Waldemar

Variants and diminutives: Valdemar, Wald, Waldo, Walter.

Meaning: 'power' or 'rule' (Germanic).

Notable namesakes: four kings of Denmark.

Walden

Variants and diminutives: Wald, Waldon.

Meaning: 'Welsh' or 'serfs' and 'valley' (Old English); derived from an English family name, in turn derived from a number of English place names.

Waldo

Variants and diminutives: Wald, Waldemar, Walter.

Meaning: 'power' or 'rule' (Germanic) as a diminutive of Waldemar.

Notable namesakes: Ralph Waldo Emerson (US writer and transcendentalist).

Walker

Variants and diminutives: Wal.

Meaning: 'fuller [of cloth]' (Old English); derived from an English family name.

Notable namesakes: Walker Percy (US writer); Walker Evans (US photographer).

Wallace

Variants and diminutives: Wal, Wall, Wallache, Wallas, Wallie, Wallis, Wally, Walsh, Welch, Welsh.

Meaning: 'Celt', 'Breton', 'Welshman' or 'foreigner' (Old French) as a Scottish variant of Wallis; derived from an English family name.

Notable namesakes: Wallace Stevens, Wallace Irwin and Wallace Stegner (US writers).

Walter

Variants and diminutives: Dima, Dimka, Gauther, Gauthier, Gautier, Gualberto, Gualterio, Gualtiero, Gutierre, Landislaus, Vacys, Valdemar, Valter, Valters, Valtr, Vanda, Vandele, Vladimir, Vladko, Volya, Vova, Vovka, Wal, Wald, Waldemar, Walden, Waldo, Waldron, Walli, Wallie, Wally, Walt, Walther, Waltili, Waltr, Wat, Watkins, Watley, Watly, Watson, Wattie, Watty, Waud, Wilt, Wolli, Wollie, Wolly.

Meaning: 'power' or 'rule' and 'people' or 'army' (Germanic).

Notable namesakes: Walther von der Vogelweide (German *Minnesinger*, or poet); Sir Walter Raleigh (English explorer and adventurer); Sir Walter Scott (Scottish writer); Walt Whitman (US poet); Walter Crane and Walter Sickert (British artists); Walter Gropius (German architect); Walter Savage Landor and Walter De La Mare (English writers); Walt Disney (US animator and film producer); Walter Matthau (US actor); the eponymous hero of the novel *The Secret Life of Walter Mitty*, by US writer James Thurber, whose name is now used to describe a fantasist or daydreamer.

Wapi
Meaning: 'fortunate' (Native American).

Ward
Variants and diminutives: Warde, Warden, Winward, Wordon.
Meaning: 'watchman', 'protector' or 'guard' (Old English); derived from an English family name.
Notable namesakes: various types of administrative district; a hospital or prison division; an open enclosure within a castle; a person under the protection of a guardian or institution.

Warner
Variants and diminutives: Garnier, Warren, Warrener, Werner, Wernher.
Meaning: 'Warin's' or 'protector's' and 'army' or 'people' (Germanic); 'warrener' or 'keeper of the game preserve' (Old French) as a diminutive of Warrener; derived from an English family name.

Warren
Variants and diminutives: Varner, Vaney, Walena, Ware, Waring, Warner, Warrener.
Meaning: 'game preserve', 'wasteland' or 'sandy soil' (Gaulish) when derived from a French and English family name, in turn derived from name of the French town La Varenne; 'to protect' or 'to preserve' (Germanic).
Notable namesakes: a complex of underground tunnels inhabited by rabbits; a preserve dedicated to game animals or birds; a city in the US state of Michigan; Warren Hastings (English administrator of Bengal); Warren Harding (US president); Warren Mitchell (British actor); Warren Beatty (US actor).

Warwick
Variants and diminutives: Wick, Wickie, Wicky.
Meaning: 'dairy farm' and 'belonging to Wary's people', 'at the dam' or 'at the weir' (Old English);

derived from an English family name, in turn derived from two English place names.

Washington
Variants and diminutives: Wash, Washburn.
Meaning: 'Wassa's kin's' and 'farm' or 'place' (Old English); derived from an English family name, in turn derived from two English place names.
Notable namesakes: the US state of Washington, which was named for the US President George Washington, as was Washington, DC, the capital of the USA, along with Mount Washington, a peak in the US state of New Hampshire, and Lake Washington, in the US state of Washington; Washington Irving (US writer).

Wat
Variants and diminutives: Walter, Watly, Wattie, Watty.
Meaning: 'power' or 'rule' and 'people' or 'army' (Germanic) as a diminutive of Walter.
Notable namesakes: Wat Tyler, the leader of the Peasants' Revolt against King Richard II of England.

Wayne
Variants and diminutives: Dwaine, Dwayne, Lewayne, Vaino, Wain, Waine, Wainwright, Wene.
Meaning: 'wain' or 'farm wagon', (Old English); denoting a maker or driver of wagons or carts derived from an English family name.
Notable namesakes: Wayne Thiebaud (US artist); Wayne Sleep (British dancer).

Webster
Variants and diminutives: Web, Webb, Weeb.
Meaning: 'weaver' (Old English); derived from an English family name.

Welby
Variants and diminutives: Welbon, Welburn, Weldon, Welford, Welham.
Meaning: 'spring' and 'farm' (Old Norse and Old English); derived from an English family name, in turn derived from two English place names.

Wendell

Variants and diminutives: Wendayne, Wendel, Wendelin, Wenford, Wentford, Wynn.
Meaning: 'wanderer' (Germanic); derived from an English family name.
Notable namesakes: Wendell Phillips (US anti-slavery reformer); Oliver Wendell Holmes (US writer).

Wesley

Variants and diminutives: Lee, Leigh, Wellesley, Wes, Wesleigh, Wesly, Wessley, West, Westbrook, Westcott, Westleigh, Westley, Weston, Wezley.
Meaning: 'western' and 'wood', 'meadow' or 'clearing' (Old English); derived from an English family name, in turn derived from a number of English place names.
Notable namesakes: Wesley Snipes (US actor).

Wilbert

Variants and diminutives: Bert, Bertie, Berty, Gilbert, Wilber, Wilbur, Wilburt.
Meaning: 'will' and 'bright' (Germanic and Old English); 'pledge' or 'hostage' and 'bright' (Germanic) or 'servant', 'servant of Saint Bridget' or 'servant of Saint Gilbert' (Scots Gaelic) as a variant of Gilbert.

Wilbur

Variants and diminutives: Gilbert, Wilbert, Wilburh, Wilburn, Wilburt, Wiley, Wilford, Wilgburh, Willard, Willmer, Wilmar, Wilmer, Wilt, Wilton, Wilver, Wylie.
Meaning: uncertain; possibly 'will' and 'defence' (Germanic and Old English); possibly derived from the English family name Wildbore, meaning 'wild' and 'boar' (Old English); possibly 'will and 'bright' (Germanic and Old English) as a variant of Wilbert; possibly 'pledge' or 'hostage' and 'bright' (Germanic) or 'servant', 'servant of Saint Bridget' or 'servant of Saint Gilbert' (Scots Gaelic) as a variant of Gilbert.
Notable namesakes: Wilbur Wright (US aviation pioneer); Wilbur Daniel Steele (US writer); Wilbur Smith (Zambian-born writer).

Wilfred

Variants and diminutives: Wilf, Wilfrid, Wilfried, Wilfredo.
Meaning: 'will' and 'peace' (Germanic).

Notable namesakes: Saint Wilfrid (or Wilfrith); the hero of the novel *Ivanhoe*, by Scottish writer Sir Walter Scott; Wilfred Blunt (English writer and explorer); Wilfred Owen (English soldier-poet); Wilfred Thesiger (British explorer and writer); Wilfred Lawson and Wilfred Hyde White (British actors).

Willard

Variants and diminutives: Will, Willie, Willy.
Meaning: 'will' and 'bold' or 'hard' (Old English).
Notable namesakes: Willard Motley (US writer).

William

Variants and diminutives: Bill, Billie, Billy, Giermo, Gigermo, Gijermo, Gillermo, Guglielmo, Guilermon, Guillamus, Guillaume, Guille, Guillelmo, Guillemot, Guillermino, Guillermo, Guillim, Guillo, Guillot, Guirmo, Gullermo, Gwilim, Gwilym, Gwylim, Gwyllim, Ilermo, Liam, Memo, Quillermo, Uilleam, Uilliam, Vas, Vasilak, Vasili, Vasilios, Vasiliy, Vaska, Vassili, Vassily, Vassos, Vasya, Vasyl, Vila, Vilek, Vilem, Vilhelm, Vili, Viliam, Viljo, Vilko, Ville, Vilmos, Vilous, Welfel, Wil, Wile, Wilem, Wilhelm, Will, Willard, Wille, Willem, Willi, Williamson, Willie, Willis, Willmer, Wills, Willy, Wilmar, Wilmer, Wilmot, Wilson, Wolf.
Meaning: 'will' and 'helmet' or 'protection' (Germanic).
Notable namesakes: four kings of England, including William I, 'the Conqueror', and William of Orange, William III; William 'the Bad', King of Sicily; William, 'the Lion', King of Scotland; William Wallace (Scottish nationalist leader); a number of saints, including Saint William Fitzherbert; William of Malmesbury (English historian); William of Wykeham, English politician and founder of the boy's school Winchester College, as well as of New College, Oxford University; William Byrd (English composer); William Shakespeare and William Congreve (English playwrights); William Tell, a legendary Swiss patriot and expert crossbowman; Will Scarlet, one of Robin Hood's band of Merry Men in English folklore; as Willem, three kings of the Netherlands; William Harvey (English physician); William Herschel, the German-born British astronomer who discovered the planet Uranus; as Wilhelm, two emperors of Germany; William Hogarth (English painter and engraver); Williamsburg, a town in the US

state of Virginia; Williams pear, a variety of pear also known as William's Bon Chrétien; William Blake (English artist, poet and mystic); William Makepeace Thackeray (English writer); Wilhelm Busch (German caricaturist and poet); William Wordsworth (English poet); William Morris (English designer, poet and socialist); William Gladstone (British politician); William Bramwell Booth (British founder of the Salvation Army); the schoolboy hero of the 'Just William' series of children's books, by British writer Richmal Crompton; William Faulkner and William Burroughs (US writers); William Hague (British politician); Willem de Kooning (Dutch-born US artist); Willem Dafoe (US actor); Prince William of the United Kingdom.

Willis
Variants and diminutives: William, Wills, Willison.
Meaning: 'son of William'; derived from an English family name.

Willoughby
Variants and diminutives: Will.
Meaning: 'willow trees' and 'farm' (Old English and Old Norse); derived from an English family name, in turn derived from a number of English place names.

Wilmer
Variants and diminutives: Will, William.
Meaning: 'will' and 'fame' (Germanic).

Wilmot
Variants and diminutives: Will, William, Willmot, Willmott, Wilmut.
Meaning: 'will' and 'helmet' or 'protection' (Germanic) as a diminutive of William; derived from an English family name.

Windsor
Variants and diminutives: Win, Winsor.
Meaning: 'windlass' or 'winch' and 'riverbank' (Old English); derived from an English family name (including, since 1917, that of the British royal family), in turn derived from a number of English place names.
Notable namesakes: Windsor Castle, a residence of

the British monarch in the English town of Windsor; a town in the Canadian province of Ontario; Windsor chair and Windsor rocker, types of wooden chair; Windsor knot and Windsor tie, tie-tying styles; Windsor Davies (Welsh actor).

Winfred
Variants and diminutives: Fred, Freddie, Freddy, Win, Winfield, Winford, Winfrid.
Meaning: 'friend' and 'peace' (Old English).
Notable namesakes:
Saint Winfred (or Boniface).

Winston
Variants and diminutives: Win, Winfield, Wingate, Winn, Winnie, Winny, Winslow, Winsten, Winthrop, Winton, Wyn, Wystan, Wynston.
Meaning: 'Win's' or 'friend's' and 'place' or 'farm' (Old English); derived from an English family name, in turn derived from a number of English place names.
Notable namesakes: Winston Churchill (British statesman and writer); Winston-Salem, a tobacco-manufacturing city in the US state of North Carolina; Gary Winston Lineker (British footballer).

Winthrop
Variants and diminutives: Win, Winfield, Wingate, Winnie, Winny, Winslow, Winston, Winton, Wystan.
Meaning: 'Win's' or 'friend's' and 'farm' or 'village' (Old English and Old Norse); derived from an English family name, in turn derived from two English place names.

Wolf
Variants and diminutives: Wilf, Wolfe, Wolfgang, Wolfhart, Wolfie, Wolfy, Wulf.
Meaning: 'wolf' (Old English).
Notable namesakes: Wolfe Tone (Irish nationalist and revolutionary); Wolf Huber (German artist).

Wolfgang
Variants and diminutives: Wolf, Wolfhart, Wolfie,

Wolfy, Wulf.
Meaning: 'wolf' and 'path' (Germanic).
Notable namesakes: Saint Wolfgang, patron saint of people suffering from stomach disorders; Wolfgang Amadeus Mozart (Austrian composer); Johann Wolfgang von Goethe (German writer).

Woodrow

Variants and diminutives: Wood, Woodie, Woodruff, Woodson, Woody.
Meaning: 'wood' and 'lane' or 'row [of cottages]' (Old English); derived from an English family name, in turn derived from a number of English place names.
Notable namesakes: (Thomas) Woodrow Wilson (US president); Woodrow Wyatt (British politician and journalist).

Woody

Variants and diminutives: Wood, Woodie, Woodrow, Woodruff, Woodson..
Meaning: 'wood' and 'lane' or 'row [of cottages]' (Old English) as a diminutive of Woodrow; also an adjective relating to wood.
Notable namesakes: Woody (Woodrow Wilson) Guthrie (US folk musician); Woody (Woodrow) Herman (US clarinetist and band leader); Woody Allen (US film director and actor); Woody Harrelson (US actor).

Wyatt

Variants and diminutives:
Guy, Wayman, Wiatt, Wyat, Wyatte, Wyeth, Wyman.
Meaning: 'wood', 'wide', 'warrior' or 'guide' (Germanic) as a variant of Guy; derived from an English family name.
Notable namesakes: Wyatt Earp (US marshal of the Wild West era).

Wybert

Variants and diminutives: Bert, Bertie, Berty.
Meaning: 'battle' and 'bright' (Old English).

Wyndham

Variants and diminutives: Wyn.
Meaning: 'Wyman's' and 'homestead' or 'settlement' (Old English), Wyman meaning 'battle' and 'protector' (Old English); derived from an English family name, in turn derived from an English place name.
Notable namesakes: Wyndham Lewis and John Wyndham (British writer).

Wynford

Variants and diminutives: Ford, Winford, Wyn.
Meaning: 'white' or 'holy' and 'stream' (Old Welsh); derived from an English family name, in turn derived from an English place name.
Notable namesakes: Wynford Vaughan-Thomas (Welsh broadcaster and writer).

Wynne

Variants and diminutives: Gwyn, Gwynfor, Win, Winn, Winne, Winnie, Winny, Wyn, Wynn.
Meaning: 'fair' (Welsh); 'friend' (Old English); derived from a British family name. Also a girl's name.

Wystan

Variants and diminutives: Wigstan.
Meaning: 'battle' and 'stone' (Old English).
Notable namesakes: Saint Wigstan (or Wystan); W(ystan) H(ugh) Auden (British-born US writer).

X

Xanthus

Variants and diminutives: Zanth, Zanthos.
Meaning: 'yellow' or 'bright' (Greek). A male version of Xantha.
Notable namesakes: a king of the Pelasgians, the son of Triopas and Oreasis, as well as one of the immortal horses of the hero Achilles in Greek mythology; the capital city of the ancient kingdom of Lydia, in Asia Minor.

Xavier

Variants and diminutives: Javier, Saviero, Xaver, Zever.
Meaning: 'new house' (Basque) when derived from a Basque and Spanish family name; 'bright' or 'brilliant' (Arabic). Also a girl's name.
Notable namesakes: Saint Francis Xavier, the 'Apostle of the Indies', a Spanish missionary and founding member of the Jesuits, or Society of Jesus; Xavier Herbert (Austrian writer).

Xenophon

Variants and diminutives: Zeno, Zennie.
Meaning: 'strange' and 'voice' or 'sound' (Greek).
Notable namesakes: a Greek soldier, historian and philosopher.

Xenos

Variants and diminutives: Zeno, Zenos.
Meaning: 'strange' (Greek).

Xerxes

Variants and diminutives: Circs.
Meaning: uncertain; possibly 'ruler' (Persian).
Notable namesakes: Xerxes I, a king of Persia, the son of Darius and Atossa.

Xylon

Variants and diminutives: Xylo.
Meaning: 'wood' (Greek).

Yakir

Variants and diminutives: Yaki.
Meaning: 'precious' or 'beloved' (Hebrew). A male version of Yakira.

Yale

Meaning: 'fertile upland' (Welsh); derived from a Welsh family name.
Notable namesakes: Yale lock, a type of cylinder lock invented by Linus Yale Jr; a university in the US state of Connecticut founded by Elihu Yale.

Yannis

Variants and diminutives: Ioannis, Yanni, John.
Meaning: 'God has favoured', 'God is gracious' or 'God is merciful' (Hebrew) as a Greek variant of John.

Yardley

Variants and diminutives: Lee, Leigh, Yard.
Meaning: 'sticks' and 'wood' or 'clearing' (Old English); derived from an English family name, in turn derived from a number of English place names.

Yarkon

Meaning: 'green' (Hebrew). A male version of Yarkona.

Yasar

Variants and diminutives: Yaser, Yasir, Yasser.
Meaning: 'wealth' (Arabic).
Notable namesakes: Yasser Arafat (Palestinian politician and leader of the Palestine Liberation Organisation).

Yehudi

Variants and diminutives: Judah, Jude, Yehuda, Yehudah.
Meaning: 'Jewish man' (Hebrew); 'praise' (Hebrew) as a variant of Judah or Jude.
Notable namesakes: Yehudi Menuhin (US-born British violinist).

Yigal

Variants and diminutives: Yagel, Yigael, Yigdal.
Meaning: 'God will redeem' (Hebrew).

Yora

Variants and diminutives: Jorah.
Meaning: 'to teach' (Hebrew).

Yorath
Variants and diminutives: Iolo, Iowerth.
Meaning: 'lord' and 'value' (Welsh) as an anglicised version of Iorwerth.

Yorick
Variants and diminutives: George, York, Yorke.
Meaning: 'farmer' (Greek) as a Danish variant of George.
Notable namesakes: a character in William Shakespeare's play *Hamlet*.

Yoshi
Variants and diminutives: Yoshie, Yoshiko, Yoshio, Yoshiyo.
Meaning: 'respectful', 'well-behaved' or 'good' (Japanese). Also a girl's name.

Yukio
Variants and diminutives: Yuki, Yukiko.
Meaning: 'boy of the snow' (Japanese). A male version of Yuki.
Notable namesakes: Yukio Mishima, the pseudonym of the Japanese writer Kimitake Hiraoka.

Yule
Variants and diminutives: Yul, Youl.
Meaning: 'Christmas' or 'yuletide' (Old English), although the original yule referred to a Norse pagan feast rather than a Christian one.

Yuma
Meaning: 'son of the chief' (Native American).

Yuri
Variants and diminutives: George, Yura, Yurchik, Yuri, Yurik, Yurko, Yusha.
Meaning: 'farmer' (Greek) as a Russian variant of George.
Notable namesakes: Yuri Andropov (Soviet politician); Yuri Gagarin (Russian cosmonaut).

Yusef
Variants and diminutives: Joseph, Yousef, Yusif, Yussuf, Yusuf.

Meaning: 'God will increase' (Hebrew) as an Arabic variant of Joseph.

Yves
Variants and diminutives: Evan, Ives, Ivo, John.
Meaning: 'yew' or 'small archer' (Germanic) as a French variant of Ivo; 'God has favoured', 'God is gracious' or 'God is merciful' (Hebrew) as a French variant of John.
Notable namesakes: Saint Yves (or Ives) of Brittany, patron saint of lawyers and judges; Yves Klein (French artist); Yves Saint-Laurent (French fashion designer).

Zacchaeus
Variants and diminutives: Zacc, Zach, Zachariah, Zacharias, Zacharie, Zachary, Zack, Zak, Zakarias, Zecharia, Zecharia, Zecharias, Zeke.
Meaning: uncertain; possibly 'pure' (Aramaic); possibly 'God has remembered' (Hebrew) as a variant of Zachariah.
Notable namesakes: a tax collector in the New Testament.

Zachariah
Variants and diminutives: Benzecry, Sachar, Sacharja, Sakari, Sakarias, Sakarja, Zacaria, Zacarias, Zaccaria, Zacchaeus, Zach, Zacharia, Zacharias, Zacharie, Zachary, Zack, Zak, Zakarias, Zakhar, Zako, Zakris, Zecharia, Zechariah, Zecharias, Zeke.
Meaning: 'God has remembered' (Hebrew).
Notable namesakes: a king of Israel, sometimes also called Zechariah, in the Old Testament.

Zacharias
Variants and diminutives: Benzecry, Sachar, Sacharja, Sakari, Sakarias, Sakarja, Zacaria, Zacarias, Zaccaria, Zacchaeus, Zach, Zacharia, Zachariah, Zacharie,

Zachary, Zack, Zak, Zakarias, Zakhar, Zako, Zakris, Zecharia, Zechariah, Zecharias, Zeke.
Meaning: 'God has remembered' (Hebrew) as a variant of Zachariah.
Notable namesakes: the father of John the Baptist, sometimes also called Zachary or Zechariah, in the New Testament; Zacharias Werner (German playwright).

Zachary

Variants and diminutives: Benzecry, Sachar, Sacharja, Sakari, Sakarias, Sakarja, Zacaria, Zacarias, Zaccaria, Zacchaeus, Zach, Zacharia, Zachariah, Zacharias, Zacharie, Zack, Zak, Zakarias, Zakhar, Zako, Zakris, Zecharia, Zechariah, Zecharias, Zeke.
Meaning: 'God has remembered' (Hebrew) as a variant of Zachariah.
Notable namesakes: the father of John the Baptist, sometimes also called Zacharias or Zechariah, in the New Testament; Saint Zachary (or Zacharias); Zachary Taylor (US president); Zachary Scott (US actor).

Zahid

Meaning: 'ascetic' (Arabic).

Zahur

Meaning: 'flower' (Swahili – Africa). A male version of Zahara.

Zak

Variants and diminutives: Sachar, Sacharja, Sakari, Sakarias, Sakarja, Zacaria, Zacarias, Zaccaria, Zacchaeus, Zach, Zacharia, Zachariah, Zacharias, Zacharie, Zachary, Zack, Zakarias, Zakhar, Zako, Zakris, Zecharia, Zecharias, Zeke.
Meaning: 'God has remembered' (Hebrew) as a diminutive of Zachariah and its variants; 'laughter' (Hebrew) as a diminutive of Isaac.

Zamir

Variants and diminutives: Samir, Zemer.
Meaning: 'song' or 'bird' (Hebrew); 'entertainment' (Arabic) as a variant of Samir.

Zane

Variants and diminutives: John, Zan.
Meaning: uncertain; possibly 'God has favoured', 'God is gracious' or 'God is merciful' (Hebrew) as a Danish variant of John; possibly derived from a US family name of uncertain meaning.
Notable namesakes: Zane Grey, the US writer of Westerns who, along with his home town of Zanesville, Ohio, was named for his forebear, Ebenezer Zane.

Zared

Meaning: 'ambush' (Hebrew).

Zebedee

Variants and diminutives: Zeb.
Meaning: 'God has given' (Hebrew).
Notable namesakes: the father of the apostles James and John in the New Testament; a character in the British children's animated television series *The Magic Roundabout*.

Zebulun

Variants and diminutives: Zeb, Zebulon, Zev, Zevulum, Zubin.
Meaning: 'to praise' or 'to honour' (Hebrew).
Notable namesakes: a son of Jacob and Leah in the Old Testament.

Zechariah

Variants and diminutives: Zacchaeus, Zachariah, Zacharias, Zachary, Zack, Zak.
Meaning: 'God has remembered' (Hebrew) as a variant of Zachariah.
Notable namesakes: a prophet and a king of Israel, sometimes also called Zachariah, in the Old Testament; the father of John the Baptist, sometimes also called Zacharias or Zachary, in the New Testament.

Zedekiah

Variants and diminutives: Zed.
Meaning: 'God is

righteousness' or 'God is goodness' (Hebrew).
Notable namesakes: the last king of Judah in the Old Testament.

Zeke
Variants and diminutives: Ezekiel, Zacchaeus, Zachariah, Zacharias, Zachary, Zack, Zak.
Meaning: 'shooting star' or 'spark' (Aramaic); 'God give strength' (Hebrew) as a diminutive of Ezekiel; 'God has remembered' (Hebrew) as a diminutive of Zachariah and its variants.

Zeno
Variants and diminutives: Cenon, Zenas, Zenon, Zenus, Zeus, Zewek, Zinon.
Meaning: 'given life by Zeus' (Greek), referring to the supreme god of Greek mythology, whose name means 'shining', 'bright' or 'bright sky', (Greek).
Notable namesakes: Zeno of Citium and Zeno of Elea, Greek philosophers; Saint Zeno of Rome; Saint Zeno, patron saint of fishermen.

Zenos
Variants and diminutives: Zenas, Zeno, Zenon, Zenus, Zeus.
Meaning: 'gift of Zeus' (Greek), referring to the supreme god of Greek mythology, whose name means 'shining', 'bright' or 'bright sky', (Greek).

Zephaniah
Variants and diminutives: Zevadia.
Meaning: 'God has hidden' or 'God has protected' (Hebrew).
Notable namesakes: an Old Testament prophet.

Zephyr
Variants and diminutives: Zephyr, Zephyrinus, Zephyrus.
Meaning: 'the west wind' (Greek); derived from the name of the god of the west wind in Greek mythology.
Notable namesakes: a gentle breeze, as well as various types of delicate fabric; Saint Zephyrinus.

Zeus
Variants and diminutives: Zeno, Zenon, Zenos.
Meaning: 'shining', 'bright' or 'bright sky' (Greek); derived from the name of the supreme god of Greek mythology.

Zev
Variants and diminutives: Seef, Sef, Sif, Zeeb, Zeev.
Meaning: 'wolf' (Hebrew).

Zinan
Meaning: 'second son' (Japanese).

Ziv
Variants and diminutives: Zivi.
Meaning: 'to shine radiantly' (Hebrew). A male version of Ziva.

Ziven
Variants and diminutives: Ziv, Zivon.
Meaning: 'vigorous' (Slavic).

Zohar
Meaning: 'brilliant light' (Hebrew).
Notable namesakes: a mystical Hebrew commentary on sections of the Pentateuch and the Hagiographa.

Girls' Names

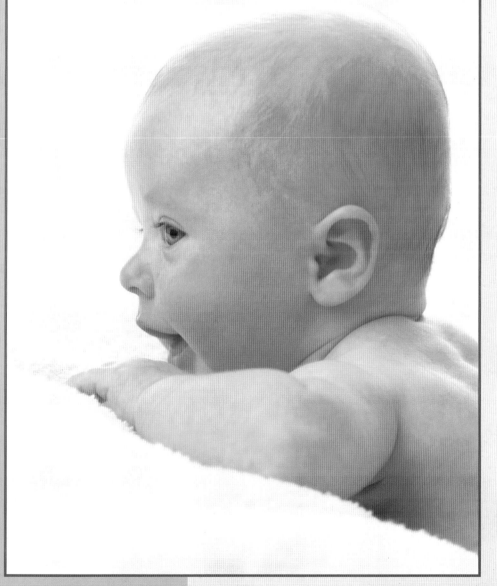

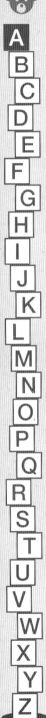

Abigail

Variants and diminutives: Abagael, Abagail, Abagil, Abaigeal, Abbe, Abbey, Abbie, Abby, Abigael, Gael, Gail, Gayle.
Meaning: 'my father rejoices' or 'source of joy' (Hebrew).
Notable namesakes: the wife of Nabal and later King David in the Old Testament; the lady's maid in Francis Beaumont and John Fletcher's play *The Scornful Ladie*, hence, since the 18th century, the generic name for a female servant or handmaid; Abigail Smith, wife of the US President John Adams.

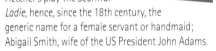

Abiola

Meaning: 'born into nobility' (Yoruban – West Africa).

Abira

Variants and diminutives: Adira, Amiza.
Meaning: 'strong' or 'heroic' (Hebrew).

Acacia

Variants and diminutives: Acaysha, Akaysha, Cacia, Casey, Casia, Kacie, Kasi, Kassie, Kassya.
Meaning: 'thorny' or 'without guile' (Greek).
Notable namesakes: the *Acacia* genus of plans.

Adah

Variants and diminutives: Ada, Adie, Adina, Dena, Dina.
Meaning: 'lovely ornament' (Hebrew); 'noble' (Latin); 'happy' (Old English).
Notable namesakes: the wife of Lamech in the Old Testament; Adah Isaacs (US actress).

Adamina

Variants and diminutives: Adama.
Meaning: 'red' or 'red earth' (Hebrew). A female version of Adam.

Adara

Meaning: 'loveliness' (Greek); 'exalted nobility' (Hebrew); 'virgin' (Arabic).

Adelaide

Variants and diminutives: Ada, Adalheid, Adalia, Addie, Addy, Adela, Adelaida, Adèle, Adelle, Adelheid, Adelia, Adelina, Adeline, Della, Heidi.
Meaning: 'noble' or 'nobility' (Germanic).
Notable namesakes: Queen Adelaide of Britain (wife of William IV and namesake of Adelaide, Australia).

Adeline

Variants and diminutives: Ada, Addie, Addy, Adelin, Adelina, Adelind, Alina, Aline, Alyna, Della, Dellene, Edelin, Edalina, Edeline, Edolina, Lina.
Meaning: 'noble' or 'nobility' (Germanic). A variant of Adelaide.

Adesina

Meaning: 'my arrival opens the way for more' (Yoruba – of West Africa).

Adina

Variants and diminutives: Adie, Ady.
Meaning: 'desire' or 'noble' (Hebrew).
Notable namesakes: the heroine of Gaetano Donizetti's opera *L'Élisir d'amore*.

Aditi

Meaning: 'free abundance' or 'unbounded creativity' (Sanskrit).
Notable namesakes: the mother of the Hindu deities.

Adrienne

Variants and diminutives: Adriana, Adriane, Adrianna, Adrianne, Adrina, Drena, Drina.
Meaning: 'from Adria' (a city in northern Italy) or 'dark one' (Latin). A female version of Adrian.
Notable namesakes: Adrienne Rich (US poet).

Affrica

Variants and diminutives: Africa.
Meaning: 'beloved' and 'free' (Anglo-Saxon).
Notable namesakes: the African continent; Queen Affrica (wife of King Semerled of the Isle of Man, Lord of the Isles).

Agate

Meaning: 'precious stone' (Greek); derived from the gemstone of the same name.

Agatha

Variants and diminutives: Agacia, Agata, Agathe, Aggie, Aggy.
Meaning: 'good' or 'a good woman' (Greek).
Notable namesakes: Saint Agatha, patron saint of bell-founders, firefighters, nurses and women suffering from breast disease; Agatha Christie (British crime novelist).

Aglaia

Variants and diminutives: Aglae.
Meaning: 'brilliant' and 'splendour' (Greek).
Notable namesakes: one of the three Graces, or Chantes, in Greek mythology.

Agnes

Variants and diminutives: Aggie, Agna, Agnella, Agnesa, Agneta, Agnette, Annais, Anis, Annice, Annis, Ina, Inez, Nessa, Nessie, Nessy, Nest, Nesta, Senga, Ynes, Ynez.
Meaning: 'pure' or 'chaste' (Greek); 'lamb' (Latin).
Notable namesakes: Saint Agnes, patron saint of girls; Agnès, a naïve character in the play L'École des femmes, by French playwright Molière; the eponymous heroine of the novel Agnes Grey, by English writer Anne Brontë; Agnes Martin (US artist).

Ahimsa

Meaning: 'reverence of harmony' (Hindi).
Notable namesakes: in Hindu belief, the principle of respect for life and peace.

Aida

Variants and diminutives: Iraida, Zaida.
Meaning: 'modesty' (Greek); 'reward' (Arabic); 'to assist' (French); 'happy' (Old English).
Notable namesakes: the heroine of Giuseppe Verdi's opera Aida.

Aiko

Meaning: 'little beloved' (Japanese).

Ailsa

Variants and diminutives: Allile, Elsa.
Meaning: uncertain; derived from the Scottish island Ailsa Craig.

Aine

Variants and diminutives: Aithne, Ann, Anne, Annie, Ethne, Hannah.
Meaning: 'brightness', 'splendour', 'delight' or 'little fire' (Irish Gaelic).
Notable namesakes: queen of the fairies of southern Munster in Irish mythology.

Aisha

Variants and diminutives: Aesha, Asha, Ayasha, Ayesha, Aysha.
Meaning: 'woman' (Arabic); 'life' (Swahili).
Notable namesakes: the wife of the Prophet Mohammed; a character in Rider Haggard's novel She ('who must be obeyed').

Aisling

Variants and diminutives: Aislin, Aislinn, Ashlin, Ashling, Islinn.
Meaning: 'vision' or 'dream' (Irish Gaelic).

Aiyana

Meaning: 'eternal little flower' (Native American).
Notable namesakes: a North American flower.

Akako

Meaning: 'red' (Japanese).

Aki

Meaning: 'autumn' (Japanese).

A B C D E F G H I J K L M N O P Q R S T U V W X Y Z

Alamea
Meaning: 'precious' or 'ripe' (Hawaiian).

Alana
Variants and diminutives: Alaina, Alaine, Alane, Alanis, Alanna, Alayne, Alina, Allanna, Alannah, Lana, Lane.
Meaning: 'rock' (Breton), 'harmony' (Celtic), 'good-looking' or 'cheerful' (Irish Gaelic) as a female version of Alan; 'child' or 'darling' (Irish Gaelic); 'an offering' or 'light' (Hawaiian).
Notable namesakes: Alanis Morissette (US musician).

Alaula
Meaning: 'light of the dawn' or 'the sunset's glow' (Hawaiian). Also a boy's name.

Alberta
Variants and diminutives: Alba, Albertha, Albertina, Albertine, Albertyna, Ali, Alli, Allie, Alverta, Auberta, Berta, Berti,.Berty, Elba, Elberta, Elbertina, Elbertine, Elbi, Elbie, Elby, Elverta.
Meaning: 'noble' and 'notable' or 'brilliant' (Old English). A female version of Albert.
Notable namesakes: Princess (Louise) Alberta, daughter of Queen Victoria of Great Britain and Prince Albert, for whom the Canadian province of Alberta was named.

Albina
Variants and diminutives: Alba, Albigna, Albinia, Albinka, Alva, Alvina, Alvinia, Alwine, Aubine, Bina.
Meaning: 'white' (Latin). A female version of Albin.

Alcina
Variants and diminutives: Alcie, Alcine, Alcinia, Alzina, Elsie.
Meaning: 'strong-willed' (Greek). A female version of Alcander.
Notable namesakes: the sister of Morgan Le Fay and King Arthur's half-sister; a fairy in poems by Italian poets Matteo Maria Boiardo (*Orlando Innamorato*) and Lodovico Ariosto (*Orlando Furioso*).

Alcyone
Variants and diminutives: Halcyone.
Meaning: 'sea' and 'I am pregnant' (Greek).
Notable namesakes: the star that shines the brightest in the Pleiades, in the constellation of Taurus; the daughter of Aeolus, King of Thessaly, and wife of Ceyx in Greek mythology.

Alda
Variants and diminutives: Aldabella, Aldas, Aldina, Aldine, Aldis, Aldona, Aldya, Aldyne, Aldys, Aude, Auld.
Meaning: 'old and wise' (Germanic). A female version of Aldous.

Aldith
Variants and diminutives: Adelid, Aethelgith, Aild, Ailith, Alda, Aldis, Alditha.
Meaning: 'old or 'experienced' and 'battle' (Old English).

Alethea
Variants and diminutives: Alatheia, Aletea, Aletha, Aletheia, Alethia, Aletta, Alithia, Allathea, Letitia, Letty.
Meaning: 'truth' (Greek).

Alexandra
Variants and diminutives: Al, Alejandra, Alejandrina, Alejo, Aleksandrina, Alessandra, Alex, Alexa, Alexandria, Alexandrina, Alexandrine, Alexia, Alexina, Alexis, Alescha, Ali, Alisaundre, Alix, Lexie, Lexine, Lexy, Lysandra, Sacha, Sandie, Sandra, Sandy, Sondra, Zandra.
Meaning: 'defender of men' or 'warrior' (Greek). A female version of Alexander.
Notable namesakes: Queen Alexandra of Britain (wife of Edward VII); Empress Alexandra of Russia (wife of Tsar Nicholas II), who was murdered during the Russian Revolution.

Alfreda
Variants and diminutives: Aelfreda, Al, Albreda, Alfie, Alfy, Elfreda, Elfrieda, Elfrida, Freda, Freddie, Freddy, Frieda.
Meaning: 'elf' or 'good' and 'counsel' (Old English). A female version of Alfred.

Alice

Variants and diminutives: Al, Ali, Alicia, Allie, Allis, Alisa, Alise, Alison, Alissa, Alix, Allison, Ally, Alyce, Alys, Alyssa, Elsa, Lissie, Lissy.

Meaning: 'truthful' (Greek); 'noble' or 'nobility' (Germanic) as a variant of Adelaide.

Notable namesakes: English writer Lewis Carroll's heroine in the children's books *Alice's Adventures in Wonderland* and *Through the Looking Glass,* named for Alice Liddell; the eponymous heroine of the novel *Alice Adams,* by US writer Booth Tarkington; Alice Thompson Meynell (English writer); Alicia Markova (British ballerina); Alice B Toklas, the companion of the US writer Gertrude Stein, who was the actual author of *The Autobiography of Alice B Toklas;* Alice Munro (Canadian writer); Alice Walker (US writer); Alice Neel (US painter).

Alida

Variants and diminutives: Aleda, Aleta, Aletta, Alette, Alidia, Alidita, Alita, Elida, Elita, Leda, Leeta, Lita, Oleda, Oleta.

Meaning: 'small winged one' (Latin); 'noble' (Spanish).

Notable namesakes: a Greek city in Asia Minor noted for its elegant clothes.

Alima

Meaning: 'expert in dancing and music-making' or 'sea maiden' (Arabic).

Alina

Variants and diminutives: Aleen, Aleena, Aleene, Alena, Alene, Aline, Alya, Lina.

Meaning: 'noble' (Arabic); 'small noble one' (Germanic); 'fair' (Celtic); 'bright' or 'lovely' (Slavic).

Alison

Variants and diminutives: Al, Ali, Alice, Alicia, Allie, Allis, Alisa, Alise, Alissa, Alix, Allison, Ally, Alyce, Alys, Alyssa, Elsa, Lissie, Lissy.

Meaning: 'truthful' (Greek) or 'noble' or 'nobility' (Germanic) as a variant of Alice.

Notable namesakes: Alison Lurie (US writer); Alison Wilding (British sculptor).

Allegra

Meaning: 'cheerful', 'joyful' or 'lively' (Italian).

Notable namesakes: a musical instruction.

Alma

Meaning: 'maiden' (Hebrew); 'caring' or 'kind' (Latin); 'soul' (Italian); 'apple' (Turkish).

Notable namesakes: *Alma Mater* ('bounteous mother'), a name given to the Roman nature goddess Ceres, now used to denote educational establishments; the Crimean War's battle of Alma (1854), fought at the river Alma; Alma Thomas (US artist).

Almira

Meaning: 'princess' or 'unquestioning truth' (Arabic); 'basket for clothes' (Hindi).

Aloha

Meaning: a word used to convey warmth when greeting and parting (Hawaiian).

Alphonsine

Variants and diminutives: Alfonsina, Alphonsina.

Meaning: 'noble' and 'ready' (Germanic). A female version of Alphonse.

Altair

Meaning: 'bird' (Arabic). Also a boy's name.

Notable namesakes: the star that shines the brightest in the constellation of Aquila (the Latin for 'eagle').

Althea

Meaning: 'wholesome', 'good' or 'to heal' (Greek).

Notable namesakes: the mother of Meleager in Greek mythology; *Althaea officinalis,* the name of the curative marshmallow plant; *To Althea from Prison,* the title of a poem by English poet Richard Lovelace.

Alyssum

Variants and diminutives: Alison, Alissa, Ilyssa, Lyssa.
Meaning: 'sensible' (Greek).
Notable namesakes: *Allysum*, a herb once thought to cure rabies and other forms of madness.

Amabel

Variants and diminutives: Amabil, Amiable, Bel, Bell, Belle, Annabel, Annabella, Annabelle, Arabella, Mabel, Mabella, Mabelle, Mable.
Meaning: 'lovable' (Latin).

Amalia

Variants and diminutives: Amaliah, Amalthea, Amelia.
Meaning: 'God's labour' (Hebrew); 'hard-working' (Latin).

Amanda

Variants and diminutives: Amandine, Amata, Manda, Mandi, Mandie, Mandy.
Meaning: 'lovable' or 'fit to be loved' (Latin).
Notable namesakes: characters in plays by British playwrights Colley Cibber (*Love's Last Shift*) and Noël Coward (*Private Lives*); Amanda Donahoe (British actress).

Amaryllis

Meaning: 'I sparkle' (Greek); often used to describe country girls in classical poetry.
Notable namesakes: the belladonna lily (*Amaryllis belladona*).

Amber

Variants and diminutives: Amberlea, Amberlee, Amberly, Ambur, Amby.
Meaning: 'jewel' (Arabic); 'fierce' (Old French); derived from the decorative resin of the same name.

Amelia

Variants and diminutives: Amali, Amalia, Amalie, Amelina, Emilia, Emily, Millie, Milly.
Meaning: 'working hard' (Latin).
Notable namesakes: the heroine of Henry Fielding's eponymous novel; Amelia Earhart (US aviator).

Aminta

Variants and diminutives: Amynta, Arminta, Minty.
Meaning: uncertain; possibly coined by Italian writer Torquato Tasso for the title of his eponymous play; possibly derived from Greek and Latin words for 'protector'.

Amira

Meaning: 'utterance' (Hebrew); 'princess' (Arabic).

Amy

Variants and diminutives: Aimée, Amata, Ami, Amice, Amie, Amicia, Esme, Esmee, Ismay.
Meaning: 'beloved' (French).
Notable namesakes: characters in *Kenilworth*, by the Scottish writer Sir Walter Scott, *Little Dorrit*, by the English writer Charles Dickens, and *Little Women*, by the US author Louisa M Alcott; Amy Lowell (US writer); Amy Tan (Chinese-American writer).

Ananda

Meaning: 'joy' (Sanskrit); 'bliss' (Hindi).
Notable namesakes: a cousin and disciple of Buddha.

Anastasia

Variants and diminutives: Anastace, Anastice, Anastasie, Anastassia, Anastatia, Anstey, Anstice, Anya, Asia, Nastassia, Nastassja, Nastasya, Natia, Nestia, Stacey, Stacie, Stacy, Stasa, Stasya, Tansy, Tasia, Tasya.
Meaning: 'resurrection' or 'awakening' (Greek).
Notable namesakes: Saint Anastasia; Grand Duchess Anastasia, the daughter of Tsar Nicholas II, who was murdered during the Russian Revolution.

Andrea

Variants and diminutives: Aindrea, Anndee, Andie, Andra, Andreanna, Andrée, Andria, Andy.
Meaning: 'manly' (Greek) the female version of Andreas (Andrew).

Andromache

Variants and diminutives: Andromaque
Meaning: 'she who fights men' (Greek).
Notable namesakes: the wife of Hector in Greek mythology, whose story is told in *The Iliad*, by the Greek poet Homer, and in the plays *Andromache*, by the Greek playwright Euripedes, and *Andromaque*, by the French playwright Jean Racine.

Andromeda

Meaning: 'ruler of men' (Greek).
Notable namesakes: the daughter of Cepheus and Cassiopeia and wife of Perseus in Greek mythology; the title of a poem by English writer Charles Kingsley.

Anemone

Meaning: 'windflower' (Greek).
Notable namesakes: the *Anemone* flower genus, named both for a nymph transformed into this bloom and the flower that sprang from the blood of Adonis in Greek mythology.

Angela

Variants and diminutives: Angel, Angelina, Angeline, Angie, Anjela, Anjelika.
Meaning: 'messenger' (Greek). A female version of Angel.
Notable namesakes: Saint Angela Merici, who founded the Ursuline order of nuns; Angela Lansbury (US actress).

Angelica

Variants and diminutives: Angelique, Angie, Anjelica.
Meaning: 'angelic' (Latin).
Notable namesakes: the *Angelica* genus of curative herbs; the heroine of the poems by Italian poets Matteo Maria Boiardo (*Orlando Innamorato*) and Lodovico Ariosto (*Orlando Furioso*); a leading character in the play *Love for Love*, by English playwright William Congreve; 'the fairest of her sex' in John Milton's poem *Paradise Regained*; Angelica Kauffmann (Swiss artist); Anjelica Huston (US actress).

Angharad

Variants and diminutives: Angahard.
Meaning: 'beloved' or 'without reproach' (Welsh).
Notable namesakes: a character in *The Mabinogion*, a collection of medieval Welsh folk tales; Angharad Rees (Welsh actress).

Anika

Variants and diminutives: Anneka, Annika.
Meaning: 'sweet face' (Hausa). Also a variant of Anna.

Anita

Meaning: 'little Ann' (Spanish).
Notable namesakes: Anita Loos (US writer); Anita Ekberg (Scandinavian actress); Anita Desai (Indian writer).

Anna

Variants and diminutives: Aine, Anika, Ann, Anne, Anneka, Annette, Annie, Annika, Anita, Anoushka, Anya, Hannah, Nan, Nancy, Nanette, Nannie, Nanny, Nina.
Meaning: 'I have been favoured (by God)' (Hebrew). A variant of Hannah.
Notable namesakes: Saint Anne, the mother of the Virgin Mary in the New Testament and patron saint of women, pregnancy, childbirth and Canada; Anne Hathaway, the wife of English playwright William Shakespeare; Anne Boleyn and Anne of Cleves, queens of England as wives of King Henry VIII; Queen Anne of Great Britain; Ann Lee (English-born founder of the American society of Shakers); Anne Brontë (English writer); the eponymous heroine of the novel *Anna Karenina*, by Russian writer Leo Tolstoy; Annie Oakley (US marksperson); Annie Besant (English Theosophist); Anna Livia Plurabelle, the heroine of novel *Finnegans Wake*, by Irish writer James Joyce; Anna Pavlova (Russian ballerina); the eponymous heroine of the novel *Anna of the Five Towns*, by English writer Arnold Bennett; the eponymous heroine of the children's book *Anne of Green Gables*, by Canadian writer L M Montgomery; the eponymous heroine of the novel *Ann Veronica*, by English writer H G Wells; the eponymous heroine of the play *Anna Christie*, by US playwright Eugene O'Neill; the eponymous heroine of the poem *Little Orphan Annie*, by US writer James Whitcomb Riley, on which US cartoonist Harold Gray

based his cartoon-strip character; Anne Frank (Dutch–Jewish diarist); Anna Akhmatova (Russian poet); Princess Anne of the United Kingdom; Anne Robinson (British television presenter); Anna Friel (British actress).

Annabella

Variants and diminutives: Anabel, Annabel, Annabelle, Annaple, Barabel, Bel, Bell, Bella, Belle.
Meaning: Anna: 'I have been favoured (by God)' (Hebrew); -bella: 'beautiful' (Italian). Possibly also a variant of Amabel.
Notable namesakes: Annabel Drummond, the mother of King James I of Scotland; *Annabel Lee*, the title of a poem by US writer Edgar Allan Poe.

Annalisa

Variants and diminutives: Annaliese, Annelies, Anneliese, Annelisa.
Meaning: Anna: 'I have been favoured (by God)' (Hebrew); -lisa (Elizabeth): 'God is perfection', 'God is satisfaction', 'dedicated to God' or 'God's oath' (Hebrew).

Annwyl

Meaning: 'beloved' (Welsh).

Anona

Meaning: 'pineapple' or 'grain harvest' (Latin).

Anselma

Variants and diminutives: Selma, Zelma.
Meaning: 'divine' and 'helmet' (Germanic) or 'related to nobility' (Old French) as a female version of Anselm.

Anthea

Meaning: 'flowery' (Greek).

Antigone

Variants and diminutives: Tiggie, Tiggy.
Meaning: 'contrary-born' (Greek).
Notable namesakes: Antigone, the daughter of Oedipus and Jocasta in Greek mythology; the title of a play by French dramatist Jean Anouilh.

Antoinette

Variants and diminutives: Antonetta, Antonette, Antonietta, Netta, Nettie, Toinetta, Toinette, Toni.
Meaning: 'flourishing' (Greek); 'without price' (Latin); derived from the Roman family name Antonius. A female version of Anthony.
Notable namesakes: Queen Marie Antoinette, wife of Louis XVI, guillotined during the French Revolution.

Antonia

Variants and diminutives: Toni, Tonia, Tonya.
Meaning: 'flourishing' (Greek); 'without price' (Latin); derived from the Roman family name Antonius. A female version of Anthony.
Notable namesakes: Antonia Shimerda, the heroine of the novel *My Antonia*, by US writer Willa Cather; Antonia White and Antonia Fraser (English writers).

Anwen

Meaning: 'very beautiful' (Welsh).

Anzu

Meaning: 'apricot' (Japanese).

Aphra

Variants and diminutives: Affery, Afra.
Meaning: 'dust' (Hebrew).
Notable namesakes: Aphra Behn (English playwright and novelist).

Aphrodite

Meaning: 'sea foam' or 'foam-born' (Greek).
Notable namesakes: the Greek goddess of love, fertility and beauty.

Apollonia

Variants and diminutives: Appolina, Appoline.
Meaning: 'of Apollo' (Greek); 'to push back' or 'destroy' (Greek) as a female version of Apollo.
Notable namesakes: Saint Apollonia, patron saint of toothache-sufferers and dentists.

April

Variants and diminutives: Aprilette, Aprille, Averil, Averyl, Avril.

Meaning: 'to open' (Latin); derived from the name of the fourth month, April.

Arabella
Variants and diminutives: Amabel, Annabel, Ara, Arabel, Arabela, Arabelle, Arbela, Arbell, Bella, Belle.
Meaning: Ara: 'altar', 'obliging' or 'ceding to prayers' (Latin); 'eagle' (Germanic); -bella: 'beautiful' (Italian).
Notable namesakes: Lady Arabella Stuart, King James VI of Scotland's cousin; Arabella Fermor, to whom Alexander Pope's poem *The Rape of the Lock* was dedicated.

Araminta
Variants and diminutives: Minty.
Meaning: coined by English playwright Sir John Vanbrugh for a character in *The Confederacy* (possibly derived from Torquato Tasso's play *Aminta*).

Aranrhod
Variants and diminutives: Arianrhod.
Meaning: 'silver coin' or 'silver wheel' (Welsh).

Aretha
Variants and diminutives: Areta, Aretta, Arette.
Meaning: 'virtue' or 'best' (Greek).
Notable namesakes: Aretha Franklin (US singer).

Aria
Meaning: 'melody' (Latin).
Notable namesakes: a solo song sung in opera.

Ariadne
Variants and diminutives: Ariane, Arianna, Arianne.
Meaning: 'very sacred', 'to delight' or 'very pure' (Greek).
Notable namesakes: the daughter of King Minos of Crete, who helped Theseus escape the Minotaur's labyrinth, and the wife of Dionysus in Greek mythology on whose story the German composer Richard Strauss based his opera *Ariadne auf Naxos*.

Arianwen
Variants and diminutives: Argenta, Ariana.
Meaning: 'silver, beautiful and blessed' (Welsh).

Ariel
Variants and diminutives: Ariela, Ariella, Arielle.
Meaning: 'hearth of the altar' or 'lion of the earth or God' (Hebrew). Also a boy's name.
Notable namesakes: an air spirit in William Shakespeare's play *The Tempest*; the title of an essay by Uruguayan essayist José Enrique Rodó; the title of a collection of poems by US poet Sylvia Plath.

Arista
Meaning: 'best' (Greek); 'grain harvest' (Latin). A female version of Aristo.

Arline
Variants and diminutives: Aline, Arleen, Arlene, Lene, Lena, Lina.
Meaning: uncertain; possibly 'man' or 'free man' (Germanic) when derived from Karolina (Caroline), a Hungarian female version of Karl (Charles); coined by Irish composer Michael Balfe for a character in his opera *The Bohemian Girl*.

Armina
Variants and diminutives: Armine, Arminel.
Meaning: 'army' and 'man' (Germanic). A female version of Herman.

Artemis
Variants and diminutives: Arta, Arte, Artema, Artamas, Artemisa, Artemisia.
Meaning: 'strong-limbed', 'she who cuts up' or 'high law-giver' (Greek).
Notable namesakes: the goddess of the moon, hunt and chastity in Greek mythology; Artemisia Gentileschi (Italian artist).

Asha
Meaning: 'woman' (Arabic); 'life' (Swahili).

Asoka
Variants and diminutives: Ashok, Ashoka.
Meaning: 'the flower that doesn't sorrow' (Hindi).

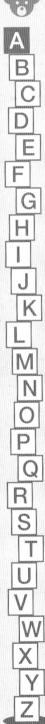

Aspasia

Variants and diminutives: Spase, Spasia.
Meaning: 'welcome' (Greek).
Notable namesakes: the cultivated Milesian mistress of the Athenian statesman Pericles; the heroine of Francis Beaumont and John Fletcher's play *The Maid's Tragedy*.

Astra

Variants and diminutives: Asta, Astera, Asteria, Astra, Astrea, Esther, Hester.
Meaning: 'of the stars' (Latin).

Astrid

Variants and diminutives: Asta, Astrud, Astyr.
Meaning: 'divine' and 'beauty' or 'strength' (Old Norse).

Atalanta

Meaning: 'full of joy' or 'of equal weight' (Greek).
Notable namesakes: a huntress and champion runner in Greek mythology, on whom English poet Algernon Charles Swinburne based his dramatic poem *Atalanta in Calydon*.

Atara

Variants and diminutives: Ataret.
Meaning: 'crown' (Hebrew).
Notable namesakes: a wife of Jerahmeel in the Old Testament.

Athena

Variants and diminutives: Athene.
Meaning: 'unnursed' or 'immortal' (Greek).
Notable namesakes: the Greek goddess of wisdom, arts and crafts and war for whom the Greek capital city, Athens, was named.

Atida

Meaning: 'the future' (Hebrew).

Aude

Meaning: 'blessed' (Gaelic).
Notable namesakes: Aude the Fair, a heroine of the romance *The Song of Roland*.

Audrey

Variants and diminutives: Aude, Audey, Audra, Audree, Audrie, Ethel, Etheldreda.
Meaning: 'noble' and 'strength' (Old English). A variant of Etheldreda.
Notable namesakes: Saint Audrey (Etheldreda), Queen of Northumbria; Audrey Hepburn (British actress).

Augusta

Variants and diminutives: Augustina, Austine, Gus, Gussie, Gusta.
Meaning: 'venerable' or 'great' (Latin). A female variant of Augustus; a title assumed by female members of the Roman imperial family.

Aurelia

Variants and diminutives: Arelia, Aura, Aurea, Aurelie, Aureola, Aureole, Auria, Auriel, Auriol, Auriole, Ora, Oralia, Oralie, Orelie, Oriel, Orielle.
Meaning: 'gold' (Latin); derived from the Roman family name Aurelius.

Aurora

Variants and diminutives: Aurore, Ora, Rora, Rory.
Meaning: 'dawn' (Latin).
Notable namesakes: the Roman goddess of the dawn; heroines of the fairy tale 'The Sleeping Beauty', by Frenchman Charles Perrault, and the poem *Aurora Leigh*, by English poet Elizabeth Barrett Browning.

Ava

Variants and diminutives: Eva, Eve.
Meaning: 'life' (Hebrew). A variant of Eva (Eve).
Notable namesakes: Ava Gardner (US actress).

Avalon

Variants and diminutives: Avallon.
Meaning: 'apple' (Old Welsh).
Notable namesakes: the island to which King Arthur was taken after he was mortally wounded, according

to Arthurian legend.

Averil

Variants and diminutives: Averill, Averyl, Avril, Avrill, Eberhilda, Everild.
Meaning: 'boar' and 'protect' or 'battle' (Old English) when derived from Saint Everild's name. Also a variant of Avril, in turn the French variant of April.
Notable namesakes: Saint Everild.

Aviva

Variants and diminutives: Abibi, Abibiti, Avivah, Avivi, Avivice, Avivit, Avrit.
Meaning: 'springtime' (Hebrew).

Aziza

Variants and diminutives: Asisa.
Meaning: 'beloved' (Arabic); 'precious' (Swahili).

Bakula

Meaning: 'bakula flower' (Hindi).
Notable namesakes: a flower that blooms when misted with wine by a lovely girl in Hindu mythology.

Barbara

Variants and diminutives: Bab, Babara, Babb, Babbie, Babette, Babica, Babie, Babita, Babola, Babs, Bairbre, Bara, Barb, Barba, Barbarella, Barbarette, Barbary, Barbata, Barbe, Barbette, Barbi, Barbie, Barbo, Barbora, Barborka, Barbot, Barbota, Barbra, Barby, Barica, Barra, Barushka, Baubie, Bob, Bobbie, Bobby, Bobs, Vara, Varenka, Varina, Varinka, Varka, Varvara, Varya, Voska.
Meaning: 'foreign' or 'strange' and 'woman' (Greek).
Notable namesakes: Saint Barbara, patron saint of architects, builders, engineers, artillerymen, miners and the prevention of lightning, thunderstorms and fire; the eponymous heroine of the poem *Barbara*

Frietchie, by US poet John Greenleaf Whittier; Barbara Undershaft, the subject of the play *Major Barbara*, by Irish writer George Bernard Shaw; Barbara Pym (British writer); Barbara Woodhouse (British dog trainer); Barbara Hepworth (British sculptor); Barbara Castle (British politician); Barbara Tuchman (US historian); Barbra Streisand (US singer); Barbara Bloom (US artist); Barbara Kingsolver (US writer); the Barbie doll.

Basilia

Variants and diminutives: Basilie, Basilla, Basilly.
Meaning: 'kingly' or 'royal' (Greek); 'war' (Irish Gaelic). A female version of Basil.

Bathsheba

Variants and diminutives: Barsabe, Bathshua, Bathsua, Batsheva, Batsua, Sheba, Sheva.
Meaning: 'daughter of riches', 'daughter of a pledge', 'seventh daughter' or 'voluptuous' (Hebrew).
Notable namesakes: the wife of Uriah, and later King David, and mother of King Solomon in the Old Testament; a character in the poem *Absalom and Achitophel*, by English writer John Dryden; Bathsheba Everdene, a character in English author Thomas Hardy's novel *Far From the Madding Crowd*.

Batya

Variants and diminutives: Basia, Basya, Batia, Bethia, Bithia, Bitya.
Meaning: 'daughter of God' (Hebrew).

Beata

Variants and diminutives: Beate.
Meaning: 'blessed' or 'happy' (Latin).
Notable namesakes: *Beata Virgo*, the 'Blessed Virgin', a name for the Virgin Mary.

Beatrice

Variants and diminutives: Bea, Beah, Beat, Beata, Beate, Beaten, Beathy, Beatie, Beatisa, Beatrica, Beatrika, Beatriks, Beatrisa, Beatrise, Beatrix, Beatriz, Beattie, Beatty, Beautrice, Bebe, Bee, Beitris, Bertrice, Bettris, Bettrys, Betune, Bice, Blaza, Blazena, Ticha, Tris, Trisa, Trissie, Trissy, Trix, Trixie, Trixy.

Meaning: 'bringer of blessings' or 'traveller' (Latin).
Notable namesakes: characters in Italian poet Dante Alighieri's *The Divine Comedy* (Beatrice Portinari was probably Dante's real-life beloved) and William Shakespeare's play *Much Ado About Nothing*; Beatrice Webb (English social reformer and founder of the London School of Economics); Beatrix Potter (English writer and illustrator of children's books); Princess Beatrice of the United Kingdom.

Becky

Variants and diminutives: Becca, Beckie, Becks, Rebecca.
Meaning: 'binding' (Hebrew). A variant of Rebecca.
Notable namesakes: Becky Sharp, a character in *Vanity Fair*, a novel by English author William Makepeace Thackeray; Becky Thatcher, a character in the novel *The Adventures of Tom Sawyer*, by US writer Mark Twain.

Behira

Meaning: 'brilliant' or 'clear' (Hebrew); 'dazzling' (Arabic).

Belinda

Variants and diminutives: Bel, Bell, Bella, Bellalinda, Belle, Bellinda, Bindy, Blenda, Linda, Lindi, Lindie, Lindy, Lynda, Lynde, Velinda.
Meaning: Bel: 'beautiful' (French); -linda: 'snake (Germanic), 'pretty' (Spanish) or 'neat' (Italian).
Notable namesakes: the heroine of the poem *The Rape of the Lock*, by English poet Alexander Pope; the title of a play by English writer A A Milne and of a novel by English writer Hilaire Belloc.

Bella

Variants and diminutives: Amabel, Annabel, Annabella, Arabella, Bel, Bela, Belicia, Belinda, Bell, Belle, Belvia, Isabel, Isabella, Isabelle, Isobel, Rosabella.
Meaning: 'beautiful' (Italian). Also a diminutive of any name ending in '-bella', such as Annabella.
Notable namesakes: Bella Akhmadulina (Russian poet).

Benedicta

Variants and diminutives: Bena, Bendetta, Bendite, Benedetta, Benedictine, Benedikta, Benet, Benetta, Benicia, Benita, Bennedett, Bennedette, Bennet, Bennie, Bennie, Bennitt, Benoite, Betta, Bettina, Binnie, Binny, Dixie.
Meaning: 'blessed' (Latin). A female version of Benedict.

Berengaria

Meaning: 'bear' and 'spear' (Germanic). A female version of Berenger.
Notable namesakes: Berengaria of Navarre, the wife of the English king Richard I, 'the Lionheart'.

Berenice

Variants and diminutives: Bérénice, Bernice, Bernie, Berniece, Bernine, Bernita, Berny, Neigy, Nicia, Nixie, Pherenice, Vernice.
Meaning: 'bringer of victory' (Greek).
Notable namesakes: Bernice, the sister of King Herod Agrippa II in the New Testament; the eponymous queen of Palestine in the plays *Bérénice*, by French playwright Jean Racine, and *Tite et Bérénice*, by French playwright Pierre Corneille; the eponymous leading character of the short story *Berenice*, by US writer Edgar Allan Poe.

Bernardette

Variants and diminutives: Bena, Berna, Bernadina, Bernadine, Bernadot, Bernadotte, Bernandina, Bernandine, Bernada, Bernadina, Bernela, Berneta, Bernetta, Bernette, Berni, Bernie, Bernine, Bernita, Berny, Dina, Ina, Nadette.
Meaning: 'bear' and 'strength' (Germanic). A female version of Bernard.
Notable namesakes: Saint Bernadette (Marie Bernarde Soubirous), the visionary of Lourdes and patron saint of shepherds, who inspired the Austrian writer Franz Werfel to write his novel *Das Lied von Bernadette* (*The Song of Bernadette*).

Bertha

Variants and diminutives: Berta, Berte, Berthe, Bertie, Bertina.

Meaning: 'bright' or 'famous' (Germanic).
Notable namesakes: Berchta (Perchta), an earth and fate goddess of Teutonic mythology; the mother of Charlemagne, the first Holy Roman emperor; Berthe Morisot (French artist); 'Big Bertha', the nickname of the infamous German howitzers used during World War I.

Beryl

Variants and diminutives: Berura, Beruria, Berylla.
Meaning: 'precious gem' (Sanskrit); 'crystal clear' (Arabic); 'sea-green gem' (Greek); derived from the name of the family of precious minerals.
Notable namesakes: Beryl Reid (British actress); Beryl Bainbridge (British writer); Beryl Cook (British artist).

Beth

Variants and diminutives: Bess, Bessie, Bessy, Beta, Bethan, Bethany, Bethesda, Bethia, Bethseda, Elizabeth.
Meaning: 'God gave a pledge', 'house' or 'God's worshipper' (Hebrew); 'life's breath' (Scots Gaelic). Also a diminutive of Elizabeth.
Notable namesakes: a character in the novel *Little Women*, by US author Louisa M Alcott.

Bethan

Variants and diminutives: Beth, Bethany, Elizabeth.
Meaning: 'life' (Scots Gaelic). Also a diminutive of Bethany and Elizabeth.

Bethany

Variants and diminutives: Beth, Bethan.
Meaning: 'house of figs' (Hebrew); 'poor house' (Arabic); derived from a place name in Israel.
Notable namesakes: the village where Lazarus was raised from the dead in the New Testament.

Bette

Variants and diminutives: Betsie, Betsy, Bettie, Bettina, Betty, Elizabeth.
Meaning: 'God is perfection', 'God is satisfaction', 'dedicated to God' or 'God's oath' (Hebrew). A diminutive of Elizabeth.
Notable namesakes: a character in the novel *La Cousine Bette*, by French writer Honoré de Balzac; Betty Grable, Bette Davis and Bette Middler (US actresses).

Bettula

Variants and diminutives: Betula.
Meaning: 'maiden' (Hebrew and Persian).

Beulah

Meaning: 'married' (Hebrew).
Notable namesakes: a name for Israel in the Old Testament; the heavenly land in English author John Bunyan's Christian allegory *The Pilgrim's Progress*.

Beverley

Variants and diminutives: Bev, Beverie, Beverlee, Beverlie, Beverly, Buffy.
Meaning: 'beaver' and 'stream' or 'meadow' (Old English); derived from an English family name, itself derived from a town in Yorkshire. Also a boy's name.

Bianca

Variants and diminutives: Biancha, Blanche.
Meaning: 'white' (Italian).
Notable namesakes: characters in William Shakespeare's plays *Othello* and *The Taming of the Shrew*; Bianca Jagger (Nicaraguan-born socialite and social activist).

Bibi

Meaning: 'bauble' (French); 'lady' (Arabic).

Billie

Meaning: 'will' and 'helmet' or 'protection' (Germanic). A female version of Billy (William).
Notable namesakes: Billie-Jean King (US tennis player).

Bina

Variants and diminutives: Bena, Binah, Buna, Bunie.
Meaning: 'wisdom' (Hebrew); 'dance' (various African languages); 'fruits' (Arapaho).

A B C D E F G H I J K L M N O P Q R S T U V W X Y Z

Blanche

Variants and diminutives: Balaniki, Bela, Bellanca; Bianca, Blanca, Blanch, Blanchi, Blandina, Blanka, Blanquita, Blanshe, Blenda, Branca.
Meaning: 'white' (Old French).
Notable namesakes: Blanche of Castile, wife of King Louis VIII of France and mother of King Louis IX; Blanche DuBois, a leading character in the play *A Streetcar Named Desire*, by US writer Tennessee Williams.

Blodwedd

Variants and diminutives: Blod.
Meaning: 'flower' and 'face' (Welsh).
Notable namesakes: a character created from flowers in Welsh mythology.

Blodwen

Variants and diminutives: Blod.
Meaning: 'flower' and 'white' (Welsh).

Blossom

Variants and diminutives: Blom, Bloom, Blum, Bluma.
Meaning: 'flower' (Old English).

Bo

Variants and diminutives: Bonita.
Meaning: 'precious' (Chinese); 'house-owner' (Old Norse).
Notable namesakes: Bo Derek (US actress).

Bonita

Variants and diminutives: Boni, Bonie, Bonnie, Bonny, Nita.
Meaning: 'pretty' (Spanish).

Bonnie

Variants and diminutives: Bonita, Bonnee, Bonni, Bonny, Bunni, Bunnie, Bunny.
Meaning: 'good' or 'lovely' (Middle English).
Notable namesakes: Bonnie Parker, the American female outlaw whose partner in crime was Clyde Barrow; the nickname of Rhett and Scarlett Butler's daughter in the novel *Gone With the Wind*, by US author Margaret Mitchell; Bonnie Raitt (US musician).

Brandy

Variants and diminutives: Brandee, Brandi, Brandie.
Meaning: 'to burn wine' (Old English); 'brandy wine' (Dutch).

Branwen

Meaning: 'blessed' or 'beautiful' and 'raven' (Welsh).
Notable namesakes: the wife of a king of Ireland in Welsh legends, as recounted in The *Mabinogion*.

Brenda

Meaning: 'prince' or 'royal' (Irish Gaelic) as a female version of Brendan; 'fiery sword' or 'torch' (Old Norse).
Notable namesakes: a heroine in the novel *The Pirate*, by Scottish author Sir Walter Scott.

Brianna

Variants and diminutives: Brenna, Briana.
Meaning: 'strong', 'hill' or 'elevated' (Irish Gaelic) as a female version of Brian.

Bridget

Variants and diminutives: Bedelia, Berek, Beret, Berget, Bergette, Bergit, Biddie, Biddu, Biddy, Bidu, Birget, Birgit, Birgitta, Birte, Breeda, Brid, Bride, Bridgid, Bridgit, Bridie, Bridita, Brietta, Brigada, Briget, Brigette, Bridghde, Brighid, Brigid, Brigida, Brigide, Brigidita, Brigita, Brigit, Brigitta, Brigitte, Brit, Brita, Britt, Bryde, Brydie, Bryga, Brygida, Brygitka, Gidita, Gitta.
Meaning: 'strength' or 'high one' (Irish Gaelic); 'protection' (Scandinavian languages).
Notable namesakes: Brid, or Brighid, the goddess of fire and poetry in Irish mythology; Saint Brigid (Bride) of Ireland, patron saint of dairymaids and scholars; Saint Bridget (Birgitta) of Sweden, patron saint of healers; Brigid Brophy (Anglo-Irish writer); Bridget Riley (British artist); Brigitte Bardot and Britt Ekland (French and Swedish actresses); the eponymous heroine of the novel *Bridget Jones' Diary*, by British writer Helen Fielding, and subsequently also of the film.

Britanny

Variants and diminutives: Brit, Brita, Britany, Britney, Britt, Britta, Brittni.
Meaning: 'Breton' or 'Briton' (Latin); 'the ardent one's child' (Celtic). A female version of Brett.
Notable namesakes: Britney Spears (US singer).

Bronwen

Variants and diminutives: Bron, Bronnie, Bronny, Bronwyn.
Meaning: 'white' and 'breast' (Welsh); 'robust friend' (Middle English).
Notable namesakes: the wife of a king of Ireland in Welsh legend.

Brook

Variants and diminutives: Brooke, Brooks.
Meaning: 'stream' (Old English). Also a boy's name.
Notable namesakes: Brooke Shields (US actress).

Brunella

Variants and diminutives: Brunetta, Nella, Netta.
Meaning: 'brown' or 'like a bear' (Germanic). A female version of Bruno.

Bryony

Variants and diminutives: Briony.
Meaning: uncertain; derived from the name of a climbing plant, *Bryonia cretica*.

Bunty

Variants and diminutives: Buntie.
Meaning: uncertain, probably derived either from the English word 'bunny', denoting a rabbit, or from the traditional English name for a pet lamb.

Cadenza

Variants and diminutives: Cadence, Cadina.
Meaning: 'to fall' (Latin).

Caitlin

Variants and diminutives: Cathleen, Kathleen.
Meaning: 'pure' (Greek). An Irish Gaelic variation of Catherine.

Calandra

Variants and diminutives: Cal, Calander, Calandré, Calandria, Cali, Calie, Calla, Calley, Calli, Callie, Cally, Kalandra, Kali, Kalie, Kalley, Kalli, Kallie, Kally, Kolandra, Landra.
Meaning: 'lark' or 'beauty' (Greek).

Calantha

Variants and diminutives: Cal, Calanthe, Calli, Callie, Cally.
Meaning: 'lovely flower' (Greek).

Calida

Meaning: 'warm' or 'loving' (Spanish).

Calista

Variants and diminutives: Calesta, Calisto, Calla, Calli, Callie, Callista, Cally, Calysta, Kallista.
Meaning: 'most beautiful' (Greek).
Notable namesakes: Calista Flockhart (US actress).

Calliope

Meaning: 'lovely voice' (Greek).
Notable namesakes: the muse of epic poetry and leader of the Muses in Greek mythology.

Callula
Meaning: 'lovely little girl' (Latin).

Calypso
Meaning: 'to cover' or 'to hide' (Greek).
Notable namesakes: in *The Odyssey*, by Greek poet Homer, a sea nymph who confined Odysseus to the island of Ogygia; a West Indian song genre.

Camellia
Variants and diminutives: Cam, Camel, Camille, Cammie, Cammy, Melia, Millie, Milly.
Meaning: derived from the name of the *Camellia* genus of flowering shrubs named for botanist Joseph Kamel.
Notable namesakes: Camille (or Marguerite), the heroine of the play *La Dame aux Camélias*, by French writer Alexandre Dumas.

Camilla
Variants and diminutives: Cam, Cama, Camala, Camel, Cami, Camila, Camille, Cammi, Cammie, Cammy, Kamila, Kamilka, Kamilla, Milla, Milli, Millie, Milly.
Meaning: 'messenger' or 'attendant at ritual' (Latin); derived from the Roman family name Camillus. A female version of Camillus.
Notable namesakes: an attendant of the moon and hunt goddess Diana in Roman mythology and a character in the *Aeneid*, by the Roman poet Virgil; Camille, a sorceress in Arthurian legend; the eponymous heroines of the novels *Camilla*, by French writer Madame D'Arblay and English writer Fanny Burney; Camilla Parker Bowles, companion of Charles, Prince of Wales.

Candice
Variants and diminutives: Candace, Candance, Candase, Candee, Candi, Candida, Candie, Candis, Candy, Candyce, Kandace, Kandee, Kandi, Kandice, Kandie, Kandy.
Meaning: 'to glow white hot' (Greek)or 'white' (Latin) as a variant of Candida.
Notable namesakes: a title used by the queens of Ethiopia; Candice Bergen (US actress).

Candida
Variants and diminutives: Candide, Candee, Candi, Candice, Candie, Candra, Candy, Kandee, Kandi, Kandie, Kandy.
Meaning: 'to glow white hot' (Greek); 'white' (Latin).
Notable namesakes: the eponymous heroine of Irish writer George Bernard Shaw's play *Candida*.

Caprice
Meaning: 'a hedgehog-like head' (Latin); 'fanciful' (Italian and French).

Cara
Variants and diminutives: Carabelle, Carina, Carine, Carita, Carra, Carrie, Kara, Karina, Karine, Karra.
Meaning: 'dear' (Latin and Italian); 'friend' (Irish Gaelic); 'diamond' (Vietnamese).

Cari
Meaning: 'keel' (Latin); 'flowing' (Turkish). Also a diminutive of many girls' names beginning with 'Car-'.

Carla
Variants and diminutives: Arla, Carleen, Carlene, Carley, Carlia, Carli, Carlie, Carlita, Carlotta, Carly, Karla, Karli, Karlie, Karly.
Meaning: 'man' or 'free man' (Germanic) as a female version of Carl (Charles).
Notable namesakes: Carly Simon (US singer-songwriter); Carla Lane (British television scriptwriter).

Carmel
Variants and diminutives: Carma, Carmania, Carmela, Carmelina, Carmelita, Carmelle, Carmen, Carmi, Carmie, Carmine, Carmit, Carmita, Carmiya, Carmy, Kaarmia, Karma, Karmel, Karmela, Karmelit, Karmit, Lita, Melina.
Meaning: 'fertile field' or 'garden' (Hebrew); 'fruit garden' or 'vineyard' (Arabic).
Notable namesakes: Mount Carmel in Israel, where the Carmelite order of friars and nuns was founded; a town in the American state of California.

Carmen
Variants and diminutives: Carma, Carmel, Carmena,

Carmencita, Carmia, Carmine, Carmino, Carmita, Chamain, Charmaine, Charmian, Charmion, Karma, Karmen, Karmia, Karmina, Karmine, Karmita, Mina.
Meaning: 'song' (Latin); 'crimson' (Spanish). Also a variant of Carmel.
Notable namesakes: the eponymous heroine of the novel by French author Prosper Mérimée and the opera by French composer Georges Bizet; Carmen Miranda (Portuguese dancer and singer).

Carol

Variants and diminutives: Carel, Carey, Caro, Carola, Carole, Carolee, Carrie, Carroll, Carry, Caryl, Kalola, Karel, Karol, Karole, Karyl, Sharyl, Sherrie, Sherry, Sherye, Sheryl.
Meaning: 'brave in battle' (Welsh); 'round dance' (Old French); 'man' or 'free man' (Germanic) as a female version of Charles. Also a diminutive of Caroline.
Notable namesakes: Christmas carols; Carole Lombard (US actress); Carole King (US singer-songwriter).

Caroline

Variants and diminutives: Arla, Cara, Carey, Cari, Carla, Carlana, Carleen, Carlen, Carlene, Carlera, Carley, Carli, Carlia, Carlie, Carlin, Carlina, Carline, Carlita, Carlite, Carley, Carlota, Carlotta, Carly, Carlyn, Carlynne, Caro, Carol, Carola, Carole, Caroleen, Carolina, Carolinda, Carolly, Caroly, Carolyn, Caron, Carona, Carri, Carrie, Carroll, Carry, Cary, Caryl, Cassie, Chariena, Charla, Charlayne, Charleen, Charlen, Charlena, Charlene, Charlet, Charline, Charlot, Charlotte, Charo, Cherlene, Ina, Inka, Kari, Karie, Karila, Karla, Karleen, Karlene, Karli, Karlie, Karlinka, Karlita, Karly, Karola, Karole, Karolina, Karoline, Karolinka, Karolyn, Lina, Linchen, Line, Linka, Lola, Lolita, Lolo, Lotchen, Lotta, Sharleen, Sharlene, Sharline, Tota.
Meaning: 'man' or 'free man' (Germanic) as a female version of Charles.
Notable namesakes: Caroline of Brandenburg-Anspach, wife of King George II of Great Britain; the American states North and South Carolina, named for King Charles I of England; Lady Caroline Lamb (English writer); Caroline Norton (English writer); Caroline Gordon (US writer); Princess Caroline of Monaco.

Caron

Variants and diminutives: Carren, Karen.
Meaning: 'pure' (Greek). A variant of Karen (Catherine).

Carys

Variants and diminutives: Caryl, Cerys, Cheryl.
Meaning: 'love' (Welsh).

Casey

Variants and diminutives: Cace, Case, Cassandra, Casi, Casie, Casy, Kace, Kacey, Kaci, Kacie, Kacy, Kase, Kasey, Kasy, KC.
Meaning: 'brave' (Irish Gaelic). Also a boy's name.

Cassandra

Variants and diminutives: Caasi, Casandra, Case, Casey, Cash, Caso, Cass, Cassander, Cassandre, Cassandry, Cassi, Cassie, Casson, Cassy, Kassandra, Sandi, Sandie, Sandra, Sandy.
Meaning: 'ensnarer of men' (Greek).
Notable namesakes: the daughter of Hecuba and King Priam of Troy, whose prophesies were fated not to be believed in Greek mythology, whose name is now used to describe any prophet of doom.

Catherine

Variants and diminutives: Caitlin, Caitlon, Caitria, Caitrin, Caren, Cari, Carin, Carina, Carita, Carolly, Caroly, Caronia, Caryn, Casey, Cass, Cassi, Cassie, Cassy, Casy, Cat, Catalina, Catant, Catarina, Cate, Caterina, Cath, Catha, Catharina, Catharine, Cathe, Cathee, Catheline, Cathi, Cathie, Cathleen, Cathlene, Cathlin, Cathrine, Cathryn, Cathy, Cati, Catie, Caton, Catlin, Catling, Catrin, Catrina, Catriona, Cattie, Caty, Caye, Cayla, Ekaterina, Kaety, Kaisa, Kaki, Kara, Karen, Karena, Karin, Karina, Kasia, Kasienka, Kasin, Kaska, Kassia, Kat, Kata, Katalin, Katarina, Katchen, Kate, Katee, Katelin, Katenka, Katerina, Katerine, Katerinka, Kateryn, Kath, Katha, Katharina, Katharine, Kathchen, Kathe, Katherin, Katherine, Kathi, Kathie,

Kathleen, Kathlene, Kathline, Kathrene, Kathrina, Kathryn, Kathy, Kati, Katica, Katie, Katika, Katina, Katinka, Katja, Katka, Katla, Kato, Katoka, Katri, Katrin, Katrina, Katrine, Katrinka, Katryna, Katsa, Katty, Katus, Katuska, Katy, Katja, Katya, Kay, Kayce, Kaye, Kayla, Kaytlin, Kerry, Ketty, Ketya, Kinny, Kisa, Kiska, Kit, Kitti, Kittie, Kitty, Kofryna, Kolina, Kotinka, Kytte, Rina, Thrine, Treinel, Trina, Trinchen, Trine, Trinette, Trini.

Meaning: 'pure' (Greek).

Notable namesakes: Saint Catherine of Alexandria, for whom the Catherine-wheel firework was named, patron saint of girls, students, philosophers, preachers, nurses and those who work with wheels; Saint Catherine of Bologna, patron saint of art and artists; Saint Catherine of Siena, patron saint of Italy, fire prevention and the Dominican order; Saint Catherine of Sweden, patron saint of warding off miscarriages; Catherine de Medici, wife of King Henri II of France; Catherine of Aragon, Catherine Howard and Catherine Parr, three wives of King Henry VIII of England; Catherine II, 'the Great', Russian empress; Lady Catherine de Bourgh, a character in the novel *Pride and Prejudice*, by English writer Jane Austen; Catherine Barkley, the heroine of the novel *A Farewell to Arms*, by US writer Ernest Hemingway; Katharine Hepburn (US actress); Catherine Deneuve (French actress); Catherine Zeta Jones (Welsh actress).

Catriona

Variants and diminutives: Cat, Catrina, Katrina, Triona.

Meaning: 'pure' (Scots Gaelic). A variant of Catherine.

Cecilia

Variants and diminutives: Cacilia, Cacilie, Cecelia, Cecely, Cecil, Cecile, Cecilie, Cecilla, Cecille, Cecillia, Cecily, Cecilya, Cecyl, Cecyle, Cecylia, Ceil, Cele, Celia, Celie, Ces, Cesia, Chela, Chila, Cicely, Cicily, Ciel, Cile, Cili, Cilka, Cilly, Cis, Ciss, Cissi, Cissie, Cissy, Cycalye, Cycly, Kikelia, Kikilia, Sela, Sely, Sesilia, Sheila, Sile, Sileas, Sis, Sisile, Sisley, Sissela, Sissi, Sissie, Sissy.

Meaning: 'blind' (Latin) or 'sixth' (Welsh) as a female version of Cecil. Also a variant of Celia.

Notable namesakes: Saint Cecilia, patron saint of music and musicians; the eponymous heroine of the novel *Cecilia, or Memoirs of an Heiress*, by English writer Fanny Burney; the subject of a song by US musicians Paul Simon and Art Garfunkel.

Ceinwen

Meaning: 'lovely jewels' (Welsh).

Celeste

Variants and diminutives: Cela, Cele, Celesta, Céleste, Celestia, Celestin, Celestina, Celestine, Celestyn, Celestyna, Celia, Celie, Celina, Celinka, Cesia, Inka, Selinka, Tyna, Tynka.

Meaning: 'celestial' or 'heavenly' (Latin).

Notable namesakes: the 'ghost ship' *Marie Celeste*.

Celia

Variants and diminutives: Caelia, Cecilia, Celie, Celina, Celinda, Selen, Selina, Sheelagh, Sheila, Shelagh, Sile.

Meaning: derived from the Roman family name Caelius, itself possibly meaning 'celestial' or 'heavenly' (Latin). Also a diminutive of Cecilia.

Notable namesakes: the subject of the poem *To Celia*, by English writer Ben Jonson; Caelia, a character in *The Faerie Queen*, by English playwright Sir Edmund Spenser; a character in William Shakespeare's play *As You Like It*; Celia Brooke, a character in the novel *Middlemarch*, by English writer George Eliot; Celia Johnson (British actress).

Celine

Variants and diminutives: Celina, Celinda, Céline, Celinka, Celka, Selen, Selena, Selene, Seline, Selina.

Meaning: 'celestial' or 'heavenly' (Latin).

Notable namesakes: Celine Dion (Canadian singer).

Ceridwen

Meaning: 'beautiful poetry' (Welsh).

Notable namesakes: the goddess of wisdom, poetry and grain in Welsh mythology.

Chandelle
Variants and diminutives: Chan, Chandell, Shan, Shandell, Shandelle.
Meaning: 'candle' (Old French).

Chandra
Variants and diminutives: Chan, Chandra, Chandah, Shan, Shanda, Shandah, Shandra.
Meaning: 'illustrious' or 'like the moon' (Sanskrit).

Chantal
Variants and diminutives: Chantel, Chantele, Chantell, Chantelle, Shantal, Shantalle, Shantel, Shantell, Shantelle.
Meaning: 'to sing' or 'stone' (Old French) when derived from a French family name; 'to sing clearly' (Old French) as a female variant of Chanticleer.
Notable namesakes: Saint Jean de Chantal.

Charity
Variants and diminutives: Carita, Carity, Charis, Charissa, Charita, Charito, Charry, Chattie, Cherry, Karita.
Meaning: 'grace' (Greek); 'kindness' (Latin); 'Christian love' (Old French).
Notable namesakes: Charis, the Greek goddess of grace and beauty described by the Greek poet Homer in *The Iliad*; the Charites, personifications of grace, charm and beauty in Greek mythology; one of the three Christian virtues, the other two being faith and hope, according to the New Testament; a character in the novel *Martin Chuzzlewit*, by English writer Charles Dickens.

Charlotte
Variants and diminutives: Cara, Carla, Carlene, Carli, Carlie, Carlota, Carlotta, Carly, Char, Charley, Charil, Charla, Charlayne, Charleen, Charlen, Charlena, Charlene, Charlet, Charlie, Charline, Charlot, Charlotta, Charlotty, Charly, Charyl, Chattie, Cheryl, Karla, Karlene, Karli, Karlicka, Karlie, Karline, Karlotta, Karlotte, Karly, Lola, Loleta, Loletta, Lolita, Lolotte, Lotta, Lottchen, Lotte, Lotti, Lottie, Lotty, Salote, Sari, Sarlote, Sarolta, Sharleen, Sharlene, Sharline, Sharyl, Sheree, Sheri, Sherisa, Sherissa, Sherri, Sherrie, Sherrill, Sherry, Sherrye, Sheryl, Totly, Totti, Tottie, Totty.
Meaning: 'man' or 'free man' (Germanic) as a female version of Charles.
Notable namesakes: the wife of King George III of Britain, for whom Charlotte, North Carolina, USA, and Charlottetown, Prince Edward Island, Canada, were named; the disgruntled French patriot Charlotte Corday, who dispatched Jean Paul Marat in his bath; the heroine of the play *The Sorrows of the Young Werther*, by German writer Johann Wolfgang von Goethe, whose real-life beloved was another Charlotte, Charlotte von Stein; the eponymous heroine of the novel *Charlotte Temple*, by US writer Susannah Haswell Rowson; Charlotte Brontë (English novelist); the eponymous heroine of the novel *Charlotte Gray*, by British writer Sebastian Faulks; Charlotte Church (Welsh singer).

Charmaine
Variants and diminutives: Carman, Charmain, Charmayne, Charmian, Sharmain, Sharmaine, Sharmayne.
Meaning: 'joy' (Greek); 'song' (Latin).
Notable namesakes: Charmian, a character in William Shakespeare's play *Anthony and Cleopatra*.

Chastity
Meaning: 'pure' or 'chaste' (Latin).
Notable namesakes: Chastity Bono (US gay-rights activist).

Chaya
Variants and diminutives: Kaija.
Meaning: 'life' (Hebrew). A female version of Chaim.

Chelsea
Variants and diminutives: Chelse, Chelsey, Chelsi.
Meaning: 'landing place of chalk' or 'port' (Old English); derived from the name of the London district and football club.
Notable namesakes: Chelsea Clinton (daughter of Bill and Hillary Clinton, US politicians).

Chenoa
Meaning: 'white dove' (Native American).

A
B
C
D
E
F
G
H
I
J
K
L
M
N
O
P
Q
R
S
T
U
V
W
X
Y
Z

Chérie

Variants and diminutives: Ceri, Cher, Cherami, Chere, Cheri, Cherie, Cherrie, Cherry, Chery, Cherye, Cheryl, Cheryle, Cherylie, Sharol, Sher, Sheral, Shere, Sheree, Sherell, Sheri, Sherelle, Sherri, Sherry, Sherye, Sheryl, Sheryle.

Meaning: 'darling' (French).

Notable namesakes: Cher (US singer and actress); Cherie Booth (British lawyer and wife of Tony Blair, British politician).

Cherry

Variants and diminutives: Cerise, Cherie, Chérie, Cheryl, Charity.

Meaning: derived from the Greek, Latin and Old English words for the fruit. Also a diminutive of Charity.

Notable namesakes: the nickname of Charity, a character in the novel *Martin Chuzzlewit*, by English writer Charles Dickens.

Cheryl

Variants and diminutives: Sheryl.

Meaning: uncertain; coined during the twentieth century, possibly by combining Cherry, 'cherry' (Greek, Latin and Old English) and Beryl, 'precious gem' (Sanskrit), 'crystal clear' (Arabic) or 'sea-green gem' (Greek).

Chloë

Variants and diminutives: Clela, Clo, Cloe.

Meaning: 'green' (Hebrew); 'tender green shoot' (Greek).

Notable namesakes: a name of the earth goddess Demeter in Greek mythology; the lover of Daphnis in the prose romance *Daphnis and Chloë*, by Greek writer Longus, on which the French composer Maurice Ravel based his ballet; a character in the novel *Uncle Tom's Cabin*, by US writer Harriet Beecher Stowe.

Christabel

Variants and diminutives: Christa, Christabell, Christabella, Christabelle, Christable, Christey, Christie, Christobelle, Christobella, Christy, Cristemberga, Cristemia, Cristie, Cristy, Bel, Bell, Bell.

Meaning: 'beautiful Christian' (Latin); possibly coined for his poem of the same name by English poet Samuel Taylor Coleridge.

Notable namesakes: Christabel Pankhurst (British suffragette); Christabel Bielenberg (British writer).

Christine

Variants and diminutives: Cairistine, Cairistiona, Cauline, Chris, Chrissie, Chrissy, Christa, Christal, Christeen, Christeena, Christel, Christen, Christi, Christiana, Christiane, Christiania, Christie, Christina, Christy, Chrystal, Chryste, Chrystel, Ciorsdan, Crestienne, Crete, Crissie, Crista, Cristi, Cristiana, Cristin, Cristina, Cristine, Cristiona, Cristy, Crystal, Crystina, Kersti, Khristina, Khristya, Kina, Kirsteen, Kirsten, Kirstin, Kirstie, Kirsto, Kirsty, Kris, Kriska, Kriss, Krissi, Krissie, Krissy, Krista, Kristel, Kristen, Kristi, Kristia, Kristian, Kristin, Kristina, Kristine, Kristinka, Kristin, Krysia, Krysta, Kryska, Krystyna, Krystynka, Stina, Stine, Teenie, Tina, Tinah, Tine, Tiny, Tyna, Xena, Xina.

Meaning: 'Christian' (Latin). A female version of Christian.

Notable namesakes: Christina de Pisan (Italian-born French poet); Queen Christina of Sweden; Christiana, a character in the Christian allegory *The Pilgrim's Progress*, by English writer John Bunyan; Christina Rossetti (English poet); Christina Stead (Australian writer); Chris Evert (US tennis player).

Ciara

Variants and diminutives: Ciar, Keera, Kiera, Kira, Kyara.

Meaning: 'dark' (Irish Gaelic).

Notable namesakes: Saint Ciara.

Cilla

Variants and diminutives: Priscilla.

Meaning: 'of ancient times' (Latin). A diminutive of Priscilla.

Notable namesakes: the sister of King Priam of Troy in Greek mythology; Cilla Black (British singer and television presenter).

Cindy

Variants and diminutives: Cindi, Cyndi, Sindy, Syndi.
Meaning: 'light' (Latin) as a diminutive of Lucinda
(Lucia, in turn a female version of Lucius); possibly also
a diminutive of Cinderella ('little cinder girl') and
Cynthia (of Cynthus', Greek).
Notable namesakes: Cindy Sherman (US artist); the
Sindy doll; Cyndi Lauper (US singer).

Clare

Variants and diminutives: Clara, Claramae, Clair,
Claire, Clairene, Clairene, Clairette, Clareta, Claretha,
Clarette, Clarey, Clari, Claribel, Claribele, Clarabella,
Clarice, Claricia, Clarie, Clarimond, Clarina, Clarinda,
Clarine, Claris, Clarisa, Clariscia, Clarissa, Clarisse,
Clarita, Clarrie, Clarrie, Clarrisse, Clarus, Clary, Clerissa,
Klara, Klarika, Klarissa, Larisa, Sorcha.
Meaning: 'clear', 'bright' or 'famous' (Latin).
Notable namesakes: an Irish county; Claire, the sister
of Sagremor in Arthurian legend; Saint Clare of Assisi,
founder of the Poor Clares, an order of nuns, and
patron saint of television, eye disorders and
embroiders; Clarissa Harlowe, the heroine of the novel
Clarissa, by English writer Samuel Richardson; Clara
Peggotty, a character in the novel *Davd Copperfield*, by
English writer Charles Dickens; Clara Wieck, the pianist
wife of the German composer Robert Schumann; Clare
Boothe Luce (US writer and diplomat); Clarice Cliff
(British pottery designer).

Claudia

Variants and diminutives: Claude, Claudeen,
Claudella, Claudeta, Claudette, Claudi, Claudie,
Claudina, Claudine, Claudita, Clodia, Gladys, Gwladys.
Meaning: 'lame' (Latin), derived from a Roman family
name as a female version of Claude.
Notable namesakes: a friend of Saint Paul in the New
Testament; Claudette Colbert (French-born US
actress); Claudine, the heroine of novels by the French
writer Colette.

Cleantha

Variants and diminutives: Cleanthe, Cliantha.
Meaning: 'flower of glory' (Greek).

Clementine

Variants and diminutives: Clem, Clemence, Clemency,
Clemense, Clementia, Clementina, Clemmie, Clemmy,
Klementine, Klementina, Tina.
Meaning: 'merciful' or 'mild' (Latin). A female version
of Clement.
Notable namesakes: Clemence, the goddess of mercy
in Roman mythology; the citrus fruit; the American
song 'Oh my Darling Clementine'; Clementine
Churchill (wife of British politician Sir
Winston Churchill).

Cleopatra

Variants and diminutives:
Cleo, Cleta.
Meaning: 'fame of my
father' (Greek).
Notable namesakes:
Cleopatra VII, the Egyptian
queen and lover of Julius
Caesar and Mark Anthony;
Cleopatra's Needle, Egyptian obelisks in London and
New York; a genus of yellow butterflies, *Gonepteryx
cleopatra*; Cleo Lane (British singer).

Clio

Variants and diminutives: Cleo, Cleon, Cleona,
Cleone, Cleora.
Meaning: 'fame-proclaimer' (Greek).
Notable namesakes: one of the Muses – that of
history and poetry – in Greek mythology.

Clotilda

Variants and diminutives: Clothild, Clothilda,
Clothilde, Clotilde, Klothilde, Klothilda.
Meaning: 'famous' and 'battle' (Germanic).
Notable namesakes: Saint Clotilda, wife of the
Frankish king, Clovis.

Clytie

Meaning: 'splendour' (Greek).
Notable namesakes: a nymph of Greek mythology
whose love for the sun god Helios was unrequited,
causing her to turn into a sunflower or heliotrope.

Colette

Variants and diminutives: Colecta, Colet, Coleta, Collect, Collett, Collette, Cosette, Cosetta, Kalotte.
Meaning: 'victory of the people' (Greek) as a diminutive of Nicolette, a female version of Nicholas.
Notable namesakes: Saint Colette; the pseudonym of the French novelist Sidonie Gabrielle Claudine Colette.

Colleen

Variants and diminutives: Coleen, Colena, Colene, Coline, Collen, Collene, Collice, Colline.
Meaning: 'girl' (Irish Gaelic).
Notable namesakes: Colleen McCullough (Australian writer).

Columbine

Variants and diminutives: Columba, Columbia, Columbina.
Meaning: 'dove-like' (Latin); 'little dove' (Italian). A female version of Columba.
Notable namesakes: the common name of the *Aquilegia* genus of flowering plants; the sweetheart of Harlequin in English pantomine, derived from a character in Italian *commedia dell'arte*.

Concepta

Variants and diminutives: Conception, Concepcion, Concetta, Concha, Conchita.
Meaning: 'conceived' (Latin).

Constance

Variants and diminutives: Con, Concettina, Conetta, Conni, Connie, Conny, Constancia, Constancy, Constanta, Constantia, Constantina, Constanz, Constanza, Conte, Custance, Custancia, Custans, Custins, Kani, Konstantin, Konstanze, Kosta, Kostatina, Kostenka, Kostya, Kostyusha, Kotik, Tina.
Meaning: 'constancy' (Latin). A female version of Constantine.
Notable namesakes: Constance M Rourke (US writer).

Consuela

Variants and diminutives: Consolata, Consuelo.
Meaning: 'free of sadness', 'consoling' (Latin).
Notable namesakes: the eponymous heroine of the novel *Consuelo*, by French writer George Sand.

Cora

Variants and diminutives: Corabelle, Coralie, Corella, Corene, Coretta, Corette, Corey, Cori, Corie, Corin, Corina, Corine, Corinn, Corinna, Corinne, Corita, Correen, Correne, Corri, Corrina, Corrine, Corinna, Corrine, Corry, Cory, Kora, Korey, Kori, Korrie, Korry, Kory.
Meaning: uncertain; coined by US writer James Fennimore Cooper for his novel *The Last of the Mohicans*, probably drawing inspiration from the Greek word for 'maiden' (Greek).
Notable namesakes: Cora Sandel (Norwegian writer).

Coral

Variants and diminutives: Coralie, Coraline.
Meaning: 'pebble' (Greek); derived from the name of the prized material produced by the aggregated skeletons of corals.
Notable namesakes: the Coral Sea; the colour coral.

Cordelia

Variants and diminutives: Cordeilia, Cordeilla, Cordelie, Cordell, Cordelle, Cordie, Cordula, Cordy, Delia, Della, Kordel, Kordula.
Meaning: 'heart' or 'from her heart' (Latin); 'harmony' or 'daughter of the sea' (Celtic).
Notable namesakes: Saint Cordula; a character in William Shakespeare's play *King Lear*.

Corinna

Variants and diminutives: Cora, Corene, Corey, Cori, Corin, Corinn, Corinne, Correnen, Correne, Corri, Corrie, Corrina, Corrine, Corrinna, Corry, Cory, Kora, Korey, Kori, Korrie, Korry.
Meaning: 'maiden' (Greek).
Notable namesakes: a poetess of ancient Greece; *Corinna's Going A-Maying*, the title of a poem by English poet Robert Herrick; the heroine of the novel *Corinne*, by French writer Madame de Staël.

Cornelia

Variants and diminutives: Cornela, Cornelie, Cornella, Cornelle, Cornie, Corny, Kornelia, Kornelis, Melia, Neely, Neila, Nele, Nelia, Nell, Nelli, Nellie, Nelly.
Meaning: 'horn' or 'cornel tree' (Latin), derived from a Roman family name as a female version of Cornelius.
Notable namesakes: Cornelia Otis Skinner (US actress and writer).

Cosima

Variants and diminutives: Cosi.
Meaning: 'order' (Greek). A female version of Cosmo.
Notable namesakes: Cosima Wagner (daughter of Hungarian composer Franz Liszt and wife of German conductor Hans von Bülow before her marriage to German composer Richard Wagner).

Courtney

Variants and diminutives: Courtenay, Courtny.
Meaning: 'short nose', 'court-dweller' or 'the domain of Curtius' (Old French), derived from a French place name. Also a boy's name.
Notable namesakes: Courtney Cox (US actress), Courtney Love (US singer and actress).

Cressida

Variants and diminutives: Briseida, Cressid, Criseida, Criseyde.
Meaning: 'golden' or 'stronger' (Greek).
Notable namesakes: in medieval romance, the lover of Troilus, son of King Priam of Troy, whose story is told in Italian writer Giovanni Boccaccio's romance *Il Filostrato*, English poet Geoffrey Chaucer's *Troilus and Criseyde* and William Shakespeare's play *Troilus and Cressida*.

Crystal

Variants and diminutives: Chris, Chrissie, Christal, Christel, Christelle, Christie, Christy, Chrys, Chrystal, Chrystie, Cristal, Cristel, Cristol, Cyrstle, Chrystol, Kristell, Krys, Krystal, Krystle, Kristol.
Meaning: 'ice' (Greek); derived from the name of the clear mineral.
Notable namesakes: Crystal Gayle (US singer); good-quality glassware.

Cynthia

Variants and diminutives: Cinda, Cindee, Cindi, Cindie, Cindy, Cinta, Cintia, Cyndi, Cyndie, Cyndy, Cynth, Cynthiana, Cynthie, Kynthia, Sindee, Sindy.
Meaning: 'of Cynthus' (Greek), Cynthus being Mount Cynthus, on the Greek island of Delos (Dhilos).
Notable namesakes: a name of Artemis, the Greek goddess of hunting, the moon and chastity, whose brother was Cynthus (Apollo); a character in the novel *Wives and Daughters*, by the British writer Mrs Gaskell.

Cytherea

Meaning: 'of Cynthera', (Greek), Cynthera being equated with the island of Cyprus.
Notable namesakes: a name of Aphrodite, the goddess of love and beauty in Greek mythology.

Daffodil

Variants and diminutives: Daff, Daffie, Daffy, Dilly, Margaret, Marguérite.
Meaning: 'asphodel' (Greek); derived from the name of the spring flower *Narcissus pseudonarcissus*.

Dagmar

Variants and diminutives: Daga, Dagi, Daggi, Dagmara, Dasa.
Meaning: 'maid of the famous day' or 'the Dane's joy' (Old Norse).

Dahlia

Variants and diminutives: Dalia, Daliah, Dahla.
Meaning: 'from the valley' (Old Norse).
Notable namesakes: the *Dahlia* genus of flowers named for the Swedish botanist Anders Dahl.

Daisy

Variants and diminutives: Daisee, Daisey, Daisi,

Daisia, Daisie, Dasey, Dasi, Dasie, Dasy, Daysee, Daysie, Daysy.

Meaning: 'day's eye' (Old English); derived from the name of the flower *Bellis perennis*.

Notable namesakes: the eponymous heroine of the novel *Daisy Miller*, by US writer Henry James; Daisy Ashford (English writer); Daisy Buchanan, a character in the novel *The Great Gatsby*, by US author F Scott Fitzgerald; Daisy Donovan (British television presenter).

Dakota

Meaning: 'friend' (Native American Sioux). Also a boy's name.

Dalila

Variants and diminutives: Dalilah, Lila, Lilah.
Meaning: 'gentle' (Swahili). Also a variant of Dahlia, Delia and Delilah.

Damaris

Variants and diminutives: Damara, Damaras, Damaress, Damiris, Demaras, Demaris, Mara, Mari, Maris.
Meaning: 'calf' or 'heifer' (Greek).
Notable namesakes: an Athenian woman whom Saint Paul converted to Christianity in the New Testament.

Dana

Variants and diminutives: Daina, Danae, Dane, Dania, Danice, Danit, Danita, Danna, Danni, Dannie, Dansy, Danu, Danuta, Danny, Dannye, Danya, Dayna.
Meaning: 'Dane' or 'from Denmark' (Celtic); 'mother of the gods', 'poet' or 'courageous' (Irish Gaelic); 'judgement of God' (Hebrew) as a diminutive of Danielle, in turn a female version of Daniel.
Notable namesakes: an earth goddess and ancestress of the Tuatha Dé Danaan, the divine race of Ireland in Irish mythology.

Danica

Variants and diminutives: Dan, Dani, Dany.
Meaning: 'morning star' (Old Slavic).

Danielle

Variants and diminutives: Dana, Danae, Danela, Danell, Danella, Danelle, Danette, Dani, Dania, Danica, Danice, Danika, Danikla, Danielka, Daniela, Daniele, Daniell, Daniella, Danila, Danilla, Danille, Danit, Danita, Danka, Danuta, Danya, Danyel, Danyell, Danyelle, Danni, Dannie, Danny, Dannye, Danya.
Meaning: 'judgement of God' (Hebrew). A female version of Daniel.
Notable namesakes: Danielle Steele (US writer).

Daphne

Variants and diminutives: Daff, Daffi, Daffie, Daffy, Dafna, Dafne, Dafnee, Dafnit, Daph, Daphe, Daphna, Daphnee, Daphnit.
Meaning: 'laurel' (Greek).
Notable namesakes: a nymph who was spared the attentions of Apollo by being transformed into a laurel tree in Greek mythology; Daphne du Maurier (British writer).

Dara

Variants and diminutives: Darah, Daralice, Daralis, Darda, Dare, Darelle, Dareth, Daria, Darice, Darissa, Darra, Darryl, Darya, Daryl.
Meaning: 'fount of wisdom' (Hebrew); 'compassionate' or 'daring' (Middle English).

Darcy

Variants and diminutives: Dar, Darce, Darcey, Darci, Darcie, D'arcy, D'Arcy, Darsey, Darsi, Darsie, Darsey.
Meaning: 'dark' (Irish Gaelic); 'of the fortress' or 'of Arcy' (Old French); derived from an Irish family name, in turn derived from the French place name Arcy. Also a boy's name.
Notable namesakes: Darcy Bussell (British ballerina).

Daria

Variants and diminutives: Darice, Darya.
Meaning: 'rich' (Greek). A female version of Darius.

Darlene

Variants and diminutives: Dareen, Darelle, Dari, Darilyn, Darilynn, Darla, Darleen, Darlin, Darline, Darling, Darilynn, Darlyn, Darylyne, Darragh,

Darrilyn, Daryl.
Meaning: 'darling' (Old English).

Davina

Variants and diminutives: Davene, Davi, Davida, Davinia, Davita, Devina, Veda, Veta, Vida, Vina, Vita, Vitia.
Meaning: 'beloved' or 'friend' (Hebrew). A female version of David.
Notable namesakes: Davina McCall (British television presenter).

Dawn

Variants and diminutives: Aurora, Dawna, Dawne, Dawnelle, Dawnette, Dawnta, Dawnyelle, Orrie, Rora.
Meaning: 'daybreak' (Old English).
Notable namesakes: Dawn French (British comic actress).

Daya

Variants and diminutives: Dayah.
Meaning: 'bird' (Hebrew).

Deanna

Variants and diminutives: Dea, Deana, Deane, Deann, Deanne, Deena, Dena, Diana.
Meaning: uncertain; possibly 'one in charge of ten' or 'dean' (Latin) or 'valley' (Old English) as a female version of Dean; possibly a variant of Diana.
Notable namesakes: Deanna Durbin (Canadian actress and singer).

Deborah

Variants and diminutives: Deb, Debbe, Debbee, Debbi, Debbie, Debby, Debera, Debi, Debire, Debo, Debor, Debora, Deboran, Debra, Debralee, Debs, Deva, Devera, Devora, Devorah, Devorit, Devra, Dobra, Dovra, Dvera, Dvorit, Dwora, Kepola.
Meaning: 'bee' (Hebrew).
Notable namesakes: the wife of Lapidoth, a prophetess and judge in the Old Testament; Rebecca's nurse in the Old Testament; a character in the novel *Cranford*, by English writer Mrs Gaskell; Debbie Reynolds and Debra Winger (US actresses).

Decima

Variants and diminutives: Deci, Deka.
Meaning: 'tenth' (Latin). A female version of Decimus.

Dee

Variants and diminutives: DD, Dede, Dee Dee, Didi.
Meaning: a diminutive of any name beginning with 'D-'; 'dark' (Welsh). Also a boy's name.

Deirdre

Variants and diminutives: Dede, Dedra, Dee, Deerdre, Deirdra, Deirdrie, Diedra, Dierdra, Dierdre, Dierdrie.
Meaning: 'broken-hearted', 'raging one', 'fearful' or 'wanderer' (Irish Gaelic).
Notable namesakes: Deirdre of the Sorrows, a tragic, suicidal character of Irish and Scottish legend, a symbol of Ireland and the subject of the plays *Deirdre*, by Irish poet W B Yeats, and *Deirdre of the Sorrows*, by Irish playwright J M Synge; a character in the British television soap opera *Coronation Street*.

Delia

Variants and diminutives: Adelia, Bedelia, Cordelia, Dahla, Dede, Dee, Dehlia, Delinda, Della, Didi.
Meaning: 'visible' or 'of Delos' (Greek), the former name of the Greek island of Dhilos.
Notable namesakes: a name of Artemis, the Greek goddess of the moon, chastity and the hunt, who is said to have been born on Delos; the subject of *Sonnets to Delia*, by the English poet Samuel Daniel; Delia Smith (British cookery writer and television presenter).

Delicia

Variants and diminutives: Dee, Dela, Delesha, Delia, Delice, Delight, Delisa, Delise, Delisha, Delisiah, Delissa, Delizia, Delycia, Delys, Delyse, Delysha, Delysia, Delyssa.
Meaning: 'delight' (Latin).

Delilah

Variants and diminutives: Dalila, Delila, Lila, Lilah.
Meaning: 'delightful', 'amorous', 'hair', 'night' or

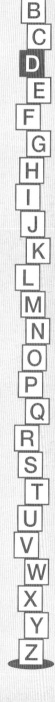

'poor' (Hebrew); 'leader' or 'flirt' (Arabic).
Notable namesakes: Samson's treacherous Philistine mistress in the Old Testament; a generic name for a temptress; the title of a song performed by Welsh singer Tom Jones.

Della
Variants and diminutives: Adela, Dela, Dell, Delle.
Meaning: 'noble' or 'nobility' (Germanic) as a diminutive of Adela (Adelaide).

Delma
Variants and diminutives: Delmar, Delmi, Delmira.
Meaning: 'noble' and 'defender' (Germanic) as a diminutive of Adelma; 'of the sea' (Spanish).

Delphine
Variants and diminutives: Delfine, Delpha, Delphina, Delphinie, Delphinium.
Meaning: 'of Delphi' (Latin), Delphi ('dolphin' in Greek) being the site of the ancient Greek Delphic oracle on Mount Parnassus; also a variant of the botanical name of the larkspur flowering plant *Delphinium* (also etymologically derived from the Greek word for dolphin).
Notable namesakes: the eponymous heroine of the novel *Delphine*, by French writer Madame de Staël.

Delyth
Meaning: 'lovely' or 'tidy' (Welsh).

Demelza
Meaning: uncertain; derived from a Cornish place name.
Notable namesakes: the heroine of the 'Poldark' series of novels, by British writer Winston Graham, and of the subsequent television series.

Demeter
Variants and diminutives: Demetra, Demetria, Demetris, Dimitra, Dimity.
Meaning: 'earth mother' (Greek).

Notable namesakes: the goddess of the earth in Greek mythology.

Dena
Variants and diminutives: Dea, Deana, Deane, Deann, Deanna, Deanne, Deena, Dena, Dene, Denna, Dina.
Meaning: 'valley' (Old English and Native American). Also a female version of Dean.

Denise
Variants and diminutives: Danice, Danise, Deneice, Denese, Deney, Denice, Deniece, Deniese, Denis, Denisha, Denisse, Denize, Dennet, Dennie, Dennise, Denny, Denyce, Denyse, Deonysia, Dinnie, Dinny, Dion, Dione, Dionetta, Dionis, Dionise, Dionycia, Dionysia, Diot.
Meaning: 'deity of the Nysa' (Greek), Nysa being the birthplace of Dionysus, the Greek god of wine, fecundity, vegetation and revelry, as a variant of Dionysia and a female version of Dennis.
Notable namesakes: Denise Levertov (US writer); Denise van Outen (British television presenter).

Derora
Variants and diminutives: Deroit, Derorice, Derorit.
Meaning: 'flowing stream', 'the swallow' (Hebrew).

Dervla
Meaning: 'poet's daughter' (Irish Gaelic).

Desdemona
Variants and diminutives: Desmona.
Meaning: 'unhappiness' or 'bad luck' (Greek).
Notable namesakes: the heroine of William Shakespeare's play *Othello*.

Désirée
Variants and diminutives: Desarae, Desaree, Desi, Desideria, Desiraye, Desirita, Desiré, Dezarae, Dezaray, Dezirae, Deziree.
Meaning: 'desired' (French).
Notable namesakes: the mistress of Napoleon Bonaparte and later wife of Jean-Baptiste Jules Bernadotte, King Charles XIV of Sweden.

Deva

Variants and diminutives: Devaki, Devanee, Devi, Devika, Dewi.
Meaning: 'divine' (Sanskrit).
Notable namesakes: Devi, a mother goddess, as well as the name for any goddess, in Hinduism; the goddess of the river Dee in Scotland in Celtic mythology.

Dia

Meaning: 'divine' (Greek); 'middle child' (Mende, Africa). Also a variant of Diana.
Notable namesakes: a name of Hera, the supreme goddess of Greek mythology.

Diamond

Variants and diminutives: Diámanta.
Meaning: 'hardest' or 'unconquerable' (Greek); derived from the name of the precious stone.

Diana

Variants and diminutives: Deana, Deane, Deanna, Deanne, Deannis, Dede, Dee, Denna, Di, Dia, Diahann, Dian, Diandra, Diane, Diani, Dianna, Dianne, Didi, Diona, Dione, Dionne, Dionetta, Dyan, Dyana, Dyane, Dyann, Dyanna, Dyanne, Kiana.
Meaning: 'divine' (Latin).
Notable namesakes: the Roman goddess of the moon, hunting and chastity; Diane de Poitiers, mistress of King Henri II of France; Diana Ross (US singer); Dyan Cannon (US actress); Diana (Spencer), Princess of Wales; Diana Krall (Canadian singer).

Dido

Meaning: 'bold' (Phoenician).
Notable namesakes: the Phoenician princess who founded Carthage in Roman mythology, whose story is told by the Roman poet Virgil in *The Aeneid*; Dido Armstrong (British singer).

Dilys

Variants and diminutives: Dalice, Dalicia, Dalisha, Delicia, Delisha, Dilees, Dylice.
Meaning: 'sincere', 'genuine' or 'perfect' (Welsh).

Dinah

Variants and diminutives: Deanna, Deanne, Deena, Dena, Dina.
Meaning: 'proved right', 'revenged' or 'judged' (Hebrew).
Notable namesakes: a daughter of Jacob and Leah in the Old Testament; Dinah Sheridan (British actress); Dinah Washington (US singer).

Dion

Variants and diminutives: Diona, Dionaea, Diondra, Dione, Dionée, Dionis, Dionna, Dionne.
Meaning: 'divine' or 'deity of the Nysa' (Greek), Nysa being the birthplace of Dionysus, the Greek god of wine, fecundity, vegetation and revelry, as a variant of Dionysia and a female version of Dennis.
Notable namesakes: Dione, the Titan mother of Aphrodite (sometimes called Dionaea), the goddess of beauty, love and fertility in Greek mythology, Dionne Warwick (US singer).

Dixie

Variants and diminutives: Dis, Disa, Dix.
Meaning: 'goddess' or 'sprite' (Old Norse). Also a boy's name.
Notable namesakes: Dis, a talent-bestowing goddess in Norse mythology; a name for the southern states of the USA (either derived from the Mason-Dixon Line or the French word for ten, *dix*, that was printed on $10 banknotes in New Orleans); Dixieland, a jazz style that originated in Dixie.

Dolina

Variants and diminutives: Donalda, Donaldina
Meaning: 'global might' (Scots Gaelic). A female version of Donald.

Dolores

Variants and diminutives: Dalores, Dela, Delora, Delores, Deloris, Delorita, Dola, Dolly, Dolo, Dolorcitas, Dolore, Dolorita, Doloritas, Dolours, Kololeke, Lo, Lola, Lolita, Lora, Loras.
Meaning: 'sorrows' (Spanish).
Notable namesakes: *Santa Maria de los Dolores* (literally 'Saint Mary of the Sorrows' or 'Lady of

Sorrows'), a title given to the Virgin Mary by the Spanish; Dolores O'Riordan (Irish singer).

Dominique

Variants and diminutives: Chumina, Dom, Doma, Domek, Domenica, Domeninga, Domina, Dominee, Dominga, Domini, Dominic, Dominica, Dominick, Dominik, Dominika, Domka, Dumin, Mika, Nika, Niki

Meaning: 'of the lord' (Latin). A female version of Dominic.

Notable namesakes: the Caribbean states Dominica and the Dominican Republic.

Donna

Variants and diminutives: Domella, Dona, Donalie, Donella, Donelle, Donetta, Donia, Donica, Doniella, Donita, Donnel, Donni, Donnie, Donnis, Donny, Kona, Ladonna.

Meaning: 'lady' (Italian).

Notable namesakes: Donna Summer (US singer); Donna Karan (US fashion designer); Donna Leon (British crime writer).

Dora

Variants and diminutives: Dorah, Doralin, Doralyn, Doralynne, Doreen, Dorelia, Dorena, Dorette, Dori, Dorind, Dorinda, Dorita, Dorothy, Dorrie, Dorry, Theodora.

Meaning: 'God's gift' (Greek) as a diminutive of both Theodora (and other '-doras') and Dorothy.

Notable namesakes: Dora Spenlow, a character in *David Copperfield*, by English writer Charles Dickens; Dora Carrington (British artist); Dora Jessie Saint, the British writer better known as Miss Read.

Dorcas

Variants and diminutives: Dorcia.

Meaning: 'gazelle' or 'doe' (Greek).

Notable namesakes: a woman (also called Tabitha) raised by the dead by Saint Peter in the New Testament.

Doris

Variants and diminutives: Dorea, Dori, Doria, Dorice, Dorie, Dorinda, Dorisa, Dorise, Dorit, Dorita, Dorith, Doritt, Dorri, Dorrie, Dorris, Dorrit, Dory, Kolika, Rinda.

Meaning: 'bountiful sea', 'sacrificial knife' or 'of Doris' (Greek), Doris being a Greek region north of the Gulf of Corinth. Also a female version of Dorian.

Notable namesakes: a sea nymph in Greek mythology; Doris Day (US actress and singer); Doris Lessing (British writer).

Dorit

Variants and diminutives: Dorice, Dorrit.

Meaning: 'generation' (Hebrew). Also a diminutive of Dorothy.

Notable namesakes: *Little Dorrit*, the novel by English writer Charles Dickens.

Dorothy

Variants and diminutives: Dahtee, Dasha, Dasya, Dede, Derede, Dode, Dodi, Dodie, Dodo, Dody, Doe, Doioreann, Dol, Doll, Dolley, Dolli, Dollie, Dolly, Dora, Doralane, Doraleen, Doralene, Doralia, Doralice, Doralyn, Dorann, Dorat, Dore, Doreen, Dorelia, Dorene, Doretta, Dorette, Dori, Dorinda, Dorisia, Dorit, Dorita, Dorka, Dorle, Dorlisa, Doro, Dorolice, Dorosia, Dorota, Dorotea, Doroteya, Doroteyo, Dorothea, Dorothee, Dorothiea, Dorotthea, Dorrie, Dorrie, Dorrit, Dorte, Dorthea, Dorthy, Dory, Dosi, Dosya, Dot, Dotti, Dottie, Dotty, Lolotea, Koleka, Kolokea, Thea, Theadora, Tiga, Tigo, Tio, Totie.

Meaning: 'God's gift' (Greek). A female variant of Theodore.

Notable namesakes: Saint Dorothea (or Dorothy), patron saint of florists; Dorothea Brooke, the heroine of the novel *Middlemarch*, by English writer George Eliot; Dorothy Wordsworth (English writer); Dorothy Parker (US writer); the heroine of the *The Wizard of Oz*, a children's story by US writer Frank Baum and subsequently a US film; Dorothy L Sayers, Dodie Smith and Dorothy Richardson (British writers); Dorothea Tanning (US artist); Dorothea Rockburne (US-Canadian artist).

Drisa

Variants and diminutives: Dreesa, Dreesha, Drisana, Drisanna, Drisha, Risa, Risha.

Meaning: 'the sun's daughter' (Hindi).

Drusilla

Variants and diminutives: Dru, Druci, Drucilla, Drusa, Drusie, Drusus, Drusy.
Meaning: uncertain; possibly 'soft-eyed' (Greek); derived from the Roman family name Drusus.
Notable namesakes: a sister of Caligula, the infamous Roman emperor; the wife of Felix, the governor of Jerusalem converted by Saint Paul in the New Testament.

Dulcie

Variants and diminutives: Delcina, Delcine, Dulce, Dulcea, Dulcee, Dulcia, Dulciana, Dulcibella, Dulcine, Dulcinea, Dulcy.
Meaning: 'sweet' (Latin).
Notable namesakes: Dulcinea del Toboso, the hero's idealised object of affection in the novel *Don Quixote*, by Spanish writer Miguel de Cervantes.

Duscha

Variants and diminutives: Dusha.
Meaning: 'soul' (Russian).

Dymphna

Variants and diminutives: Damhnait, Daunat, Dympna.
Meaning: 'eligible' or 'little fawn' (Irish Gaelic).
Notable namesakes: Saint Dymphna, patron saint of epileptics, sufferers of neurological disorders and mentally ill people.

Eartha

Variants and diminutives: Erda, Erde, Erna, Ertha, Herta, Hertha.
Meaning: 'earth' (Old English).
Notable namesakes: Eartha Kitt (US singer).

Easter

Variants and diminutives: Esther.
Meaning: 'radiant dawn' (Germanic). Also a variant of Esther.
Notable namesakes: the name of the Christian festival commemorating Christ's death and resurrection, in turn derived from Eastre (or Ostara), the pagan goddess who was venerated in northern Europe at the vernal equinox.

Ebony

Variants and diminutives: Ebbony, Ebonee, Eboney, Eboni, Ebonie.
Meaning: 'the ebony tree' (Greek), derived from the name of the *Diospyros* genus of trees that produce dark hardwood.

Edda

Meaning: 'great-grandmother', 'poetry' or 'song-writer' (Old Norse); 'striver' (Germanic).
Notable namesakes: a Norse goddess, ancestor of the Thralls; two collections of early Icelandic mythology: *The Younger Edda* (or *The Prose Edda*) and *The Elder Edda* (or *The Poetic Edda*).

Eden

Meaning: 'delight' or 'paradise' (Hebrew). Also a boy's name.
Notable namesakes: the Garden of Eden – paradise – in the Old Testament.

Edith

Variants and diminutives: Ardith, Dita, Ditka, Duci, Eade, Eadita, Eady, Eda, Edda, Edde, Ede, Edetta, Edi, Edie, Edit, Edita, Edite, Editha, Edithe, Ediva, Edka, Edon, Edy, Edyta, Edyth, Edytha, Edythe, Eidita, Ekika, Eyde..
Meaning: 'happiness' or 'riches' and 'war' (Old English).
Notable namesakes: Saint Edith; Edith Wharton (US writer); Edith Sitwell (British poet); Edith Evans (British actress); Edith Piaf (French singer).

A B C D E F G H I J K L M N O P Q R S T U V W X Y Z

Edna

Variants and diminutives: Adena, Adina, Eda, Edana, Edena, Ednah, Eithne.
Meaning: 'delight' or 'rejuvenation' (Hebrew); 'pleasing gift' (Old English); 'kernel' or 'small fire' (Irish Gaelic) as a variant of Ethne.
Notable namesakes: Edna St Vincent Millay (US poet); Edna Ferber (US writer); Edna O'Brien (Irish novelist).

Edwina

Variants and diminutives: Edina, Edna, Edweena, Edwene, Edwyna.
Meaning: 'happiness' or 'riches' and 'friend' (Old English). A female version of Edwin.
Notable namesakes: Edwina, Countess Mountbatten; Edwina Currie (British politician and novelist).

Eileen

Variants and diminutives: Aibhilin, Aileen, Eibhilin, Eila, Eilean, Eiley, Eilidh, Eilleen, Eily, Elie, Eveleen, Evelyn, Helen, Ilean, Ileen, Ileene, Ilene.
Meaning: 'bright' (Greek) as an Irish Gaelic variant of Helen; 'hazelnut' (Germanic) or 'bird' (Latin) as an Irish Gaelic variant of Evelyn.
Notable namesakes: Eileen Gray (Irish architect and designer).

Eira

Meaning: 'snow' (Welsh).

Eirian

Meaning: 'silver' (Welsh).

Elain

Meaning: 'fawn' (Welsh).

Elaine

Variants and diminutives: Elain, Elaina, Elane, Elayne, Ellaine, Helen.
Meaning: 'bright' (Greek) as an Old French variant of Helen.
Notable namesakes: the lover of Sir Lancelot and mother of Sir Galahad in Arthurian legend; Elaine Stritch (US comic actress).

Elana

Variants and diminutives: Ilana.
Meaning: 'tree' (Hebrew); 'spirited' (Latin); 'friendly' (Native American). A female version of Elan.

Eleanor

Variants and diminutives: Alianora, Alienor, Alienora, El, Ele, Elanora, Eleanora, Eleanore, Elen, Elena, Eleni, Elenor, Elenora, Elenorah, Eleonora, Eleonore, Eli, Elianor, Elianora, Elie, Elien, Elin, Elinor, Elinora, Elinore, Elinorr, Ella, Ellen, Ellenor, Ellenora, Ellenore, Ellette, Ellie, Ellin, Elly, Ellyn Elnore, Elnora, Elyenora, Elyn, Elynn, Heleanor, Leanor, Lennie, Lenora, Lenore, Leonora, Leonore, Leora, Nelda, Nora, Nell, Nella, Nellie, Nelly, Nora, Norah, Noreen, Norene, Norina, Norine, Nureen.
Meaning: 'bright' (Greek) as an Old French variant of Helen; 'foreign' (Germanic).
Notable namesakes: Eleanor of Aquitaine, wife of King Louis VII of France and King Henry II of England; Eleanor of Castile, wife of King Edward I of England, whose death prompted the raising of 'Eleanor crosses' (including Charing Cross) in England; Elena Stakhova, the heroine of the novel *On the Eve*, by Russian writer Ivan Turgenev; Elinor Wylie (US writer); Elinor Glyn (English writer); Eleanor Roosevelt (US social worker and wife of President Franklin D Roosevelt); Eleanor Hibbert (English writer).

Electra

Variants and diminutives: Electre, Elektra.
Meaning: 'amber' or 'radiant' (Greek).
Notable namesakes: the daughter of Agamemon and Clytemnestra in Greek mythology, whose fixation on her father inspired Austrian psychoanalyst Sigmund Freud to name a complex after her, her story also being used as the basis of plays by the Greek dramatists Aeschylus (*Oresteia*), Sophocles and Euripedes (both called *Electra*), of the opera *Elektra* by German composer Richard Strauss, of the trilogy *Mourning Becomes Electra*, by US playwright Eugene O'Neill, and of the play *Électre*, by French playwright Jean Giraudoux; one of the Pleiades, the 'lost Pleiad', the daughter of Atlas and Pleione and mother of Dardanus in Greek mythology.

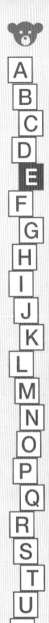

Elfrida

Variants and diminutives: Alfreda, Elfie, Eldreda, Frida, Freda.
Meaning: 'elf' and 'strength' (Old English).
Notable namesakes: the mother of King Ethelred II, 'the Unready', of England.

Elissa

Variants and diminutives: Elisabeth, Lisa, Lissa.
Meaning: uncertain; possibly 'heroic' (Phoenician); possibly 'God is perfection', 'God is satisfaction', 'dedicated to God' or 'God's oath' (Hebrew) as a diminutive of Elizabeth.
Notable namesakes: a name of Dido, Queen of Carthage, in Greek mythology; a character in the moral allegory *The Faerie Queene*, by English poet Edmund Spenser.

Elita

Meaning: 'selected' (Latin).

Elizabeth

Variants and diminutives: Alzbeta, Bab, Babette, Bela, Belicia, Belita, Bella, Bess, Bessi, Bessie, Bessy, Bet, Beta, Beth, Bethan, Betka, Betsey, Betsi, Betsie, Betssy, Betsy, Bett, Betta, Bette, Betti, Bettina, Bettine, Betty, Betuska, Boski, Bozsi, Buffy, Chabica, Chavelle, Chela, Ealasaid, Eilie, Eilis, Ela, Elese, Elikapeka, Elis, Elisa, Elisabet, Elisabeta, Elisabeth, Elisabetta, Elisavet, Elise, Elisheba, Elisheva, Eliska, Elissa, Elisveta, Eliza, Elizabet, Elizabete, Elizbez, Elize, Elka, Ellie, Elsa, Elsavetta, Elsbet, Else, Elsebeth, Elschen, Elsebin, Elsey, Elsi, Elsie, Elspet, Elspeth, Elspie, Elsye, Elts, Elysa, Elyse, Elyssa, Elza, Elzbieta, Elsbietka, Elzunia, Erzebet, Erzsebet, Etti, Etty, Helsa, Ila, Ilisa, Ilise, Ilsa, Ilse, Ilyse, Isa, Isabel, Isabelita, Isabella, Isabelle, Isobel, Issa, Iza, Izabel, Izabela, Izabella, Letha, Lety, Libbi, Libbie, Libby, Lieschen, Liese, Liesel, Liesl, Liisa, Liisi, Lili, Lilian, Lilibet, Lila, Lilla, Lillah, Lisa, Lisbet, Lisbeth, Lise, Liselotta, Lieselotte, Lisbete, Lise, Lisenka, Liseta, Lisette, Lisettina, Lisl, Lista, Liszka, Liz, Liza, Lizabeth, Lizanka, Lizbeth, Lize, Lizette, Lizka, Lizzi, Lizzie, Lizzy, Lusa, Orse, Sabela, Tetsy, Tetty, Tibby, Yelisabeta, Yelizaveta, Ysabel, Yza, Yzabel, Yzabela, Zizi.
Meaning: 'God is perfection', 'God is satisfaction', 'dedicated to God' or 'God's oath' (Hebrew).
Notable namesakes: Elisheva, the wife of Aaron in the Old Testament; the mother of Saint John the Baptist in the New Testament; Saint Elizabeth of Portugal, patron saint of peace-making during war; Saint Elizabeth of Hungary, patron saint of charities, bakers and nurses; Queen Elizabeth I of England; Saint Elizabeth Seton, patron saint of those whose parents, husbands or children have died and those having problems with their in-laws; Elisabeth Vigée-Lebrun (French artist); Elizabeth Cleghorn Gaskell (English writer); Elizabeth Fry (English philanthropist and prison reformer); Elizabeth Barrett Browning (English poet); Eliza Doolittle, the heroine of the play *Pygmalion*, by Irish dramatist George Bernard Shaw and the subsequent film and musical *My Fair Lady*; Elizabeth Bowes-Lyon, the Queen Mother, mother of Queen Elizabeth II of the United Kingdom; Elizabeth Bowen (British writer); Elisabeth Frink (British sculptress); Elizabeth Bishop (US poet); Elizabeth David (British food writer); Elizabeth Taylor (US actress); Elizabeth Murray (US artist).

Ella

Variants and diminutives: Ala, Ela, Elizabeth, Ellen, Hela, Hele.
Meaning: 'all' (Germanic); 'fairy' and 'maiden' (Old English). Also a variant of Elizabeth and Ellen.
Notable namesakes: Ella Fitzgerald (US singer).

Ellama

Meaning: 'mother goddess' (Hindi).
Notable namesakes: a mother goddess of southern India, invoked for health and luck.

Ellen

Variants and diminutives: Elea, Elen, Elin, Ella, Ellan, Elli, Ellie, Ellin, Ellon, Elly, Elyn, Nell, Nellie, Nelly.
Meaning: 'bright' (Greek) as a variant of Helen.
Notable namesakes: a daughter of King Arthur in Arthurian legend; Ellen Terry (British actress); Ellen Glasgow (US writer); Ellen MacArthur (British yachtswoman).

A B C D E F G H I J K L M N O P Q R S T U V W X Y Z

Elma

Variants and diminutives: Alma.
Meaning: 'apple' (Turkish).

Eloise

Variants and diminutives: Eloisa, Heloise, Lois, Louise.
Meaning: 'hale' and 'wide' (Germanic); 'famed' and 'warrior' (Germanic) as a variant of Louise.
Notable namesakes: Héloïse, the lover of the French scholastic philosopher Abelard and abbess of Paraclete, France.

Elsa

Variants and diminutives: Ailsa, Aliza, Else, Elsie, Elza.
Meaning: 'truthful' (Greek), 'noble' or 'nobility' (Germanic) as a variant of Alice (Adelaide); 'swan' (Anglo-Saxon); 'God is my joy' (Hebrew). Also a diminutive of Elizabeth.
Notable namesakes: Princess Elsa of Brabant, the wife of the legendary German hero Lohengrin, and, as such, the heroine of the opera *Lohengrin*, by German composer Richard Wagner; Elsie Dinsmore, the eponymous heroine of the 'Elsie' books by US writer Martha Finley; the leading character of the novel *Elsie Venner: A Romance of Destiny*, by US writer Oliver Wendell Holmes; Elsa Schiaparelli (Italian fashion designer); Elsa Morante (Italian writer); the lioness whose story was told in the book (and subsequent film) *Born Free*, by the German-born writer Joy Adamson.

Eluned

Variants and diminutives: Eiluned, Elined, Linet, Linette, Linnet, Lyn, Lynette, Lynne, Lynnette.
Meaning: 'idol' or 'adored one' (Welsh).

Elvira

Variants and diminutives: Ela, Elvire, Wirke, Wira.
Meaning: uncertain; possibly 'elf' or 'good' and 'counsel' (Germanic) as a variant of Alfreda; possibly 'white' (Latin).
Notable namesakes: the Spanish town of Elvira; characters in the operas *Don Giovanni*, by Austrian composer Wolfgang Amadeus Mozart, and *Ernani*, by Italian composer Giuseppe Verdi; characters in the poem *Don Juan'*, by the English poet Lord Bryon, and in the plays *Dom Juan ou le Festin de Pierre*, by French playwright Molière, and *Blithe Spirit*, by English playwright Noël Coward.

Emily

Variants and diminutives: Aimil, Amalea, Amalie, Ameldy, Amelia, Amelie, Amella, Amilia, Amilie, Amma, Eimile, Em, Ema, Emalia, Emaline, Eme, Emele, Emelin, Emelina, Emeline, Emera, Emi, Emie, Emilia, Emilie, Emiley, Emilia, Emilie, Emiliia, Emilita, Emilka, Emlyn, Emlynn, Emlynne, Emm, Emma, Emmaline, Emmeleia, Emmeline, Emmi, Emmie, Emmy, Imma, Mema, Milka, Millie, Milly, Neneca, Nuela, Ymma.
Meaning: 'eager', 'flatter' or 'rival' (Latin); derived from the Roman family name Aemilius. A female version of Emile.
Notable namesakes: as Emilia, characters in the epic *Teseida*, by Italian writer Giovanni Boccaccio, 'The Knight's Tale' (part of *The Canterbury Tales*), by English poet Geoffrey Chaucer, and William Shakespeare's play *Othello*, as well as the eponymous heroine of the play *Emilia Galotti*, by German writer Gotthold Ephraim Lessing; Emily Brontë (English writer); Emily Dickinson (US poet); Emily Pankhurst (British suffragette); Emily Watkins (British actress).

Emma

Variants and diminutives: Em, Emmeline, Emmi, Emmie, Emmy, Irma.
Meaning: 'whole' or 'universal' (Germanic).
Notable namesakes: Emma of Normandy, the wife of King Ethelred II, 'the Unready', and King Canute (Knut), of England; Lady Emma Hamilton, mistress of the English admiral Horatio Nelson; heroines of the novel *Emma*, by English writer Jane Austen, and *Madame Bovary*, by French writer Gustave Flaubert; Emma Lazarus (US poet); Emma Peel, a character in the British television series *The Avengers*; Emma Freud (British broadcaster).

Emmeline

Variants and diminutives: Amelia, Ameline, Em, Emaline, Emblem, Emblyn, Emelen, Emeline, Emelyn, Emiline, Emma, Emmie, Emmy, Emylynn.

Meaning: 'work' (Germanic). Also a variant of Emma and Emily.
Notable namesakes: Emmeline Pankhurst (British suffragette).

Ena
Variants and diminutives: Aine, Aithne, Enya, Ethne, Eugénie, Helena, Ina.
Meaning: 'bright' (Greek) as a diminutive of Helena (Helen); 'kernel' or 'small fire' (Irish Gaelic) as a diminutive of Ethne; 'well-born' (Greek) as a diminutive of Eugénie.
Notable namesakes: Princess Ena, wife of King Alfonso XIII of Spain; Ena Sharples, a character in the British television soap opera *Coronation Street*.

Enid
Meaning: 'soul' or 'life force' (Welsh).
Notable namesakes: an Arthurian character whose story is told in 'Geraint and Enid', part of English poet Alfred, Lord Tennyson's, series of poems *The Idylls of the King*; Enid Bagnold and Enid Blyton (British writers).

Enya
Variants and diminutives: Eithne, Ena, Etha, Ethenia, Ethna, Ethne, Etna, Etney.
Meaning: 'small fire' or 'kernel' (Irish Gaelic) as a diminutive of Ethne.
Notable namesakes: Enya (Eithne) Ni Bhraonain (Irish singer).

Erica
Variants and diminutives: Elika, Ericka, Erika, Errika, Rica, Rickee, Ricki, Rickie, Ricky, Rika, Rikki, Rikky.
Meaning: 'eternal', 'honourable' or 'island' and 'ruler' (Old Norse). A female version of Eric.
Notable namesakes: the *Erica* genus of heathers; Erica Jong (US writer).

Erin
Variants and diminutives: Eri, Erina, Erinn, Erinna, Errin, Eryn.
Meaning: 'western island' or 'from Ireland' (Irish Gaelic); 'peace' (Old Norse).

Notable namesakes: an ancient and poetic name for Ireland, derived from the name of the goddess Eriu (as is another of Ireland's names, Eire).

Ermintrude
Variants and diminutives: Armigil, Ermegarde, Ermengarde, Ermyntrude, Trudi, Trudie, Trudy.
Meaning: 'universal' and 'strength' (Germanic).

Ernestina
Variants and diminutives: Erna, Ernesta, Ernestine.
Meaning: 'earnest' (Old English). A female version of Ernest.

Ersa
Variants and diminutives: Erse.
Meaning: 'dew' (Greek).
Notable namesakes: the daughter of Zeus and Selene in Greek mythology.

Esmé
Variants and diminutives: Amy, Amyas, Esmee.
Meaning: 'esteemed' (French). Also a boy's name.

Esmeralda
Variants and diminutives: Emerald, Emeralda, Emeraldine, Emerlin, Emerline, Esmeraldah, Esmaralda, Esmarelda, Esmerelda, Meraud.
Meaning: 'emerald' (Greek); derived from the name of the green precious stone, a variety of beryl.
Notable namesakes: a character in the novel *The Hunchback of Notre Dame*, by French writer Victor Hugo; the 'Emerald Isle', a poetic name for Ireland.

Estelle
Variants and diminutives: Essie, Estella, Estrelita, Estrella, Estrelletta, Estrellita, Stella, Stelle.
Meaning: 'star' (Latin).
Notable namesakes: Estella Havisham, a character in the novel *Great Expectations*, by English writer Charles Dickens; Estelle Morris (British politician).

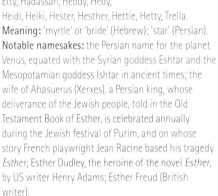

Esther

Variants and diminutives: Easter, Eister, Eistir, Essa, Essi, Essie, Essy, Esta, Estee, Estella, Ester, Estercita, Estralita, Estrella, Etti, Ettie, Etty, Hadassah, Heddy, Hedy, Heidi, Heiki, Hester, Hesther, Hettie, Hetty, Trella.

Meaning: 'myrtle' or 'bride' (Hebrew); 'star' (Persian).

Notable namesakes: the Persian name for the planet Venus, equated with the Syrian goddess Eshtar and the Mesopotamian goddess Ishtar in ancient times; the wife of Ahasuerus (Xerxes), a Persian king, whose deliverance of the Jewish people, told in the Old Testament Book of Esther, is celebrated annually during the Jewish festival of Purim, and on whose story French playwright Jean Racine based his tragedy *Esther*; Esther Dudley, the heroine of the novel *Esther*, by US writer Henry Adams; Esther Freud (British writer).

Ethel

Variants and diminutives: Adal, Adale, Adela, Adeline, Alice, Edel, Eth, Ethelda, Etheldreda, Ethelinda, Etheline, Ethelyn, Ethyl.

Meaning: 'noble' (Germanic).

Notable namesakes: characters in the novels *The Newcomes*, by the English writer William Makepeace Thackerary, and *The Daisy Chain*, by the English writer Charlotte M Yonge; Ethel M Dell (British writer); Ethel Barrymore and Ethel Merman (US actresses).

Etheldreda

Variants and diminutives: Audrey, Dreda, Ethel.

Meaning: 'noble' and 'strength' (Old English).

Notable namesakes: Saint Etheldreda (Audrey), Queen of Northumbria.

Ethne

Variants and diminutives: Aine, Aithne, Eithne, Ena, Ethlinn, Ethnea, Ethnee.

Meaning: 'kernel' or 'small fire' (Irish Gaelic).

Notable namesakes: Ethlinn, the daughter of Balor of the Evil Eye in Irish Celtic mythology; the mother of Saint Aidan.

Eudora

Variants and diminutives: Dora.

Meaning: 'beneficial' and 'gifted' (Greek).

Notable namesakes: a sea goddess in Greek mythology; Eudora Welty (US writer).

Eugénie

Variants and diminutives: Ena, Eugenia, Gene, Genie, Ina

Meaning: 'well-born' (Greek). A female version of Eugene.

Notable namesakes: Saint Eugenia; Eugénie de Montijo, wife of Emperor Napoleon III of France; the eponymous heroine of the novel *Eugénie Grandet*, by French writer Honoré de Balzac; Princess Eugenie of the United Kingdom.

Eulalia

Variants and diminutives: Eula, Eulalie.

Meaning: 'sweet talker' (Greek).

Notable namesakes: Saint Eulalia.

Eunice

Variants and diminutives: Niki, Nikki, Unice, Younice.

Meaning: 'victorious' (Greek).

Notable namesakes: the mother of Timothy in the New Testament.

Euphemia

Variants and diminutives: Eadaoine, Effie, Effim, Effum, Epham, Eppie, Eufemia, Eupham, Eupheme, Femie, Fanny, Oighrig, Phamie, Phemie.

Meaning: 'well thought of' or 'auspicious talk' (Greek).

Notable namesakes: Saint Euphemia.

Eustacia

Variants and diminutives: Stacey, Stacia, Stacie, Stacy.

Meaning: 'fruitful', 'good' or 'ear of corn' (Greek). A female version of Eustace.

Evangeline

Variants and diminutives: Angela, Eva, Evangela, Evangelia, Evangelina, Eve, Lia, Litsa.

Meaning: 'gospel' or 'good news' (Greek); 'messenger'

(Greek) as a variant of Angela.

Notable namesakes: Evangeline Bellefontaine, the heroine of the poem *Evangeline, A Tale of Acadie*, by US poet Henry Wadsworth Longfellow; a character in the novel *Uncle Tom's Cabin*, by US writer Harriet Beecher Stowe.

Eve

Variants and diminutives: Aoiffe, Ava, Chava, Eba, Ebba, Eeva, Eeve, Eubha, Ev, Eva, Evadne, Evaine, Evalina, Evaline, Evathia, Evchen, Eveleen, Evelin, Evelina, Evelyn, Evetta, Evette, Evi, Evia,, Eviana, Evicka, Evie, Eviene, Evike, Evin, Evita, Evka, Evleen, Evlyn, Evonne, Evota, Evuska, Evy, Ewa, Ewalina, Ina, Lina, Vica, Yeva, Yevka, Zoe.

Meaning: 'life' (Hebrew).

Notable namesakes: the first woman and wife of Adam in the New Testament; Little Eva, a character in the novel *Uncle Tom's Cabin*, by US writer Harriet Beecher Stowe; Eva Gonzalèz (French painter); Eva Braun, the mistress of the German dictator Adolf Hitler; Eva Perón (see Evita, below); Eva Hesse (German-born US artist).

Eveline

Variants and diminutives: Avelina, Aveline, Eileen, Eve, Eveleen, Evelina, Evelyn, Evie.

Meaning: 'hazelnut' (Germanic) or 'bird' (Latin) as a variant of Evelyn (also a boy's name).

Notable namesakes: Evelina Anville, the heroine of the novel *Evelina*, by English writer Fanny Burney.

Evita

Variants and diminutives: Eva, Eve.

Meaning: 'life' (Hebrew) as a diminutive of Eva (Eve).

Notable namesakes: Evita (Eva) Perón, the Argentinian populist leader and wife of President Juan Perón, whose life story was dramatised in the British musical *Evita*, by Andrew Lloyd Webber and Tim Rice, subsequently also made into a film.

Fabiola

Variants and diminutives: Fabia, Fabiana.

Meaning: uncertain; possibly 'bean' or 'skilful' (Latin); derived from the Roman family name Fabius. A female version of Fabian.

Notable namesakes: Saint Fabiola; Fabiola de Mora y Aragón, wife of Baudouin, King of the Belgians.

Faith

Variants and diminutives: Fae, Fay, Faye, Fayth, Faythe, Fe, Fidelia, Fidelity.

Meaning: 'trust' or 'faithful' (Latin). A female version of Fidel.

Notable namesakes: Fides, one of the three goddesses of transactions in Roman mythology; one of the three Christian virtues, the other two being charity and hope, according to the New Testament.

Farrah

Variants and diminutives: Fara, Farah, Farra.

Meaning: 'happiness' (Arabic); 'lovely' (Middle English).

Notable namesakes: Farrah Fawcett (US actress).

Fatima

Variants and diminutives: Fatimah, Fatma.

Meaning: 'weaner' or 'abstainer' (Arabic).

Notable namesakes: the favourite daughter of the Prophet Mohammed, for whom the Portuguese village of Fatima, famed for visions of the Virgin Mary, was named; the last wife of the fairy-tale villain Bluebeard; Fatima Whitbread (British athlete).

Fawn

Variants and diminutives: Fauna, Fawna, Fawnah, Fawniah.

Meaning: 'offspring' (Latin).
Notable namesakes: a generic name given to young deer.

Fay

Variants and diminutives: Fae, Faye, Fayette, Fayina.
Meaning: 'fairy' (Old French); 'trust' or 'faithful' (Latin) as a diminutive of Faith, in turn a female version of Fidel.
Notable namesakes: Morgan le Fay ('the fairy'), an enchantress and half-sister of King Arthur in Arthurian legend; Fay Compton (British actress); Faye Dunaway (US actress); Fay Weldon (British writer).

Felicity

Variants and diminutives: Falice, Falicia, Falasha, Fela, Felcia, Felecia, Felice, Felicia, Feliciana, Felicidad, Felicie, Felicite, Felicitas, Felis, Felise, Felisha, Felisia, Felisse, Felita, Feliz, Feliza, Felka, Filicie, Filisia, Fillys, Flick, Lisha, Liss, Lissa, Lissie, Phelicia, Phil, Philicia.
Meaning: 'happy' or 'fortunate' (Latin). A female version of Felix.
Notable namesakes: Felicitas, the Roman goddess of happiness; Felicia Hemans (British poet); Felicity Kendal (British actress).

Fenella

Variants and diminutives: Finella, Finnuala, Finola, Fionnghuala, Fionila, Fionnuala, Fionnula, Fionuala, Nuala.
Meaning: 'fair-shouldered' (Irish Gaelic) as an anglicised version of Fionnuala.
Notable namesakes: Fionnuala, a character in Irish legend who was transformed into a swan; a character in the novel *Peveril of the Peak*, by Scottish writer Sir Walter Scott; Fenella Fielding (British actress).

Fern

Variants and diminutives: Ferne.
Meaning: 'leaf' (Old English); derived from the *Filicinophyta* phylum of plants.

Fifi

Variants and diminutives: Fi.
Meaning: 'God will increase' (Hebrew) as a diminutive of Josephine, in turn a female version of Joseph.
Notable namesakes: Fifi Trixibelle Geldof (daughter of the Irish musician Bob Geldof and British television presenter Paula Yates).

Fiona

Variants and diminutives: Fee, Ffion, Fi, Fio, Fionna, Fione.
Meaning: 'fair' (Scots Gaelic); a name coined for his pseudonym, Fiona Macleod, by Scottish poet William Sharp.
Notable namesakes: Ffion Hague, the wife of British politician William Hague.

Flavia

Variants and diminutives: Flavus.
Meaning: 'yellow' (Latin) as the female version of Flavius.

Fleur

Variants and diminutives: Fflur, Fleurette, Flora, Flower.
Meaning: 'flower' or 'blossom' (French). A variant of Flora.
Notable namesakes: Fleur Forsyte, a character in the collection of novels *The Forsyte Saga*, by British writer John Galsworthy.

Flora

Variants and diminutives: Eloryn, Fflur, Fiora, Fiore, Fleur, Fleure, Fleurette, Flo, Flor, Flore, Florella, Flores, Floressa, Floretta, Florette, Flori, Floria, Floriana, Florianne, Florida, Floridita, Florie, Florinda, Floris, Florita, Florri, Florrie, Flory, Florry, Floss, Flossie, Flower, Kveta, Kvekta, Lora, Lorka.
Meaning: 'flower' or 'blossom' (Latin).
Notable namesakes: the goddess of spring and flowers in Roman mythology; Saint Flora; the Scottish heroine Flora MacDonald, who effected the escape of Prince Charles Edward Stuart ('Bonnie Prince Charlie' or the 'Young Pretender') to France; the leading character of the novel *Cold Comfort Farm*, by British writer Stella Gibbons; Flora Robson (British actress); Flora Nwapa (Nigerian writer).

Florence

Variants and diminutives: Fiorella, Fiorenza, Flann, Flo, Flonda, Flor, Flora, Florance, Flore, Floreen, Floren, Florencia, Florentia, Florentina, Florenz, Florina, Florinda, Florine, Florri, Florrie, Floryn, Floss, Flossi, Flossie, Flossy.

Meaning: 'flowering' or 'blossoming' (Latin).

Notable namesakes: the Italian town of Florence (Firenze), where Florence Nightingale, the English founder of professional nursing, was born.

Fortuna

Variants and diminutives: Faustina, Faustine, Fortune, Fortunata.

Meaning: 'luck' (Latin).

Notable namesakes: Fortuna, the Roman goddess of luck.

Frances

Variants and diminutives: Cella, Chica, Fan, Fanchette, Fanchon, Fancy, Fanechka, Fani, Fania, Fanni, Fannie, Fanny, Fannye, Fanya, Fedora, Ferike, Fotina, Fraka, Fran, Franca, France, Francesca, Franci, Francie, Francina, Francine, Francisca, Franciska, Franciszka, Francise, Francka, Françoise, Franconia, Francyne, Frania, Franika, Frank, Frankey, Frankie, Franni, Frannie, Franny, Franja, Franny, Fanz, Franze, Franziska, Franziske, Fronia, Paca, Pancha, Panchita, Paquita, Ranny.

Meaning: 'French' (Latin). A female version of Francis.

Notable namesakes: Saint Francesca Romana (Frances of Rome), patron saint of motorists, wives and widows; Francesca, the lover of Paolo in Italian poet Dante's *Inferno*, the first part of the epic poem *The Divine Comedy*; the eponymous heroine of the novel *Fanny Hill, Memoirs of a Woman of Pleasure*, by English writer John Cleland; Fanny Burney (English writer); Frances Brooke (English-born Canadian writer); Fanny Adams, a murdered woman whose name gave rise to the expression 'sweet Fanny Adams'; Saint Frances Cabrini, founder of the religious order the Missionary Sisters of the Sacred Heart and patron saint of emigrants and immigrants; Fanny Kemble (British actress); Frances Hodgson Burnett (English-born US writer); Frances Hodgkins (New Zealand painter); Françoise Sagan (French writer); Francesca Annis (British actress).

Freda

Variants and diminutives: Elfrida, Fred, Fredda, Freddie, Freddy, Fredi, Fredie, Fredyne, Freida, Freide, Frieda, Friede, Frida, Fritzi, Fryda.

Meaning: 'peace' (Germanic); 'elf' and 'strength' (Old English) as a diminutive of Elfrida; 'reconciliation' (Welsh) and 'peace' (Old English) as a diminutive of Winifred. Also a female version of Frederick.

Notable namesakes: Frieda von Richthofen, wife of the English writer D H Lawrence; Frida Kahlo (Mexican artist).

Frederica

Variants and diminutives: Farica, Federica, Fedriska, Feriga, Fred, Freda, Fredda, Freddi, Freddie, Freddy, Fredericka, Frederika, Frederique, Fredrica, Fredrika, Frerika, Frici, Frida, Friederike, Fritze, Frizinn, Fryda, Fryderyka, Frydryka, Rica, Ricki, Ricky, Rika, Rike, Rikki.

Meaning: 'peace' and 'ruler' (Germanic). A female version of Frederick.

Freya

Variants and diminutives: Freja, Freyja, Froja.

Meaning: 'noble lady' (Old Norse).

Notable namesakes: Freyja, a fertility goddess and Vanir of Norse mythology; Freya Stark (English travel writer).

Fulvia

Meaning: 'tawny' (Latin); derived from the Roman family name Fulvius.

G

Gabrielle

Variants and diminutives: Gabay, Gabbie, Gabby, Gabel, Gabell, Gabey, Gabi, Gabie, Gabriel, Gabriela, Gabriella, Gabryell, Gaby, Gavi, Gavra, Gavriela, Gavriella, Gavrielle, Gavrila, Gavrilla, Gay, Gaye, Gigi.
Meaning: 'man of God' or 'my strength is God' (Hebrew). A female version of Gabriel.
Notable namesakes: Gabrielle d'Estrées, mistress of King Henri IV of France; Gabrielle, also known as Coco, Chanel (French fashion designer); Gabrielle Roy (Canadian writer); Gabriela Mistral (Chilean poet); Gabriela Sabatini (Argentinian tennis player); Gabriela, a leading chracter of the novel *Gabriela, Clove and Cinnamon*, by Brazilian writer Jorge Amado.

Gaia

Meaning: 'earth' (Greek).
Notable namesakes: the primeval earth goddess of Greek mythology, also called Ge, for whom James Lovelock named the holistic ecological Gaia theory.

Gail

Variants and diminutives: Gael, Gale, Gayel, Gayelle, Gayle, Gayleen, Gaylin, Gayline, Gaylyn, Gaylynn.
Meaning: 'my father rejoices' or 'source of joy' (Hebrew). A diminutive of Abigail.
Notable namesakes: Gail Godwin (US writer).

Gardenia

Meaning: derived from the name of the *Gardenia* genus of flowering plants named for the botanist Dr Alexander Garden.

Garnet

Variants and diminutives: Garnett, Grania.
Meaning: 'grain' (Latin); 'pomegranate' (Old French); derived from the name of the silicate-mineral gemstone that ranges from pink to dark red in colour. Also a boy's name.

Gay

Variants and diminutives: Gae, Gaye.
Meaning: 'merry' (Old French). Also a diminutive of Gabrielle and Gaynor and a boy's name, although recently rendered unfashionable by its homosexual connotations.

Gaynor

Variants and diminutives: Gaenor, Gainer, Gaenor, Gay, Gayner.
Meaning: 'fair' and 'yielding' or 'ghost' (Welsh) as a diminutive of Guinevere.

Gemma

Variants and diminutives: Gem, Jem, Jemma.
Meaning: 'jewel' (Latin and Italian).
Notable namesakes: Saint Gemma Galcani; Gemma Craven (British actress).

Geneva

Variants and diminutives: Gena, Genève, Genevia, Genna, Janeva, Janevra.
Meaning: 'juniper' or 'river mouth' (Latin).
Notable namesakes: Geneva (Genève), a Swiss canton, city and lake (also known as Lac Léman); the Geneva Convention, an international agreement regulating certain rules of war.

Genevieve

Variants and diminutives: Gen, Gena, Genavieve, Gene, Geneva, Geneveeve, Genevra, Genie, Genivieve, Ginette, Genni, Gennie, Genny, Genovefa, Genovera, Genoveva, Gina, Guenevere, Guinevere, Janeva, Jen, Jenevieve, Jenni, Jennie, Jenny.
Meaning: uncertain; possibly 'race' and 'woman' (Germanic).
Notable namesakes: Saint Geneviève, patron saint of Paris and disasters.

Georgia

Variants and diminutives: George, Georgea,

Georgeanna, Georgeanne, Georgeen, Georgeene, Georgena, Georgene, Georgess, Georgett, Georgetta, Georgette, Georgi, Georgiana, Georgianna, Georgianne, Georgie, Georgienne, Georgina, Georgine, Georginita, Georgy, Gerda, Gigi, Gina, Gyorci, Gyorgyi, Jirca, Jirina, Jirka, Jorgina.
Meaning: 'farmer' (Greek). A female version of George.
Notable namesakes: the US state of Georgia; the Russian republic of Georgia; Georgia O'Keeffe (US artist).

Georgina
Variants and diminutives: George, Georgea, Georgeanna, Georgeanne, Georgeen, Georgeene, Georgena, Georgene, Georgess, Georgett, Georgetta, Georgette, Georgi, Georgia, Georgiana, Georgianna, Georgianne, Georgie, Georgienne, Georgine, Georginita, Georgy, Gerda, Gigi, Gina, Gyorci, Gyorgyi, Jirca, Jirina, Jirka, Jorgina.
Meaning: 'farmer' (Greek). A female version of George.
Notable namesakes: Georgina, Duchess of Devonshire; Georgette Heyer (British writer).

Geraldine
Variants and diminutives: Deena, Dina, Geralda, Geraldene, Geraldina, Gerarda, Gerardine, Gerardine, Gererdina, Gererdine, Gerhardina, Gerhardine, Geri, Gerldine, Gerri, Gerrie, Gerry, Giralda, Jeralee, Jere, Jeri, Jerri, Jerrie, Jerry.
Meaning: 'spear' and 'rule' (Germanic). A female version of Gerald.
Notable namesakes: 'The Fair Geraldine', the name by which the English poet Henry Howard, Earl of Surrey, addressed Lady Elizabeth Fitzgerald in his sonnet; a character in the poem *Christabel*, by English poet Samuel Taylor Coleridge; the heroine of the poem *Lady Geraldine's Courtship*, by English poet Elizabeth Barrett Browning; Geri Halliwell (British singer).

Gerda
Variants and diminutives: Gerde.
Meaning: 'protector' or 'enclosure' (Old Norse).

Notable namesakes: a name of Freyja, a fertility goddess and Vanir of Norse mythology; a character in the fairy story 'The Snow Queen', by the Danish writer Hans Christian Andersen.

Germaine
Variants and diminutives: Germain, Germana, Germane, Germayne, Jermain, Jermaine, Jermane, Jermayn, Jermayne.
Meaning: 'brother' (Latin) or 'German' (Old French). A female version of Germain (Jermaine).
Notable namesakes: Germaine Greer (Australian feminist writer).

Gertrude
Variants and diminutives: Gatt, Gatty, Gerda, Gert, Gerte, Gertie, Gertruda, Gertrudis, Gerty, Jara, Jera, Jerica, Truda, Trude, Trudel, Trudi, Trudie, Trudy, Trula, Truta.
Meaning: 'spear' and 'strength' (Germanic).
Notable namesakes: Saint Gertrude of Nivelles, patron saint of travellers and those who fear rats and mice; Saint Gertrude the Great; Hamlet's mother in William Shakespeare's play *Hamlet*; Gertrude Jekyll (English garden designer); Gertrude Bell (English writer, explorer and archaeologist); Gertrude Stein (US writer); Gertrude Lawrence (British actress).

Ghislaine
Variants and diminutives: Ghislain.
Meaning: 'pledge' (Germanic).

Gilberta
Variants and diminutives: Gil, Gilbertine.
Meaning: 'pledge' or 'hostage' and 'bright' (Germanic); 'servant', 'servant of Saint Bridget' or 'servant of Saint Gilbert' (Scots Gaelic). A female version of Gilbert.

Gilda
Variants and diminutives: Gilde, Gildi, Gildie, Gildita, Gildy, Gill, Gill, Jil, Jill.
Meaning: uncertain; possibly 'to gild' (Old English).
Notable namesakes: the US film *Gilda*; Gilda Radner (US actress and comedienne).

Gillian

Variants and diminutives: Gilian, Gill, Gillan, Gilli, Gilianne, Gillie, Gilly, Gillyanne, Jil, Jili, Jill, Jilli, Jillian, Jilliann, Jillianne, Jillie, Jilly, Jillyan, Juliana, Lian.
Meaning: uncertain; possibly 'fair-skinned' (Latin); derived from the Roman family name Julianus. A female version of Julian.
Notable namesakes: Gillian Andersen (US actress); Jilly Cooper (British writer).

Gina

Variants and diminutives: Geena, Ginat.
Meaning: 'garden' (Hebrew); 'silvery' (Japanese); otherwise dependent on the name from which it is derived: for example, 'farmer' (Greek) as a diminutive of Georgina.
Notable namesakes: Gina Lollobrigida (Italian actress).

Gisela

Variants and diminutives: Ghislaine, Gigi, Gisele, Gisella, Giselle, Giza, Gizela, Gizi, Gizike, Gizus.
Meaning: 'pledge' or 'hostage' (Germanic).
Notable namesakes: *Giselle*, a ballet inspired by the French writer Théophile Gautier.

Gladys

Variants and diminutives: Glad, Gladi, Gladis, Gleda, Gwladys.
Meaning: uncertain; possibly 'small sword' (Latin); possibly 'lame' (Latin), derived from a Roman family name, as the Welsh version of Claudia, in turn a female version of Claude; possibly 'territorial ruler' or 'delicate flower' (Welsh).
Notable namesakes: Gladys Cooper (British actress); Gladys Knight (US singer).

Glenda

Variants and diminutives: Glen, Glennie, Glenny.
Meaning: 'pure' or 'holy' and 'good' (Welsh).
Notable namesakes: Glenda Jackson (British actress and politician).

Glenna

Variants and diminutives: Glen, Glena, Gleneen,
Glenesha, Glenice, Glenine, Glenisha, Glenn, Glenne, Glenneen, Glennette, Glenni, Glennie, Glennine.
Meaning: 'valley' (Scots Gaelic); derived from a Scottish family name, in turn derived from a geographical feature. A female version of Glen.

Glenys

Variants and diminutives: Glen, Glenis, Glinys, Glyn, Glynis.
Meaning: 'pure' or 'holy' (Welsh).
Notable namesakes: Glenys Kinnock (Welsh politician).

Gloria

Variants and diminutives: Glora, Gloree, Glori, Gloriana, Gloriane, Glorianna, Glorianne, Glorie, Glorria, Glory.
Meaning: 'glory' (Latin).
Notable namesakes: Gloriana, Queen of the Faeries, in the moral allegory *The Faerie Queen*, by English poet Edmund Spenser; Gloriana, a flattering name referring to Elizabeth I, Queen of England; a character in the play *You Never Can Tell*, by the Irish writer George Bernard Shaw; Gloria Swanson (US actress); the title of a song by Northern Irish musician Van Morrison.

Glynis

Variants and diminutives: Glenice, Glenis, Glenise, Glennice, Glennis, Glennys, Glenwys, Glenys, Glenyse, Glinnis, Glinys, Glyn, Glynn, Glynnis.
Meaning: 'little valley' (Welsh).
Notable namesakes: Glynis Johns (British actress).

Golda

Variants and diminutives: Goldarina, Goldi, Goldia, Goldie, Goldina, Goldy.
Meaning: 'golden' (Germanic).
Notable namesakes: Golda Meir (Israeli politician); Goldie Hawn (US actress).

Grace

Variants and diminutives: Arete, Engracia, Giorsal, Graca, Gracia, Graciana, Gracie, Graciela, Gráinne, Grania, Grata, Gratia, Gratiana, Grayce, Grazia, Graziella, Grazielle, Grazina, Graziosa, Kaleki.

Meaning: 'grace' (Latin).

Notable namesakes: the three Graces, or Chantes, of Greek mythology (the goddesses Aglaia, Euphrosyne and Thalia), who personified grace and beauty; Grace O'Malley (or Gráine Ni Maille), a sea-faring princess of Irish legend; Grace Darling (Scottish life-saving heroine); Grazia Deledda (Italian writer); Gracie Fields (British singer and actress); Grace Hartigan (US artist); Grace Kelly (the actress who became Princess Grace of Monaco on her marriage to Prince Rainier III of Monaco); Grace Jones (US singer).

Gráinne

Variants and diminutives: Grace, Gráine, Grania, Granya.

Meaning: 'love', 'terrifier' or 'goddess of grain' (Irish Gaelic).

Notable namesakes: the daughter of Cormac Mac Airt, who eloped with Diarmuid in Irish mythology; Gráine Ni Maille (or Grace O'Malley), a sea-faring princess of Irish legend.

Greta

Variants and diminutives: Gretal, Gretchen, Grete, Gretel, Grethal, Grethel, Gretta, Grette, Gryta, Margareta, Margarete.

Meaning: 'pearl' (Greek) as a German and Scandinavian diminutive of Margareta (Margaret).

Notable namesakes: Gretel, the young heroine of the fairy tale 'Hansel and Gretel', popularised by the German folklorists the Brothers Grimm; Gretchen, a character in the play Faust, by German writer Johann Wolfgang von Goethe; Greta Garbo (Swedish actress).

Griselda

Variants and diminutives: Chriselda, Criselda, Griseldis, Grishilda, Grishilde, Grissel, Grittie, Grizel, Grizelda, Grizzel, Grizzie, Selda, Zelda.

Meaning: 'grey' and 'battle' (Germanic).

Notable namesakes: 'the patient' Griselda, the heroine of Italian poet Giovanni Boccaccio's The Decameron, adapted by English poet Geoffrey Chaucer for 'The Clerk's Tale (part of The Canterbury Tales).

Guadelupe

Variants and diminutives: Guada, Guadaloupa, Guadaloupe, Guadaloupa, Guadalupi, Guadelupe, Guadolupa, Guadolupe, Lupe, Lupeta, Lupina, Lupita.

Meaning: 'the world's valley' (Spanish); derived from the name of the West Indian island group in the Leeward Islands.

Notable namesakes: 'The Virgin of Guadelupe', a name for the Virgin Mary.

Guinevere

Variants and diminutives: Gaenor, Gaynor, Genevra, Ginevra, Guener, Guenever, Guenevere, Guenievre, Guinever, Gweniver, Jenifer, Jennifer, Jenniver.

Meaning: 'fair' and 'yielding' or 'ghost' (Welsh).

Notable namesakes: the wife of King Arthur and lover of Sir Lancelot in Arthurian legend.

Gwen

Variants and diminutives: Gwena, Gwenna, Gwinn, Gwynn, Gwynne, Wynne.

Meaning: 'fair' (Welsh). Also a diminutive of Gwendolyn and other names beginning with 'Gwen-'. A female version of Gwyn.

Notable namesakes: a grandmother of King Arthur in Arthurian legend; Gwen John (British artist).

Gwendolyn

Variants and diminutives: Guendolen, Gwen, Gwena, Gwenda, Gwendaline, Gwendeth, Gwendi, Gwendolen, Gwendolin, Gwendolina, Gwendoline, Gwendolyne, Gwendolynn, Gwenna, Gwennie, Gwenny, Wenda, Wendi, Wendie, Wendoline, Wendy, Wyn, Wynelle, Wynette, Wynne.

Meaning: 'fair' and 'ring' (Welsh).

Notable namesakes: a number of characters of Welsh legend; Gwendolina, the wife of Merlin in Arthurian legend; Gwendolyn Harleth, the heroine of the novel Daniel Deronda, by English writer George Eliot; Gwendolen Fairfax, a character in the play The Importance of Being Earnest, by Irish writer Oscar Wilde;

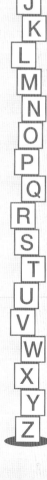

Gwendolyn Brooks (US writer); Gwendolyn MacEwen (Canadian writer).

Gwyneth

Variants and diminutives: Gwen, Gwenda, Gwenith, Gwenn, Gwenne, Gwennie, Gwenny, Gwenth, Gwyn, Gwynne, Gwynedd, Gwynneth, Wendi, Wendie, Wendy, Winni, Winnie, Winny, Wynne.
Meaning: 'happiness' or 'luck' (Welsh).
Notable namesakes: the Welsh county of Gwynedd; Gwyneth Paltrow (US actress).

Habiba

Variants and diminutives: Haviva.
Meaning: 'lover' or 'beloved' (Arabic). A female version of Habib.

Hadara

Meaning: 'bedeck with loveliness' (Hebrew).

Hadassah

Variants and diminutives: Dasi, Dassi, Hadassa.
Meaning: 'myrtle' or 'bride' (Hebrew).
Notable namesakes: another name of Esther, the wife of Ahasuerus (Xerxes), a Persian king, whose deliverance of the Jewish people, told in the Old Testament Book of Esther, is celebrated annually during the Jewish festival of Purim.

Hagar

Meaning: 'abandoned' (Hebrew).
Notable namesakes: the Egyptian maid of Sarah and mother of Ishmael by Abraham in the Old Testament.

Hana

Variants and diminutives: Hanae, Hanako.
Meaning: 'blossom' (Japanese); 'sky' or 'dark cloud' (Arapaho).

Hannah

Variants and diminutives: Anci, Aniko, Ann, Anna, Anne, Annuska, Chana, Chanah, Chani, Hana, Hania, Hanicka, Hanita, Hanka, Hanna, Hanne, Hannele, Hanni, Hannie, Hanny, Johannah, Nan, Nana, Nina, Ninascka, Nusi, Ona.
Meaning: 'I have been favoured (by God)' (Hebrew).
Notable namesakes: the wife of Elkanah and mother of Samuel in the Old Testament; Hannah Cowley (English playwright); Hannah Adams (US historian); the eponymous heroine of the drama *Hannele*, by German playwright Gerhart Hauptmann; Hannah Arendt (German-born US political philosopher); Hannah Höch (German artist); Hannah Wilke (US artist).

Harmony

Variants and diminutives: Harmonee, Harmoni, Harmonia, Harmonie.
Meaning: 'harmony' (Greek).
Notable namesakes: Harmonia, the daughter of Aphrodite and Ares and wife of Cadmus in Greek mythology.

Harriet

Variants and diminutives: Arriet, Enrica, Enrichetta, Enrieta, Enriqueta, Enriquita, Etta, Etti, Ettie, Haliaka, Harri, Harrie, Harrietta, Harriette, Harriot, Harriott, Hatti, Hattie, Hatty, Hendrike, Henia, Henka, Henrie, Henrieta, Henriete, Henrietta, Henriette, Henrinka, Henriqueta, Hetta, Hetti, Hettie, Hetty, Jarri, Jindraska, Kika, Kiki, Minette, Queta, Yetta, Yettie, Yetty.
Meaning: 'home' and 'ruler' (Germanic) as a female version of Harry (Henry).
Notable namesakes: Harriet Beecher Stowe (US writer); Harriet Tubman (US slavery abolitionist); Harriet Martineau (English writer); Hattie Jacques (British actress and comedienne).

Hasika
Meaning: 'laughter' (Sanskrit).

Hayat
Meaning: 'life' (Arabic).

Hayley
Variants and diminutives: Haile, Hailey, Haley, Hali, Halie, Halli, Hallie, Hally, Haylie.
Meaning: 'hay' and 'meadow' (Old English); derived from an English family name, in turn derived from a place name; 'hero' (Norse); 'ingenious' (Irish Gaelic).
Notable namesakes: Hayley Mills (British actress).

Hazel
Meaning: 'hazelnut' (Old English); derived from the common name of the *Corylus* genus of nut-bearing trees.
Notable namesakes: a greeny-brown eye colour.

Heather
Meaning: 'flowering heath' or 'heather' (Middle English); derived from the common name of ericaceous shrubs, such as *Calluna vulgaris* and *Erica*.

Hebe
Meaning: 'young' (Greek).
Notable namesakes: the goddess of youth and cupbearer of the Olympian gods in Greek mythology; the botanical name of the shrubby veronica genus of flowering shrubs.

Hedwig
Variants and diminutives: Eda, Heda, Hedda, Heddi, Heddie, Heddy, Hede, Hedi, Hedvick, Hedvika, Hedy.
Meaning: 'struggle' or 'refuge' and 'during war' (Germanic).
Notable namesakes: the eponymous heroine of the play *Hedda Gabler*, by Norwegian playwright Henrik Ibsen; Hedy Lamarr (Austrian actress); Harry Potter's owl in the 'Harry Potter' series of children's books by British writer J K Rowling.

Heidi
Variants and diminutives: Heide, Heidie.
Meaning: 'noble' or 'nobility' (Germanic) as a diminutive of Adelheid (Adelaide).
Notable namesakes: the eponymous young heroine of *Heidi*, a children's story by the Swiss writer Johanna Spyri.

Helen
Variants and diminutives: Ailie, Ale, Alena, Alenka, Aliute, Eileen, Eilidh, Elaina, Elaine, Elana, Elane, Elayne, Eleanor, Eleanora, Eleanore, Elen, Elena, Elene, Eleni, Elenita, Elenitsa, Elenka, Elenoa, Elenola, Elenor, Elenora, Elenore, Elenuta, Eleonor, Eleonora, Elia, Elianora, Elin, Elinor, Elle, Ellen, Elli, Ellie, Ellin, Elly, Ellyn, Elnora, Elyn, Ena, Halina, Hela, Helaine, Helayne, Hele, Helena, Hélène, Helenka, Helina, Hella, Helli, Heluska, Jelena, Jelika, Ila, Ileana, Ileanna, Ilena, Iliana, Ilka, Ilona, Ilonka, Iluska, Laina, Lana, Léan, Leena, Lena, Lenci, Lene, Leni, Lenka, Lenni, Lenore, Leona, Leonora, Leonor, Leonore, Leontina, Leora, Liana, Lili, Lina, Lino, Liolya, Liora, Nel, Nell, Nella, Nellene, Nelli, Nellie, Nelly, Nelya, Nitsa, Nora, Norah, Olena, Olenka, Yelena.
Meaning: 'bright' (Greek).
Notable namesakes: Helen, daughter of Zeus and Leda, wife of Menelaus, King of Sparta, and mistress of Paris, a prince of Troy, in Greek mythology, who is referred to in many plays, including those by the Greek playwright Euripides and the English playwrights William Shakespeare (*All's Well That Ends Well* and *A Midsummer Night's Dream*) and Christopher Marlowe (*Faustus*); Saint Helena, mother of the Roman emperor Constantine, 'the Great'; the lover of Adam Flemming in the Scottish ballad *Helen of Kirconnell*; the eponymous title character of the ballad *Sister Helen*, by English poet and artist Dante Gabriel Rossetti; Helen Hunt Jackson and Helen MacInnes (US writers); Helena Petrovna Blavatsky (Russian spiritualist and occultist); Helen Keller (blind and deaf US author); Helen Frankenthaler (US artist); Helen Mirren and Helena Bonham Carter (British actresses); Helena Christensen (Danish model); Helen Hunt (US actress).

Helga
Variants and diminutives: Olga.
Meaning: 'prosperous' or 'pious' (Old Norse).

Henrietta

Variants and diminutives: Enrica, Enrichetta, Enrieta, Enriqueta, Enriquitta, Etta, Etti, Ettie, Etty, Haliaka, Harri, Harrie, Harriet, Harrietta, Harriette, Harriot, Harriott, Hatti, Hattie, Hatty, Hen, Hendrike, Henia, Henka, Henni, Hennie, Henny, Henrie, Henrieta, Henriete, Henriette, Henrinka, Henriqueta, Hetta, Hetti, Hettie, Hetty, Jarri, Jindraska, Kika, Kiki, Minette, Netta, Nettie, Netty, Oighrig, Queta, Yetta, Yettie, Yetty.

Meaning: 'home' and 'ruler' (Germanic) as a female variant of Henry.

Notable namesakes: Henrietta Maria, daughter of King Henri IV of France and wife of King Charles I of England.

Hephzibah

Variants and diminutives: Eppie, Eppy, Hephziba, Hepsey, Hepsie, Hepsy, Hepzi, Hepziba, Hepzibah, Hesba.

Meaning: 'she is my delight' or 'she is my desire' (Hebrew).

Notable namesakes: Hephzibah Menuhin (US pianist).

Hera

Meaning: 'lady' (Greek).

Notable namesakes: the queen of heaven, wife of Zeus and goddess of marriage in Greek mythology.

Hermione

Variants and diminutives: Erma, Herma, Hermia, Hermina, Hermine, Herminia, Mina.

Meaning: 'support' or 'stone' (Greek). A female variant of Hermes.

Notable namesakes: a name of Persephone, goddess of the underworld in Greek mythology; the daughter of Menelaus and Helen in Greek mythology; a character in William Shakespeare's play *The Winter's Tale*; Hermia, a character in William Shakespeare's play *A Midsummer Night's Dream*; Hermione Gingold and Hermione Baddeley (British actresses); Hermione Granger, a character in the 'Harry Potter' series of children's books by British writer J K Rowling.

Hero

Meaning: 'hero' (Greek).

Notable namesakes: a priestess of Aphrodite and lover of Leander, whose tragic story is told in the plays *Hero and Leander*, by English playwright Christopher Marlowe, and *Des Meeres und der Liebe Wellen* (*The Waves of Sea and Love*), by Austrian playwright Franz Grillparzer.

Hesper

Variants and diminutives: Hespera, Hesperia.

Meaning: 'evening' or 'evening star' (Greek).

Notable namesakes: Hesperus, a name for an evening star, particularly Venus; the Hesperides, the guardians of the golden-apple-bearing tree on the Islands of the Blessed, or the Hesperides, in Greek mythology; Hesperia, the poetic Greek name for Italy and the poetic Roman name for Spain and lands beyond.

Hester

Variants and diminutives: Esther, Hettie, Hetty.

Meaning: 'myrtle' or 'bride' (Hebrew) or 'star' (Persian) as a variant of Esther.

Notable namesakes: Lady Hester Stanhope (English traveller); Hester Prynne, a leading character in the novel *The Scarlet Letter*, by US writer Nathaniel Hawthorne; Hester Lynch Thrale (English bluestocking).

Hestia

Meaning: 'hearth' (Greek).

Notable namesakes: the goddess of the hearth flame and protector of the home in Greek mythology.

Hilary

Variants and diminutives: Hilaire, Hilaria, Hilarie, Hillarie, Hillary, Ilaria.

Meaning: 'cheerfulness' (Latin). Also a boy's name.

Notable namesakes: Hillary Rodham Clinton (US politician).

Hilda

Variants and diminutives: Hild, Hilde, Hildegard, Hildi, Hildie, Hildy, Hylda.

Meaning: 'battle' (Germanic).

Notable namesakes: Hild, the leader of the Valkyries in Norse mythology; Saint Hilda; Hilda Doolittle (US poet); Hilda Ogden, a character in the British television soap opera *Coronation Street;* Hylda Baker (British actress and comedienne).

Hippolyta
Variants and diminutives: Pollie, Polly.
Meaning: 'horse' and 'release' (Greek) as a female version of Hippolytus.
Notable namesakes: queen of the Amazons and mother of Hippolytus in Greek mythology; a character in William Shakespeare's play *A Midsummer Night's Dream.*

Holly
Variants and diminutives: Holley, Holli, Hollie, Hollye.
Meaning: 'holy' or 'holly tree' (Old English); derived from the common name of the *Ilex* genus of plants.
Notable namesakes: Holly Forsyte, a character in *The Forsyte Saga*, a collection of novels by the British writer John Galsworthy; a character in the novel *Tender is the Night*, by US writer F Scott Fitzgerald.

Honey
Meaning: 'honey' (Old English); derived from the name of the bee-produced food-stuff.

Honor
Variants and diminutives: Annora, Honora, Honoria, Honorine, Honour, Nora, Norah, Noreen, Norine, Norrie, Nureen, Onóra.
Meaning: 'honour' (Latin).
Notable namesakes: Honor Tracy (British writer); Honor Blackman (British actress).

Hope
Variants and diminutives: Esperance, Esperanza, Hopi, Hopie.
Meaning: 'hope' (Old English); 'little valley' (Old English) when derived from an English family name and place name.
Notable namesakes: one of the three Christian virtues, the other two being charity and faith, according to the New Testament.

Horatia
Meaning: uncertain; possibly 'time' or 'hour' (Latin); derived from the Roman family name Horatius. A female version of Horatio (Horace).

Hortensia
Variants and diminutives: Hortense, Ortense, Ortensia.
Meaning: 'garden' (Latin); derived from the Roman family name Hortensius.
Notable namesakes: the common name of the mophead hydrangea, *Hydrangea macrophylla;* Hortense de Beauharnais, wife of Louis Bonaparte and mother of Emperor Napoleon III of France; Hortense Calisher (US writer).

Hoshi
Variants and diminutives: Hoshie, Hoshiko, Hoshiyo.
Meaning: 'star' (Japanese).

Hulda
Variants and diminutives: Hildie, Huldah, Huldi, Huldy.
Meaning: 'weasel' (Hebrew); 'covered' or 'muffled' (Old Norse); 'beloved' or 'gracious' (Germanic).
Notable namesakes: Huldah, a female prophet in the Old Testament; a goddess of marriage in Teutonic mythology.

Hyacinth
Variants and diminutives: Cinthie, Cynthia, Cynthie, Giacinta, Hy, Hyacintha, Hyacinthe, Hyacinthia, Jacenta, Jacinda, Jacinta, Jacinth, Jacintha, Jacinthe, Jackie, Jacky.
Meaning: 'precious blue stone' (Greek); derived from the name of the *Hyacinthus* genus of flowering plants. Once also a boy's name.
Notable namesakes: Hyacinthus, a young man inadvertently killed by Apollo in Greek mythology, from whose spilled blood the first hyacinths were said

A B C D E F G H I J K L M N O P Q R S T U V W X Y Z

to have sprung; Saint Hyacinth; another name for the red gemstone jacinth; Hyacinth Bucket, the leading character of the British television sitcom *Keeping up Appearances*.

Hypatia

Meaning: 'highest' (Greek).
Notable namesakes: a Greek philosopher, 'the Divine Pagan', whose story – and sticky end – is told in the novel *Hypatia*, by English writer Charles Kingsley.

Ianthe

Variants and diminutives: Iantha, Iola, Iolanthe, Iole, Ione.
Meaning: 'violet' or 'dawn cloud' (Greek).
Notable namesakes: as a daughter of the sea deities Oceanus and Tethys, one of the Oceanides, or water nymphs, of Greek mythology; a character in the poem *Queen Mab*, by English poet Percy Bysshe Shelley.

Ida

Variants and diminutives: Aida, Edonia, Edony, Idalee, Idaleene, Idalene, Idalia, Idalina, Idaline, Idalou, Idana, Idande, Idane, Iddes, Ide, Idel, Idella, Idelle, Idena, Ideny, Idette, Idhuna, Idina, Idona, Idonea, Idonia, Idony, Idun, Iduna, Idunn, Iduska, Ita, Itka, Ydonea.
Meaning: 'work' (Germanic); 'protection' or 'prosperity' (Old English).
Notable namesakes: a number of nymphs in Greek mythology; Mount Ida, a mountain on the Greek island of Crete, supposedly the birthplace of Zeus, the supreme god of Greek mythology; Idun, the goddess

of the seasons and keeper of the golden apples of immortality in Norse mythology; Idane, the heroine of the poem *The Princess*, by English poet Alfred, Lord Tennyson; the eponymous heroine of the opera *Princess Ida*, by the British collaborators W S Gilbert and Arthur Sullivan; Ida Applebroog (US artist).

Ilia

Meaning: 'from Ilium' (Latin), Ilium being Troy, the ancient city in Asia Minor.
Notable namesakes: also known as Rhea Silvia, the mother of Romulus and Remus, founders of Rome, in Roman mythology.

Ilka

Variants and diminutives: Ilke.
Meaning: 'striving' or 'flattering' (Slavic).

Ilona

Variants and diminutives: Helen, Ili, Ilonka, Lonci.
Meaning: 'bright' (Greek) as a Hungarian variant of Helen; 'beautiful' (Hungarian).

Ilse

Variants and diminutives: Ilsa.
Meaning: 'God is perfection', 'God is satisfaction', 'dedicated to God' or 'God's oath' (Hebrew). A German variant of Elizabeth.
Notable namesakes: Ilse Aichinger (Austrian writer).

Imogen

Variants and diminutives: Emogene, Imagina, Immie, Immy, Imogene, Imogine, Imojean, Innogen, Inogen.
Meaning: uncertain; possibly 'innocent' or 'image' (Latin); possibly 'daughter' (Irish Gaelic) as a misprint of Innogen that first appeared as the name of the daughter of Cymbeline in William Shakespeare's play *Cymbeline*.
Notable namesakes: Imogen Stubbs (British actress).

India

Variants and diminutives: Indie, Indy.
Meaning: 'river' (Sanskrit); derived from the name of the country, itself derived from the river Indus.
Notable namesakes: India Wilkes, a character in the

novel *Gone With the Wind*, by US author Margaret Mitchell; India Hicks (British model).

Indigo
Variants and diminutives: Indie, Indy.
Meaning: 'from India' (Greek).
Notable namesakes: a dark-blue colour.

Indira
Variants and diminutives: Indie, Indy.
Meaning: 'splendid' (Hindi).
Notable namesakes: Indira Gandhi (Indian politician).

Inez
Variants and diminutives: Ines, Inesita, Inessa, Ynes, Ynesita, Ynez.
Meaning: 'pure' or 'chaste' (Greek) or 'lamb' (Latin) as a Spanish version of Agnes.
Notable namesakes: Donna Inez, the mother of Don Juan in the poem *Don Juan*, by English poet George, Lord Byron.

Ingeborg
Variants and diminutives: Inga, Ingaberg, Inge, Ingeberg, Inger, Ingmar, Ingunna, Inky.
Meaning: 'Ing's protection' (Old Norse), Ing being a Norse fertility god.
Notable namesakes: several characters in Norse legend, including the daughter of King Bele of Norway, whose story is told in the *Frithiof Saga*.

Ingrid
Variants and diminutives: Inga, Inge, Inger, Ingerith, Ingmar, Ingrede, Ingunna, Inky.
Meaning: 'Ing's beautiful one', 'Ing's daughter' or 'Ing's ride [referring to a golden boar]' (Old Norse), Ing being a Norse fertility god.
Notable namesakes: Ingrid Bergman (Swedish actress); Ingrid Pitt (British actress).

Iolanthe
Variants and diminutives: Ianthe, Iola, Iole, Yolanda, Yolande.
Meaning: 'violet' or 'dawn cloud' (Greek) as a variant of Iole.

Notable namesakes: the eponymous heroine of the opera *Iolanthe*, by the British collaborators W S Gilbert and Arthur Sullivan.

Iole
Variants and diminutives: Ianthe, Iola, Iolanthe, Iona, Ione.
Meaning: 'violet' or 'dawn cloud' (Greek).
Notable namesakes: the daughter of Antioche and Eulytus, King of Oechalia, who was beloved by Heracles, (Hercules) in Greek mythology.

Iona
Variants and diminutives: Ione, Ionia.
Meaning: uncertain; possibly 'violet' or 'dawn cloud' (Greek); possibly 'island' (Old Norse); derived from the name of the Scottish Hebridean island.

Iphigenia
Variants and diminutives: Iffie, Iphie, Iphy.
Meaning: 'sacrifice' (Greek).
Notable namesakes: the daughter of Agamemnon and Clytemnestra, who was sacrificed to Artemis, the goddess of the moon, chastity and the hunt, in Greek mythology, whose story was told in the plays *Iphigenia in Aulis* and *Iphigenia in Tauris* (also the title of a play by German writer Johann Wolfgang von Goethe), by Greek playwright Euripedes, and *Iphigénie en Aulide*, by French playwright Jean Racine.

Irene
Variants and diminutives: Ailine, Arina, Arinka, Eireen, Eirena, Eirene, Eireni, Erena, Erene, Ereni, Ira, Ireen, Iren, Irena, Irenea, Irenee, Irenka, Irenke, Iriana, Irin, Irina, Irine, Irini, Irisha, Irka, Irusya, Irynam Jereni, Nitsa, Orina, Orya, Oryna, Rena, Rene, Renette, Reney, Renie, Renny, Rina, Yarina, Yaryna.
Meaning: 'peace' (Greek).
Notable namesakes: Eirene, the goddess of peace and daughter of Themis and Zeus in Greek mythology.

Iris
Variants and diminutives: Irisa, Irisha, Irissa, Irita, Iryl, Irys, Risa, Risha, Rissa.
Meaning: 'messenger of light' or 'rainbow' (Greek).

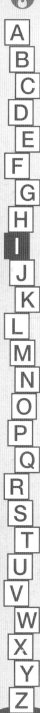

Notable namesakes: the messenger goddess of the rainbow, daughter of Electra and Thaumus, in Greek mythology; the coloured part of the eye; the *Iris* genus of flowering plants; Iris Murdoch (British writer).

Irma

Variants and diminutives: Emma, Erma, Irmina, Irmintrude.
Meaning: 'universal' or 'whole' (Germanic).

Isabel

Variants and diminutives: Bel, Bela, Belia, Belica, Belicia, Belita, Bell, Bella, Belle, Chabela, Chabi, Chava, Elisa, Ella, Ezabel, Ib, Ibbie, Ibbot, Ibby, Isa, Isabeau, Isabele, Isabelita, Isabella, Isabelle, Isbel, Iseabal, Iseabail, Ishbel, Isla, Isobel, Isopel, Issabell, Issi, Issie, Issy, Iza, Izabel, Izabela, Izabele, Izabella, Izzie, Izzy, Liseta, Nib, Tibbi, Tibbie, Tibbs, Tibby, Ysabel.
Meaning: 'God is perfection', 'God is satisfaction', 'dedicated to God' or 'God's oath' (Hebrew) as a variant of Elizabeth, the '-bel' (and also '-bella' and '-belle') additionally signifying 'beautiful' in Romance languages.
Notable namesakes: Isabella of France ('the She-wolf of France'), the daughter of King Philip IV of France and the unfaithful wife of King Edward II of England; two Spanish queens, including Isabella I, 'the Catholic', Queen of Castile and the first queen of Spain; Isabella, the heroine of William Shakespeare's play *Measure for Measure*; the heroine of the poem *Isabella, or the Pot of Basil*, by English poet John Keats; Isabel Archer, the heroine of the novel *Portrait of a Lady*, by US writer Henry James; Lady Isabella Gregory (Irish playwright); Isabel Bishop (US artist).

Ishana

Variants and diminutives: Ishani.
Meaning: 'desirable' (Sanskrit).

Isidora

Variants and diminutives: Dora, Isadora, Isadore, Isidore, Izzy.
Meaning: 'gift of Isis' (Greek), Isis being the supreme goddess of Egyptian mythology whose cult was subsequently adopted by the Greeks and Romans. A

female version of Isidore.
Notable namesakes: Isadora Duncan (US dancer).

Isla

Meaning: uncertain; possibly 'God is perfection', 'God is satisfaction', 'dedicated to God' or 'God's oath' (Hebrew) as a Scots Gaelic version of Isabel (Elizabeth); possibly derived from the name of the Scottish Hebridean island of Islay or a Scottish river.

Isolde

Variants and diminutives: Isaut, Iseult, Iseut, Isola, Isolda, Isolt, Yseult.
Meaning: 'ice' and 'rule' (Germanic); 'lovely' (Welsh).
Notable namesakes: Iseult, the Irish princess and lover of Tristan in Celtic legend and medieval Arthurian romance, on whose story the German composer Richard Wagner based his opera *Tristan and Isolde*.

Ita

Variants and diminutives: Ide.
Meaning: 'thirst' (Irish Gaelic).
Notable namesakes: Saint Ita.

Ivana

Variants and diminutives: Ivania, Ivanka, Ivanna, Ivannia, Ivanya, Vana.
Meaning: 'God has favoured', 'God is gracious' or 'God is merciful' (Hebrew) as a female version of Ivan, in turn a Slavic version of John.
Notable namesakes: Ivana Trump (Czech-born US socialite), whose model daughter is called Ivanka.

Ivy

Variants and diminutives: Iva, Ivie, Ivi.
Meaning: 'plant' (Greek); derived from the common name of the *Hedera* genus of climbing plants.
Notable namesakes: Ivy Compton-Burnett (English writer).

Jacinta

Variants and diminutives: Cinthie, Cynthia, Cynthie, Giacinta, Hy, Hyacinth, Hyacintha, Hyacinthe, Hyacinthia, Jacenta, Jacinda, Jacinna, Jacinta, Jacinth, Jacintha, Jacinthe, Jackie, Jacky, Jacyth.
Meaning: 'precious blue stone' (Greek); derived from the name of the *Hyacinthus* genus of flowering plants. A Spanish version of Hyacinth.
Notable namesakes: another name for the hyacinth flower; the red gemstone jacinth.

Jacqueline

Variants and diminutives: Jacaline, Jacalyn, Jackalin, Jackalyn, Jackelyn, Jacket, Jackey, Jacki, Jackie, Jacklyn, Jacky, Jaclyn, Jacoba, Jacobina, Jacolyn, Jacquelyn, Jacquelynne, Jacquenetta, Jacquenette, Jaqueta, Jacquetta, Jacquette, Jacqui, Jacquie, Jaculyn, Jakelyn, Jakolina, Jaqualine, Jaqueline, Jaquelina, Jaquetta, Jaquith.
Meaning: 'supplanter' (Hebrew) as a female French version of Jacques, in turn derived from Jacob via James.
Notable namesakes: Jaquetta Hawkes (British archaeologist and writer); Jacqueline Bouvier Kennedy Onassis (wife of US President John F Kennedy and Greek shipping tycoon Aristotle Onassis); Jackie Collins (British-born US writer); Jacqueline du Pré (British cellist); Jaclyn Smith (US actress).

Jade

Variants and diminutives: Jayde.
Meaning: 'flank' or 'groin' (Latin); derived from the name of the jadeite or nephrite semi-precious stone that was once believed to cure renal colic.
Notable namesakes: Jade Jagger (daughter of British musician Mick Jagger and his Nicaraguan-born former

wife Bianca).

Jael

Meaning: 'wild goat' or 'mountain goat' (Hebrew).
Notable namesakes: the woman who killed Sisera with a tent peg in the Old Testament.

Jaime

Variants and diminutives: Jaimee, Jaimi, Jaimie, Jaimy, Jamee, Jamey, Jami, Jamie, Jamielee, Jaymee, Jaymi, Jaymie, Jymie.
Meaning: 'supplanter' (Hebrew) as a Spanish and Portuguese variant of James (Jacob) and thus also a boy's name.

Jamesina

Variants and diminutives: Jaime, Jamie, Jamesena, Jamie, Ina.
Meaning: 'supplanter' (Hebrew) as a female version of James (Jacob).

Jamila

Variants and diminutives: Jameela, Jameelah, Jamilah, Jamillah, Jamillia.
Meaning: 'beautiful' (Arabic). A female version of Jamal.

Jan

Variants and diminutives: Jane, Janet.
Meaning: 'God has favoured', 'God is gracious' or 'God is merciful' (Hebrew), both as a female version of John and a diminutive of Janet and of other names beginning with 'Jan-'. Also a boy's name.
Notable namesakes: Jan Morris (British writer).

Jane

Variants and diminutives: Gian, Giann, Gianna, Giannetta, Giannina, Giovanna, Hanne, Ioanna, Iva, Ivana, Ivanka, Ivanna, Jama, Jan, Jana, Janae, Janean, Janee, Janeen, Janel, Janela, Janella, Janelle, Janerette, Janess, Janessa, Janet, Janeta,

Janetta, Janette, Janey, Jani, Jania, Janica, Janice, Janie, Janina, Janine, Janis, Janita, Janith, Janka, Janna, Janne, Janessa, Janissa, Jantina, Jany, Jasia, Jasisa, Jatney, Jayne, Jaynell, Jayney, Jayni, Jaynie, Jean, Jeanette, Jeani, Jeanie, Jeanine, Jeanne, Jehane, Jehanne, Jene, Jenica, Jenine, Jenka, Jenni, Jennie, Jenny, Jensine, Jess, Jessi, Jessie, Jessy, Jinni, Jinnie, Jinny, Joan, Joana, Joanka, Joanna, Joanne, Joasta, Joeann, Johanka, Johanna, Johanne, Jone, Joni, Jonie, Jony, Jovanna, Juana, Juanita, Jutta, Nita, Ohanna, Seini, Seonaid, Sheena, Shena, Sian, Sine, Sinéad, Siobhan, Vania, Yoana, Zaneta, Zanna, Zannz, Zsanett.

Meaning: 'God has favoured', 'God is gracious' or 'God is merciful' (Hebrew) as a female version of John.

Notable namesakes: Jane Seymour, wife of King Henry VIII of England and mother of King Edward VI of England; Lady Jane Grey, Queen of England for nine days; Jane Austen (English writer); the eponymous heroine of the novel *Jane Eyre*, by English writer Charlotte Brontë; Crazy Jane, the heroine of a number of poems by Irish writer W G Yeats; Jayne Mansfield (US actress); Jane Doe, the US generic name for an unidentified woman; Miss Jane Marple, an amateur detective created by English crime-writer Agatha Christie; Jane Mander (New Zealand writer); Jane Bowles (US writer); Jane Seymour (British-born US actress).

Janet

Variants and diminutives: Jan, Jane, Janella, Janelle, Janeta, Janete, Janetta, Janette, Janice, Janis, Janot, Jeanette, Jenetta, Jennie, Jennit, Jenny, Jessie, Netta, Nettie, Netty, Seonaid, Shona, Sinéid.

Meaning: 'God has favoured', 'God is gracious' or 'God is merciful' (Hebrew) as a female version of John.

Notable namesakes: Janet Flanner (US writer); Janet Frame (New Zealand writer); Janet Jackson (US singer).

Janice

Variants and diminutives: Jan, Jane, Janess, Janessa, Janis, Janissa, Janith, Janissa, Jansisa.

Meaning: 'God has favoured', 'God is gracious' or 'God is merciful' (Hebrew) as a female version of John.

Notable namesakes: the eponymous heroine of the novel *Janice Meredith,* by British writer Paul Leicester Ford; Janis Joplin (US singer).

Janine

Variants and diminutives: Jan, Jane, Janeen, Janina, Janita, Jeanine, Jeannine, Jenine.

Meaning: 'God has favoured', 'God is gracious' or 'God is merciful' (Hebrew) as a female version of John.

Jardena

Variants and diminutives: Jordan, Jordana, Jordane, Jordann, Jordanne, Jordyn.

Meaning: 'to flow down' (Hebrew), a female variant of the boy's (and increasingly girl's) name Jordan.

Jasmine

Variants and diminutives: Jasmin, Jasmina, Jazmin, Jazmina, Jesmond, Jess, Jessamine, Jessamy, Jessamyn, Jessi, Jessie, Jessy, Yasiman, Yasmin, Yasmina, Yasmine.

Meaning: 'jasmine flower' (Persian and Arabic) as an anglicised form of Yasmin; derived from the common name of the *Jasminum* genus of fragrant flowering plants.

Jean

Variants and diminutives: Gene, Genie, Genna, Gianina, Giovanna, Giovanni, Ivana, Jana, Jane, Janeska, Janina, Janka, Janne, Jasia, Jeane, Jeanette, Jeani, Jeanice, Jeanie, Jeanine, Jeanne, Jeannette, Jeannie, Jeannine, Jehane, Jehanne, Jen, Jena, Jenalyn, Jenat, Jenda, Jenica, Jenni, Jennica, Jennie, Jennine, Jinny, Joan, Joanna, Joanne, Johanna, Johanne, Kini, Netta, Nettie, Netty, Nina.

Meaning: 'God has favoured', 'God is gracious' or 'God is merciful' (Hebrew) as a female Scottish version of John.

Notable namesakes: the eponymous heroine of the novel, and subsequent film, *The Prime of Miss Jean Brodie*, by Scottish writer Muriel Spark; Jean Rhys (British writer); Jean Stafford (US writer); Jean Plaidy, a pseudonym of the English writer Eleanor Hibbert; Jean Simmons (British actress).

Jeanette

Variants and diminutives: Janet, Jean, Jeannette.
Meaning: 'God has favoured', 'God is gracious' or 'God is merciful' (Hebrew) as a female version of John, as well as a variant of Janet and Jean.

Jemima

Variants and diminutives: Jem, Jemimah, Jemma, Jona, Jonati, Jonina, Jonit, Mima, Yonina, Yemima.
Meaning: 'dove' (Hebrew and Arabic).
Notable namesakes: a daughter of Job in the Old Testament; Jemima Puddleduck, a character that features in the children's books by Beatrix Potter, the British writer and illustrator; Jemima Khan (wife of the Pakistani former cricketer Imran Khan).

Jenna

Variants and diminutives: Genna, Janet, Jen, Jennabel, Jennalee, Jennalyn, Jennanne, Jennarae, Jenni, Jennie, Jennifer, Jenniver, Jenny.
Meaning: 'God has favoured', 'God is gracious' or 'God is merciful' (Hebrew) as a variant of Janet, in turn a female version of John; 'fair' and 'yielding' or 'ghost' (Welsh) as a Cornish variant of Jenny, a diminutive of Jennifer, in turn derived from Guinevere.

Jennifer

Variants and diminutives: Gaenor, Ganor, Gaynor, Genevra, Genn, Gennfer, Genny, Ginevra, Ginnifer, Ginny, Guener, Guenever, Guenevere, Guenievre, Guinever, Guinivere, Gweniver, Gwinny, Gwyneth, Jen, Jenefer, Jenifer, Jeniffer, Jenn, Jennelle, Jenni, Jennie, Jennilee, Jenniver, Jenny, Jeny, Jinny, Vanora.
Meaning: 'fair' and 'yielding' or 'ghost' (Welsh) as a Cornish variant of Guinevere.
Notable namesakes: Jennifer Saunders (British comic actress); Jennifer Anniston and Jennifer Jason Leigh (US actresses); Jennifer Capriati (US tennis player); Jennifer Lopez (US singer and actress).

Jenny

Variants and diminutives: Genn, Genny, Ginny, Jen, Jenn, Jenna, Jenni, Jennie, Jenifer, Jennifer, Jenniver, Jenny, Jeny, Jinny.
Meaning: 'God has favoured', 'God is gracious' or 'God

is merciful' (Hebrew) as a variant of Janet, in turn a female version of John; 'fair' and 'yielding' or 'ghost' (Welsh) as a diminutive of Jennifer, in turn derived from Guinevere.
Notable namesakes: the spinning jenny, a spinning frame devised by the English inventor James Hargreaves; the eponymous leading character of the novel *Jennie Gerhardt*, by US writer Theodore Dreiser; Jenny Holzer (US artist); Jenny Agutter (British actress).

Jessica

Variants and diminutives: Gessica, Iscah, Janka, Jesca, Jess, Jessalyn, Jesse, Jessi, Jessie, Jesslyn, Jessy.
Meaning: uncertain; possibly 'God sees' or 'wealthy' (Hebrew) as a variant of Iscah.
Notable namesakes: Iscah, the sister of Lot in the Old Testament; a character in William Shakespeare's play *The Merchant of Venice*; Jessica Mitford (British-born US writer, one of the celebrated Mitford sisters); Jessica Lange (US actress).

Jessie

Variants and diminutives: Jess, Jesse, Jessey, Jessi, Jessica, Jessy.
Meaning: 'God has favoured', 'God is gracious' or 'God is merciful' (Hebrew) as a Scottish version of Janet, in turn a female version of John; possibly 'God sees' or 'wealthy' (Hebrew) as a diminutive of Jessica, in turn a possible variant of Iscah; 'gift' or 'God exists' (Hebrew) as a female version of Jesse.

Jetta

Variants and diminutives: Jet, Jette, Jetti, Jettie, Jetty.
Meaning: 'stone of Gagai' (Greek), Gagai being a town in Lycia, Asia Minor, where jet, a decorative black variety of lignite, was once mined.

Jewel

Variants and diminutives: Jewell.
Meaning: 'plaything' (Old French); 'jewel' (Old English).
Notable namesakes: Jewel Kilcher (US singer).

A B C D E F G H I J K L M N O P Q R S T U V W X Y Z

A B C D E F G H I J K L M N O P Q R S T U V W X Y Z

Jezebel

Meaning: 'domination' or 'impure' (Hebrew).
Notable namesakes: the Baal-worshipping daughter of the king of Sidon and wife of King Ahab of Israel in the Old Testament, whose name has become the generic word for a scheming or shameless woman.

Jill

Variants and diminutives: Gill, Gilli, Gillian, Gillie, Gilly, Jilli, Jillian, Jilliana, Jillie, Jilly.
Meaning: uncertain; possibly 'fair-skinned' (Latin) as a diminutive of Jillian (Gillian, in turn a female variant of Julian).
Notable namesakes: the Jill of nursery-rhyme fame who went up the hill with Jack; Jil Sander (German fashion designer).

Joan

Variants and diminutives: Giovanna, Giovannina, Hanne, Ione, Ivanna, Jane, Janis, Janna, Jean, Jehane, Jenise, Jhone, Jo, Joanie, Joann, Joanna, Joanne, Joeann, Joeanna, Joeanne, Johan, Johanna, Johannah, Johanne, Johna, Johnna, Johnnie, Jonet, Joni, Jonie, Jonnie, Jovana, Jovanna, Juan, Juana, Juanita, Nita, Seonag, Siobhan, Zaneta.
Meaning: 'God has favoured', 'God is gracious' or 'God is merciful' (Hebrew) as a female variant of John.
Notable namesakes: Saint Joan of Arc (Jeanne d'Arc), patron saint of France, soldiers and rape victims, the 'Maid of Orléans' who led a French army during the Hundred Years War and whose story inspired the play *St Joan*, by the Irish writer George Bernard Shaw; the 'Fair Maid of Kent', wife of Edward, the Black Prince, and mother of King Richard II of England; Pope Joan, a legendary female pope; Joan Crawford (US actress); Joan Collins (British actress); Joan Didion (US writer); Joni Mitchell (US singer-songwriter); Joan Rivers (US comedienne).

Joanna

Variants and diminutives: Giovanna, Giovannina, Hanne, Ivanna, Janna, Jo, Joan, Joanie, Joann, Joanne, Joeann, Joeanna, Joeanne, Johan, Johanna, Johannah, Johanne, Johna, Johnna, Johnnie, Joni, Jonnie, Jonnie, Jovana, Jovanna.
Meaning: 'God has favoured', 'God is gracious' or 'God is merciful' (Hebrew) as a female variant of John.
Notable namesakes: the wife of the manager of King Herod's household and a witness to Christ's resurrection in the New Testament; Joanna, 'the Mad', the Spanish mother of Charles V, a Holy Roman emperor; Joanna Lumley (British actress); Joanna Trollope (British writer).

Jobina

Variants and diminutives: Jobey, Jobi, Jobie, Joby.
Meaning: 'persecuted' (Hebrew). A female version of Job.

Jocasta

Meaning: 'shining moon' or 'woe adorned' (Greek).
Notable namesakes: the mother and wife of Oedipus, King of Thebes.

Jocelyn

Variants and diminutives: Jocelin, Joceline, Jocelynd, Jocelyne, Jos, Joscelin, Joscelind, Josceline, Joscelyn, Josceline, Joslyn, Joss.
Meaning: uncertain; possibly 'a Goth' or 'a Gaut' (Germanic), referring to a Germanic tribe; possibly 'champion' (Celtic). Also a boy's name.

Jodie

Variants and diminutives: Jodi, Jody.
Meaning: 'Jewish woman' (Hebrew) as a diminutive of Judith; 'praise' (Hebrew) as a female version of Jude, a diminutive of Judah.
Notable namesakes: Jodie Foster (US actress).

Joella

Variants and diminutives: Joel, Joela, Joelle, Joellen, Joellyn.
Meaning: 'Jehovah is God' or 'God is willing' (Hebrew) as a female version of Joel.

Jolie

Variants and diminutives: Joleen, Jolene, Joletta, Joliet, Jolly.
Meaning: 'pretty' (Old French); 'jolly' (Middle English).

Joline

Variants and diminutives: Josepha, Josephine, Joleen, Jolene.
Meaning: 'God will increase' (Hebrew). A female version of Joseph.

Jonquil

Variants and diminutives: Jonquilla, Jonquille.
Meaning: 'reed' (Spanish); derived from the common name of the *Narcissus jonquilla* flowering plant.

Josephine

Variants and diminutives: Fife, Fifi, Fifine, Jo, Joe, Josepha, Josèphe, Josephina, Josette, Josie, Pepita, Peppie, Peppy, Pheenie, Pheeny, Posie, Posy, Yosepha, Yosifa.
Meaning: 'God will increase' (Hebrew). A female version of Joseph.
Notable namesakes: Joséphine de Beauharnais, wife of Emperor Napoleon I (Napoleon Bonaparte) of France; Josephine Tey (Scottish writer); Josephine Baker (US dancer); Josephine Miles (US writer).

Joy

Variants and diminutives: Joia, Joya, Joye, Joyita.
Meaning: 'happiness' (Old French).

Joyce

Variants and diminutives: Jocea, Jocey, Jocosa, Joice, Jolia, Jooss, Josse, Jossi, Jossie, Jossy.
Meaning: uncertain; possibly 'Lord' (Breton); derived from a British family name, in turn derived from the Latin name Jodocus via the French Breton name Joisse. Also a boy's name.
Notable namesakes: Saint Joyce (also known as Judoc, Judocus, Joisse or Josse), a male hermit; Joyce Carol Oates (US writer).

Juanita

Variants and diminutives: Juana, Nita, Wanika, Wanita.
Meaning: 'God has favoured', 'God is gracious' or 'God is merciful' (Hebrew) as a female Spanish variant of Juan (John).

Judith

Variants and diminutives: Eudice, Giulia, Ioudith, Jodette, Jodi, Jodie, Jody, Juci, Jicika, Jude, Judi, Judie, Judit, Judita, Judite, Judithe, Jitka, Judy, Jutka, Yehudit, Yudif, Yudit, Yudita, Yuta.
Meaning: 'Jewish woman' (Hebrew); 'praise' (Hebrew) as a female version of Jude, a diminutive of Judah.
Notable namesakes: a wife of Esau in the Old Testament; Judith of Bethulia, the Old Testament Jewish heroine who killed the Assyrian general Holofernes as told in the Book of Judith in the Apocrypha, as well as in plays by the German writer Friedrich Hebbel and the French writer Jean Giraudoux; Judith of Bavaria, wife of Louis I, 'the Pious', and mother of Charles II, 'the Bald', both Holy Roman emperors; Judith Leyster (Dutch artist); Judy, the wife of Punch in the English children's puppet show; judy, a generic slang word for a girl or woman; Judy Garland (US actress); Judi Dench (British actress); Judy Chicago (US artist).

Julia

Variants and diminutives: Gillie, Giula, Giulia, Giuletta, Iulia, Jula, Julca, Julcia, Jule, Jules, Juli, Juliaca, Juliana, Juliane, Julianna, Julianne, Julie, Julienne, Juliet, Julieta, Julietta, Juliette, Julina, Julinda, Juline, Julinka, Juliska, Julissa, Julita, Julitta, Julka, Julyann, Sheila, Sile, Sileas, Utili, Yula, Yulinka, Yuliya, Yulka, Yulya.
Meaning: uncertain; possibly 'fair-skinned' (Latin). A female version of Julian.
Notable namesakes: a character in William Shakespeare's play *Two Gentlemen of Verona*; Julia Ward Howe (US poet); Julia Roberts (US actress); Julia Sawalha (British actress).

Juliana

Variants and diminutives: Julia, Jule, Jules, Juliane, Julianna, Julianne, Julie, Julienne, Juliet, Julitta, Liana, Lianne, Julyan.

Meaning: uncertain; possibly 'fair-skinned' (Latin). A female version of Julian.
Notable namesakes: Saint Juliana; Queen Juliana of the Netherlands; Julianne Moore (US actress).

Julie

Variants and diminutives: Juli, Julia, Juliana, Julianne, Jule, Jules, Julienne, Juliet, Julitta.
Meaning: uncertain; possibly 'fair-skinned' (Latin). A French version of Julia, in turn derived from Julian.
Notable namesakes: Julie d'Etranges, the leading character of the novel *Julie ou la Nouvelle Héloïse*, by French philosopher and writer Jean Jacques Rousseau; the leading character of the play *Miss Julie*, by Swedish writer August Strindberg; Julie Andrews and Julie Christie (British actresses).

Juliet

Variants and diminutives: Giuletta, Giulietta, Juet, Juetta, Jule, Jules, Julia, Juliana, Julie, Julieta, Julietta, Juliette, Julitta, Jules.
Meaning: uncertain; possibly 'fair-skinned' (Latin). A French version of Julia, in turn derived from Julian.
Notable namesakes: Juliet
Capulet, the heroine of
William Shakespeare's play
Romeo and Juliet, for whom
the Juliet cap was named;
the wife of Claudio in
William Shakespeare's play
Measure for Measure; the
code for the letter 'J' in
verbal communications.

June

Variants and diminutives: Juno, Junella, Unella.
Meaning: 'younger' or 'the month of June' (Latin); probably derived from the Roman family name Junius, but also linked with Juno, the Roman supreme goddess for whom the month of June may have been named.
Notable namesakes: June Whitfield (British actress).

Justine

Variants and diminutives: Jestine, Jestina, Jussie, Jussy, Justeen, Justina, Justyne.
Meaning: 'just' (Latin). A female version of Justin.
Notable namesakes: Saint Justina; the eponymous heroine of the novel *Justine*, part of the *Alexandria Quartet*, by the British writer Lawrence Durrell; Justine Frischman (British musician).

Kagami

Meaning: 'mirror' (Japanese).

Kalinda

Variants and diminutives: Kaleenda.
Meaning: 'the sun' (Hindi).
Notable namesakes: the mountains of Kalinda in Hindu mythology.

Kalindi

Variants and diminutives: Kali, Lindi.
Meaning: 'the Jumna' (Hindi), Jumna being a sacred Hindu river.

Kalyca

Variants and diminutives: Kali, Kalica, Kalie, Kalika, Kaly.
Meaning: 'rosebud' (Greek).

Kamea

Variants and diminutives: Kameo.
Meaning: 'the one' (Hawaiian).

Kammile

Variants and diminutives: Kameel, Kamil, Kamila, Kamilla, Kamillah.
Meaning: 'perfection' (Arabic) as a female version of Kamil.

Kanani
Variants and diminutives: Ani, Nani.
Meaning: 'beautiful' (Hawaiian).

Karen
Variants and diminutives: Caren, Carin, Caron, Carren, Caryn, Kaarina, Kalena, Kalina, Kar, Kari, Karin, Karina, Karine, Karon, Karyn, Karyna, Kaz.
Meaning: 'pure' (Greek) as a Danish diminutive of Katherine (Catherine).
Notable namesakes: the Karen people of the Far East; Karen Blixen (Danish writer).

Karima
Variants and diminutives: Kareema, Karimah.
Meaning: 'noble' or 'generous' (Arabic). A female version of Karim.

Karita
Variants and diminutives: Cara, Cari, Carita, Carity, Charis, Charissa, Charita, Charito, Charry, Chattie, Cherry, Kara, Kari, Karina.
Meaning: 'grace' (Greek); 'kindness' (Latin); 'Christian love' (Old French). A variant of Charity.

Karma
Meaning: 'action' (Sanskrit).
Notable namesakes: the principle of retributive justice in Hinduism and Buddhism, with particular reference to reincarnation.

Kasimira
Variants and diminutives: Kasi, Mira.
Meaning: 'peace is proclamed' (Old Slavic). A female version of Kasimir (Casimir).

Kasota
Meaning: 'cloudless sky' (Native American).

Kassia
Variants and diminutives: Kasia, Kasienka, Kasin, Kaska.
Meaning: 'pure' (Greek) as a Polish version of Katherine (Catherine).

Kate
Variants and diminutives: Cate, Catey, Catharine, Catherine, Cathy, Catie, Kadee, Kadi, Kadia, Kadiane, Kadianne, Kadie, Kadienne, Kady, Kaety, Kaiti, Kaity, Kassia, Kat, Katelyn, Katey, Katharine, Käthe, Katherine, Katee, Kati, Katie, Katy, Kay, Keti, Kit, Kittie, Kitty.
Meaning: 'pure' (Greek) as a diminutive of Katherine (Catherine).
Notable namesakes: a character in the play *Henry V*, by William Shakespeare, and the leading female character in Shakespeare's play *The Taming of the Shrew*, on which the musical *Kiss Me Kate* is based; Kate Greenaway (British artist); Kate Chopin (US writer); Käthe Kollwitz (German artist); the eponymous heroine of the children's books 'What Katy Did', by US writer Susan Coolidge; Kate Bush (British musician); Kate Moss (British model); Cate Blanchett (Australian actress); Kate Winslet (British actress).

Katherine
Variants and diminutives: Caitlin, Caitlon, Caitria, Caitrin, Cari, Cass, Cassi, Cassie, Cassy, Casy, Catalina, Catant, Cate, Catey, Catarina, Caterina, Cath, Catharin, Catharina, Catharine, Cathe, Catheline, Catherine, Cathi, Cathie, Cathleen, Cathy, Catie, Catrin, Catriona, Cayla, Ekaterina, Kaety, Kaisa, Kara, Karen, Karena, Karin, Karina, Kasia, Kasienka, Kasin, Kaska, Kassia, Kat, Kata, Katalin, Katarina, Katchen, Kate, Katee, Katelyn, Katenka, Katerina, Katerinka, Katey, Kath, Katharina, Katharine, Kathe, Katherin, Kathi, Kathie, Kathleen, Kathryn, Kathy, Kati, Katica, Katie, Katika, Katinka, Katka, Katla, Kato, Katoka, Katri, Katrin, Katrina, Katrine, Katryna, Katsa, Katus, Katuska, Katy, Katya, Kay, Kayce, Kayla, Ketya, Kisa, Kiska, Kit, Kitti, Kittie, Kitty, Kofryna, Kolina, Kotinka, Rina, Trina, Trinchen, Trine, Trinette.
Meaning: 'pure' (Greek) as a variant of Catherine.
Notable namesakes: Katharina (Kate), the shrewish character in William Shakespeare's play *The Taming of the Shrew*; Katherine Mansfield (New Zealand-born British writer); Katharine Susannah Prichard (Australian writer); Katharine Hepburn (US actress).

Kathleen
Variants and diminutives: Caitlin, Cath, Catharin,

Catharine, Catherin, Catherine, Cathleen, Cathy, Kaitlan, Kaitleen, Kaitlen, Kaitlin, Kaitlinn, Kaitlyn, Kaitlynn, Kate, Katelyn, Kath, Kathie, Kathlee, Kathy, Katie, Katlin, Katy, Kay, Kit, Kittie, Kitty.
Meaning: 'pure' (Greek) as an Irish variant of Katherine (Catherine).
Notable namesakes: the eponymous heroine of the poetic drama *The Countess Cathleen*, by Irish writer W B Yeats; Kathleen Raine (English poet); Kathleen Turner (US actress).

Kathy

Variants and diminutives: Cath, Catharine, Catherine, Cathy, Kat, Kath, Katharine, Katerine, Kath, Katherine, Kathie, Kay.
Meaning: 'pure' (Greek) as a diminutive of Katherine (Catherine).
Notable namesakes: Kathy Bates (US actress); Kathy Reichs (US crime writer); Kathy Burke (British actress).

Katrina

Variants and diminutives: Cat, Catrina, Catrine, Catriona, Kat, Katrine, Trina.
Meaning: 'pure' (Greek) as a variant of Katherine (Catherine).
Notable namesakes: Loch Katrine, a lake in central Scotland.

Katya

Variants and diminutives: Ekaterina, Katenka, Kaaterinka, Katinka, Katka, Katryna, Katya, Ketya, Kisa, Kiska, Kitti, Kotinka.
Meaning: 'pure' (Greek) as a diminutive of Ekaterina, a Russian variant of Katherine (Catherine).

Kay

Variants and diminutives: Kai, Kailee, Kailey, Kailin, Kaye, Kayla, Kaylee, Kayley, Kaylin, Kayly, Kaylyn, Kaylynn.
Meaning: 'pure' (Greek) as a diminutive of Katherine (Catherine); 'rejoice' (Greek); 'fence' (Old Breton); 'quay' (Old French); 'spear' (Middle Low German); 'key' (Old English). Also a boy's name (see Kai).
Notable namesakes: Kay Boyle (US writer); Kay Sage (US artist and poet).

Kayley

Variants and diminutives: Kailee, Kailey, Kay, Kayla, Kaylee, Kayleigh, Kayley, Kayly.
Meaning: 'slim' (Irish Gaelic); derived from an Irish family name.

Keely

Variants and diminutives: Keelin, Keelyn.
Meaning: 'beautiful' (Irish Gaelic).

Kelda

Variants and diminutives: Keli, Kelie, Kelli, Kellie, Kelley, Kelly.
Meaning: uncertain; possibly 'fountain', 'well' or 'spring' (Old Norse).

Kelila

Variants and diminutives: Kaila, Kaile, Kayle, Kelilah, Kelula, Kyla, Kyle, Kylene, Lylia.
Meaning: 'crowned with laurel' (Hebrew). Also a female version of Kyle.

Kelly

Variants and diminutives: Kaley, Keeley, Keely, Keli, Kelia, Kellee, Kellen, Kelley, Kelli, Kellia, Kellie, Kellina, Kelisa, Kelton, Kylie.
Meaning: uncertain; possibly 'Celtic warrior' (Greek); possibly 'warrior' or 'attender of church' (Irish Gaelic) when derived from an Irish family name; possibly 'wood' (Scots Gaelic) when derived from a Scottish family name, in turn derived from a British place name. Also a boy's name.
Notable namesakes: Kelly Preston (US actress).

Kendra

Variants and diminutives: Ken, Kendis, Kenna.
Meaning: uncertain; possibly 'knowledge' (Old English).

Kenina

Variants and diminutives: Kenna, Nina.
Meaning: 'born of fire' or 'handsome' (Scottish and Irish Gaelic); 'royal oath' (Old English). A female version of Kenneth.

Keren

Variants and diminutives: Kaaren, Kareen, Karen, Karin, Karon, Karyn, Kerenhappuch, Kyran.
Meaning: 'animal horn' or 'horn of antimony' (Hebrew), antimony being a metal that was once used to beautify the eyes. A dimutive of Kerenhappuch.
Notable namesakes: Kerenhappuch, a daughter of Job in the Old Testament.

Kerry

Variants and diminutives: Ceri, Cerrie, Cerry, Keree, Keri, Kerie, Kerrey, Kerri, Kerrie.
Meaning: 'descendants of Ciar' or 'dark children' (Irish Gaelic); derived from the name of the Irish county. Also a boy's name.
Notable namesakes: the Kerry blue terrier, a breed of dog.

Keshisha

Meaning: 'an elder' (Aramaic).

Keturah

Meaning: 'fragrance' or 'incense' (Hebrew).
Notable namesakes: a wife of Abraham in the Old Testament.

Kezia

Variants and diminutives: Kerzia, Kesia, Kesiah, Ketzi, Ketzia, Kez, Kezi, Keziah, Kezzie, Kezzy, Kissie, Kiz, Kizzie, Kizzy.
Meaning: 'cassia tree', 'fragrant bark' or 'bark like cinnamon' (Hebrew).
Notable namesakes: a daughter of Job in the Old Testament.

Kim

Variants and diminutives: Kimberlee, Kimberley, Kimberli, Kimberlie, Kimberly, Kimmi, Kimmie, Kym.
Meaning: 'ruler' (Old English); 'Cyneburga's clearing' (Old English), Cyneburga being a 7th century English abbess and saint, as a diminutive of Kimberley. Also a boy's name.
Notable namesakes: Kim Novak (US actress).

Kimberley

Variants and diminutives: Kim, Kimberlee, Kimberli, Kimberlie, Kimberly, Kimmi, Kimmie, Kym.
Meaning: 'Cyneburga's clearing' (Old English), Cyneburga being a 7th century English abbess and saint; derived from an English family name, in turn derived from a number of English place names. Also a boy's name.
Notable namesakes: a diamond-mining town in South Africa; the Kimberleys, a plateau in north-western Australia.

Kimi

Variants and diminutives: Kimie, Kimoko, Kimiyo.
Meaning: 'without equal' (Japanese).

Kira

Variants and diminutives: Kiran, Kiri, Kiriana, Kirina, Kirini, Klla, Kirra, Kyra.
Meaning: 'sun', 'throne' or 'shepherd' (Persian) as a female variant of Cyrus.

Kirby

Variants and diminutives: Kirbie.
Meaning: 'church village' (Old Norse); derived from an English family name, in turn derived from a number of English place names. Also a boy's name.

Kirsten

Variants and diminutives: Christine, Keirstan, Kersten, Kerstine, Kireen, Kirsteen, Kirstene, Kirstie, Kirstien, Kirstin, Kirstine, Kirston, Kirsty, Kirstyn.
Meaning: 'Christian' (Latin) as a Scandinavian variant of Christine (Christian).

Kirsty

Variants and diminutives: Christine, Kersty, Kirsteen, Kirsten, Kirsti, Kirstie, Kirstene, Kyrsty.
Meaning: 'Christian' (Latin) as a Scottish diminutive of Kirstene (Christine, in turn derived from Christian).
Notable namesakes: Kirstie

Alley (US actress); Kirsty Wark and Kirsty Young (British broadcasters).

Kismet
Meaning: 'destiny' (Arabic).

Kitty
Variants and diminutives: Catherine, Kit, Kittie.
Meaning: 'pure' (Greek) as a diminutive of Katherine (Catherine).

Koko
Meaning: 'stork' (Japanese).

Kristen
Variants and diminutives: Christin, Christine, Krista, Kristan, Kristene, Kristin, Kristina, Kristine, Krysta, Krystena.
Meaning: 'Christian' (Latin) as a Danish version of Christine (Christian).
Notable namesakes: Kristin Lavransdatter, the heroine of a trilogy of novels by Norwegian writer Sigrid Undset; Kristin Scott Thomas (British actress).

Kylie
Variants and diminutives: Keeley, Kellie, Kelly, Kilie.
Meaning: 'boomerang' (Western Australian Aboriginal); as a variant of Kelly, possibly 'Celtic warrior' (Greek); 'warrior' or 'attender of church' (Irish Gaelic) when derived from an Irish family name; 'wood' (Scots Gaelic) when derived from a Scottish family name, in turn derived from a British place name.
Notable namesakes: Kylie Tennant (Australian writer); Kylie Minogue (Australian singer).

Lacey
Variants and diminutives: Lacee, Lacie, Lacy, Larissa.
Meaning: uncertain; possibly 'merry' (Latin) or 'citadel' (Greek) as a diminutive of Larissa; possibly 'frisky' or 'noose' (Latin) when derived from a British family name. Also a boy's name.

Laelia
Variants and diminutives: Lelia.
Meaning: 'jolly' or 'garrulous' (Latin).
Notable namesakes: Saint Lelia.

Lalage
Variants and diminutives: Lala.
Meaning: 'babbling' or 'chattering' (Greek).
Notable namesakes: characters in the poems of the Roman poet Horace; a character in the novel *The French Lieutenant's Woman*, by the British writer John Fowles.

Lalita
Variants and diminutives: Lal, Lalie, Lita.
Meaning: 'honest' or 'charming' (Sanskrit).

Lana
Variants and diminutives: Alana, Lanna, Lanne, Lannie, Lanny.
Meaning: uncertain; possibly 'woolly' (Latin); possibly 'buoyant' (Hawaiian); possibly 'rock' (Breton), 'harmony' (Celtic), 'good-looking', 'cheerful', 'child' or 'darling' (Irish Gaelic), 'an offering' or 'light' (Hawaiian) as a diminutive of Alana (Alan).
Notable namesakes: Lana Turner (US actress).

Lara
Variants and diminutives: Larissa.
Meaning: uncertain; possibly 'merry' (Latin) or 'citadel'

(Greek) as a Russian diminutive of Larissa.
Notable namesakes: a goddess of the underworld in Roman mythology; a character in the novel *Dr Zhivago*, by Russian writer Boris Pasternak, and in the subsequent film.

Larissa

Variants and diminutives: Lacey, Lara, Laris, Larisa, Larochka, Lissa.
Meaning: uncertain; possibly 'merry' (Latin); possibly 'citadel' (Greek).

Lark

Meaning: 'lark' (Germanic); derived from the common name of the *Alaudidae* family of songbirds.

Laura

Variants and diminutives: Lara, Laraine, Lari, Larilia, Larinda, Lauraine, Lauran, Laurane, Laure, Laureana, Laureen, Laurel, Laurella, Lauren, Laurena, Laurene, Laurestine, Lauretta, Laurette, Lauri, Laurice, Laurie, Lauriette, Laurina, Laurinda, Laurine, Laurka, Lawrie, Lavra, Lola, Lollie, Lolly, Lora, Lorain, Loraine, Loral, Lorann, Lorayne, Loree, Loreen, Lorell, Loren, Lorena, Lorene, Lorenza, Loretah, Loretta, Lorette, Lori, Lorie, Lorinda, Lorine, Lorita, Lorna, Lorraine, Lorri, Lorrie, Lorry, Loura, Lourana.
Meaning: 'laurel' (Latin); 'from Laurentum' (Latin), Laurentum being the Roman name of an Italian town, as a female version of Laurence.
Notable namesakes: the idealised woman to whom the Italian poet Francesco Petrarch dedicated his *Il Canzoniere*; Laura Jackson (US writer); Laura Wheeler Waring (US artist); Laura Ashley (British fashion designer); Laura Dern (US actress).

Laurel

Variants and diminutives: Laura, Laure, Laurella, Loral, Lorell.
Meaning: 'laurel' (Latin) as a variant of Laura; 'from Laurentum' (Latin), Laurentum being the Roman name of an Italian town, as a female version of Laurence.
Notable namesakes: a character in Arthurian legend.

Lauren

Variants and diminutives: Laura, Lauran, Laurena, Laurene, Laurencia, Laurentia, Laurenza, Laurie, Laurin, Laurine, Lauryn, Loreen, Loren, Lorena, Lorene, Lorenza, Lorin, Lorine, Lorrin, Loryn, Lorynn, Lorynne.
Meaning: 'laurel' (Latin) as a variant of Laura; 'from Laurentum' (Latin), Laurentum being the Roman name of an Italian town, as a female version of Laurence.
Notable namesakes: Lauren Bacall (US actress); Lauren Hutton (US model).

Lavender

Meaning: 'to wash' (Latin); derived from the common name of the *Lavandula* genus of fragrant plants.
Notable namesakes: a pale shade of purple.

Laverne

Variants and diminutives: Lavern, Laverna, LaVerne, La Verne, Luvern.
Meaning: 'the springtime' (Latin); 'the green one' (Old French).
Notable namesakes: Laverna, the goddess of thieves in Roman mythology; La Verne, a place in California.

Lavinia

Variants and diminutives: Lavena, Lavina, Lavinie, Vin, Vina, Vinia, Vinnie, Vinny.
Meaning: uncertain; possibly 'woman of Rome' (Latin).
Notable namesakes: the daughter of King Latinus and wife of Aeneas in Greek and Roman mythology; Lavinia Fontana (Bolognese artist).

Leah

Variants and diminutives: Lea, Lee, Leigh, Lia, Liah.
Meaning: 'weary', 'gazelle' or 'cow' (Hebrew).
Notable namesakes: the daughter of Laban and first wife of Jacob in the Old Testament.

Leanne

Variants and diminutives: Ann, Anne, Lee, Leeanne, Lee-Ann, Leigh-Anne, Liane, Lianne.
Meaning: uncertain; probably a compound name comprising Lee, 'meadow', 'clearing' or 'wood' (Old English), and Anne (Hannah), 'I have been favoured (by God)' (Hebrew).

Leda

Variants and diminutives: Ledah, Lida, Lidah, Lidia.
Meaning: 'woman' (Lycian).
Notable namesakes: the daughter of Eurythemis and Thestrius and queen of Sparta who was seduced by Zeus, who assumed the form of a swan for the purpose, in Greek mythology.

Leeba

Variants and diminutives: Liba, Luba.
Meaning: 'heart' (Hebrew); 'dear one' (Yiddish).

Leila

Variants and diminutives: Laila, Laili, Lailie, Laleh, Layla, Leila, Leilah, Leilia, Lela, Lelah, Lelia, Lila, Leyla.
Meaning: 'dark' or 'night' (Arabic).
Notable namesakes: a legendary Persian heroine; characters in the poems *The Giaour* and *Don Juan*, by English poet George, Lord Byron; the eponymous heroine of the novel *Leila*, by English writer Lord Edward Lytton; the eponymous subject of the song 'Leila', by British musician Eric Clapton.

Leilani

Variants and diminutives: Lei, Lelani.
Meaning: 'heavenly' and 'child' or 'flower' (Hawaiian).

Lelia

Variants and diminutives: Lela, Lélia.
Meaning: uncertain; derived from the Roman family name Laelius.
Notable namesakes: the eponymous heroine of the novel *Lélia*, by French writer George Sand.

Lena

Variants and diminutives: Galina, Helena, Leena, Lenah, Lene, Lenea, Lenette, Liene, Lina, Linah, Magdalene.
Meaning: 'lodging place' (Hebrew); 'seductress' (Latin); 'bright' (Greek) as a diminutive of Helena (Helen).
Notable namesakes: a Siberian river; Lena Grove, a chracter in the novel *Light in August*, by US writer William Faulkner.

Leona

Variants and diminutives: Leola, Leoma, Leonarda, Leone, Leonel, Leonia, Leonice, Léonie, Leonina, Leonine, Leonora, Leontine, Leontyne, Leora, Leota, Liona, Lona, Loni.
Meaning: 'lion' (Latin) as a female variant of Leo.

Léonie

Variants and diminutives: Leona, Leone, Leonia, Leonice, Leonina, Leonine, Liona, Lona.
Meaning: 'lion' (Latin) as a female French variant of Leo.

Leonora

Variants and diminutives: Eleanora, Leonarda, Lenora, Lenore, Nora, Norah, Nornie.
Meaning: 'bright' (Greek) as a diminutive of Eleanora (Helen via Eleanor), and, as such, also 'foreign' (Germanic); 'lion' (Latin) as a variation of Leona (Leo).
Notable namesakes: the heroine of the opera *Fidelio*, by German composer Ludwig van Beethoven; Leonora Carrington (British artist).

Leora

Meaning: 'light' (Hebrew) as a female version of Leor; 'lion' (Latin) as a variant of Leona (Leo).

Leta

Variants and diminutives: Letitia.
Meaning: 'joyful' (Latin) as a diminutive of Letitia; 'bringer' (Swahili).

Letifa

Variants and diminutives: Letipha.
Meaning: 'gentle' (Arabic).

Letitia

Variants and diminutives: Laetitia, Latisha, Laytisha, Lece, Lecelina, Lecia, Leda, Leetice, Leta, Lethia, Letice, Leticia, Letisha, Letizia, Letti, Lettice, Lettie, Letty, Letycia, Loutitia, Tish, Tisha, Titia.
Meaning: 'joyful' (Latin).
Notable namesakes: Letitia Dean (British actress).

Levana

Variants and diminutives: Levanna, Levona, Livana, Livona.
Meaning: 'rising sun' or 'lifter' (Latin).
Notable namesakes: Levanna, the goddess of newborn babies in Roman mythology.

Levia

Variants and diminutives: Livia, Liviya.
Meaning: 'attached' or 'pledged' (Hebrew) as a female version of Levi.

Lexa

Variants and diminutives: Lecksi, Leksi, Leksie, Lexi, Lexie, Lexia.
Meaning: 'word' (Greek) as a female version of Lex; 'defender of men' or 'warrior' (Greek) as a diminutive of Alexandra (Alexander).

Liana

Variants and diminutives: Juliana, Lean, Leana, Leane, Leanna, Leanne, Lia, Liane, Lianna, Lianne, Oliana.
Meaning: uncertain; possibly 'fair-skinned' (Latin) as a diminutive of Juliana (Julian); 'to bind' (French).
Notable namesakes: the common name of various tropical climbing plants.

Libby

Variants and diminutives: Elizabeth, Lib, Libbie.
Meaning: 'God is perfection', 'God is satisfaction', 'dedicated to God' or 'God's oath' (Hebrew) as a diminutive of Elizabeth.

Liberty

Variants and diminutives: Lib, Libbie, Libby.
Meaning: 'freedom' (Latin).

Liesel

Variants and diminutives: Elizabeth, Liese, Lieselotte, Liesl, Lise, Lisette.
Meaning: 'God is perfection', 'God is satisfaction', 'dedicated to God' or 'God's oath' (Hebrew) as a German diminutive of Elizabeth.
Notable namesakes: Liesl von Trapp, the eldest of the Austrian singing children popularised by the British film *The Sound of Music*.

Lilac

Variants and diminutives: Lila, Lilah.
Meaning: 'bluish' (Persian); derived from the common name of the *Syringa* genus of flowering shrubs.
Notable namesakes: a shade of purple.

Lilith

Variants and diminutives: Lilis, Lilita, Lillith, Lillus.
Meaning: uncertain; possibly 'storm goddess' or 'of the night' (East Semitic).
Notable namesakes: a female demon said to have been Adam's first wife in Jewish folklore and Talmudic

literature; a character in the US television series *Cheers* and *Frasier*.

Lillian

Variants and diminutives: Boske, Bozsi, Elizabeth, Leka, Lelya, Lena, Lenka, Liana, Lieschen, Liesel, Lil, Lila, Lilana, Lileana, Lili, Lilia, Lilian, Liliana, Liliane, Lilias, Lilie, Lilike, Lilion, Liliosa, Liljana, Lill, Lilla, Lilli, Lillias, Lillie, Lillis, Lilly, Lily, Lilyan, Olena, Olenka.
Meaning: 'lily' (Greek) as a variant of Lily; 'God is perfection', 'God is satisfaction', 'dedicated to God' or 'God's oath' (Hebrew) as a variant of Elizabeth.
Notable namesakes: Lillian Gish (US actress); Lillian Hellman, Lillian Smith and Lillian O'Donnell (US writers).

Lily

Variants and diminutives: Boske, Bozsi, Elizabeth, Leka, Lelya, Lena, Lenka, Liana, Lieschen, Liesel, Lil, Lila, Lilana, Lileana, Lili, Lilia, Lilian, Liliana, Liliane, Lilias, Lilie, Lilike, Lilion, Liliosa, Liljana, Lilla, Lillah, Lilli, Lillian, Lillie, Lillis, Lilly, Lilya, Lilyan, Olena, Olenka.
Meaning: 'lily' (Greek) when derived from the common name of the *Lilium* genus of flowering plants; 'God is perfection', 'God is satisfaction',

'dedicated to God' or 'God's oath' (Hebrew) as a variant of Elizabeth.

Notable namesakes: Lillie Langtry, the British actress known as the 'Jersey Lily'; Lily Briscoe, a character in the novel *To the Lighthouse*, by British writer Virginia Woolf.

Linda

Variants and diminutives: Belinda, Lin, Lindi, Lindia, Lindie, Lindita, Lindy, Lyn, Lynda, Lynn, Lynne.

Meaning: 'snake' (Germanic); 'pretty' (Spanish); 'neat' (Italian); also a diminutive of any name ending in '-linda', such as Belinda.

Notable namesakes: Linda Hamilton (US actress); Linda McCartney (US photographer, singer and vegetarian-food campaigner).

Lindsay

Variants and diminutives: Linda, Lindsey, Lindsie, Linsey, Linsi, Linsie, Linsy, Lyndsay, Lyndsey, Lyndsy, Lynsey.

Meaning: 'island' or 'wetland' and 'of lime trees' or 'of Lincoln' (Old English); derived from a Scottish family name, in turn derived from the English place name Lindsey. Also a boy's name.

Linnea

Variants and diminutives: Linea, Linna, Linnae, Linnaea, Lynea, Lynnea.

Meaning: derived from the *Linnaea* (twin flower) genus of flowering plants named for the Swedish botanist Carolus Linnaeus (Carl von Linné).

Lirit

Variants and diminutives: Lyra, Lyre, Lyris.

Meaning: 'lyrical' (Hebrew).

Liron

Variants and diminutives: Lirone.

Meaning: 'my song' (Hebrew) or 'the circle' (Old French) as a female version of Leron.

Lisa

Variants and diminutives: Elizabeth, Liese, Lis, Lisbeth, Lise, Liseta, Lisette, Liza, Lizette.

Meaning: 'God is perfection', 'God is satisfaction', 'dedicated to God' or 'God's oath' (Hebrew) as a diminutive of Elizabeth.

Notable namesakes: the subject of the painting *Mona Lisa*, by Italian artist Leonardo da Vinci; Lisa Kudrow (US actress).

Livia

Variants and diminutives: Olivia, Levia, Liv, Livie, Liviya, Livy, Livvie, Livvy

Meaning: 'black and blue' (Latin) when derived from the Roman family name Livius; 'olive' (Latin) as a diminutive of Olivia; 'crown' (Hebrew).

Notable namesakes: Livia Drusilla, wife of the Roman emperor Augustus and mother of the Roman emperor Tiberius; Liv Tyler (US actress).

Liz

Variants and diminutives: Elizabeth, Lisa, Lisabet, Lisabeth, Lisabette, Lisbet, Lisbeth, Liz, Liza, Lizana, Lizanne, Lizabeth, Lizabette, Lizbeth, Lizbett, Lizet, Lizette, Lizina, Lizzie, Lizzy, Lyza, Lyzbeth, Lyzet, Lyzett, Lyzette.

Meaning: 'God is perfection', 'God is satisfaction', 'dedicated to God' or 'God's oath' (Hebrew) as a diminutive of Elizabeth.

Notable namesakes: Lizzie Borden (alleged US axe-murderer); Liza Minelli (US singer and actress).

Llewella

Variants and diminutives: Lewella, Louella, Luella.

Meaning: 'leader' or 'lion' and 'resemblance' (Welsh) as a female version of Llewellyn.

Lois

Variants and diminutives: Eloise, Louise.

Meaning: uncertain; possibly 'desirable' or 'good' (Greek); possibly 'famed' and 'warrior' (Germanic) as a variant of Louise, in turn a female version of Louis (Ludwig).

Notable namesakes: a grandmother of Timothy and a convert of Saint Paul in the New Testament; Lois Jones

(US artist and designer); Lois Lane, the girlfriend of Clark Kent, the Superman comic-strip hero originally created by US writer Jerome Siegel and illustrator Joseph Shuster, later also of television and cinematic fame.

Lola

Variants and diminutives: Dolores, Lo, Lolita, Lita, Loleta, Luchel, Lurleen, Lurline.
Meaning: 'sorrows' (Spanish) as a diminutive of Dolores.
Notable namesakes: Lola Montez (Irish dancer); Lolita, the eponymous subject of the novel *Lolita*, by Russian-born US writer Vladimir Nabokov; the subject of the song 'Lola', by the British band The Kinks.

Lorelei

Variants and diminutives: Lorelie, Lorilee, Lura, Lurette, Lurleen, Lurlene, Lurline.
Meaning: uncertain; derived from Lurlei, the name of a rock on the German river Rhine, south of Koblenz.
Notable namesakes: a siren who combs her hair while perched on the Lurlei, who lures sailors to their deaths, as told in poems by the German writers Clemens Brentano and Heinrich Heine.

Lorna

Variants and diminutives: Lona, Lornna.
Meaning: uncertain; possibly 'forlorn' (Old English); possibly 'from Laurentum' (Latin), Laurentum being the Roman name of an Italian town, as a variant of Laura (Laurence); possibly derived from a Scottish place name; coined by the English writer R D Blackmore for the eponymous heroine of his novel *Lorna Doone, A Romance of Exmoor*.

Lorraine

Variants and diminutives: Laraine, Larraine, Lauraine, Laurraine, Lorain, Loraine, Lorayna, Lorayne, Lorrane, Lorrayne, Raina, Rayna.
Meaning: 'Lothar's kingdom' (Latin); derived from the name of the Lorraine region of eastern France that was once ruled by the Holy Roman emperor Lothar (Lothair) I.
Notable namesakes: Lorraine Hansberry (US playwright); Lorraine Chase (British model).

Lottie

Variants and diminutives: Charlotte, Elizabeth, Lieselotte, Lotta, Lotte, Lotty.
Meaning: 'man' or 'free man' (Germanic) as diminutive of Charlotte, in turn a female version of Charles; 'God is perfection', 'God is satisfaction', 'dedicated to God' or 'God's oath' (Hebrew) as a diminutive of Lieselotte (Elizabeth).
Notable namesakes: Lotte Lenya (Austrian singer and actress).

Louella

Variants and diminutives: Llewella, Lewella, Luella.
Meaning: a compound name comprising Lou, 'famed' and 'warrior' (Germanic) as a diminutive of Louise, in turn a female version of Louis (Ludwig), and Ella, 'all' (Germanic) or 'fairy' and 'maiden' (Old English), also a variant of Elizabeth and Ellen.
Notable namesakes: Louella Parsons (US gossip columnist).

Louise

Variants and diminutives: Aloisa, Aloise, Aloisia, Alouise, Aloys, Aloyse, Aloysia, Aluisa, Eloisa, Eloise, Eloisia, Heloise, Isa, Iza, Lewes, Lisette, Lodoiska, Lois, Loise, Lou, Louie, Louisa, Louisetta, Louisette, Lovisa, Loyce, Lu, Ludka, Ludwika, Luisa, Luisana, Luisanna, Luise, Luisetta, Luisina, Luiza, Lujza, Lula, Lulita, Lulu, Lutza, Luyiza, Ouida.
Meaning: 'famed' and 'warrior' (Germanic) as a female version of Louis (Ludwig).
Notable namesakes: Louise Labé (French poet); Saint Louise de Marillac, co-founder of the religious order the Daughters of Charity and patron saint of social workers and widows; Louise de Kéroualle, Duchess of Portsmouth, a mistress of King Charles II of Britain; Louisa M Alcott (US writer); Louise Bogan (US poet and critic); Louise Nevelson (Russian-born US sculptor); Louise Bourgeois (French-born US sculptor). Louise Glück (US poet).

Lourdes

Meaning: uncertain; derived from the name of the French place of pilgrimage.
Notable namesakes: Lourdes Ciccone, the daughter of the US singer Madonna and Carlos Leon.

Loveday

Variants and diminutives: Lovdie, Lowdy, Luveday.
Meaning: 'day of love' (Old English).
Notable namesakes: in English tradition, a day dedicated to reconciliation.

Lucia

Variants and diminutives: Cindie, Cindy, Lu, Luce, Lucetta, Lucette, Luci, Luciana, Lucie, Lucienne, Lucija, Lucile, Lucilla, Lucille, Lucina, Lucinda, Lucine, Lucita, Lucky, Lucy, Lusita, Luz, Luzia, Luzija, Luzine.
Meaning: 'light' (Latin) as a female version of Lucius.
Notable namesakes: Lucina, a goddess of childbirth in Graeco-Roman mythology; Saint Lucia of Syracuse, patron saint of blind people and the prevention of eye disease; Saint Lucia, an island state in the Caribbean.

Lucilla

Variants and diminutives: Cilla, Lu, Luce, Lucia, Lucile, Lucille, Lucy.
Meaning: 'light' (Latin) as a variant of Lucia, in turn a female version of Lucius.
Notable namesakes: Saint Lucilla; Lucille Ball (US actress and comedienne).

Lucinda

Variants and diminutives: Cindie, Cindy, Lu, Lucia, Lucinde, Lucy.
Meaning: 'light' (Latin) as a diminutive of Lucia, in turn a female version of Lucius.
Notable namesakes: a character in the novel *Don Quixote*, by Spanish writer Miguel de Cervantes.

Lucretia

Variants and diminutives: Lucrece, Lucrecia, Lucretzia, Lucrezia.
Meaning: uncertain; possibly 'gain' (Latin); derived from the Roman family name Lucretius.
Notable namesakes: the Roman wife of Tarquinius Collatinus who was raped by Sextus, as told in William Shakespeare's poem *The Rape of Lucrece* and the opera *The Rape of Lucretia*, by British composer Benjamin Britten; Lucrezia Borgia, the daughter of the Italian Pope Alexander VI and sister of Cesare Borgia.

Lucy

Variants and diminutives: Cindy, Laoise, Lu, Luca, Luce, Lucetta, Lucette, Luci, Lucia, Luciana, Luciane, Lucida, Lucie, Lucienne, Lucija, Lucika, Lucila, Lucile, Lucilla, Lucille, Lucina, Lucinda, Lucine, Lucita, Lucka, Lucky, Lucya, Lulu, Lusita, Luz, Luzi, Luzie, Luzia, Luzija, Luzine.
Meaning: 'light' (Latin) as an English variant of Lucia, in turn a female version of Lucius.
Notable namesakes: Lucy Stone (US suffragette); the US television series *I Love Lucy*, starring Lucille Ball.

Ludmilla

Variants and diminutives: Ludie, Ludmila, Ludovika.
Meaning: 'people' and 'grace' or 'beloved' (Slavonic).
Notable namesakes: Saint Ludmilla.

Lulu

Variants and diminutives: Lleulu, Louise, Lu, Lucy.
Meaning: 'rabbit' (Native American); 'famed' and 'warrior' (Germanic) as a diminutive of Louise, in turn a female version of Louis (Ludwig); 'light' (Latin) as a diminutive of Lucy (Lucia), in turn a female version of Lucius.
Notable namesakes: a Scottish singer.

Luna

Variants and diminutives: Lunette.
Meaning: 'moon', 'month' or 'crescent' (Latin).
Notable namesakes: a goddess of the moon in Roman mythology.

Lydia

Variants and diminutives: Liddie, Liddy, Lida, Lidi, Lidia, Lidie, Lidiya, Lidka, Lidochka, Lyda, Lydda, Lydie.
Meaning: 'from Lydia' (Greek), Lydia being an ancient region of Asia Minor.
Notable namesakes: a convert of Saint Paul's in the New Testament; Lydia Languish, a character in the play *The Rivals*, by the Irish-born English playwright Richard Brinsley Sheridan; the heroine of the novel *Love for Lydia*, by the British writer H E Bates.

Lynette

Variants and diminutives: Eiluned, Eluned, Lanette,

Linet, Linetta, Linette, Linnet, Linnett, Linette, Luned, Lyn, Lynette, Lynn, Lynne, Lynnet, Lynnette.
Meaning: uncertain; possibly 'flax' (Latin) as a variant of Linnet, linnet being the common name of the flax-eating finch *Acanthis cannabina*; possibly 'idol' or 'adored one' (Welsh) as a variant of Eluned.
Notable namesakes: an Arthurian character whose story is told in 'Gareth and Lynette', part of the poetic series of poems *The Idyll of the King*, by English poet Alfred, Lord Tennyson.

Lynn

Variants and diminutives: Carolyn, Eluned, Lin, Lina, Linda, Linell, Linelle, Linn, Linne, Linnet, Lyn, Lynda, Lyndel, Lyndell, Lyndelle, Lynell, Lynelle, Lynette, Lynna, Lynne, Lynelle.
Meaning: 'lake' (Celtic); 'snake' (Germanic), 'pretty' (Spanish) or 'neat' (Italian) as a diminutive of Lynda (Linda); 'flax' (Latin), 'idol' or 'adored one' (Welsh) as a diminutive of Lynette; also a diminutive of a number of names containing the '-lyn-' element, such as Carolyn. Also a boy's name (generally Lyn).
Notable namesakes: Lynn Redgrave (British actress).

Lyra

Variants and diminutives: Lirit, Lyre, Lyris.
Meaning: 'lyre' (Greek).

Lysandra

Variants and diminutives: Sandie, Sandra, Sandy.
Meaning: 'freer of men' (Greek) as a female version of Lysander.

Mabel

Variants and diminutives: Amabel, Amabella, Maeve, Mab, Mabb, Mabbit, Mabbot, Mabbs, Mabell, Mabella, Mabelle, Mabilia, Mabilla, Mable, Mably, Mapp, Mappin, Mapps, Mave, Mavis.
Meaning: 'lovable' (Latin) as a diminutive of Amabel; 'intoxicating' (Irish Gaelic) as a variant of Maeve.
Notable namesakes: Queen Mab, another name for the Irish goddess Mebd (Maeve), a fairy who bestows dreams on sleeping people and who features William Shakespeare's play *Romeo and Juliet*.

Madeleine

Variants and diminutives: Lena, Lenna, Lina, Linn, Lynn, Lynne, Mada, Madia, Madaleine, Madalina, Madaliene, Madaline, Madalyn, Madalyne, Madalynn, Madalynne, Maddi, Maddie, Maddy, Madelaine, Madelena, Madelina, Madeline, Madena, Madge, Madina, Madlen, Madlin, Madlyn, Mady, Magaly, Magda, Magdalen, Magdalena, Magdalene, Magdalina, Magola, Mahda, Mala, Malena, Marla, Marleen, Marlena, Marlene, Marlina, Marline.
Meaning: 'woman from Magdala' (Hebrew), Magdala being a place on the Sea of Galilee, as a French variant of Magdalene.
Notable namesakes: Madeleine de Scudéry (French writer); madeleine cakes, possibly invented by the French pastry cook Madeleine Paulmier; Madeleine Smith (British actress).

Madonna

Variants and diminutives: Donna, Maria, Mary.
Meaning: 'my lady' (Italian), usually referring to the Virgin Mary.
Notable namesakes: the generic name for artistic depictions of the Virgin Mary; the Madonna lily, *Lilium candidum*; Madonna Ciccone (US singer).

Maeve

Variants and diminutives: Mab, Mabel, Madhbh, Mauve, Mave, Mavis, Meadhbh, Meave, Medb.
Meaning: 'intoxicating' (Irish Gaelic).
Notable namesakes: a queen of Connacht (Connaught) and goddess of sovereignty in Irish legend; Maeve Binchy (Irish writer).

Magdalene

Variants and diminutives: Delenna, Leli, Lena, Lene, Lenna, Lina, Linn, Lynn, Lynne, Mada, Madaleine, Madalena, Madaliene, Madaline, Madalyn, Madalyne, Madeline, Madalynne, Maddalena, Maddi, Maddie, Maddy, Madeena, Madel, Madelaine, Madeleine, Madelena, Madelia, Madelina, Madeline, Madella, Madelle, Madelon, Madelyn, Madge, Madia, Madina, Madlen, Madli, Madlin, Madlyn, Madlynn, Madlynne, Mady, Mag, Magaly, Magda, Magdale, Magdalen, Magdalena, Magdalina, Magdaline, Magdelina, Magia, Magli, Magola, Mahda, Mai, Mala, Malena, Mali, Malin, Manda, Marla, Marleen, Marlena, Marlene, Marlie, Marlina, Marline, Marlo, Marlowe, Marlys, Maudlin, Migdana.

Meaning: 'woman from Magdala' (Hebrew), Magdala being a place on the Sea of Galilee.

Notable namesakes: Saint Mary Magdalene (see also Mary), the woman who anointed Christ's feet and witnessed his resurrection in the New Testament, and inspired the generic name magdalen, or madgalene, for reformed prostitutes, and the word maudlin, meaning 'tearful'; the Magdalena river in Colombia, Magdalena Bay in Mexico; the Palaeolithic Magdalenian culture, named for the French village La Madeleine; the eponymous heroine of the play *Magda* (or *Die Heimat*), by German writer Hermann Sudermann.

Maggie

Variants and diminutives: Mag, Maggi, Maggy, Margaret.

Meaning: 'pearl' (Greek) as a diminutive of Margaret.

Notable namesakes: Maggie Johnson, the subject of the novel *Maggie: A Girl of the Streets*, by US writer Stephen Crane; Maggie Smith (British actress).

Magnolia

Variants and diminutives: Lia.

Meaning: uncertain; derived from the *Magnolia* genus of flowering shrubs named for the French botanist Pierre Magnol.

Mahala

Variants and diminutives: Mahalah, Mahalia, Mahela, Mahelia, Mahila, Mahilia, Mehala, Mehalah, Mehalia.

Meaning: 'tenderness' or 'infertile' (Hebrew); 'woman' (Native American).

Mahina

Variants and diminutives: Hina.

Meaning: 'moon' (Hawaiian).

Mahira

Variants and diminutives: Mehira.

Meaning: 'energetic' or 'quick' (Hebrew).

Maia

Variants and diminutives: Mae, Mai, May, Maya.

Meaning: 'mother' or 'nurse' (Greek).

Notable namesakes: one of the Pleiades and the mother of Hermes by Zeus in Greek mythology; the goddess of spring growth in Roman mythology, for whom the month of May is named.

Maidie

Variants and diminutives: Maddie, Maddy, Maid, Maida, Maidel, Maidie, Maidey, Margaret, Mary.

Meaning: uncertain; possibly 'little maid' (Old English); possibly 'pearl' (Greek) as a diminutive of Margaret; possibly 'longed-for child' or 'rebellion' (Hebrew) as a diminutive of Mary (Miriam).

Maire

Variants and diminutives: Mair, Mary.

Meaning: 'dark' (Celtic); 'longed-for child' or 'rebellion' (Hebrew) as an Irish Gaelic variant of Mary (Miriam).

Maisie

Variants and diminutives: Mairead, Maise, Margaret, Mysie.

Meaning: 'pearl' (Greek) as a diminutive of Margaret; 'maize' (French).

Notable namesakes: Maisie Farange, the title character of the novel *What Maisie Knew*, by US writer Henry James; the leading character – a mouse – of British writer Aileen Paterson's series of children's books.

Maja
Variants and diminutives: Majidah.
Meaning: 'splendid' (Arabic).

Malka
Variants and diminutives: Malkah.
Meaning: 'queen' (Hebrew and Arabic).

Malu
Variants and diminutives: Malulani.
Meaning: 'peace' (Hawaiian).

Malvina
Variants and diminutives: Melvina, Vina.
Meaning: uncertain; possibly 'smooth' and 'brow'
(Scots Gaelic); coined by the Scottish writer James
Macpherson.
Notable namesakes: Islas Malvinas, the Argentinian
name for the Falkland Islands in the South Atlantic.

Mamie
Variants and diminutives: Mary, Miriam.
Meaning: 'my darling' (French); 'longed-for child' or
'rebellion' (Hebrew) as a diminutive of Mary (Miriam).
Notable namesakes: Mamie Eisenhower (wife of US
President Dwight D Eisenhower).

Mandy
Variants and diminutives: Amanda, Armanda, Mand,
Manda, Mandi, Mandie.
Meaning: 'lovable' or 'fit to be loved' (Latin) as a
diminutive of Amanda.
Notable namesakes: the title of a song by the British
band 10cc.

Mangena
Variants and diminutives: Mangena.
Meaning: 'song' or 'melody' (Hebrew).

Manuela
Variants and diminutives: Emanuella, Emmanuela.
Meaning: 'God is with us' (Hebrew) as a female
version of Manuel (Emmanuel).

Mara
Variants and diminutives: Marah.
Meaning: 'bitter' (Hebrew).
Notable namesakes: a name used for herself by the
grieving Naomi in the Old Testament.

Marcella
Variants and diminutives: Malinda, Marcela,
Marcelia, Marcelinda, Marcelle, Marcellina, Marcelline,
Marcelyn, Marcha, Marci, Marcia, Marcie, Marcile,
Marcilen, Marcille, Marcy, Marisella, Marquita, Marsha,
Marshe, Melinda.
Meaning: uncertain; possibly 'martial' (Latin) through
association with Mars, the god of war in Roman
mythology, as a female version of Marcellus.
Notable namesakes: Saint Marcella; a character in the
novel *Don Quixote*, by Spanish writer Miguel de
Cervantes.

Marcia
Variants and diminutives: Marcelia, Marcella,
Marcelle, Marcha, Marci, Marcie, Marcile, Marcille,
Marcy, Marquita, Marsha, Marshe, Marsi, Marsie,
Marsy.
Meaning: uncertain; possibly 'martial' (Latin) through
association with Mars, the god of war in Roman
mythology, as a female version of Marcus.
Notable namesakes: Marsha Hunt (US actress).

Margaret
Variants and diminutives: Daisy, Ghita, Gita, Gitka,
Gitta, Gituska, Gogo, Greta, Gretal, Gretchen, Grete,
Gretel, Gretie, Gretta, Grieta, Gritty, Madge, Madie,
Mady, Mae, Maergrethe, Mag, Magge, Maggi, Maggie,
Maggy, Mago, Maidie, Maiga, Mairead, Maisie, Maisy,
Makelesi, Mamie, Manci, Mared, Marga, Margalit,
Margalith, Margara, Margareta, Margarete,
Margaretha, Margarethe, Margaretta, Margarette,
Margarid, Margarida, Margarinda, Margarita,
Margaritis, Margaro, Margat, Margaux, Marge,
Margebelle, Marged, Margene, Margerie, Margery,
Marget, Marghanita, Margherita, Margiad, Margie,
Margisia, Margit, Margita, Margo, Margot, Margret,
Margreta, Margrete, Margrethe, Margrieta,
Marguarita, Marguerita, Marguerite, Marquita, Margy,

Mari, Marjarie, Marjary, Marjatta, Marje, Marjie, Marjorie, Marjory, Marka, Marketa, Marleah, Marles, May, Meaghan, Meeri, Meg, Megan, Meggi, Meggie, Meggy, Meghan, Mergret, Meta, Midge, Mittie, Mog, Moggie, Moggy, Molly, Mysie, Peg, Peggi, Peggie, Peggy, Penina, Perla, Polly, Reatha, Reet, Reta, Rita, Tita.
Meaning: 'pearl' (Greek).
Notable namesakes: the marguerite genus of flowering plants, *Leucanthemum vulgare*; Saint Margaret of Antioch, patron saint of pregnant women, women in labour and dying people; Saint Margaret of Scotland, wife of King Malcolm III of Scotland and patron saint of Scotland; Saint Margaret of Clitherow, patron saint of business women; Saint Margaret of Cortona, patron saint of repentant prostitutes; Queen Margaret of Scotland, 'the Maid of Norway'; Margaret of Anjou, wife of King Henry VI of England; Margaret Tudor, daughter of King Henry VII of England and wife of King James IV of Scotland; Margaret d'Angoulême, also known as Marguerite of Navarre, sister of King François I of France, wife of King Henri II of Navarre, poet and writer; Margaret of Valois, daughter of King Henri II of France and wife of King Henri IV of France; Margaret Fuller (US writer and teacher); Margaret Mitchell (US author); Margaret Mead (US anthropologist); Margaret Rutherford (British actress); Marguerite Duras (French writer and film-maker); Margaret Bourke-White (US photographer); Margaret Burroughs (US artist); Princess Margaret of the United Kingdom; Margot Fonteyn (British ballerina); Margaret Laurence and Margaret Atwood (Canadian writers); Margaret Drabble (British writer); Margaret Thatcher (British politician); Queen Margrethe II of Denmark; the island of Margarita in the Caribbean Sea; margarita, the name of a cocktail.

Maria

Variants and diminutives: Carmen, Dolores, Jesusa, Lucita, Luz, Mareea, Mariabella, Mari, Mariah, Mariamne, Mary, Marya, Mia, Mitzi.
Meaning: 'longed-for child' or 'rebellion' (Hebrew) as the Latin form of Mary (Miriam).
Notable namesakes: the Virgin Mary (see Mary); Maria Theresa, daughter of Emperor Charles VI of Austria, wife of Emperor Francis I and mother of Emperor Joseph II of Austria; Saint Maria Faustina Kowalska, patron saint of mercy; Saint Maria Goretti, patron saint of young people, girls and rape victims; a character in William Shakespeare's play *Twelfth Night*; the eponymous heroine of the novel *Maria*, by Colombian writer Jorge Isaacs; Maria Edgeworth (Irish writer); Maria Callas (Greek singer); the heroine of the musical *West Side Story*, by US composer Leonard Bernstein; Mariah Carey (US singer)

Marian

Variants and diminutives: Ann, Anna, Anne, Mari, Mariamne, Mariane, Mariann, Marianne, Marien, Marion, Meirion, Mor, Morag.
Meaning: 'longed-for child' or 'rebellion' (Hebrew) as a variant of Marianne and Mary (Miriam).
Notable namesakes: an adjective relating to the Virgin Mary, but also to Mary, Queen of Scots, and Queen Mary of England; Maid Marian, Robin Hood's love interest in English folklore.

Marianne

Variants and diminutives: Ann, Anna, Anne, Mari, Mariamne, Marian, Mariana, Mariane, Mariann, Marianna, Marien, Mary, Maryam, Maryann, Maryanna, Maryanne.
Meaning: a compound name comprising Marie (Miriam via Mary), 'longed-for child' or 'rebellion' (Hebrew), and Anne (Hannah via Anna), 'I have been favoured (by God)' (Hebrew).
Notable namesakes: the female personification of the Republic of France; the Mariana Trench, the deepest part of the sea floor; the Mariana Islands (or Marianas) in the Pacific Ocean; a character in the novel *Sense and Sensibility*, by English writer Jane Austen; Marianne Moore (US poet); Marianne Faithfull (British singer).

Marie

Variants and diminutives: Maree, Maree, Mari, Marietta, Mariette.
Meaning: 'longed-for child' or 'rebellion' (Hebrew) as a French variant of Mary (Miriam).
Notable namesakes: Marie Galante, an island in the Caribbean Sea; Marie de France (French poet); Marie

de' Medici, wife of King Henri IV and mother of King Louis XIII of France; Marie Antoinette, wife of King Louis XVI of France, who was guillotined after the French Revolution; Madame Marie Tussaud, founder of the waxwork exhibition in London; Marie Louise, daughter of Emperor Francis I of Austria and wife of Emperor Napoleon I (Napoleon Bonaparte) of France; Marie, wife and consort of King Ferdinand I of Romania; Marie Corelli, the pseudonym of the British writer Mary Mackay; Marie Stopes (British birth-control pioneer); Marie Curie (Polish scientist); Marie Laurencin (French artist and designer).

Marigold

Variants and diminutives: Goldie, Goldy, Mari, Marie, Mary, Marygold.
Meaning: 'Mary's gold' (Old English); derived from the common name of the *Tagetes* genus of flowering plants.

Marilyn

Variants and diminutives: Maralin, Maralyn, Mara-Lyn, MaraLyn, Maralyne, Maralynn, Mari, Marilee, Marilene, Marilin, Marillin, Marillyn, Marilynn, Marilynne, Marlyn, Marolyn, Marrilyn, Marylin, Maryline, Marylyn, Marylynn, Merili, Merilyn, Merilynn, Merrilyn.
Meaning: a composite name comprising Mary (Miriam), 'longed-for child' or 'rebellion' (Hebrew), and Lyn (Lynn), 'lake' (Celtic), 'snake' (Germanic), 'pretty' (Spanish), 'neat' (Italian), 'flax' (Latin), 'idol' or 'adored one' (Welsh).
Notable namesakes: Marilyn Monroe (US actress).

Marina

Variants and diminutives: Mare, Maren, Marena, Marie, Maris, Marisa, Marisella, Marissa, Marna, Marne, Marni, Marnie, Marnina, Marys, Meris, Rina.
Meaning: 'of the sea' (Latin).
Notable namesakes: Saint Marina; the generic name for a docking facility for pleasure boats; Marina Ivanovna Tsvetayevna (Russian poet); Princess Marina of Greece, wife of the Duke of Kent, who, in Britain, gave her name to a shade of blue.

Marisa

Variants and diminutives: Mareesa, Mari, Maris, Marissa, Marisella, Marita, Maritza, Marrisa, Mary, Marysa, Maryse, Maryssa, Meris, Merisa, Merissa, Morissa, Risa, Rissa.
Meaning: 'longed-for child' or 'rebellion' (Hebrew) as a variant of Mary (Miriam).

Marjorie

Variants and diminutives: Margaret, Marge, Margerie, Margery, Margie, Marjarie, Marjary, Marje, Marjie, Marjory, Marsali.
Meaning: 'pearl' (Greek) as a variant of Margaret.
Notable namesakes: Marjorie Bruce, daughter of King Robert the Bruce of Scotland and wife of Walter the Steward, founder of the Stewart (Stuart) dynasty of Scottish rulers; Marjorie Kinnan Rawlings (US writer).

Marlene

Variants and diminutives: Layna, Lene, Lena, Leyna, Lina, Linn, Lynn, Lynne, Magdalena, Magdalene, Mala, Malena, Marla, Marlaina, Marlaine, Marlane, Marle, Marlea, Marleah, Marlee, Marleen, Marlena, Marley, Marlie, Marlies, Marlin, Marlina, Marline, Marlyn, Mary.
Meaning: a compound name comprising Maria (Miriam via Mary), 'longed-for child' or 'rebellion' (Hebrew), and Magdalena (Magdalene), 'woman from Magdala' (Hebrew).
Notable namesakes: Marlene Dietrich (German-born US actress and singer); 'Lili Marlene', a song popular among both German and British combatants during World War II.

Marnie

Variants and diminutives: Marina, Marna, Marni.
Meaning: 'of the sea' (Latin) as a variant of Marina.
Notable namesakes: the title of a film by the British film director Alfred Hitchcock.

A
B
C
D
E
F
G
H
I
J
K
L
M
N
O
P
Q
R
S
T
U
V
W
X
Y
Z

Marnina

Variants and diminutives: Marni, Marnie, Marny, Nina.

Meaning: 'rejoicer' or 'singer' (Hebrew). A female version of Marnin.

Martha

Variants and diminutives: Maita, Marcia, Mardeth, Mardie, Mart, Marta, Martelle, Marthe, Marthena, Marti, Marticka, Martie, Martina, Martita, Martus, Martuska, Marty, Masia, Matti, Mattie, Matty, Merta, Moireach, Pat, Pattie, Patty.

Meaning: 'lady' (Aramaic).

Notable namesakes: Saint Martha, the house-proud sister of Mary and Lazarus in the New Testament, patron saint of home-makers, cooks, hoteliers, servants and lay-sisters; the wife of US President George Washington; Martha's Vineyard, an island off the coast of Cape Cod, in the US state of Massachusetts; the title of an opera by German composer Friedrich von Flotow; Martha Finley (US writer).

Martina

Variants and diminutives:
Marta, Martella, Marti,
Martie, Martine, Marty,
Martyna, Martyne, Tina.

Meaning: uncertain;
possibly 'martial' (Latin)
through association with
Mars, the god of war in
Roman mythology, as a
female version of Martin.

Notable namesakes: Martina Navratilova (Czech-born US tennis player); Martina Hingis (Swiss tennis player); Martine McCutcheon (British actress).

Mary

Variants and diminutives: Macia, Mae, Mai, Maidie, Maie, Maija, Maijii, Maikki, Mair, Maire, Mairi, Mairin, Maisie, Malia, Maralou, Mame, Mamie, Manette, Manka, Manon, Manya, Mara, Marabel, Marca, Marcsa, Mare, Maree, Mareea, Marella, Maren, Marenka, Mari, Maria, Mariah, Mariam, Mariamne, Marian, Mariana, Mariane, Marianna, Marianne, Maribel, Maribella, Maribeth, Maricara, Marice, Maridel, Marie, Mariel, Mariele, Mariene, Marienka, Mariesa, Mariessa, Marietta, Mariette, Marija, Marijon, Marijune, Marika, Marilee, Marilin, Marilu, Marilyn, Marinka, Marion, Mariquilla, Mariquita, Marisa, Marisha, Mariska, Marissa, Marita, Mariwin, Mariya, Marja, Marla, Marlo, Maroula, Maruca, Maruja, Maruska, Marya, Maryalice, Maryam, Maryann, Maryanna, Maryanne, Marybeth, Marye, Maryla, Marylin, Marylinn, Marylois, Marylou, Marylyn, Maryna, Maryse, Masha, Mashenka, Mashka, Maura, Maure, Maureen, Maurene, Maurine, May, Meirion, Mele, Meli, Meri, Meriel, Merrill, Meryl, Mhairi, Miliama, Millie, Mim, Mimi, Min, Minette, Minni, Minnie, Mira, Miri, Miriam, Mirit, Mirjam, Mirjana, Mirra, Miryam, Mitzi, Mo, Moira, Moire, Moll, Molli, Mollie, Molly, Mollye, Morine, Moya, Moyra, Muire, Mura, Muriel, Muriell, Poll, Polli, Pollie, Polly, Roula.

Meaning: 'longed-for child' or 'rebellion' (Hebrew) as a variant of Miriam.

Notable namesakes: Saint Mary, the Virgin Mary, mother of Christ in the New Testament, patron saint of mothers, virgins and nuns; Saint Mary Magdalene, the woman who anointed Christ's feet and witnessed his resurrection in the New Testament, patron saint of the contemplative life, hairdressers, repentant prostitutes, sinners and penitents (see also Magdalene); Mary of Bethany, sister of Martha and Lazarus in the New Testament; the mother of James and Joseph in the New Testament; the mother of Mark in the New Testament; Saint Mary of Egypt, patron saint of repentant prostitutes; Marie of Guise (or Mary of Lorraine), wife of King James V of Scotland and mother of Mary, Queen of Scots; the *Mary Rose*, King Henry VIII of England's flagship, which sank and was subsequently raised from the sea and restored; Queen Mary I ('Bloody Mary') of England; Mary, Queen of Scots; Mary of Modena, wife of King James II of Britain; Queen Mary II, co-ruler of Britain with her husband, King William III; Mary Wortley Montagu (English writer); Mary Wollstonecraft and her daughter Mary Wollstonecraft Shelley (English writers); Mary Cassatt (US artist); Mary Baker Eddy, the US founder of the Christian Science movement; Mary of Teck, wife of King George V of Britain; Maryland, a US state; Mary

Stewart and Mary Renault (British writers); Mary Poppins, the leading character of the eponymous children's book (and subsequent film) created by British author P L Travers; Mary Peters (British athlete); Mary J Blige (US singer).

Matana
Meaning: 'gift' (Hebrew).

Matilda
Variants and diminutives: Hilda, Hilde, Macia, Maddy, Mahaut, Mala, Malkin, Mat, Matelda, Mathilda, Mathilde, Mati, Matilde, Matilldis, Matti, Mattie, Matty, Mattye, Matya, Matylda, Maud, Maude, Maudene, Maudie, Mawde, Mechthild, Metilda, Mold, Pattie, Patty, Tila, Tilda, Tilde, Tildie, Tildy, Tillie, Tilly, Tylda.
Meaning: 'mighty' and 'battle' (Germanic).
Notable namesakes: Matilda, wife of King William I, 'the Conqueror', of England; Matilda, also known as the Empress Maud, the daughter of King Henry I of England who unsuccessfully challenged her cousin Stephen for the English throne, wife of the Holy Roman emperor Henry V and Geoffrey Plantagenet, Count of Anjou; in Australia, a bushman's swag popularised by the song 'Waltzing Matilda'; Matilde Serao (Italian writer); the eponymous leading character of the children's book by British writer Roald Dahl.

Maud
Variants and diminutives: Matilda, Maude, Maudie.
Meaning: 'mighty' and 'battle' (Germanic) as a variant of Matilda.
Notable namesakes: the Empress Maud (see Matilda); the title of a poem by English poet Alfred, Lord Tennyson; the heroine of the poem *Maud Muller*, by US poet John Greenleaf Whittier; Maud Gonne (Irish patriot).

Maura
Variants and diminutives: Maire, Mary, Maureen, Maurene, Maurine, Moira, Mora.
Meaning: 'dark' (Celtic); 'longed-for child' or 'rebellion' (Hebrew) as an anglicised form of Maire, an Irish Gaelic variant of Mary (Miriam).
Notable namesakes: Saint Maura.

Maureen
Variants and diminutives: Maire, Mairin, Mary, Maura, Maurene, Maurine, Mo, Moira, Mora, Moreen, Morena.
Meaning: 'dark' (Celtic); 'longed-for child' or 'rebellion' (Hebrew) as an anglicised form of Maire, an Irish Gaelic variant of Mary (Miriam).
Notable namesakes: Maureen O'Sullivan and Maureen O'Hara (Irish-born US actresses).

Mavis
Variants and diminutives: Maeve, Mave.
Meaning: 'song thrush' (Old French); derived from the common name of the song thrush, *Turdus philomelos*.
Notable namesakes: a character in the novel *The Sorrows of Satan*, by British writer Marie Corelli; Mavis Gallant (Canadian writer).

Maxine
Variants and diminutives: Max, Maxencia, Maxi, Maxie, Maxima, Maxime, Maxy.
Meaning: 'great' (Latin).

May
Variants and diminutives: Mae, Maia, Margaret, Mary, Maya, Maybelle, Mei.
Meaning: 'the month of Maia' (Latin); 'longed-for child' or 'rebellion' (Hebrew) as a diminutive of Mary (Miriam); 'pearl' (Greek) as a diminutive of Margaret.
Notable namesakes: the name of the fifth month of the year (see Maia), the first day of which is known as May Day (also the name of a radiotelephonic distress signal, from the French *m'aidez*); may blossom, a common name of the hawthorn, *Crataegus*; Mae West, the US actress whose ample figure gave rise to the slang term for an inflatable life jacket; Louisa May Alcott and May Sarton (US writers).

Maya
Variants and diminutives: Maia, May.
Meaning: 'illusion' (Sanskrit).
Notable namesakes: the goddess of illusion, after whom the principle of maya, or illusion, is named in Hinduism and Buddhism; the Maya (or Mayan) peole of South America; Maya Angelou (US writer).

A
B
C
D
E
F
G
H
I
J
K
L
M
N
O
P
Q
R
S
T
U
V
W
X
Y
Z

Meena
Variants and diminutives: Mina.
Meaning: 'precious stone' or 'fish' (Sanskrit).

Megan
Variants and diminutives: Meagan, Meaghan, Meaghen, Meg, Megen, Meggie, Meggy, Meghan, Meghann.
Meaning: 'pearl' (Greek) as a Welsh variant of Margaret.
Notable namesakes: Megan Lloyd George (British political activist).

Meira
Variants and diminutives: Meera, Mira.
Meaning: 'radiant' or 'light' (Hebrew).

Meirion
Variants and diminutives: Merrion.
Meaning: 'longed-for child' or 'rebellion' (Hebrew) as a Welsh variant of Marian (Miriam via Mary).
Notable namesakes: the former Welsh county of Merionethshire.

Melanie
Variants and diminutives: Ela, Mel, Mela, Melana, Melani, Melania, Melaniya, Melanka, Melantha, Melany, Melanya, Melashka, Melasya, Melena, Melenia, Melka, Melli, Mellie, Melloney, Mellony, Melly, Meloni, Melonie, Meloney, Melony, Milena, Milya.
Meaning: 'black' or 'dark' (Greek).
Notable namesakes: as Melania, two saints; Melanie Wilkes, a character in the novel *Gone With the Wind*, by US writer Margaret Mitchell; Melanie Klein (Austrian psychoanalyst).

Melinda
Variants and diminutives: Linda, Lynda, Malinda, Malinde, Mallie, Mally, Mel, Meli, Melissa, Melli, Mellie, Melly, Melynda.
Meaning: a composite name comprising 'Mel', 'honey' (Greek), and '-linda', 'snake' (Germanic), 'pretty' (Spanish), or 'neat' (Italian).

Meliora
Meaning: 'better' (Latin).

Melissa
Variants and diminutives: Lissa, Lisse, Malina, Malinda, Malinde, Malissa, Mallie, Mally, Mel, Melesa, Melessa, Meli, Melina, Melinda, Melisa, Melisande, Melise, Melisenda, Mell, Melli, Mellie, Melly, Melynda, Misha, Missie, Missy.
Meaning: 'bee' (Greek).
Notable namesakes: the daughter of Melissus, King of Crete, who nourished Zeus, the supreme god of Greek mythology, with honey; a name of Artemis, the goddess of the moon, chastity and hunting in Greek mythology, whose priestesses were the Melissae; a prophetess who features in the epic poem *Orlando Furioso*, by Italian poet Lodovico Ariosto.

Melody
Variants and diminutives: Medosa, Mel, Melina, Melodi, Melodie, Melodye, Meldoy.
Meaning: 'harmonious tune' or 'singer of songs' (Greek).

Melora
Variants and diminutives: Mel, Lora.
Meaning: uncertain; possibly 'honey' and 'gold' (Greek).
Notable namesakes: the daughter of King Arthur and lover of Orlando in Arthurian legend.

Melosa
Variants and diminutives: Mel.
Meaning: 'honey-sweet' or 'gentle' (Spanish).

Melvina
Variants and diminutives: Malva, Malvina, Malvinda, Melevine, Melva, Melveen, Melvene, Melvine.
Meaning: uncertain; possibly 'smooth' and 'brow' (Scots Gaelic) as a variant of Malvina; possibly 'Amalo's settlement' (Germanic) or 'bad' and 'town' (Old French) as a female version of Melvin.

Menora
Variants and diminutives: Menorah.

Meaning: 'candelabrum' (Hebrew).
Notable namesakes: the menorah, a seven-branched candelabrum that was historically used in the Temple and is now the badge of the modern state of Israel, as well as a Jewish emblem.

Mercedes

Variants and diminutives: Mercy, Sadie.
Meaning: 'mercy' (Spanish).
Notable namesakes: *Santa Maria de las Mercedes* (literally 'Saint Mary of the Mercies'), a title of the Virgin Mary in Spain; the German car-manufacturing company Mercedes-Benz.

Mercia

Variants and diminutives: Mercy.
Meaning: 'people of the borderland' (Old English); derived from the name of an Anglo-Saxon kingdom.

Mercy

Variants and diminutives: Mercedes, Mercia, Mercille, Merri, Merry.
Meaning: 'recompense' (Latin); 'clemency' (English).
Notable namesakes: a Christian virtue; Merry Pecksniff, a character in the novel *Martin Chuzzlewit*, by English writer Charles Dickens; Mercy Warren (US writer).

Meredith

Variants and diminutives: Bedo, Maredudd, Meri, Merideth, Meridith, Merri, Merridie, Merrie, Merry.
Meaning: 'great' and 'chief' or 'lord' (Old Welsh). Also a boy's name.

Merle

Variants and diminutives: Meriel, Muriel, Merla, Merlina, Merline, Merola, Merril, Merrill, Merryl, Meryle, Morell, Murle.
Meaning: 'blackbird' (Latin); 'sea' and 'bright' (Irish Gaelic) as a variant of Muriel. Also a boy's name.
Notable namesakes: a Scottish common name for the blackbird, *Turdus merula*; a term used to describe a dog's speckled coat; Merle Oberon (US actress).

Merry

Variants and diminutives: Marrilee, Mercy, Meredith, Meri, Merie, Meridee, Merri, Merrie, Merrielle, Merrili, Merris, Merrita.
Meaning: 'agreeable' or 'jolly' (Old English); 'recompense' (Latin) or 'clemency' (English) as a diminutive of Mercy; 'great' and 'chief' or 'lord' (Old Welsh) as a diminutive of Meredith.

Meryl

Variants and diminutives: Maryl, Meriel, Merilyn, Merril, Merrill, Merrilyn, Merryl, Merle, Meryle, Muriel.
Meaning: 'sea' and 'bright' (Irish Gaelic) as a variant of Muriel; 'longed-for child' or 'rebellion' (Hebrew) as a variant of Mary (Miriam).
Notable namesakes: Meryl Streep (US actress).

Mia

Variants and diminutives: Maria.
Meaning: 'my' (Italian and Spanish); 'longed-for child' or 'rebellion' (Hebrew) as a diminutive of Maria, the Latin form of Mary (Miriam).
Notable namesakes: Mia Farrow (US actress).

Michaela

Variants and diminutives: Miia, Mica, Michael, Michaelle, Michal, Michel, Michele, Michelina, Micheline, Michelle, Micki, Mickie, Micky, Miguella, Mikaela, Mikelina.
Meaning: 'who is like God?' (Hebrew) as a female version of Michael.

Michelle

Variants and diminutives: Michael, Michaela, Michaelle, Michal, Michel, Michèle, Michelina, Micheline, Micki, Mickie, Micky.
Meaning: 'who is like God?' (Hebrew) as a female French version of Michael.
Notable namesakes: the title of a song by the British band The Beatles; Michelle Pfeiffer (US actress).

A B C D E F G H I J K L M N O P Q R S T U V W X Y Z

Mignon

Variants and diminutives: Mignonette.
Meaning: 'darling' (French).
Notable namesakes: a heroine of the novel

Wilhelm Meisters Lehrjahre
(*Wilhelm Meister's Apprenticeship*), by German writer
Johann Wolfgang von Goethe, on which the opera
Mignon, by French composer Ambroise Thomas, is
based; mignonette, the common name of the *Reseda
odorata* flowering plant.

Mildred

Variants and diminutives: Melicent, Mélisande,
Melisent, Mil, Milda, Millie, Milly, Mindy.
Meaning: 'mild' and 'strength' (Old English).
Notable namesakes: Saint Mildred; the leading
female character in the British television sitcom
George and Mildred.

Millicent

Variants and diminutives: Mel, Meli, Melicent,
Mélisande, Melisent, Melita, Melleta, Melli, Mellicent,
Mellie, Mellisent, Melly, Melusine, Mil, Mili, Milli, Millie,
Millisent, Milly.
Meaning: 'work' and 'strength' (Germanic).
Notable namesakes: as Mélisande, the heroine of the
play *Pelléas et Mélisande*, by the Belgian writer Count
Maurice Maeterlinck, and of the opera of the same
name by the French composer Claude Debussy.

Mima

Variants and diminutives: Jemima.
Meaning: 'dove' (Hebrew and Arabic) as a diminutive
of Jemima.

Mimi

Variants and diminutives: Helmine, Maria, Mary,
Miriam.
Meaning: 'longed-for child' or 'rebellion' (Hebrew) as
an Italian diminutive of Maria, the Latin form of Mary
(Miriam).
Notable namesakes: the heroine of the opera *La
Bohème*, by the Italian composer Giacomo Puccini.

Mina

Variants and diminutives: Helmine, Hermina, Meena,
Mena, Minna, Wilhelmina.
Meaning: 'will' and 'helmet' or 'protection' (Germanic)
as a diminutive of Wilhelmina (William). Also a
diminutive of any other name ending in '-mina'.

Minerva

Variants and diminutives: Min, Minette, Minni,
Minnie, Minny.
Meaning: uncertain; possibly 'mind' or 'remember'
(Latin); derived from the name of the goddess of
wisdom, martial skills and household arts and crafts in
Roman mythology.

Minna

Variants and diminutives: Helmine, Mina, Minda,
Mindi, Mindie, Mindy, Minee, Minetta, Minette, Minne,
Minnie, Minny, Wilhelmina.
Meaning: 'love' (Germanic); 'will' and 'helmet' or
'protection' (Germanic) as a diminutive of Wilhelmina
(William).
Notable namesakes: a character in the novel *The
Pirate*, by Scottish author Sir Walter Scott; the
eponymous leading character of the play *Minna von
Barnhelm*, by German writer Gotthold Ephraim
Lessing.

Minnie

Variants and diminutives: Mina, Minee, Minna,
Minni, Minny, Wilhelmina.
Meaning: 'will' and 'helmet' or 'protection' (Germanic)
as a diminutive of Wilhelmina (William). Also a
diminutive of Mary (Miriam).
Notable namesakes: Minnie Mouse, an animated
cartoon character popularised by US film producer
Walt Disney; Minnie Driver (British actress).

Mirabelle

Variants and diminutives: Bella, Belle, Mira, Mirabel,
Mirabell, Mirabella, Mirabelle, Mirella.
Meaning: 'wonderful' or 'extraordinary' (Latin);
'beautiful' (Spanish).

Miranda

Variants and diminutives: Maranda, Marenda, Meranda, Mina, Mira, Mirabel, Mirinda, Mironda, Mirranda, Myranda, Randa, Randee, Randi, Randie, Randy.
Meaning: 'wonderful' or 'admirable' (Latin); possibly coined by William Shakespeare for the heroine of his play *The Tempest.*
Notable namesakes: a satellite of the planet Uranus; Miranda Richardson (British actress).

Miriam

Variants and diminutives: Mary, Maria, Marian, Marianne, Meliame, Meryem, Mimi, Minni, Minnie, Miri, Mirjam, Mitzi, Myriam.
Meaning: 'longed-for child' or 'rebellion' (Hebrew).
Notable namesakes: the sister of Moses and Aaron in the Old Testament; a character in the novel *Sons and Lovers*, by British writer D H Lawrence; a leading character of the poem *Miriam*, by US poet John Greenleaf Whittier; Miriam Schapiro (US artist); Miriam Margolyes (British actress).

Misty

Variants and diminutives: Misti, Mistie, Mystee, Mysti, Mystie, Mystique.
Meaning: 'obscure' or 'foggy' (Old English).
Notable namesakes: *Play Misty For Me*, the title of a US film.

Mitzi

Variants and diminutives: Mitz, Mitzie, Mitzy.
Meaning: 'longed-for child' or 'rebellion' (Hebrew) as a German diminutive of Maria, the Latin form of Mary (Miriam).
Notable namesakes: Mitzi Gaynor (US actress); Mitzi Cunliffe (US sculptor).

Modesty

Variants and diminutives: Modesta, Modeste, Modestee, Modestene, Modestia, Modestina, Modestine.
Meaning: 'humble' or 'temperate' (Latin).
Notable namesakes: Modesty Blaise, a comic-strip character created by the British pairing Jim Holdaway and Peter O'Donnell.

Moira

Variants and diminutives: Maire, Mary, Maura, Moyra, Myra.
Meaning: 'dark' (Celtic); 'longed-for child' or 'rebellion' (Hebrew) as an anglicised form of Maire, an Irish Gaelic version of Mary (Miriam).
Notable namesakes: Moira Stewart (British newsreader).

Molly

Variants and diminutives: Mary, Moll, Molli, Mollie.
Meaning: 'longed-for child' or 'rebellion' (Hebrew) as a diminutive of Mary (Miriam).
Notable namesakes: the common name of the *Molliensia* genus of tropical fish; Moll Flanders, the eponymous heroine of the novel by the English writer Daniel Defoe; as Moll, the slang name for a gangster's female accomplice or a prostitute; Molly Malone, the subject of an Irish folk song; Molly Maguire, a male member of both an Irish secret society and a Pennsylvanian society of miners who disguised themselves as women; Molly Bloom, a leading character in the novel *Ulysses*, by Irish writer James Joyce.

Mona

Variants and diminutives: Madonna, Monica, Monique, Monna, Moyna, Muadhnait, Muna.
Meaning: uncertain; possibly 'alone' or 'just' (Greek); possibly 'admonish' or 'warn' (Latin); possibly 'my lady' (Italian); possibly 'noble', 'nun' or 'angel' (Irish Gaelic); possibly 'wish' (Arabic); possibly 'month' (Old English).
Notable namesakes: the Latin name of both Anglesey, the island off the northwest coast of Wales, and the Isle of Man; the subject of the painting *Mona Lisa*, by Italian artist Leonardo da Vinci.

Monica

Variants and diminutives: Mona, Monca, Monique, Monika, Monna, Muna.
Meaning: uncertain; as a variant of Mona, possibly 'alone' or 'just' (Greek), 'admonish' or 'warn' (Latin), 'my lady' (Italian) 'noble', 'nun' or 'angel' (Irish Gaelic), 'wish' (Arabic) or 'month' (Old English).
Notable namesakes: Saint Monica, patron saint of

married women, mothers and widows; Monica Lewinsky (US handbag designer and notorious former White House intern).

Morag

Variants and diminutives: Marion, Moirin, Moreen, Sarah.
Meaning: 'great' and 'sun' or 'young one' (Scottish and Irish Gaelic); 'princess' (Hebrew) as a Scots Gaelic variant of Sarah.

Morgan

Variants and diminutives: Morcant, Morgain, Morgana, Morganne, Morgen, Morgenne, Morien.
Meaning: uncertain; possibly 'morning' (Germanic); possibly 'sea' or 'great' and 'bright' (Celtic); derived from a British family name. Also a boy's name.
Notable namesakes: Morgan le Fay (or Morgana), an enchantress and half-sister of King Arthur in Arthurian legend.

Moriah

Variants and diminutives: Mariah, Morel, Moria, Morice, Moriel, Morit.
Meaning: 'my teacher is God' (Hebrew).
Notable namesakes: the mountain on which Isaac was nearly sacrificed by Abraham in the Old Testament.

Morna

Variants and diminutives: Morrow, Muirne, Myrna.
Meaning: 'spirited' or 'beloved' (Irish Gaelic).

Morven

Variants and diminutives: Morve, Ven, Venna, Venni, Vennie, Venny.
Meaning: uncertain; possibly 'big mountain' or 'sea gap' (Scots Gaelic); derived from a number of Scottish place names. Also a boy's name.

Morwenna

Variants and diminutives: Wenna, Wennie, Wenny.
Meaning: 'maiden' or 'sea' and 'wave' (Welsh).
Notable namesakes: Saint Morwenna.

Muriel

Variants and diminutives: Marial, Meriel, Merril, Merrill, Merryle, Meryl, Meryle, Miriel, Muireall, Muirgheal, Murial, Muriell, Murielle.
Meaning: 'sea' and 'bright' (Irish Gaelic).
Notable namesakes: Muriel Rukeyser (US writer); Muriel Spark (Scottish writer).

Myfanwy

Variants and diminutives: Fanni, Fannie, Fanny, Myf, Myvanwy.
Meaning: 'my fine', 'my rare' or 'my dear' and 'one' (Welsh).

Myra

Variants and diminutives: Mira.
Meaning: uncertain; as a variant of Myrna, possibly 'myrrh' (Aramaic and Arabic); 'spirited' or 'beloved' (Irish Gaelic); coined for various poems by the English poet Fulke Greville, Baron Brooke. Also a female version of Myron.
Notable namesakes: Myra Hess (British pianist).

Myrna

Variants and diminutives: Merna, Mirna, Moina, Morna, Muirna, Muirne, Murnia, Moyna.
Meaning: 'myrrh' (Aramaic and Arabic); 'spirited' or 'beloved' (Irish Gaelic) as a variant of Morna.
Notable namesakes: the mother of Finn mac Cumhail (or Finn MacCool), a hero of Irish legend; Myrna Loy (US actress).

Myrtle

Variants and diminutives: Myrta, Myrtia, Myrtice, Myrtilla.
Meaning: 'myrtle' (Greek); derived from the common name of the *Myrtus* genus of evergreen shrubs.
Notable namesakes: 'Moaning Myrtle', a character in the 'Harry Potter' series of children's books by British writer J K Rowling.

Nabila

Variants and diminutives: Nabeela, Nabiha, Nabilah.
Meaning: 'noble' (Arabic). A female version of Nabil.

Nadia

Variants and diminutives: Dusya, Nada, Nadeen, Nadenka, Nadezhda, Nadie, Nadina, Nadine, Nadiya, Nadja, Nadka, Nado, Nady, Nadya, Nata, Natka.
Meaning: 'hope' (Slavonic) as as diminutive of Nadezhda.
Notable namesakes: the heroine of the novel *Nadja*, by French writer André Breton; Nadia Boulanger (French composer, teacher and conductor); Nadia Comaneci (Romanian gymnast).

Nagida

Meaning: 'noble', 'wealthy' or 'ruler' (Hebrew). A female version of Nagid.

Nancy

Variants and diminutives: Ann, Anna, Anne, Hannah, Nan, Nana, Nance, Nancey, Nanci, Nancie, Nanette, Nani, Nanice, Nannie, Nanny.
Meaning: 'I have been favoured (by God)' (Hebrew) as a diminutive of Ann, Anna, Anne and other variants of Hannah.
Notable namesakes: a city in northeastern France; Nancy Astor (US-born British politician); Nancy Drew, the heroine of a series of books by US writer Edward L Stratemeyer; a character in the short story *That Evening Sun Go Down* and the novel *Requiem for a Nun*, by US writer William Faulkner; Nancy Mitford (British writer); a derogatory slang word for an effeminate man; Nancy Spero and Nancy Graves (US artists).

Nanette

Variants and diminutives: Ann, Anna, Anne, Annette, Hannah, Nan, Nana, Nancy, Nannette, Nannie, Nanny.
Meaning: 'I have been favoured (by God)' (Hebrew) as a diminutive of Ann, Anna, Anne and other variants of Hannah.
Notable namesakes: *No, No, Nanette*, a British musical and film; Nanette Newman (British actress).

Naomi

Variants and diminutives: Naoma, Naome, Noami, Noemi, Nomi.
Meaning: 'pleasant' or 'my delight' (Hebrew).
Notable namesakes: the mother-in-law of Ruth and wife of Boaz in the Old Testament.

Narcissa

Variants and diminutives: Narcisse.
Meaning: 'numbness' (Greek) as a female version of Narcissus.

Nasia

Variants and diminutives: Nasya.
Meaning: 'miracle of God' (Hebrew).

Natalia

Variants and diminutives: Nacia, Nat, Nata, Natacha, Natala, Natalie, Natalina, Nataline, Natalka, Natalle, Natalya, Natasa, Natasha, Nathalia, Nathalie, Nati, Natie, Natka, Nattie, Nattie, Natty, Neda, Netti, Nettie, Netty, Noel, Noelle, Novella, Talia, Talya, Tasha, Tashka, Taska, Tasya, Tata, Tuska, Tusya.
Meaning: 'birthday' (Latin); 'Christ's birthday' or 'Christmas' (Slavonic).
Notable namesakes: Saint Natalia; Natalia Gontcharova (Russian artist); Nathalie Sarraute (Russian-born French writer); Natalia Ginzburg (Italian writer); Natalie Wood (US actress).

A B C D E F G H I J K L M N O P Q R S T U V W X Y Z

Natania

Variants and diminutives: Nataniella, Natanielle, Nathania, Nathaniella, Nathanielle, Netania, Netanya, Nethania.

Meaning: 'gift' (Hebrew) as a female version of Nathan.

Natasha

Variants and diminutives: Nat, Nata, Natacha, Natala, Natalia, Natalya, Nathalie, Natasa, Nati, Natie, Natti, Nattie, Natty, Talia, Talya, Tasha, Tashka, Tashua, Taska, Tasya, Tata, Tuska, Tusya.

Meaning: 'birthday' (Latin); 'Christ's birthday' or 'Christmas' (Slavonic) as a Russian diminutive of Natalya (Natalia).

Notable namesakes: Natasha Rostova, the heroine of the novel *War and Peace*, by Russian writer Leo Nikolaievich Tolstoy; Natasha Filippovna, a character in the novel *The Idiot*, by Russian writer Fyodor Mikhailovich Dostoyevsky; Natasha Gurdin, the real name of US actress Natalie Wood.

Neala

Variants and diminutives: Nea, Neala, Neali, Nealie, Nealy, Nelda, Neela, Neeli, Neelie, Neely, Neili, Neily, Nia, Nigella.

Meaning: 'champion', 'cloud' or 'vehement' (Irish Gaelic) as a female version of Neal (Neil).

Nell

Variants and diminutives: Eleanor, Ellen, Helen, Nel, Nelli, Nellie, Nellwyn, Nelly.

Meaning: 'bright' (Greek) as a diminutive of Eleanor, Ellen and other variants of Helen; also 'foreign' (Germanic) as a diminutive of Eleanor.

Notable namesakes: Nell Gwyn, English orange-seller, actress and mistress of King Charles II of England; Mistress Nell Quickly, a character in William Shakespeare's plays *Henry IV*, *Henry V* and *The Merry Wives of Windsor*; Little Nell, a character in the novel *The Old Curiosity Shop*, by English writer Charles

Dickens; Nellie Melba (Australian opera singer); Nelly Sachs (German writer).

Neola

Variants and diminutives: Neolie, Neoly.

Meaning: 'new' (Greek).

Neoma

Meaning: 'new moon' (Greek).

Nerissa

Variants and diminutives: Nerice, Nerina, Nerine, Nerisse, Nerita, Nissa, Rissa.

Meaning: uncertain; possibly 'sea nymph' (Greek); derived from the name of the Nereides, sea nymphs of Greek mythology.

Notable namesakes: a character in William Shakespeare's play *The Merchant of Venice*.

Nerys

Meaning: 'lord' (Welsh).

Notable namesakes: Nerys Hughes (British actress).

Nesta

Variants and diminutives: Agnes, Nesha, Nessa, Nessie, Nessy, Nest.

Meaning: 'pure' or 'chaste' (Greek) or 'lamb' (Latin) as a variant of Agnes.

Netta

Variants and diminutives: Antoinetta, Antoinette, Jeanetta, Jeanette, Neata, Neta, Nettie, Netty.

Meaning: 'door' (Mende – Africa); also a diminutive of any name ending in '-netta' or '-nette', such as Jeanette, meaning 'God has favoured', 'God is gracious' or 'God is merciful' (Hebrew) as a female version of John.

Neva

Variants and diminutives: Nevada.

Meaning: 'to snow' or 'snow white' (Spanish).

Notable namesakes: a Russian river; the US state of Nevada.

Ngaio
Meaning: 'clever' (Maori).
Notable namesakes: Ngaio Marsh (New Zealand writer).

Niamh
Meaning: 'bright' (Irish Gaelic).
Notable namesakes: the lover of Ossian (Oisin) in Irish legend.

Nicola
Variants and diminutives: Colette, Collete, Cosette, Nic, Nicci, Nichele, Nichelle, Nichol, Nichola, Nichole, Nicholle, Nicki, Nickie, Nicky, Nico, Nicol, Nicole, Nicoleen, Nicolete, Nicoletta, Nicolette, Nicoli, Nicolina, Nicoline, Nicolle, Nijole, Nika, Nike, Niki, Nikki, Nikolette, Nikolia.
Meaning: 'victory of the people' (Greek) as a female Italian version of Nicholas.
Notable namesakes: Nikki Giovanni (US poet); Nicole Kidman (Australian actress).

Nigella
Variants and diminutives: Gella, Jella, Neala, Nigie.
Meaning: 'black' (Latin) when derived from the *Nigella* genus of flowering plants, commonly known as love-in-the-mist, which have black seeds; 'champion', 'cloud' or 'vehement' (Irish Gaelic) as a female version of Nigel, Neil.
Notable namesakes: Nigella Lawson (British journalist and cookery writer).

Nike
Variants and diminutives: Niki.
Meaning: 'victory' (Greek); derived from the name of the winged goddess of victory in war in Greek mythology.
Notable namesakes: a brand of sportswear.

Nina
Variants and diminutives: Nena, Nenah, Neneh, Ninetta, Ninette, Ninita, Ninnetta, Ninnette, Ninon.
Meaning: 'girl' (Spanish); 'mighty' (Native American); 'I have been favoured (by God)' (Hebrew) as a Russian form of Anna (Hannah); also a diminutive of any name ending in '-nina'.
Notable namesakes: a Mesopotamian sea goddess; the *Niña*, one of Italian explorer Christopher Columbus' America-discovering ships; Ninette de Valois (British ballerina and choreographer); Nina Simone (US singer); Nina Hagen (German singer).

Nisha
Variants and diminutives: Neesh, Neesha, Neisha, Nesha, Neshia, Nishi.
Meaning: 'night' (Sanskrit).

Nissa
Variants and diminutives: Nisa, Nisse, Nissie, Nissy.
Meaning: 'sign' or 'to test' (Hebrew); 'a never-forgotten loved one' (Hausa – Africa)
Notable namesakes: a nymph and mother of the sun in Greek mythology.

Nita
Variants and diminutives: Anita, Juanita.
Meaning: 'bear' (Chocktaw – Native American); also a diminutive of any name ending in '-nita', such as Anita (Hannah via Anna), meaning 'I have been favoured (by God)' (Hebrew).

Nitza
Variants and diminutives: Nitzana, Nizana, Zana, Zanah.
Meaning: 'bud' (Hebrew).

Nixie
Variants and diminutives: Nix, Nixe, Nixy.
Meaning: 'water spirit' or 'nymph' (German); derived from the name of the Nixen, river spirits of Germanic mythology.
Notable namesakes: the Nixi, goddesses who act as midwives in Roman mythology; the Nixie tube, a digitron or information-displaying electronic tube.

Noëlle
Variants and diminutives: Natalia, Natasha, Noel, Noele, Noeleen, Noelene, Noeline, Noell, Noella, Noelle, Nolene, Novelia, Nowlle.
Meaning: 'birthday' (Latin), 'Christ's birthday' or 'Christmas' (French) as a female version of Noël.

A
B
C
D
E
F
G
H
I
J
K
L
M
N
O
P
Q
R
S
T
U
V
W
X
Y
Z

Nofia

Variants and diminutives: Nophia.
Meaning: 'panorama' (Hebrew).

Nola

Variants and diminutives: Finnuala, Finola, Nolana, Noleen, Nolena, Nuala.
Meaning: 'son of the noble one' (Irish Gaelic) as a female version of Nolan; 'fair-shouldered' (Irish Gaelic) as a variant of Fionnuala (Fenella)
Notable namesakes: an Italian town.

Nolene

Variants and diminutives: Noalene, Noelle, Nola, Nolana, Noleen, Nolena.
Meaning: 'son of the noble one' (Irish Gaelic) as a female version of Nolan; 'birthday' (Latin), 'Christ's birthday' or 'Christmas' (French) as a female version of Noël.

Nona

Variants and diminutives: Noni, Nonie.
Meaning: 'ninth' (Latin).
Notable namesakes: one of the Parcae (Fates) and the goddess of foetal development in Roman mythology.

Nora

Variants and diminutives: Annora, Honor, Honora, Leonora, Norah, Noreen, Norene, Norine.
Meaning: 'honour' (Latin) as a diminutive of Honora (Honor); 'bright' (Greek) as a diminutive of most names ending in '-nora', such as Eleanora (Helen via Eleanor), which also means 'foreign' (Germanic).

Norma

Variants and diminutives: Normie, Normy.
Meaning: 'rule' or 'pattern' (Latin); 'north' and 'man' [Norseman or Viking] (Germanic) as a female version of Norman.
Notable namesakes: the title of an opera by Italian composer Vincenzo Bellini; Norma Shearer (US actress); Norma Jean Baker (or Mortenson), the real name of the US actress Marilyn Monroe.

Norna

Variants and diminutives: Nornie, Norny.
Meaning: 'fate' (Old Norse); derived from the name of the Norns (or Nornir), the three Fates of Norse mythology.
Notable namesakes: Norn, the medieval Norse language once spoken in the Orkneys, Shetland and northern Scotland.

Nova

Variants and diminutives: Novia.
Meaning: 'new' (Latin).
Notable namesakes: a variable type of star.

Noya

Meaning: 'bejewelled by nature' (Hebrew).

Nuala

Variants and diminutives: Fenella, Fionnghuala, Fionnuala, Nola.
Meaning: 'fair-shouldered' (Irish Gaelic) as a variant of Fionnuala (Fenella).

Nydia

Variants and diminutives: Neda, Nedda, Nydie, Nydy.
Meaning: 'nest' or 'home' (Latin).

Nyree

Variants and diminutives: Ngaire.
Meaning: uncertain; an anglicised version of the Maori name Ngaire.
Notable namesakes: Nyree Dawn Porter (New Zealand actress).

Nysa

Variants and diminutives: Nissa, Nisse, Nissie, Isy, Nyssa.
Meaning: 'beginning' (Greek); 'striving' or 'soaring' (Latin).

Nyx

Meaning: 'night' (Greek); derived from the name of the underworld goddess of the night in Greek mythology.

Obelia

Variants and diminutives: Belia, Belya.
Meaning: 'pillar', 'pointer' or 'marker' (Greek); 'off the beaten track' (Bini – Africa).

Octavia

Variants and diminutives: Octaviana, Octavie, Ottavia, Tavi, Tavia, Tavie.
Meaning: 'eighth' (Latin); derived from the Roman family name Octavius. A female version of Octavius.
Notable namesakes: the sister of Octavian, better known as the Roman emperor Augustus, and wife of Mark Anthony; the wife of the Roman emperor Nero; Octavia Hill, founder of the British heritage organisation the National Trust.

Odelia

Variants and diminutives: Delia, Detta, Oda, Odelet, Odelinda, Odell, Odella, Odelyn, Odetta, Odette, Odila, Odile, Odilia, Otha, Othelia, Othilia, Othilie, Ottilia, Ottilie, Ottoline, Uta.
Meaning: 'song' or 'ode' (Greek); 'praise be to God' (Hebrew); 'where woad grows' (Old English) or 'otter' (Danish) as a female version of Odell; 'riches' (Germanic) as a female version of Odo.
Notable namesakes: Saint Odelia, patron saint of blind people.

Odette

Variants and diminutives: Oda, Oddetta, Odelia, Odetta, Odile, Odilia, Otilie, Ottilia, Ottoline.
Meaning: 'riches' (Germanic) as a female version of Odo.
Notable namesakes: Odette de Crécy, a character in the novel *À la recherche du temps perdu* (*Remembrance of Things Past*), by French writer Marcel

Proust; Odette Churchill, a French-born British agent during World War II.

Ola

Meaning: 'protector' or 'nourisher' (Old Norse); 'forebear' and 'relics' (Old Norse) as a female version of Olaf.

Oleander

Variants and diminutives: Oliana, Olinda, Olynda.
Meaning: 'rose tree' (Greek); derived from the common name of the flowering shrub *Nerium oleander*.

Olena

Variants and diminutives: Helen, Lena.
Meaning: 'bright' (Greek) as a Russian variant of Helen.

Olga

Variants and diminutives: Elga, Helga, Lelya, Lesya, Ola, Olenka, Olesya, Olia, Olina, Olka, Olli, Ollie, Olly, Olunka, Oluska, Olva, Olya, Olyusha.
Meaning: 'prosperous' or 'pious' (Old Norse) as a Russian variant of Helga.
Notable namesakes: Saint Olga of Kiev; Olga Dmitriyevna Forsh (Russian writer); Olga Rozanova (Russian artist); Olga Korbut (Russian gymnast).

Olive

Variants and diminutives: Liv, Liva, Livie, Livrie, Livvy, Livy, Nola, Nolana, Nollie, Oli, Olia, Oliff, Oliva, Olivet, Olivette, Olivia, Oliwia, Ollett, Oli, Ollie, Olliffe, Olly, Ollye, Olva.
Meaning: 'olive' (Latin); derived from the common name of the olive-bearing *Olea europaea* genus of trees. Also a female variant of Oliver.
Notable namesakes: the olive fruit, which yields olive oil; a greeny-yellow colour; the olive branch, a symbol of peace; the Mount of Olives, a range of hills in Israel; two saints; Olive Schreiner (South African writer).

A B C D E F G H I J K L M N O P Q R S T U V W X Y Z

Olivia

Variants and diminutives: Liv, Liva, Livia, Livie, Livrie, Livvy, Llvy, Nola, Nolana, Nollie, Oli, Olia, Oliff, Oliva, Olive, Olivet, Olivette, Oliwia, Ollett, Olli, Ollie, Olliffe, Olly, Ollye, Olva.

Meaning: 'olive' (Latin) as an Italian variant of Olive. Also a female variant of Oliver.

Notable namesakes: a character in William Shakespeare's play *Twelfth Night*; a character in the novel *The Vicar of Wakefield*, by Irish writer Oliver Goldsmith; Olivia De Havilland (US actress); Olivia Hussey (British actress); Olivia Newton-John (Australian singer).

Olwen

Variants and diminutives: Olwin, Olwyn.

Meaning: 'white tracks' (Old Welsh).

Notable namesakes: the daughter of the giant Ysbaddaden, from whose footprints sprang white flowers, as told in the story 'Culhwch [or Kulhwch] and Olwen' in *The Mabinogion*, a collection of tales from Welsh legend and mythology.

Olympia

Variants and diminutives: Olimpe, Olimpia, Olimpie, Olympe, Olympias, Olympie.

Meaning: 'from Olympus' (Greek), Olympus being Mount Olympus, home of the gods in Greek mythology, or 'from Olympia' (Greek), the original site of the Olympic Games.

Notable namesakes: the Olympiades, another name for the Muses of Greek mythology; Saint Olympias, mother of Alexander the Great, King of Macedonia; Olympia Dukakis (US actress).

Omega

Variants and diminutives: Mega.

Meaning: 'great 'O'' (Greek); derived from the name of the last letter of the Greek alphabet.

Notable namesakes: a word used to describe the last of a series or an ending; a Swiss brand of watch.

Oona

Variants and diminutives: Oonagh, Oonie, Ona, Una.

Meaning: 'one' or 'together' (Latin) or 'lamb' (Irish Gaelic) as an Irish Gaelic form of Una.

Notable namesakes: Oonagh, wife of Fionnbharr, together rulers of the fairies in Irish mythology; Oona O'Neill, daughter of the US playwright Eugene O'Neill and wife of the English actor and director Charlie Chaplin.

Opal

Variants and diminutives: Opalina, Opaline.

Meaning: 'precious stone' (Sanskrit); derived from the name of the decorative iridescent mineral.

Ophelia

Variants and diminutives: Ofelia, Oilia, Ophelie.

Meaning: 'help' (Greek).

Notable namesakes: a tragic character in William Shakespeare's play *Hamlet*.

Ophira

Variants and diminutives: Ofira.

Meaning: 'gold' (Hebrew).

Oprah

Variants and diminutives: Ofra, Ophra, Ophrah, Opra, Orfa, Orpah.

Meaning: uncertain; possibly 'fawn' or 'runaway' (Hebrew) as a variant of Orpah.

Notable namesakes: Oprah Winfrey (US actress and broadcaster).

Ora

Variants and diminutives: Aurora, Cora, Dora, Orah.

Meaning: 'edge' or 'boundary' (Latin); also a diminutive of any name ending in '-ora', such as Aurora, meaning 'dawn' (Latin).

Orah

Variants and diminutives: Ora, Oralee, Orit, Orlice, Orly.

Meaning: 'light' (Hebrew).

Oriana

Variants and diminutives: Oralia, Orelda, Orella, Orelle, Oria, Oriande, Oriane, Oriente, Orlann, Orlene.
Meaning: 'to rise' or 'sunrise' (Latin).
Notable namesakes: the beloved of Amadis in the romance *Amadis de Gaul*; a poetic name for Queen Elizabeth I of England; the title of a poem by English poet Alfred, Lord Tennyson; Oriane, Duchesse de Guermantes, a character in the novel *À la recherche du temps perdu* (*Remembrance of Things Past*), by French writer Marcel Proust.

Oriel

Variants and diminutives: Auriel, Aurelia, Aurildis, Nehora, Ora, Orah, Orabel, Oralia, Orieldis, Orielle, Oriole, Orit.
Meaning: 'fire' and 'strife' (Germanic); 'niche' (Latin); 'gallery' (Old French); 'gold' (Latin) as a variant of Aurelia.
Notable namesakes: oriel window, a bay window supported by corbels or brackets; an Oxford University college.

Oriole

Variants and diminutives: Oriel.
Meaning: 'golden one' (Latin); derived from the common name of the *Oriolus* genus of songbirds.

Orla

Variants and diminutives: Oria, Orlagh, Orlaidh.
Meaning: 'golden princess' (Irish Gaelic).

Orpah

Variants and diminutives: Ofra, Ophra, Ophrah, Opra, Oprah, Orfa, Orpha, Orpra, Orphy.
Meaning: uncertain; possibly 'fawn' or 'runaway' (Hebrew).

Osanna

Variants and diminutives: Hosana, Hosanna, Osana.
Meaning: 'save now, we pray' (Hebrew); 'praise be to God' (Latin); a diminutive of Hosanna, a Judaeo-Christian exclamation of praise.

Ottilie

Variants and diminutives: Odala, Odette, Odila, Odile, Odilia, Odille, Otilie, Ottalie, Ottilia, Ottoline, Uta.
Meaning: 'of the fatherland' (Germanic); 'riches' (Germanic) as a female version of Otto (Odo).
Notable namesakes: Saint Ottilia (or Odilia), patron saint of Alsace.

Ottoline

Variants and diminutives: Odette, Odile, Otilie, Ottilie.
Meaning: 'riches' (Germanic) as a female version of Otto (Odo).
Notable namesakes: Ottoline Morrell (British literary patron).

Ouida

Variants and diminutives: Louise.
Meaning: 'famed' and 'warrior' (Germanic) as a diminutive of Louise, in turn a female version of Louis (Ludwig).
Notable namesakes: the pseudonym of the British writer Marie Louise de la Ramée.

Ova

Meaning: 'egg' or 'to celebrate a small triumph' (Latin); 'sunshine' (Bini – Africa); 'January-born' (Hausa – Africa).

Padma

Meaning: 'lotus' (Hindi).
Notable namesakes: an alternative name of many Hindu goddesses, including Lakshmi, the goddess of beauty and prosperity.

Paige

Variants and diminutives: Page, Paget, Pagett.
Meaning: 'child' (Greek); 'page boy' or 'boy attendant'

(Old French); derived from an English family name. Also a boy's name (generally Page).

Paloma

Variants and diminutives: Palometa, Palomita.
Meaning: 'dove' (Spanish).
Notable namesakes: Paloma Picasso, daughter of the Spanish artist Pablo Picasso, a jewellery designer who also markets a brand of perfumes and cosmetics.

Pamela

Variants and diminutives: Pam, Pamala, Pamelia, Pamelina, Pamella, Pammi, Pammie, Pammy.
Meaning: uncertain; possibly 'all' and 'honey' (Greek); coined by the English poet Philip Sidney for a heroine of his romance *Arcadia*.
Notable namesakes: the heroine of the eponymous novel *Pamela, or Virtue Rewarded*, by English writer Samuel Richardson; Pamela Hansford Johnson (British writer); Pamela Stephenson (Australian-born comedienne and wife of Scottish comedian Billy Connelly); Pamela Anderson (US actress).

Pandora

Variants and diminutives: Dora, Pandore, Polydora.
Meaning: 'all' and 'gift' (Greek).
Notable namesakes: the first woman in Greek mythology, who disobeyed the gods to open a tantalisingly closed box, thereby unleashing all of the ills of the world (hence the expression 'Pandora's box' for a present that turns out to be a curse); the common name of a red sea bream, *Pagellus erythrinus*.

Pansy

Variants and diminutives: Pansie.
Meaning: 'thought' (Old French); derived from the common name of the *Viola tricolor* genus of flowering plants.
Notable namesakes: a violet colour; Pansy Osmond, a character in the novel *The Portrait of a Lady*, by US writer Henry James.

Parthenia

Variants and diminutives: Partha, Parthenope, Parthenos.

Meaning: 'virgin' (Greek).
Notable namesakes: an alternative name of the goddesses Artemis, Athena and Hera, as well as the name of one of the Pleiades and a nymph of Samos (which was originally called Parthenia) in Greek mythology.

Pascale

Variants and diminutives: Pascha.
Meaning: 'to pass over' (Hebrew) or 'of Easter' (Old French) as a female version of Pascal.

Pat

Variants and diminutives: Patricia, Patsy, Patti, Pattie, Patty.
Meaning: 'noble' or 'patrician' (Latin) as a diminutive of Patricia (and of Patrick).

Patience

Variants and diminutives: Pat, Patia, Pattie, Patty.
Meaning: 'endurance' (Latin).
Notable namesakes: a Christian virtue; an opera by the British pairing Gilbert and Sullivan; a number of single-player card games.

Patricia

Variants and diminutives: Paddie, Paddy, Pat, Patia, Patrice, Patrizia, Patsy, Patti, Pattie, Patty, Tricia, Trish, Trisha.
Meaning: 'noble' or 'patrician' (Latin). A female version of Patrick.
Notable namesakes: Saint Patricia, patron saint of Naples; Patrician Cornwall (US crime writer).

Patsy

Variants and diminutives: Pat, Patricia, Patsi, Patsie, Patty.
Meaning: 'noble' or 'patrician' (Latin) as a diminutive of Patricia (and of Patrick).
Notable namesakes: a slang word for a scapegoat or, in North America, someone who is easily conned; a character in the British television comedy series *Absolutely Fabulous*; Patsy Palmer (British actress).

Patty

Variants and diminutives: Martha, Matilda, Pat, Patti, Patricia, Patsy, Patty.
Meaning: 'noble' or 'patrician' (Latin) as a diminutive of Patricia; 'lady' (Aramaic) as a diminutive of Martha; 'mighty' and 'battle' (Germanic) as a diminutive of Matilda.
Notable namesakes: Patti Smith (US poet and musician).

Paula

Variants and diminutives: Paola, Paolina, Paule, Pauleen, Paulene, Pauletta, Paulette, Pauli, Paulie, Paulina, Pauline, Paulita, Pauly, Pavia, Pavla, Pavlina, Pavlinka, Pawlina, Pola, Polcia, Polli, Pollie, Polly.
Meaning: 'small' (Latin) as a female version of Paul.
Notable namesakes: Saint Paula, patron saint of widows; the heroine of the play *The Second Mrs Tanqueray*, by British writer Arthur Wing Pinero; Paula Modersohn-Becker (German artist); Paula Rego (Portuguese artist).

Paulette

Variants and diminutives: Paula, Pauletta, Pauline, Paulita.
Meaning: 'small' (Latin) as a female version of Paul.
Notable namesakes: Paulette Goddard (US actress).

Pauline

Variants and diminutives: Paula, Pauleen, Paulene, Paulette, Pauli, Paulie, Paulina, Paulita, Pavlina, Pavlinka, Pawlina.
Meaning: 'small' (Latin) as a female version of Paul.
Notable namesakes: Pauline Fowler, a character in the British television soap opera *Eastenders*; Pauline Quirke (British actress).

Pazia

Variants and diminutives: Paz, Paza, Pazice, Pazit.
Meaning: 'gold' (Hebrew). Also a boy's name.

Peace

Variants and diminutives: Pax, Paz.
Meaning: 'peace' (English).

Pearl

Variants and diminutives: Margaret, Pearla, Pearle, Pearlie, Pearline, Perla, Perle, Perly, Perry.
Meaning: 'sea mussel' (Latin); derived from the lustrous gem produced by oysters.
Notable namesakes: a river in the US state of Mississippi; Pearl Buck (US writer); characters in the novels *The Scarlet Letter*, by US writer Nathaniel Hawthorne, and *Sacred Country*, by British writer Rose Tremain; Pearl Baily (US singer and actress).

Peggy

Variants and diminutives: Margaret, Meg, Peg, Peggi, Peggie.
Meaning: 'pearl' (Greek) as a diminutive of Margaret.
Notable namesakes: Peggy Ashcroft (British actress); Peggy Lee (US singer).

Pelagia

Variants and diminutives: Palasha, Pasha, Pashka, Pelageya.
Meaning: 'sea' (Greek).
Notable namesakes: an alternative name of Aphrodite, the sea-born goddess of love and beauty of Greek mythology; Saint Pelagia; Saint Pelagia of Antioch; the heroine of the novel *Captain Corelli's Mandolin*, by British writer Louis de Bernières, and of the subsequent film.

Penelope

Variants and diminutives: Fenella, Fionnghuala, Lopa, Pela, Pelcha, Pelcia, Pen, Peneli, Penelopa, Pénélope, Penina, Penine, Penni, Pennie, Penny, Pinelopi, Pipitsa, Popi.
Meaning: uncertain; possibly 'bobbin', 'thread' or 'weaver' (Greek).
Notable namesakes: the wife of Odysseus and mother of Telemachus in Greek mythology; Penelope Mortimer (British writer); Lady Penelope, a character in the British children's television series *The Thunderbirds*; Penelope Keith (British actress); Penélope Cruz (US actress).

A
B
C
D
E
F
G
H
I
J
K
L
M
N
O
P
Q
R
S
T
U
V
W
X
Y
Z

Penina
Variants and diminutives: Peninah, Peninit.
Meaning: 'pearl' or 'coral' (Hebrew).

Penny
Variants and diminutives: Pen, Penelope, Penney, Penni, Pennie.
Meaning: uncertain; possibly 'bobbin', 'thread' or 'weaver' (Greek) as a diminutive of Penelope.
Notable namesakes: a British unit of currency; Penny Black, the first postage stamp; penny farthing, an early type of bicycle; penny dreadful, a cheap, sensationalist book.

Peony
Variants and diminutives: Paeony, Peonie.
Meaning: 'healing' (Greek); derived from the common name of the *Paeonia* genus of flowering plants.

Pepita
Variants and diminutives: Josefina, Josephine.
Meaning: 'God will increase' (Hebrew) as a Spanish diminutive of Josefina (Josephine).

Perdita
Variants and diminutives: Purdey, Purdie.
Meaning: 'lost' (Latin); coined by William Shakespeare for the heroine of his play *A Winter's Tale*.
Notable namesakes: the pseudonym of the English actress Mary Robinson, the mistress of George, Prince of Wales (later King George IV of Britain); a canine character in the children's book *A Hundred and One Dalmatians,* by British writer Dodie Smith, as well as of the subsequent film.

Perpetua
Variants and diminutives: Pet, Petua.
Meaning: 'perpetual' (Latin).
Notable namesakes: Saint Perpetua, patron saint of cows.

Persephone
Variants and diminutives: Persephassa, Perseponeia, Proserpina.
Meaning: 'bearer of death', 'destroyer of light' or 'dazzling radiance' (Greek); derived from the name of the daughter of Demeter and Zeus, and, as the wife of Pluto or Hades, queen of the underworld for six months of the year in Greek mythology.

Peta
Variants and diminutives: Pet, Petena, Peterina, Peternella, Petie, Petra, Petrina, Petrona, Petty.
Meaning: 'rock' (Greek) as a female version of Peter.

Petal
Variants and diminutives: Pet.
Meaning: 'leaf' (Greek); derived from the name of the flower component.

Petra
Variants and diminutives: Pet, Peta, Petie, Petrina, Petrona, Petty.
Meaning: 'rock' (Greek) as a female version of Peter.

Petronella
Variants and diminutives: Parnall, Parnel, Parnell, Patch, Pernel, Peronel, Peronnelle, Perri, Perrin, Perrine, Perry, Perryne, Pet, Peta, Peternella, Petrina, Petrona, Petronel, Petronia, Petronilla, Petronille, Petty.
Meaning: uncertain; possibly 'rock' (Greek); derived from the Roman family name Petronius.
Notable namesakes: Saint Petronella (or Petronilla), protector against fevers.

Petula
Variants and diminutives: Pet.
Meaning: uncertain; possibly 'pert' or 'to assail' (Latin).
Notable namesakes: Petula Clark (British singer and actress).

Petunia
Variants and diminutives: Pet.
Meaning: 'tobacco' (Old French); derived from the name of the *Petunia* genus of flowering plants.

Phaedra

Variants and diminutives: Phaidra, Phèdre.
Meaning: 'shining brightly' (Greek).
Notable namesakes: the daughter of Pasiphaë and King Minos of Crete, wife of Theseus and admirer of Hippolytus in Greek mythology, whose story is told in works by the Greek playwright Euripedes, the Roman playwright Seneca and the French playwright Jean Racine (*Phèdre*).

Phila

Variants and diminutives: Philadelphia, Philana, Philantha, Philberta.
Meaning: 'love' or 'beloved' (Greek).

Philadelphia

Variants and diminutives: Delphia, Delphie, Delphy, Phil, Phila, Phillie, Philly.
Meaning: 'brotherly love' (Greek).
Notable namesakes: an ancient city in Asia Minor; the capital city of the US state of Pennsylvania.

Philana

Variants and diminutives: Lana, Phil, Phila, Philene, Philina, Phillie, Phillina, Philly.
Meaning: 'lover of humanity' (Greek).

Philantha

Variants and diminutives: Lantha, Phil, Phila, Phillie, Philly.
Meaning: 'flower-lover' (Greek).

Philippa

Variants and diminutives: Felipa, Fiipote, Filipa, Filippa, Filippina, Filpina, Flippa, Ina, Inka, Pelipa, Phelypp, Phil, Philipa, Philippe, Philippine, Philli, Phillie, Phillipa, Phillippa, Philly, Pine, Pip, Pippa, Pippi, Pippie, Pippy.
Meaning: 'horse-lover' (Greek) as a female version of Philip.
Notable namesakes: Philippa of Hainault, wife of King Edward III of England; Philippa Carr, a pseudonym of the English writer Eleanor Hibbert.

Philomela

Variants and diminutives: Filomela, Phil, Phillie, Philly, Mela, Mellie, Melly.
Meaning: 'loving' or 'sweet' and 'song' (Greek).
Notable namesakes: the sister of Procne, who was turned into a nightingale in Greek mythology, which is why philomela, or philomel, has become the poetic name for the nightingale, *Luscinia megarhynchos*.

Philomena

Variants and diminutives: Filomena, Phil, Phillie, Philly, Philomina.
Meaning: 'love' and 'harmony' or 'strength' (Greek); 'peace' and 'beloved' (Latin).
Notable namesakes: Saint Philomena, patron saint of impossible causes.

Phoebe

Variants and diminutives: Phebe, Pheobe, Pheoby.
Meaning: 'shining' or 'radiant' (Greek).
Notable namesakes: a Titan and, as another name for Artemis, a moon goddess of Greek mythology, which is why Phoebe has become a poetic name for the moon; an associate of Saint Paul in the New Testament; a satellite of the planet Saturn; the common name of the flycatching *Sayornis* genus of birds; one of the characters in the US television sitcom *Friends*..

Phoenix

Variants and diminutives: Phenice, Phenix.
Meaning: 'purple' (Phoenician). Also a boy's name.
Notable namesakes: a bird of Arabian legend that burns itself to death every five hundred years and arises anew from the ashes; a constellation; *The Phoenix and the Turtle*, the title of a poem by William Shakespeare; the capital city of the US state of Arizona; the Phoenix Islands, coral islands in the south Pacific; Phoenix Park in Dublin, Ireland.

Phyllida

Variants and diminutives: Filide, Phil, Phillida, Phillie, Philly, Phyllada, Phyllis.
Meaning: 'foliage' or 'leafy' (Greek) as a variant of Phyllis.
Notable namesakes: Phyllida Law (British actress).

A
B
C
D
E
F
G
H
I
J
K
L
M
N
O
P
Q
R
S
T
U
V
W
X
Y
Z

Phyllis

Variants and diminutives: Filide, Filis, Phil, Philis, Phillida, Phillie, Phillis, Philliss, Philly, Phillys, Phyl, Phylis, Phyliss, Phyllada, Phyllida, Phyllie, Phyllys, Phylys, Pilisi.
Meaning: 'foliage' or 'leafy' (Greek).
Notable namesakes: a Thracian princess and wife of Demophon who was transformed into an almond tree in Greek mythology; a name for country girls in classical and pastoral poetry; Phillis Wheatley (US poet); Phyllis Calvert (British actress); Phyllis McGinley (US poet); P[hyllis] D[orothy] James (British crime-writer).

Pia

Meaning: 'pious' or 'dutiful' (Latin). A female version of Pius.

Pilar

Meaning: 'pillar' or 'fountain base' (Spanish). Also a boy's name.

Pippa

Variants and diminutives: Philippa, Pip.
Meaning: 'horse-lover' (Greek) as a diminutive of Philippa (Philip).
Notable namesakes: the heroine of the poetic play *Pippa Passes*, by English writer Robert Browning.

Placida

Variants and diminutives: Placidia.
Meaning: 'peaceful' (Latin) as a female version of Placido.

Pleasance

Variants and diminutives: Plaisance, Pleasant.
Meaning: 'pleasure' (Old French).

Polly

Variants and diminutives: Pol, Poli, Poll, Polley, Polli, Pollie, Pollyanna.
Meaning: 'longed-for child' or 'rebellion' (Hebrew) as a variant of Molly (Miriam via Mary); 'small' (Latin) as a diminutive of Paula (Paul).
Notable namesakes: the slang name for a parrot; the heroine of *The Beggar's Opera*, by English writer John Gay; *Pollyanna*, a children's book by US writer E H Porter, a name now used to described someone who is overly optimistic.

Polydora

Variants and diminutives: Dora, Pandora, Pol, Poli, Poly.
Meaning: 'many' and 'gift' (Greek).

Pomona

Variants and diminutives: Mona, Pom, Pommie, Pommy.
Meaning: 'fruit' (Latin).
Notable namesakes: the goddess of fruit trees in Roman mythology.

Poppy

Variants and diminutives: Poppi, Poppie.
Meaning: 'poppy' (Latin); derived from the common name of the *Papaver* genus of flowering plants.
Notable namesakes: a red colour; Poppy Day, Remembrance Sunday in the UK, when red poppies are traditionally worn to recall the carnage of World War I and subsequent wars.

Pora

Meaning: 'fruitful' (Hebrew).

Portia

Variants and diminutives: Porsha.
Meaning: 'entrance', 'gate' or 'pig' (Latin); derived from the Roman family name Porcius.
Notable namesakes: the wife of Marcus Junius Brutus, a conspiritor in the plot to assassinate Julius Caesar; a heroine of William Shakespeare's play *The Merchant of Venice*.

Posy

Variants and diminutives: Poesie, Poesy, Posie.
Meaning: 'poetic creativity' (Greek); 'a small bunch of flowers' (English); 'God will increase' (Hebrew) as a diminutive of Josephine.
Notable namesakes: a short inscription; Posy Simmonds (British cartoonist).

Primrose

Variants and diminutives: Primula, Rose.
Meaning: 'first rose' (Latin); derived from the common name of the *Primula* genus of flowering plants.
Notable namesakes: a yellow colour; the primrose path, denoting a pleasant way of life.

Primula

Variants and diminutives: Primrose.
Meaning: 'little first one' (Latin); derived from the *Primula* genus of flowering plants.

Priscilla

Variants and diminutives: Cilla, Precilla, Prescilla, Pricilla, Pris, Prisca, Priscella, Priscila, Prisilla, Priss, Prissie, Prissila, Prissy, Scilla, Sila.
Meaning: 'of ancient times' (Latin).
Notable namesakes: Priscilla (or Prisca), the wife of Aquila and friend of Saint Paul in the New Testament; Saint Priscilla (or Prisca); Priscilla Presley (US actress and former wife of the singer Elvis Presley); Priscilla (Cilla) Black (British singer and television presenter).

Priya

Variants and diminutives: Priyal, Priyam, Priyanka, Priyata, Pryasha, Pryati.
Meaning: 'endearing' or 'sweet-natured' (Hindi).

Prudence

Variants and diminutives: Pru, Prude, Prudencia, Prudentia, Prudi, Prudie, Prudy, Prue, Pruedi.
Meaning: 'discretion' (Latin).
Notable namesakes: Prudence Sarn, the narrator of the novel *Precious Bane*, by English writer Mary Webb; 'Dear Prudence', a song recorded by the British bands The Beatles and Siouxie and the Banshees; Prue Leith (British cook).

Prunella

Variants and diminutives: Ella, Nella, Pru, Prue.
Meaning: 'little plum' (Latin).
Notable namesakes: the name of a strong type of fabric; *Prunella vulgaris*, a herb commonly known as selfheal; Prunella Scales (British actress).

Pyralis

Variants and diminutives: Pyrene.
Meaning: 'fire' (Greek).

Queenie

Variants and diminutives: Quanda, Queena, Queenby, Queeny, Quenie, Quinn, Regina, Victoria.
Meaning: 'wife' (Old Norse) or 'queen' (Old English) as a diminutive of the highest female rank of nobility.

Quella

Variants and diminutives: Ella.
Meaning: 'to kill' or 'to quell' (Old English).

Querida

Variants and diminutives: Rida.
Meaning: 'to query' or 'beloved' (Spanish).

Questa

Variants and diminutives: Esta.
Meaning: 'searcher' (Old French).

Quinta

Variants and diminutives: Quin, Quinci, Quincie, Quincy, Quinetta, Quinette, Quintessa, Quintilla, Quintina.
Meaning: 'fifth' (Latin) as a female variant of Quintin (Quentin).

Quintessa

Variants and diminutives: Quentessa, Quentice, Quinta, Quintice, Tess, Tessa, Tessi, Tessie, Tessy.
Meaning: 'the fifth essence' or 'quintessence' (Latin).

Quirina

Variants and diminutives: Rina.
Meaning: 'of Romulus' (Latin) as a female version of Quirinal.

Rabia

Variants and diminutives: Rabi, Rabiah.
Meaning: 'breeze' (Arabic).

Rachel

Variants and diminutives: Lahela, Lesieli, Rachael, Rachele, Racheli, Rachelle, Rachie, Rae, Ragnhildr, Rahel, Rahela, Rahil, Rakel, Rakhil, Rakhhila, Raoghnald, Raquel, Raquela, Rasnel, Ray, Raye, Rochell, Ruchel, Shell, Shelley, Shellie, Shelly.
Meaning: 'ewe' (Hebrew).
Notable namesakes: the sister of Leah, second wife of Jacob and mother of Joseph and Benjamin in the Old Testament; Rachel Ruysch (Dutch artist); the stage name of the French actress Elizabeth Félix; Raquel Welch (US actress); Rachel Whiteread (British artist).

Rae

Variants and diminutives: Rachel, Raelene, Ray, Raye.
Meaning: 'ewe' (Hebrew) as a diminutive of Rachel.

Raina

Variants and diminutives: Raine, Raini, Rainie, Rana, Rane, Rayna, Rayne, Raynell, Raynette, Regina, Reina, Reine, Reyna, Reyne.
Meaning: 'queen' (Latin) as a Russian variant of Regina; 'advice' or 'might' and 'army' (Germanic) as a female version of Rayner; 'pure' (Yiddish).

Raisa

Variants and diminutives: Raissa, Raiza, Raizel, Rayzel, Rayzil, Razil.
Meaning: 'rose' (Yiddish).
Notable namesakes: Raisa Gorbachev, wife of the Russian politician Mikhail Gorbachev.

Ramona

Variants and diminutives: Mona, Raymonda, Raymonde, Romona.
Meaning: 'advice' or 'might' and 'protector' (Germanic) as a female version of Ramon (Raymond).
Notable namesakes: the eponymous heroine of the novel *Ramona*, by US writer Helen Hunt Jackson.

Rana

Variants and diminutives: Raniyah, Ranya.
Meaning: 'pleasing to the eye' (Arabic).

Ranana

Meaning: 'fresh' (Hebrew).

Randa

Variants and diminutives: Randi, Randie, Randy.
Meaning: 'the randa tree' (Arabic); 'shield' or 'raven' and 'wolf' (Old English) as a female version of Randall.

Rani

Variants and diminutives: Raina, Rana, Rancie, Ranee, Rania, Regina.
Meaning: 'queen' (Sanskrit). A female version of Raja.
Notable namesakes: Queen Rania of Jordan.

Raphaela

Variants and diminutives: Rafaela, Rafaele.
Meaning: 'healed by God' (Hebrew) as a female version of Raphael.

Rashida

Variants and diminutives: Rasheeda, Rashi.
Meaning: 'follower of the correct path' (Sanskrit and Arabic); 'righteous' (Swahili). A female version of Rashid.

Rawnie
Variants and diminutives: Rawni, Ronni, Ronnie, Ronny.
Meaning: 'lady' (English Gypsy).

Raya
Meaning: 'friend' (Hebrew).

Raz
Variants and diminutives: Razi, Razia, Raziah, Raziel, Raziela, Razilee, Razille, Razili, Raziye.
Meaning: 'secret' (Hebrew and Aramaic). Also a boy's name.

Rea
Variants and diminutives: Poppy, Rhea, Ria.
Meaning: 'poppy' (Greek).

Rebecca
Variants and diminutives: Becca, Beck, Becka, Becki, Beckie, Becks, Becky, Bekka, Bekki, Bekkie, Bekky, Reba, Rebe, Rebeca, Rebeka, Rebekah, Rena, Reva, Reveca, Reveka, Revekka, Rifka, Rivca, Rivka.
Meaning: 'binding', 'knotted cord' or 'to fatten' (Hebrew); 'gentle' (Akkadian).
Notable namesakes: the wife of Isaac and mother of Jacob and Esau in the Old Testament; the heroine of the novel *Ivanhoe*, by Scottish writer Sir Walter Scott; Rebecca Randall, the heroine of the children's story *Rebecca of Sunnybrook Farm*, by US writer Kate Douglas Wiggin; Rebecca Harding Davis (US writer); the title of a novel by British writer Daphne du Maurier, referring to the first Mrs de Winter; Rebecca West, the pseudonym of British writer Cicily Fairfield; Rebecca Horn (German arist).

Regan
Variants and diminutives: Reagan, Reaganne, Reagen, Regen, Regin, Regina.
Meaning: uncertain; possibly 'wise' (Germanic); possibly 'queen' (Latin) as a variant of Regina; possibly 'descendant of the little king' or 'queen' (Irish Gaelic) when derived from an Irish family name; coined by William Shakespeare for a character in his play *King Lear*. Also a boy's name.

Regina
Variants and diminutives: Gina, Ina, Queenie, Raina, Raine, Raini, Rainie, Rane, Rani, Rayna, Raynell, Raynette, Reena, Reene, Regan, Regi, Regie, Reggi, Reggie, Reggy, Regine, Reina, Reine, Reinette, Rena, Rene, Renia, Reyna, Reyne, Rina.
Meaning: 'queen' (Latin). A female version of Rex.
Notable namesakes: an alternative name of Juno, the supreme goddess of Greek mythology, and Rhiannon, a moon goddess of Welsh mythology.

Renata
Variants and diminutives: Rene, Renée, Renette, Renita.
Meaning: 'reborn' (Latin); 'joyful song' (Hebrew); 'lovely melody' (Arabic).

Rene
Variants and diminutives: Irene, Reenie, Rena, Renah, Renie, Renna.
Meaning: 'peace' (Greek) as as diminutive of Irene.

Renée
Variants and diminutives: Reenie, Rena, Renata, Rene, Renette, Renita.
Meaning: 'reborn' (French). A female version of René.
Notable namesakes: Renée Zellweger (US actress).

Rhea
Variants and diminutives: Rea, Reanna, Ria.
Meaning: uncertain; possibly 'flowing' or 'protector' (Greek); derived from the name of the Titan wife of Kronos and the mother of many gods, including Zeus, in Greek mythology.
Notable namesakes: Rhea Silvia (or Rea Sylvia), the mother of Romulus and Remus in Roman legend; a satellite of the planet Saturn; the common name of two genera of flightless birds, *Rhea americana* and *Pterocnemia pennata*.

Rheta
Variants and diminutives: Reeta, Rita.
Meaning: 'well-spoken' (Greek).

Rhian
Variants and diminutives: Reanna, Rhiana, Rhianna, Rhianne, Rhianu, Rian, Riana, Riane, Rianne.
Meaning: 'maiden' (Welsh); 'great queen', 'goddess', 'moon goddess' or 'nymph' (Welsh) as a diminutive of Rhiannon.

Rhiannon
Variants and diminutives: Reanna, Rhiana, Rhianna, Rhianne, Rhona, Rian, Riana, Riane, Rianne.
Meaning: 'great queen', 'goddess', 'moon goddess' or 'nymph' (Welsh); derived from the name of a moon goddess, the daughter of Hefeydd Hen, wife of Pwyll and Manawydan fab Llyr and mother of Pryderi in Welsh mythology.

Rhoda
Variants and diminutives: Rhode, Rhodeia, Rhodope, Rhodie, Rhody, Rhona, Rhosanna, Roda, Rodina, Rona, Rosa, Rose.
Meaning: 'rose' or 'woman from Rhodes [a Greek island]' (Greek).
Notable namesakes: a maidservant in the New Testament; the leading character of the novel *Rhoda Fleming*, by English writer George Meredith; the eponymous heroine of the US television series *Rhoda*.

Rhona
Variants and diminutives: Rhon, Rhonette, Rhonni, Rhonnie, Rhonny, Ron, Rona, Ronni, Ronnie, Ronny.
Meaning: uncertain; possibly 'little seal' (Irish Gaelic) as a female version of Ronan; possibly derived from the Hebridean island of Rona.

Rhonda
Variants and diminutives: Rhon, Rhondda, Rhonnie, Rhonny, Rhonwen, Ronda.
Meaning: uncertain; possibly 'powerful river' (Celtic); possibly 'noisy' or 'gift' (Welsh); possibly derived from the Rhondda Valley in Wales.
Notable namesakes: Rhonda Fleming (US actress).

Rhonwen
Variants and diminutives: Rhona, Rowena.
Meaning: 'lance' or 'slim' and 'fair' (Welsh).

Ria
Variants and diminutives: Maria, Rhea, Victoria.
Meaning: 'little river' or 'river mouth' (Spanish). Also a diminutive of any name ending in '-ria', such as Victoria, 'victory' (Latin).

Rica
Variants and diminutives: Erica, Erika, Ricki, Ricky, Rika, Rikki, Rikkie, Rikky, Roderica.
Meaning: 'eternal', 'honourable' or 'island' and 'ruler' (Old Norse) as a diminutive of Erica. Also a diminutive of any name ending in '-rica', such as Roderica (Roderick), 'renowned' and 'ruler' (Germanic).

Ricarda
Variants and diminutives: Rica, Richanda, Richarda, Richardyne, Richela, Richella, Richelle, Richenda, Richenza, Richia, Richmal, Ricka, Ricki, Rickie, Ricky, Riki, Rikki, Rikkie, Rikky.
Meaning: 'ruler' and 'hard' (Germanic) as a female version of Richard.
Notable namesakes: Ricarda Huch (German writer).

Richmal
Variants and diminutives: Ricarda, Richarda, Richenda.
Meaning: uncertain; possibly a composite name comprising 'Rich-', 'ruler' and 'hard' (Germanic), as a diminutive of Richard, and '-mal', 'who is like God?' (Hebrew) as a diminutive of Michael.
Notable namesakes: Richmal Crompton (British children's writer).

Rilla
Meaning: 'little stream' (Low German).

Rimona
Variants and diminutives: Mona.
Meaning: 'pomegranate' (Arabic).

Rina
Variants and diminutives: Katrina, Marina, Reena, Rena, Sabrina.
Meaning: a diminutive of any name ending in '-rina', such as Marina, 'of the sea' (Latin).

Rishona

Meaning: 'first' (Hebrew).

Rita

Variants and diminutives: Margarita, Margherita, Marguerita, Reda, Reeta, Reida, Rheta.
Meaning: 'pearl' (Greek) as a diminutive of Margarita (Margaret); 'proper' (Hindi).
Notable namesakes: Saint Rita of Cascia, patron saint of desperate causes and unhappy marriages; Rita Hayworth (US actress); the heroine of the British film *Educating Rita*.

Riva

Variants and diminutives: Ree, Reeva, Reva, Rivana, River, Rivi, Rivy.
Meaning: 'river bank' (Latin).

Roberta

Variants and diminutives: Berta, Bertha, Bertunga, Bobbet, Bobbette, Bobbi, Bobbie, Bobby, Bobbye, Bobina, Bobine, Bobinetta, Bobinette, Erta, Rebinah, Roba, Robbi, Robbie, Robbin, Robby, Robena, Robenia, Robin, Robina, Robine, Robinette, Robinia, Robonia, Robyn, Robynn, Robynne, Rori, Rory, Rubinah, Ruby, Ruperta.
Meaning: 'fame' and 'bright' (Germanic) as a female version of Robert.

Robina

Variants and diminutives: Bina, Bobina, Bobine, Bobinetta, Bobinette, Robbie, Robbin, Robby, Robena, Robenia, Roberta, Robin, Robina, Robine, Robinette, Robinia, Robonia, Robyn, Robynn, Robynne.
Meaning: 'fame' and 'bright' (Germanic) as a variant of Robin (Robert).

Rochelle

Variants and diminutives: Roch, Rochele, Rochella, Rochette, Roshele, Roshelle, Shell, Shelley, Shelli, Shellie, Shelly.
Meaning: 'little rock' (French); possibly derived from the western French port La Rochelle.

Roderica

Variants and diminutives: Rod, Roddi, Roddie, Roddy, Rori, Rory.
Meaning: 'renowned' and 'ruler' (Germanic) as a female version of Roderick.

Róisín

Variants and diminutives: Rosaleen, Rose, Rosheen.
Meaning: 'little rose' (Irish Gaelic).

Rolanda

Variants and diminutives: Orlanda, Ralna, Rolaine, Rolande, Rolene, Roll, Rolleen, Rolli, Rollie, Rolly.
Meaning: 'fame' and 'land' (Germanic) as a female version of Roland.

Roma

Variants and diminutives: Romaine, Romelda, Romia, Romilda, Romola.
Meaning: 'Rome' (Latin and Italian); derived from the Latin and Italian name for the city of Rome, in turn named for Romulus, its legendary co-founder. A female version of Roman.
Notable namesakes: the goddess who personified Rome in Roman mythology.

Romaine

Variants and diminutives: Roma, Romain, Romana, Romayne, Romola, Romy.
Meaning: 'of Rome' (French). A female version of Romain.

Romelda

Variants and diminutives: Roma, Romaine, Romilda.
Meaning: 'Roman warrior' (Germanic).

Romia

Variants and diminutives: Roma, Romaine, Romelda.
Meaning: 'exalted' (Hebrew).

Ronalda

Variants and diminutives: Rona, Roni, Ronl, Ronna, Ronne, Ronnette, Ronnie, Ronny, Ronsie, Ronsy.
Meaning: 'advice' or 'might' and 'power' (Germanic) as a female version of Ronald (Reynold).

Roni

Variants and diminutives: Rani, Ranit, Ranita, Renana, Renanit, Ronia, Ronit, Ronli, Ronnit.
Meaning: 'joy' (Hebrew).

Rosa

Variants and diminutives: Rosabella, Rosaleen, Rosalie, Rosalind, Rosaline, Rosamund, Rose.
Meaning: 'rose' (Latin).
Notable namesakes: Rosa Bonheur (French artist); Rosa Luxemburg (Polish-born German founder of the German Communist Party, or Spartacus League).

Rosabella

Variants and diminutives: Bell, Bella, Belle, Ros, Rosa, Rosabel, Rosabelle, Roz.
Meaning: a composite name comprising 'Rosa-', 'rose' (Latin), and '-bella', 'beautiful' (Italian).

Rosaleen

Variants and diminutives: Rosa, Rosalie, Rosalind, Rosaline, Rose, Roseleen.
Meaning: 'little rose' (Latin) as an Irish variant of Rosa.

Rosalie

Variants and diminutives: Ros, Rosa, Rosaleen, Rosalia, Rosaline, Rose, Rosele, Roz, Rozalia, Rozalie.
Meaning: 'little rose' (Latin).
Notable namesakes: Rosalia (or Rosaria), the ancient Roman practice of commemoration with roses; Saint Rosalie (or Rosalia), patron saint of the Sicilian city of Palermo; the title of a US musical.

Rosalind

Variants and diminutives: Lindi, Lindie, Lindy, Rhodalind, Ros, Rosa, Rosaleen, Rosalin, Rosalinda, Rosalinde, Rosaline, Rosalyn, Rosalynd, Rosalynde, Rose, Roseleen, Roselyn, Rosilyn, Rosina, Roslyn, Roslyne, Roslynn, Roz, Rozalin, Rozlyn.
Meaning: 'horse' or 'fame' and 'snake' or 'tender' (Germanic); 'rose' and 'lovely' (Spanish).
Notable namesakes: a character in poetic book *Shepheard's Calendar*, by English poet Edmund Spenser; the eponymous heroine of the romance *Rosalynde*, by English writer Thomas Lodge, on which William Shakespeare based his play *As You Like It;* Rosalind Russell (US actress).

Rosaline

Variants and diminutives: Ros, Rosa, Rosaleen, Rosalin, Rosalina, Rosalind, Rosalinda, Rosalyn, Rosalynd, Roseleen, Roseline, Roselyn, Rosilyn, Roslyn, Roslyne, Roslynn, Rosslyn, Roz, Rozalin, Rozalina, Rozaline, Rozlyn.
Meaning: 'horse' or 'fame' and 'snake' or 'tender' (Germanic) or 'rose' and 'lovely' (Spanish) as a variant of Rosalind.
Notable namesakes: characters in William Shakespeare's plays *Love's Labour's Lost* and *Romeo and Juliet.*

Rosamund

Variants and diminutives: Ros, Rosamond, Rosamunda, Rosamunde, Roseaman, Roseman, Rosemunda, Rosomon, Roz, Rozamond.
Meaning: 'horse' or 'fame' and 'protection' (Germanic); 'rose' and 'of the world' or 'pure' (Latin).
Notable namesakes: Rosamond Clifford, the 'Fair Rosamond' who was the mistress of King Henry II of England; Rosamond Lehmann (British writer).

Rosanne

Variants and diminutives: Ann, Anna, Anne, Roanne, Ros, Rosa, Rosana, Rose, Roseann, Rosanna, Roseanna, Roseanne, Roz, Rozanne.
Meaning: a composite name comprising 'Rosa-', 'rose' (Latin), and '-anne' (Hannah), 'I have been favoured (by God)' (Hebrew).
Notable namesakes: Roseanne Barr (US comedienne and actress).

Rose

Variants and diminutives: Chalina, Chara, Charo, Losa, Lose, Rhoda, Ricki, Roanne, Roese, Roesia, Rohana, Rohese, Rois, Róisín, Rosa, Rosabel, Rosabella, Rosabelle, Rosabeth, Rosalba, Rosaleen, Rosalia, Rosalie, Rosalin, Rosalina, Rosalind, Rosalinda, Rosamund, Rosana, Rosanna, Rosanne, Rosaura, Roesia, Rosebud, Rosedale, Rosel, Roselani, Rosella, Rosele, Rosella, Roselle, Rosellen, Roselotte, Roselynde, Rosemary, Rosena, Rosetta, Rosette, Rosi, Rosie, Rosina, Rosine, Rosita, Roslyn, Rosy, Royse, Roza, Rozalia, Rozalie, Roze, Rozele, Rozene, Rozina, Rozsa, Rozsi, Rozy, Rozyte, Ruusu, Ruza, Ruzena, Ruzenka, Ruzha, Ruzsa, Shaba, Zita.
Meaning: 'horse' or 'fame' (Germanic); 'rose' (Latin) when derived from the common name of the *Rosa* genus of flowering plants.
Notable namesakes: a pink colour; rosé, a pink-coloured wine; rose quartz and rose topaz, pink-coloured semi-precious stones; the French medieval romance *Roman de la Rose* (*Romance of the Rose*); Saint Rose of Lima, patron saint of the Americas, the Indies, Peru and the Philippines, as well as of florists; *The Rose and the Ring*, the title of a fairy tale by English writer William Makepeace Thackeray; the title character of the play *Rose Bernd*, by German playwright Gerhart Hauptmann; Rose Macaulay (British writer).

Rosemary

Variants and diminutives: Marie, Mary, Romy, Ros, Rose, Rosemaree, Rosemaria, Rosemarie, Rosie, Rosmarie, Roz, Rozmary.
Meaning: 'sea dew' (Latin) or 'rose of the sea' (Latin) when derived from the common name of the *Rosmarinus* genus of herbs; as a composite name, 'Rose-', 'horse' or 'fame' (Germanic) or 'rose' (Latin), and '-mary' (Miriam), 'longed-for child' or 'rebellion' (Hebrew).
Notable namesakes: Rosemarie Trockel (German artist).

Rosetta

Variants and diminutives: Ros, Rose, Rosette, Rosita, Roz.
Meaning: 'rose' (Latin) as an Italian variant of Rose.
Notable namesakes: a former name of the Egyptian town of Rashid, where the Rosetta Stone, the key to the decipherment of ancient Egyptian hieroglyphics, was discovered.

Rosina

Variants and diminutives: Ros, Rose, Rosetta, Rosita, Roz.
Meaning: 'rose' (Latin) as an Italian variant of Rose.

Rosita

Variants and diminutives: Ros, Rose, Rosetta, Roz.
Meaning: 'rose' (Latin) as a Spanish variant of Rose.

Rosslyn

Variants and diminutives: Ros, Ross, Rosslinda, Rosslynda, Roz, Lyn, Lynn, Lynne.
Meaning: 'horse' or 'fame' and 'snake' or 'tender' (Germanic) or 'rose' and 'lovely' (Spanish) as a variant of Roslyn (Rosalind via Roseline); 'cape' or 'promontory' (Scots Gaelic), 'wood' (Scottish and Irish Gaelic) or 'moor' (Cornish and Welsh) as a female version of Ross.

Rowena

Variants and diminutives: Rhona, Rhonwen, Roanna, Roanne, Rowan, Weena, Wena.
Meaning: 'lance' or 'slim' and 'fair' (Welsh) as a variant of Rhonwen; 'fame' and 'joy' (Germanic); 'mountain ash' (Old Norse) or 'red' (Irish Gaelic) as a female version of Rowan.
Notable namesakes: the heroine of the novel *Ivanhoe*, by Scottish writer Sir Walter Scott.

Roxanne

Variants and diminutives: Rosana, Roxana, Roxane, Roxann, Roxanna, Roxi, Roxianne, Roxie, Roxine, Roxy.
Meaning: 'dawn' (Persian).
Notable namesakes: Roxana, a wife of Alexander the Great, King of Macedonia; the eponymous heroine of the novel *Roxana*, by English writer Daniel Defoe; the heroine of the play *Cyrano de Bergerac*, by French writer Edmond Rostand, as well as of subsequent films; the title of a song by the British band The Police.

A
B
C
D
E
F
G
H
I
J
K
L
M
N
O
P
Q
R
S
T
U
V
W
X
Y
Z

Ruby

Variants and diminutives: Rubetta, Rubette, Rubey, Rubi, Rubia, Rubie, Rubina, Rubye.
Meaning: 'red' (Latin); derived from the name of the precious stone, a variety of corunum.
Notable namesakes: a dark red colour; Ruby Keeler (US singer and dancer); Ruby Wax (American-born British comedienne).

Rula

Meaning: 'rule' or 'pattern' (Latin).
Notable namesakes: Rula Lenska (British actress).

Rumer

Meaning: 'Gypsy' (English Gypsy).
Notable namesakes: Rumer Godden (British writer).

Ruth

Variants and diminutives: Ruthann, Ruthanne, Ruthi, Ruthie, Ruthina, Ruthine, Ruthven.
Meaning: 'friend', 'companion' or 'lovely sight' (Hebrew); 'compassion', 'remorse' or 'grief' (Old English).
Notable namesakes: the daughter-in-law of Naomi and wife of Boaz, whose story is told in the Book of Ruth in the Old Testament; Ruth McKenney (US writer); Ruth Prawer Jhabvala (German-born British writer); Ruth Rendell (British crime writer).

Saada

Meaning: 'help' or 'support' (Hebrew).

Sabina

Variants and diminutives: Bina, Sabcia, Sabia, Sabin, Sabine, Sabinka, Sabka, Savina, Savya.
Meaning: 'a Sabine woman' (Latin), Sabine referring to an ancient central Italian tribe whose women were abducted by the Romans.
Notable namesakes: Saint Sabina.

Sabira

Meaning: 'patient' (Arabic).

Sabra

Variants and diminutives: Sabrina, Zabra, Zabrina.
Meaning: 'prickly pear' or 'thorny cactus' (Hebrew and Arabic).
Notable namesakes: a name for a native Israeli.

Sabrina

Variants and diminutives: Brina, Sabra, Sabreen, Sabreena, Sabrinna, Sabryna.
Meaning: 'the river Severn [in England]' (Latin).
Notable namesakes: the goddess of the river Severn in Romano-British mythology; the illegitimate daughter of Estrildis and the Welsh king Locrine, whose wife, Gwendolen, drowned Sabrina and her mother in the river Severn, according to Welsh mythology, as told in the masque *Comus*, by English poet John Milton, and referred to in the play *Sabrina Fair*, by US playwright Samuel Taylor.

Sadie

Variants and diminutives: Mercedes, Sada, Sadella, Sadi, Sady, Sadye, Saida, Saidee, Sara, Sarah, Zaidee.
Meaning: 'princess' (Hebrew) as a diminutive of Sarah; 'mercy' (Spanish) as a diminutive of Mercedes.
Notable namesakes: Sadie Frost (British actress).

Sadira

Meaning: 'lotus' (Persian).

Saffron

Variants and diminutives: Saffie, Safflower, Saffrey, Saffy.
Meaning: 'saffron' or 'crocus' (Arabic); derived from the common name of the *Crocus sativus* genus of flowers, whose dried stigmas impart a yellow colour and spicy taste to food.
Notable namesakes: a character in the British television series *Absolutely Fabulous*; Saffron Burrows (British actress).

Sagara
Meaning: 'ocean' (Hindi).

Sahara
Variants and diminutives: Zahara.
Meaning: 'desert' (Arabic), referring to the Sahara desert in North Africa, the largest in the world.

Sakura
Meaning: 'cherry blossom' (Japanese).

Sally
Variants and diminutives: Sal, Salena, Salina, Sall, Salley, Salli, Sallie, Sara, Sarah.
Meaning: 'princess' (Hebrew) as a diminutive of Sarah.
Notable namesakes: Aunt Sally, an effigy of an old woman's head used as a target in fairground games and a term that now also describes a target for criticism; Sally Field (US actress).

Salome
Variants and diminutives: Sal, Salama, Saloma, Salomi, Shulamit, Shulamith, Shuly, Zulema.
Meaning: 'peace' or 'peace of Zion' (Hebrew).
Notable namesakes: the daughter of Herodias and step-daughter of Herod Antipas, who demanded the head of John the Baptist as a reward for her dancing in the New Testament; a witness to Christ's crucifixion in the New Testament.

Samantha
Variants and diminutives: Sam, Sami, Sammi, Sammie, Sammy.
Meaning: uncertain; possibly 'to listen' (Hebrew).
Notable namesakes: a female character in the US television series *Bewitched*; Samantha Bond and Samantha Janus (British actresses).

Samara
Variants and diminutives: Mara, Sam, Sami, Sammie, Sammy.
Meaning: 'guarded by God' or 'guardian' (Hebrew).

Samira
Variants and diminutives: Mira, Sam, Sami, Sammie, Sammy.
Meaning: 'entertainment' (Arabic) as a female version of Samir.

Sanchia
Variants and diminutives: Saint, Sancha, Santa, Sayntes, Sence, Senses.
Meaning: 'holy' (Latin).
Notable namesakes: a daughter of a count of Provence who married Richard, Earl of Cornwall, in medieval times.

Sandra
Variants and diminutives: Alessandra, Alexandra, Cassandra, Sanda, Sandi, Sandie, Sandy, Saundra, Sondra, Zandra.
Meaning: 'defender of men' or 'warrior' (Greek) as a diminutive of Alexandra, in turn a female version of Alexander; 'ensnarer of men' (Greek) as a diminutive of Cassandra.
Notable namesakes: Sandra Bullock (US actress)

Sanne
Variants and diminutives: Susannah.
Meaning: 'lily' (Hebrew) as a diminutive of Susannah.

Santa
Variants and diminutives: Saint, Sancha, Sanchia, Santina.
Meaning: 'holy' (Latin); 'saint' (Portuguese and Spanish). A female version of Santo.

Sapphire
Variants and diminutives: Sapir, Sapira, Sapphira.
Meaning: 'beloved by the planet Saturn' (Sanskrit); 'sapphire' (Hebrew); derived from the common name of the blue corundum gemstone.
Notable namesakes: a deep blue colour; Sapphira, the fraudulent wife of Ananias in the New Testament.

Sarah

Variants and diminutives: Chara, Charita, Kala, Morag, Sada, Sadella, Sadie, Sady, Sadye, Saida, Saidee, Sal, Sala, Salaidh, Salcia, Saliee, Sallie, Sally, Sara, Sarai, Saran, Sarann, Saranna, Saranne, Sareen, Sarena, Sarene, Saretta, Sarette, Sari, Sarice, Sarika, Sarina, Sarine, Sarinia, Sarita, Sarka, Sarolta, Sarotte, Sarra, Sasa, Satette, Sayre, Sela, Shara, Sharai, Shari, Sher, Sherrie, Socha, Sorale, Soralie, Sorcha, Sorolie, Zaidee, Zara, Zarah, Zaria, Zora, Zorana, Zoreen, Zorene, Zorna.
Meaning: 'princess' (Hebrew).
Notable namesakes: the wife of Abraham and mother of Isaac in the Old Testament; Saint Sara, the handmaid of Mary Magdalene in the New Testament; the eponymous leading character of the play *Miss Sara Sampson*, by German writer Gotthold Ephraim Lessing; Sarah Gamp, a character in the novel *Martin Chuzzlewit*, by English writer Charles Dickens: Sarah Orne Jewett (US writer); Sarah Bernhardt (French actress); Sarah Siddons and Sarah Miles (British actresses); Sarah Vaughan (US singer); Sarah King (British publisher).

Sasha

Variants and diminutives: Alexandra, Sacha.
Meaning: 'defender of men' or 'warrior' (Greek) as a Russian diminutive of Alexandra (Alexander). Also a boy's name (generally Sacha).

Saskia

Variants and diminutives: Alexandra.
Meaning: uncertain; possibly 'Saxon' (Old Dutch); possibly 'defender of men' or 'warrior' (Greek) as a Dutch diminutive of Alexandra (Alexander).
Notable namesakes: Saskia van Uylenburgh, the wife of, and subject of paintings by, the Dutch painter Rembrandt; Saskia Reeves (US actress).

Savannah

Variants and diminutives: Sav, Savana, Savanna, Savanah, Savi, Savie, Savy.
Meaning: 'open grasslands' (Spanish); derived from the topographical feature.

Notable namesakes: the Savannah river in the American South; the port of Savannah in the US state of Georgia, from which the *Savannah*, the first steamship to cross the Atlantic, set sail for Liverpool.

Scarlett

Variants and diminutives: Scarlet.
Meaning: 'fine cloth' (Old French); derived from a British family name.
Notable namesakes: a bright red colour; scarlet woman, a sinful woman referred to in the New Testament and a name now used to describe a sexually promiscuous woman; scarlet letter, a bright-red letter used to stigmatise people convicted of adultery by US puritans, a practice made notorious by the novel *The Scarlet Letter*, by US writer Nathaniel Hawthorne; scarlet pimpernel, the common name of the *Anagallis arvensis* species of flowering plants, as well as the eponymous hero of the novel *The Scarlet Pimpernel*, by Hungarian-born British novelist Baroness Emmuska Orczy; Scarlett O'Hara, the heroine of the novel *Gone with the Wind*, by US writer Margaret Mitchell.

Scilla

Variants and diminutives: Cilla, Priscilla, Scylla, Sila.
Meaning: 'of ancient times' (Latin) as a diminutive of Priscilla.
Notable namesakes: the *Scilla* genus of flowering plants; Scylla, a daughter of King Nisus of Megara, who was transformed into a lark in Greek mythology; a six-headed monster, who, along with Charybdis, guarded the Straits of Messina in Greek mythology.

Sela

Variants and diminutives: Selena.
Meaning: 'rock' (Hebrew).

Selena

Variants and diminutives: Cela, Celena, Celene, Celie, Celina, Celinda, Celine, Cellina, Salena, Salina, Sela, Selene, Selia, Selie, Selina, Selinda, Seline, Selinka, Sena, Sillina.
Meaning: 'bright light' or 'moon' (Greek) when derived from Selene, a moon goddess of Greek mythology; 'celestial' or 'heavenly' (Latin) as a variant of Celine.

Selima

Variants and diminutives: Selimah.
Meaning: 'healthy' or 'well-made' (Arabic).

Selma

Variants and diminutives: Anselma, Aselma, Zelma.
Meaning: 'divine' and 'helmet' (Germanic) or 'related to nobility' (Old French).as a diminutive of Anselma, in turn a female version of Anselm; 'fair' (Celtic); 'secure' (Arabic).
Notable namesakes: Selma Lagerlöf (Swedish writer).

Senga

Variants and diminutives: Agnes.
Meaning: 'pure' or 'chaste' (Greek) or 'lamb' (Latin), or maybe the reverse because this name results from spelling Agnes backwards.

Septima

Meaning: 'seventh' (Latin). A female version of Septimus.

Seraphina

Variants and diminutives: Serafina, Serafine, Seraphine.
Meaning: 'winged' or 'fiery' (Hebrew); derived from the name of the highest order of angels, the seraphs, or seraphim, in Judaeo-Christian belief.
Notable namesakes: two saints.

Serena

Variants and diminutives: Reena, Rena, Rina, Saryna, Sereena, Serene, Serepta, Serina, Seryna, Sirena.
Meaning: 'calm' (Latin).
Notable namesakes: Saint Serena; Serena Williams (US tennis player).

Shani

Variants and diminutives: Shan, Shannon, Shauna.
Meaning: 'wonderful' (Swahili); 'God has favoured', 'God is gracious' or 'God is merciful' (Hebrew) as a female version of Shane (John via Sean); 'old' (Irish Gaelic) as a diminutive of Shannon.

Shanna

Variants and diminutives: Shan, Shana, Shannah, Shannan, Shannon.
Meaning: 'old' (Irish Gaelic) as a diminutive of Shannon.

Shannon

Variants and diminutives: Shan, Shani, Shanna, Shannagh, Shannah, Shannan, Shannen, Shanon, Shauna, Shawna, Shawni.
Meaning: 'old' (Irish Gaelic); derived from an Irish family name, in turn derived from the name of the longest river in Ireland. Also a boy's name.

Sharifa

Variants and diminutives: Shareefa, Shari, Sharifah.
Meaning: 'honest' or 'noble' (Arabic) as a female version of Sharif.

Sharman

Variants and diminutives: Charmian, Sherman.
Meaning: 'joy' (Greek) or 'song' (Latin) as a variant of Charmian (Charmaine); 'shears' and 'man' (Old English) when derived from an English family name, when it can also be used as a boy's name.

Sharon

Variants and diminutives: Shaaron, Shara, Sharai, Sharan, Shareen, Shari, Sharma, Sharona, Sharron, Sharry, Sharyn, Sheri, Sherisa, Sherissa, Sherry, Sherryn, Shery.
Meaning: 'a plain' (Hebrew), referring to the Plain of Sharon in Israel. Also a boy's name.
Notable namesakes: a woman described as the 'rose of Sharon' in the Old Testament Song of Solomon; sharon fruit, another name for the fruit of the persimmon tree, *Diospyros*; Sharon Stone (US actress).

Shauna

Variants and diminutives: Seana, Seanna, Shana, Shanna, Shannah, Shawna, Shawnee, Shawni, Shawnie, Siana.
Meaning: 'God has favoured', 'God is gracious' or 'God is merciful' (Hebrew) as a female version of Shaun (John via Sean); 'old' (Irish Gaelic) as a diminutive of Shannon.

A B C D E F G H I J K L M N O P Q R S T U V W X Y Z

Sheba

Variants and diminutives: Bathsheba, Sheva.
Meaning: 'daughter of riches', 'daughter of a pledge', 'seventh daughter' or 'voluptuous' (Hebrew) as a diminutive of Bathsheba.
Notable namesakes: the ancient kingdom of the Sabeans, also known as Saba, whose queen (Balkis) visited Solomon in the Old Testament.

Sheena

Variants and diminutives: Jane, Jean, Shayna, Sheenah, Sheina, Shena, Shina, Shiona, Sine.
Meaning: 'God has favoured', 'God is gracious' or 'God is merciful' (Hebrew) as an anglicised version of Sine, in turn a Scots Gaelic variant of Jane or Jean (John).

Sheila

Variants and diminutives: Cecilia, Celia, Seila, Selia, Shayla, Shaylah, Sheela, Sheelagh, Sheelah, Sheilah, Sheilla, Shela, Shelagh, Shelia, Shelley, Shelli, Shelly, Shiela, Shielah, Sighile, Sile.
Meaning: 'celestial' or 'heavenly' (Latin) as an Irish Gaelic variant of Celia; 'blind' (Latin) or 'sixth' (Welsh) as an Irish Gaelic variant of Cecilia.
Notable namesakes: a generic slang word for a girl or woman in Australia.

Shelley

Variants and diminutives: Shell, Shelli, Shellie, Shelly.
Meaning: 'bank', 'plateau' or 'ledge' and 'wood' or 'clearing' (Old English); derived from an English family name, in turn derived from a number of English place names. Also a boy's name.
Notable namesakes: Shelley Winters (US actress).

Sherry

Variants and diminutives: Chérie, Sharee, Shari, Sharie, Sher, Sheree, Sherey, Sheri, Sherie, Sherill, Sherilyn, Sherina, Sherisa, Sherissa, Sherita, Sherree, Sherrey, Sherri, Sherrie, Sherrita, Sherryn, Shery, Sherye, Sheryl.
Meaning: 'darling' (French) as an anglicised version of Chérie; 'from Jerez' (Spanish) when referring to the fortified wine, which was originally made in the Jerez region of Spain.
Notable namesakes: Sherrie Levine (US artist).

Sheryl

Variants and diminutives: Cheryl, Sharell, Sheralin, Sheralyn, Sherileen, Sherill, Sherilyn, Sherlynn, Sherrill, Sherryl, Sheryll.
Meaning: uncertain; possibly a variant of Cheryl, a composite name comprising Cherry, 'cherry' (Greek, Latin and Old English) and Beryl, 'precious gem' (Sanskrit), 'crystal clear' (Arabic) or 'sea-green gem' (Greek).

Shira

Variants and diminutives: Shirah, Shiri, Shirlee.
Meaning: 'song' (Hebrew).

Shirley

Variants and diminutives: Sher, Sheree, Sheri, Sherill, Sherline, Sherri, Sherrie, Sherry, Sherye, Sheryl, Shir, Shirl, Shirlee, Shirleen, Shirleigh, Shirlene, Shirli, Shirlie, Shirline, Shirly, Shirlyn, Shirlynn.
Meaning: 'bright' or 'shire' and 'wood' or 'clearing' (Old English); derived from an English family name, in turn derived from a number of English place names.
Notable namesakes: Shirley Keeldar, the heroine of the novel *Shirley*, by English writer Charlotte Brontë; Shirley Jackson (US writer); Shirley Temple (US child actor); Shirley Williams (British politician); Shirley Conran (British writer); the eponymous heroine of the British film *Shirley Valentine*; Shirley Bassey and Shirley Manson (British singers).

Shizu

Variants and diminutives: Shizue, Shizuka, Shizuko, Shizuyo, Suizuka.
Meaning: 'clear' or 'quiet' (Japanese).

Shona

Variants and diminutives: Janet, Seonaid, Shaina, Shaine, Shana, Shanie, Shannon, Shayna, Shayne, Shonagh, Shoni, Shonie.
Meaning: 'God has favoured', 'God is gracious' or 'God is merciful' (Hebrew) as an anglicised variant of Seonaid, in turn a Scots Gaelic version of Jane or Janet (John).

Shula
Variants and diminutives: Shulamit.
Meaning: 'peace' (Hebrew).
Notable namesakes: a character in the British radio serial *The Archers*.

Siân
Variants and diminutives: Jane.
Meaning: 'God has favoured', 'God is gracious' or 'God is merciful' (Hebrew) as a Welsh variant of Jane (John).
Notable namesakes: Siân Phillips (British actress).

Sidony
Variants and diminutives: Sidney, Sidonia, Sidonie, Sydney.
Meaning: 'from Sidon' (Latin), Sidon being a city of ancient Phoenicia, today the Lebanese city of Saïda; 'linen' (Greek).
Notable namesakes: Sidonie Gabrielle Claudine Colette, the full name of the French writer Colette.

Signy
Variants and diminutives: Signe, Signi.
Meaning: 'victory' and 'new' (Old Norse).

Sigrid
Variants and diminutives: Siggi, Siggie, Siggy, Siri.
Meaning: 'victory' and 'beautiful' or 'advice' (Old Norse); 'victory' and 'peace' (Germanic) as a female version of Siegfried.
Notable namesakes: Sigrid Undset (Norwegian writer).

Silvana
Variants and diminutives: Silva, Silvano, Silvia, Sylva, Sylvana, Sylverta, Sylvi, Sylvia, Sylvie, Vana, Xylia, Xylina, Zilvana.
Meaning: 'sylvan' or 'of the woods' (Latin) as a female version of Silvanus.
Notable namesakes: the Silvanae, the attendants of Silvanus, god of the woods, fields and flocks, in Roman mythology.

Silver
Variants and diminutives: Silva, Silveria, Silvie.
Meaning: 'silver' (Old English); derived from the name of the metal. Also a boy's name.

Silvestra
Variants and diminutives: Silvia, Sylvia, Sylvestra.
Meaning: 'sylvan' or 'of the woods' (Latin) as a female version of Silvester.

Simone
Variants and diminutives: Simeona, Simona, Simonetta, Simonette, Simonia, Simonne.
Meaning: 'God has heard', 'listening' or 'little hyena' (Hebrew) or 'snub-nosed' (Greek) as a female French version of Simon.
Notable namesakes: Simone de Beauvoir (French feminist, socialist and writer); Simone Weil (French philosopher); Simone Signoret (French actress).

Síne
Variants and diminutives:
Meaning: 'God has favoured', 'God is gracious' or 'God is merciful' (Hebrew) as a Scots Gaelic version of Jane or Janet (John).

Sinéad
Variants and diminutives: Janet, Seonaid.
Meaning: 'God has favoured', 'God is gracious' or 'God is merciful' (Hebrew) as an Irish Gaelic version of Jane or Janet (John).
Notable namesakes: Sinead Cusack (Irish actress); Sinead O'Connor (Irish singer).

Siobhán
Variants and diminutives: Charvon, Chavon, Chavonn, Chavonne, Chevon, Chevonne, Chivon, Shavon, Shavone, Shavonne, Shervan, Shevaun, Shevon, Shevonne, Siobhan, Shivohn, Siobahn, Siobhian.
Meaning: 'God has favoured', 'God is gracious' or 'God

A B C D E F G H I J K L M N O P Q R S T U V W X Y Z

is merciful' (Hebrew) as an Irish Gaelic variant of Jane or Joan (John).
Notable namesakes: Siobhán McKenna (Irish actress); Siobhan Fahey (British singer).

Sissy
Variants and diminutives: Cis, Cissie, Cissy, Sis, Sisi, Sissi, Sissie.
Meaning: 'blind' (Latin) or 'sixth' (Welsh) as a diminutive of Cecilia; 'little sister' (English).
Notable namesakes: Sisi, the nickname of Elizabeth of Wittelsbach, wife of Franz Josef, Emperor of Austria-Hungary; a derogative word for an effeminite man; Sissy Spacek (US actress).

Sita
Variants and diminutives: Zita.
Meaning: 'furrow' (Sanskrit); derived from the name of a goddess of agriculture, who arose from a furrow, beloved by Vishnu in his incarnation as Rama in Hindu mythology.

Sky
Variants and diminutives: Skye.
Meaning: 'transparent skin' (Old Norse); 'cloud' Old English.
Notable namesakes: the Isle of Skye off the north-western coast of Scotland.

Solange
Meaning: 'alone' (Latin).
Notable namesakes: Saint Solange, patron saint of rape victims and drought relief.

Soma
Meaning: 'intoxicating juice' (Sanskrit), referring to an extract of the *Asclepias acida* plant used in Vedic ritual; 'moon' (Hindi); 'body' (Greek).
Notable namesakes: a sedative drug used to control the masses in the novel *Nineteen Eighty-Four*, by British writer George Orwell.

Sonia
Variants and diminutives: Sondya, Sonja, Sonya, Sophia, Zonya.
Meaning: 'wisdom' (Greek) as a Russian variant of Sophia.
Notable namesakes: Sonya, the heroine of the novel *Crime and Punishment*, by Russian writer Fyodor Mikhailovich Dostoyevsky; the title of a novel by British writer Stephen McKenna; Sonia Delaunay (Russian-born French artist and designer).

Sophia
Variants and diminutives: Chofa, Chofie, Fifi, Sofi, Sofia, Soficita, Sofka, Sofya, Sonia, Sondya, Sonja, Sonni, Sonny, Sonya, Sophie, Sophoon, Sophronia, Sophy, Sunny, Sunya, Zocha, Zofia, Zofie, Zofka, Zonya, Zophia, Zosha, Zosia.
Meaning: 'wisdom' (Greek).
Notable namesakes: the goddess of wisdom, an Aeon (angel) and the spirit of God in Gnostic belief and Hellenic philosophy, to whom the cathedral (now a mosque) of Hagia Sophia in Constantinople (Istanbul), Turkey, was dedicated; Sophia Prunikos, an unhappy Aeon in Gnostic belief; Sophia-achamoth, an Aeon personifying the lower astral light, the daughter of Sophia and mother of God in Gnostic belief; a number of saints; Sofia, the capital of Bulgaria; Sophia, Electress of Hanover, a granddaughter of King James I of England and Scotland and the mother of King George I of Great Britain and Ireland; Sophia Loren (Italian actress); Sophie Calle (French artist); Sophie Marceau (French actress); Sophie Ellis Bextor (British singer).

Sophronia
Meaning: 'prudent' (Greek).

Sorcha
Variants and diminutives: Sarah, Sorcka, Sorka.
Meaning: 'radiant' or 'bright' (Irish Gaelic).

Sorrel
Variants and diminutives: Sorel, Sorell, Sorelle, Sorrell.
Meaning: 'sour' (Germanic) when derived from the name of both the sorrel tree (or sourwood),

Oxydendrum arboreum, and the *Rumex* genus of plants, which have edible, bitter-tasting leaves; 'chestnut-coloured' or 'reddish-brown' (Old French).
Notable namesakes: a shade of brown.

Stacey
Variants and diminutives: Anastasia, Staci, Stacia, Stacie, Stacy, Stasa, Staska, Stasya, Tasenka, Tasia, Taska, Tasya.
Meaning: 'resurrection' or 'awakening' (Greek) as a diminutive of Anastasia. Also a boy's name as a diminutive of Eustace, 'fruitful', 'good' or 'ear of corn' (Greek).

Star
Variants and diminutives: Estella, Estelle, Starla, Starlit, Starr, Starry, Stella.
Meaning: 'star' (Old English); derived from the generic name for a celestial object.
Notable namesakes: a word used to describe a celebrity or outstandingly successful person.

Stella
Variants and diminutives: Estella, Estelle, Esther, Hester, Star.
Meaning: 'star' (Latin); derived fron the generic name for a celestial object.
Notable namesakes: *Stella Maris* ('Star of the Sea'), a title of the Virgin Mary; the heroine of the sonnet cycle *Astrophel and Stella*, by English poet Philip Sidney; the title of a play by German writer Johann Wolfgang von Goethe; the recipient (actually Ester Johnson) of *Journal to Stella*, a series of letters by Irish writer Jonathan Swift.

Stephanie
Variants and diminutives: Estephania, Etienette, Stamatios, Stef, Stefa, Stefani, Stefania, Stefanida, Stefanie, Stefcia, Stefenie, Steffi, Steffie, Stefka, Stepa, Stepania, Stepanida, Stepanie, Stepanyda, Stepha, Stephana, Stephanine, Stephenie, Stesha, Steshka, Stevana, Stevena, Stevi, Stevie, Stevy, Panya, Teena, Trinette.
Meaning: 'crown' (Greek) as a female version of Stephen.

Notable namesakes: Princess Stephanie of Monaco; Steffi Graf (German tennis player); Stevie Smith (British poet).

Stina
Variants and diminutives: Christina, Stine.
Meaning: 'Christian' (Latin) as a German diminutive of Christina (Christine).

Storm
Variants and diminutives: Stormie, Stormy.
Meaning: 'storm' (Old English); derived from the name for a tempestuous weather condition. Also a boy's name.

Sukie
Variants and diminutives: Kukana, Su, Sue, Suka, Suke, Sukee, Sukey, Suki, Suky, Susan, Susannah.
Meaning: 'lily' (Hebrew) as a diminutive of Susan or Susannah.

Summer
Variants and diminutives:
Meaning: 'season' (Sanskrit); 'the season of summer' (Old English).

Susan
Variants and diminutives: Chana, Shoshan, Shoushan, Shushan, Siusan, Sonel, Su, Suanne, Sudi, Sue, Suella, Suka, Sukee, Sukey, Suki, Suki, Sukie, Suky, Susana, Susanka, Susanna, Susanne, Susannah, Suse, Susetta, Susette, Susi, Susie, Susy, Suzan, Suzana, Suze, Suzetta, Suzette, Suzi, Suzie, Suzy, Zuska, Zuza, Zuzana, Zuzanka, Zuzca, Zuzia, Zuzka.
Meaning: 'lily' (Hebrew) as a diminutive of Susannah.
Notable namesakes: Susan B Anthony (US suffragette); Suzanne Lenglen (French tennis player); Susanne Langer (US philosopher); Susan Glaspell and Susan Sontag (US writers); Susan Hayward and Susan Sarandon (US actresses); Susan Hampshire and Susan George (British actresses); Suzanne Valadon (French artist); Susan Rothenberg (US artist); Suzanne Vega (US musician).

Susannah

Variants and diminutives: Chana, Kukana, Sanne, Shoushan, Siusaidh, Siusan, Sanna, Sanne, Shoshan, Shoshana, Shoshanah, Shushan, Shushana, Shushanah, Shushanna, Siusan, Sonel, Sosanna, Su, Suanne, Sudi, Sue, Suella, Suka, Suke, Sukee, Sukey, Suki, Sukie, Sukey, Suky, Susan, Susana, Susanka, Susanna, Susanne, Suse, Susetta, Susette, Susi, Susie, Susy, Suzan, Suzana, Suzanna, Suzannah, Suzanne, Suze, Suzetta, Suzette, Suzi, Suzie, Suzy, Xuxu, Zana, Zsa Zsa, Zuska, Zuza, Zuzana, Zuzanna, Zuzia, Zuzka, Zuzanka.
Meaning: 'lily' (Hebrew).
Notable namesakes: a bathing beauty who was falsely accused of adultery as told in the Apocrypha; Susanna, a follower of Christ in the New Testament; Susana Solano (Spanish sculptor); Susannah York (British actress).

Sybil

Variants and diminutives: Cybele, Cybil, Sevilla, Sib, Sibbie, Sibby, Sibel, Sibell, Sibella, Sibelle, Sibett, Sibeal, Sibil, Sibilla, Sibille, Sibley, Sibyl, Sibylla, Sibylle, Sibyllina, Sybella, Sybilla, Sybille, Sybyl, Sybylla.
Meaning: uncertain; possibly 'prophetess' (Greek); possibly 'whistle' or 'hiss' (Latin).
Notable namesakes: as sibyl, a number of prophetesses or oracles of Graeco-Roman mythology, notably the Cumaean sibyl, who guided Aeneas through the underworld and is said to have been the source of the Sibylline Books, books of prophecy referred to in ancient Rome; the wife of King Robert II, 'Curthose', of England; the heroine of the novel *Sybil, or The Two Nations*, by British politician and writer Benjamin Disraeli; Sybil Thorndike (British actress); Sybil Colefax (British interior designer); Sybil Fawlty, a character in the British television series *Fawlty Towers*.

Sylvia

Variants and diminutives: Silivia, Silva, Silvana, Silvano, Silveria, Silvestra, Silvia, Silvie, Silvina, Sylva, Sylvana, Sylverta, Sylvestra, Sylvi, Sylvie, Xylia, Xylina, Zilvia.
Meaning: 'wood' (Latin).
Notable namesakes: Rhea Silvia, the mother of Romulus and Remus in Roman mythology; a character in William Shakespeare's play *Two Gentlemen of Verona*; Sylvia Pankhurst (British suffragette); Sylvia Townsend Warner (English writer); Sylvia Ashton-Warner (New Zealand writer); Sylvia Plath (US poet); Queen Silvia of Sweden.

Tabitha

Variants and diminutives: Tab, Tabatha, Tabbi, Tabbie, Tabbitha, Tabby.
Meaning: 'gazelle' (Aramaic).
Notable namesakes: a woman (also known as Dorcas) whom Saint Peter resurrected from the dead in the New Testament; Tabitha Bramble, a character in the novel *Humphrey Clinker*, by Scottish writer Tobias Smollett; Tabitha Twitchett, a feline character created by English children's writer and illustrator Beatrix Potter.

Tacey

Variants and diminutives: Tace, Tacie, Tacita, Tacy, Tacye.
Meaning: 'to be silent' (Latin).

Tacita

Variants and diminutives: Tacey, Tacye.
Meaning: 'the silent' (Latin).
Notable namesakes: the goddess of silence, one of the Camenae (prophetic water nymphs) in Roman mythology.

Taja

Variants and diminutives: Tajah, Talajara, Tejab, Tejal.
Meaning: 'crown' (Urdu and Arabic). A female version of Taj.

Takara
Variants and diminutives: Kara.
Meaning: 'treasure' or 'precious' (Japanese).

Talia
Variants and diminutives: Tal, Tali, Tallie, Tally, Talor, Talora, Talya, Teli, Thalia.
Meaning: 'lamb' (Aramaic); 'dew of heaven' (Hebrew); 'birthday' (Latin), 'Christ's birthday' or 'Christmas' (Slavonic) as a diminutive of Natalia.

Talitha
Variants and diminutives: Tali, Talith.
Meaning: 'little girl' (Aramaic).

Tallulah
Variants and diminutives: Lula, Lulah, Talli, Talie, Tallis, Talllou, Tally, Tallula, Talula, Talulla.
Meaning: 'spring' or 'running' or 'leaping' and 'water' (Choctaw – Native American); derived from a North American place name.
Notable namesakes: Tallulah Bankhead (US actress).

Talulla
Variants and diminutives: Lula, Lulla, Tali, Talie, Talullah.
Meaning: 'abundance' and 'princess' or 'lady' (Irish Gaelic).
Notable namesakes: two saints.

Tamar
Variants and diminutives: Tam, Tama, Tamah, Tamara, Tamarah, Tamarra, Tamer, Tami, Tamie, Tamimah, Tammi, Tammie, Tammy, Tamor, Tamour, Tamra, Tamyra, Temima, Temira, Timora, Timi.
Meaning: 'date palm' or 'palm tree' (Hebrew).
Notable namesakes: a wife of Er and mother of Perez and Zerah by Judah in the Old Testament; a daughter of David, sister of Absalom and half-sister of Amnon in the Old Testament, whose story inspired US poet Robinson Jeffers, *Tamar and Other Poems*; a daughter of Absalom in the Old Testament; an English river.

Tamara
Variants and diminutives: Mara, Tam, Tama, Tamah, Tamar, Tamarah, Tamarka, Tamarra, Tamer, Tami, Tamie, Tammara, Tammera, Tammi, Tammie, Tammy, Tamor, Tamour, Tamra, Tamyra, Temira, Timora, Tomochka.
Meaning: 'date palm' or 'palm tree' (Hebrew) as a Russian variant of Tamar.
Notable namesakes: a queen of Georgia, a former kingdom on the Black Sea; the eponymous heroine of a symphonic poem by Russian composer Mily Alexeyevich Balakirev; Tamara Karsavina (Russian ballerina) Tamara de Lempicka (Polish-born French artist).

Tamsin
Variants and diminutives: Tamasin, Tamasine, Tami, Tammie, Tammy, Tansin, Tamzin, Tamzine, Tamzon, Thomasina, Thomasine.
Meaning: 'twin' (Aramaic) as a variant of Thomasina (Thomas).

Tanith
Variants and diminutives: Tanit.
Meaning: 'great mother' (Phoenician) when derived from the name of the supreme goddess of Carthage; 'estate' (Irish Gaelic).

Tansy
Variants and diminutives: Tansie.
Meaning: 'immortality' (Greek); derived from the common name of the *Tanacetum vulgare* flowering plant, which has edible leaves.

Tanya
Variants and diminutives: Tanhya, Tania, Tatiana, Tiana.
Meaning: uncertain; possibly 'fairy queen' (Old Slavonic), 'I arrange' (Greek) or derived from the Sabine and Roman family name Tatius as a diminutive of Tatiana.

Tara
Variants and diminutives: Tarah, Tarra, Taryn, Tatiana, Teamhair, Tera, Terra.
Meaning: uncertain; possibly 'hill' (Irish Gaelic);

possibly 'star' (Sanskrit) when derived from the name of the Hindu, Jain and Buddhist Tantric mother goddess; possibly 'to carry' or 'to throw' (Aramaic).
Notable namesakes: Tara (Tea-mhair) Hill, the capital of ancient Ireland in County Meath and traditionally the site of a royal palace founded by the Irish goddesses Tea and Tephi; the estate of the O'Hara family in the novel *Gone With the Wind*, by US author Margaret Mitchell.

Tasha
Variants and diminutives: Talia, Natasha.
Meaning: 'birthday' (Latin), 'Christ's birthday' or 'Christmas' (Slavonic) as a diminutive of Natasha, in turn a diminutive of Natalya (Natalia).

Tasya
Variants and diminutives: Anastasia, Tasia.
Meaning: 'resurrection' or 'awakening' (Greek) as a diminutive of Anastasia.

Tatiana
Variants and diminutives: Tanhya, Tania, Tanya, Tara, Tiana, Tita, Titania.
Meaning: uncertain; possibly 'fairy queen' (Old Slavonic); possibly 'I arrange' (Greek); possibly derived from the Sabine and Roman family name Tatius.
Notable namesakes: Saint Tatiana; a Russian grand duchess, daughter of Tsar Nicholas II, who was murdered following the Russian Revolution.

Tatum
Variants and diminutives: Tait, Taite, Tata, Tate, Tayte.
Meaning: uncertain; possibly 'windy' or 'garrulous' (Native American), 'cheerful' (Old Norse), 'dear', 'happy', 'dice', 'hilltop', 'tress of hair', 'father' or 'teat' (Old English) as a female version of Tate.
Notable namesakes: Tatum O'Neal (US actress).

Tauba
Variants and diminutives: Dove, Taube, Toby.
Meaning: 'dove' (Germanic).

Tawny
Variants and diminutives: Tawni, Tawnie.
Meaning: 'tan' (Old French) when derived from the name of the light-orange-brown colour; 'little one' (English Gypsy).

Teal
Variants and diminutives: Teale.
Meaning: 'teal' (Middle English); derived from an English family name, in turn derived from the common name of a number of small ducks, such as *Anas crecca*.
Notable namesakes: a greenish-blue colour.

Tegan
Variants and diminutives: Taegen, Taygan, Teagan, Teegan, Tegan, Tegin, Tegwen, Tiegan, Tigan.
Meaning: 'lovely' (Welsh); 'poet' or 'philosopher' (Irish Gaelic) as a female version of Teague.

Tegwen
Variants and diminutives: Tegan.
Meaning: 'lovely' and 'fair' or 'blessed' (Welsh).

Temima
Variants and diminutives: Tamar, Tamimah.
Meaning: 'honest' or 'entire' (Hebrew and Arabic).

Temperance
Variants and diminutives: Temp, Tempi, Tempie, Tempy.
Meaning: 'to regulate' (Latin).

Tempest
Variants and diminutives: Tempestt.
Meaning: 'storm' (Old French).
Notable namesakes: *The Tempest*, a play by English playwright William Shakespeare.

Tertia
Variants and diminutives: Terti, Tertie, Terty, Tia.
Meaning: 'third' (Latin). A female version of Tertius.

Tesia
Variants and diminutives: Taisha, Taysha, Tesha, Teysha, Theophila.

Meaning: 'God-loving' (Greek) as a Polish diminutive of Theophila (Theophilus).

Tessa

Variants and diminutives: Teresa, Tersa, Tesa, Tess, Tessi, Tessia, Tessie, Tessy, Theresa, Tresa.
Meaning: uncertain; possibly 'harvest', 'reap' or 'from Thera [or Therasia]' (Greek) as a diminutive of Theresa.
Notable namesakes: Tess Durbeyfield, the heroine of the novel *Tess of the D'Urbervilles*, by English writer Thomas Hardy; Tessa Sanderson (British athlete).

Thalassa

Variants and diminutives: Thalli, Thallie, Thally, Lassa.
Meaning: 'sea' (Greek), with particular reference to the Mediterranean Sea.

Thalia

Variants and diminutives: Talia, Talya, Thaleia.
Meaning: 'to prosper', 'to flourish' or 'to bloom' (Greek).
Notable namesakes: the Muse of comedy, as well as one of the Nereides (sea nymphs) and one of the graces or Charites (personifications of grace, beauty and charm), in Greek mythology.

Thea

Variants and diminutives: Dorothea, Dorothy, Theia, Theodora.
Meaning: 'goddess' (Greek) as a female version of Theo; 'God's gift' (Greek) as a diminutive of Dorothea (Dorothy), in turn a female version of Theodore.
Notable namesakes: Theia, a Titan goddess of light and mother of Helios, Eos and Selene in Greek mythology, as well as one of the Oceanides (water nymphs).

Thekla

Variants and diminutives: Tecla, Tecle, Thecla, Thea, Theodora, Theodosia, Theophania, Theophila.
Meaning: 'God' and 'renowned' (Greek).
Notable namesakes: Saint Thekla (or Thecla).

Thelma

Variants and diminutives: Kama, Teli, Telma.

Meaning: uncertain; possibly 'will', 'wish' or 'nursling' (Greek); coined by British writer Marie Corelli for the heroine of her novel of the same name.
Notable namesakes: a heroine of the US film *Thelma and Louise*.

Theodora

Variants and diminutives: Dora, Dorothea, Dorothy, Fedora, Feodora, Ted, Tedda, Teddi, Teddy, Tedra, Teodora, Thaddea, Thadine, Thea, Theda, Thekla, Theo, Theodosia, Theophania, Theophila.
Meaning: 'God's gift' (Greek) as a female version of Theodore.
Notable namesakes: a Byzantine empress, the consort of Emperor Justinian I.

Theodosia

Variants and diminutives: Thea, Thekla, Theodora, Theophania, Theophila.
Meaning: 'given by God' (Greek).

Theophania

Variants and diminutives: Thea, Theodora, Theodosia, Theophila, Tiffany.
Meaning: 'God's manifestation' or 'epiphany' (Greek).

Theophila

Variants and diminutives: Offie, Offy, Phila, Tesia, Thea, Theodora, Theodosia, Theophania.
Meaning: 'God-loving' (Greek) as a female version of Theophilus.

Theresa

Variants and diminutives: Renia, Resel, Resi, Rezi, Riza, Rizua, Tassos, Teca, Techa, Tera, Tercsa, Tere, Terenia, Teresa, Terese, Teresina, Teresita, Tereska, Teressa, Terez, Tereza, Terezia, Terezie, Terezilya, Terezka, Teri, Terie, Terike, Terri, Terrie, Terry, Tery, Tarsa, Teruska, Tesa, Tesia, Tess, Tessa, Tessi, Tessie, Tessy, Tete, Therese, Thérèse, Theresia, Trace, Tracey, Traci, Tracie, Tracy, Tresa, Trescha, Treszka, Zilya, Zita.
Meaning: uncertain; possibly 'harvest', 'reap' or 'from Thera [or Therasia]' (Greek), Thera (Thira) being a Greek island in the Aegean Sea, also known as Santorini.
Notable namesakes: Saint Theresa, wife of Saint

A B C D E F G H I J K L M N O P Q R S T U V W X Y Z

Paulinus; Saint Teresa of Avila, patron saint of headache-sufferers; Maria Theresa, daughter of Emperor Charles VI of Austria, wife of Emperor Francis I and mother of Emperor Joseph II of Austria; Saint Thérèse of Lisieux, patron saint of aviators, missions, florists and Russia; Countess Teresa Guiccioli, the Italian mistress of the English poet George, Lord Byron; the eponymous heroine of the novels *Thérèse Aubert*, by French writer Charles Nodier, *Thérèse Raquin*, by French writer Emile Zola, and *Thérèse Desqueyroux*, by French writer François Mauriac; Mother Teresa (or Theresa), the Nobel Prize-winning founder of the Missionaries of Charity in Calcutta, India; Thérèse Oulton (British artist).

Thirza

Variants and diminutives: Thirsa, Thirzah, Thyrza, Tirza, Tirzah.
Meaning: uncertain; possibly 'pleasantness' or 'acceptance' (Hebrew).

Thomasina

Variants and diminutives: Tamanique, Tamasin, Tamasine, Tami, Tammie, Tammy, Tamsin, Tamzin, Tamzine, Tamzon, Thomasa, Thomasin, Thomasine, Thomasing, Thomassine, Thomson, Toma, Tomasa, Tomasina, Tomasine, Tommi, Tommianne, Tommy.
Meaning: 'twin' (Aramaic) as a female version of Thomas.

Thora

Variants and diminutives: Thodia, Thordis, Thyra, Tora, Tyra.
Meaning: uncertain; possibly 'of Thor' or 'the thunderer' (Old Norse), Thor being the thunder god of Norse mythology. A female version of Thor.
Notable namesakes: the goddess of spring and dawn and wife of Ragnar Löbrog in Norse and Teutonic mythology; Thora Hird (British actress).

Tiana

Variants and diminutives: Christiana, Tania, Tanya, Tatiana, Tia, Tiane, Tianna, Tianne.
Meaning: 'Christian' (Latin) as a diminutive of Christiana (Christine); possibly 'fairy queen' (Old

Slavonic), 'I arrange' (Greek) or derived from the Sabine and Roman family name Tatius as a diminutive of Tatiana.

Tibby

Variants and diminutives: Isabel, Tibbi, Tibbie, Tibbs.
Meaning: 'God is perfection', 'God is satisfaction', 'dedicated to God' or 'God's oath' (Hebrew) and 'beautiful' (French, Italian and Spanish) as a diminutive of Isabel.

Tiffany

Variants and diminutives: Teffan, Teffany, Thefania, Theophania, Tifaine, Tiff, Tiffan, Tiffani, Tiffanie, Tiffy, Tiphaine, Thiphania, Tyfanny.
Meaning: 'God's manifestation' or 'epiphany' (Greek) as a diminutive of Theophania.
Notable namesakes: the Christian feast day Epiphany (6 January); a type of gauzy fabric; the US film *Breakfast at Tiffany's*, Tiffany's referring to the US jewellery retailers founded by Charles L Tiffany; Tiffany (or Favrile) glass, a style of stained glass first manufactured by US artist and glassmaker Louis Comfort Tiffany (the son of Charles L Tiffany).

Tilda

Variants and diminutives: Matilda, Tila, Tilda, Tilde, Tildie, Tildy, Tillie, Tilly, Tylda
Meaning: 'mighty' and 'battle' as a diminutive of Matilda.
Notable namesakes: Tilda Swinton (British actress).

Timothea

Variants and diminutives: Timi, Timie, Timmie, Timmy.
Meaning: 'in honour of God' (Greek) as a female version of Timothy.

Tina

Variants and diminutives: Christina, Constantina, Tiana, Tyna, Valentina.
Meaning: a diminutive of any name ending in '-tina', such as Christina (Christine), 'Christian' (Latin).
Notable namesakes: Tina Turner (US singer); Tina Brown (a British-born US magazine editor).

Tisha
Variants and diminutives: Letitia, Tish, Titia.
Meaning: 'joyful' (Latin) as a diminutive of Letitia.

Tivona
Variants and diminutives: Tibona, Tiboni, Tivony.
Meaning: 'nature-lover' (Hebrew). A female version of Tivon.

Tonia
Variants and diminutives: Antonia, Toni, Tonie, Tonya, Tosia.
Meaning: 'flourishing' (Greek) or 'without price' (Latin) as a diminutive of Antonia (Anthony).
Notable namesakes: Toni Morrison (US writer).

Topaz
Variants and diminutives: Topaza.
Meaning: 'topaz' (Greek); derived from the name of the usually golden-coloured gemstone.

Tora
Variants and diminutives: Tori, Tory.
Meaning: 'tiger' (Japanese).
Notable namesakes: Tori Amos (US singer).

Tori
Variants and diminutives: Tora, Tory.
Meaning: 'bird' (Japanese).

Toyah
Variants and diminutives: Toya.
Meaning: 'toying' or 'trifling' (Middle English).
Notable namesakes: Toyah Wilcox (British singer and actress).

Tracy
Variants and diminutives: Teresa, Theresa, Trace, Tracey, Traci, Tracie, Trasey.
Meaning: 'Thracian' or 'of Thrace' (Latin), Thrace being an ancient kingdom in the south-eastern Balkans, when derived from an English family name, in turn derived from two French place names; possibly 'harvest', 'reap' or 'from Thera [or Therasia]' (Greek) as a diminutive of Theresa. Also a boy's name.

Notable namesakes: Tracy Lord, the heroine of the US films *The Philadelphia Story* and *High Society*; Tracey Emin (British artist).

Trina
Variants and diminutives: Catriona, Katrina, Trinete.
Meaning: 'pure' (Greek) as a diminutive of Catriona and Katrina, both variants of Catherine; 'piercing' (Hindi).

Trisha

Variants and diminutives: Patricia, Tricia, Trish.
Meaning: 'noble' or 'patrician' (Latin) as a diminutive of Patricia (Patrick); 'thirst' (Hindi).

Trixie
Variants and diminutives: Beatrice, Beatrix, Tris, Trissie, Trix, Trixy.
Meaning: 'bringer of blessings' or 'traveller' (Latin) as a diminutive of Beatrix (Beatrice).

Trudy
Variants and diminutives: Ermintrude, Gertrude, Truda, Trude, Trudey, Trudi, Trudie.
Meaning: 'spear' and 'strength' (Germanic) as a diminutive of Gertrude; 'universal' and 'strength' (Germanic) as a diminutive of Ermintrude.

Tryphena
Variants and diminutives: Phena, Truffeni, Tryphosa.
Meaning: 'delicacy' or 'daintiness' (Greek).

Twyla
Variants and diminutives: Twila, Twilla.
Meaning: 'woven with a double thread' (Old English).
Notable namesakes: Twyla Tharp (US choreographer).

Tyra
Variants and diminutives: Thora, Thyra.
Meaning: uncertain; possibly 'of Tyr' or 'warrior' (Old Norse), Tyr being a god of war in Norse mythology.

A B C D E F G H I J K L M N O P Q R S T U V W X Y Z

U

Udelle
Variants and diminutives: Ella, Elle, Udella, Ula.
Meaning: 'yew' and 'valley' (Old English) as a female version of Udell; 'wealth' (Old Norse), 'owner' (Germanic) or 'sea jewel' (Irish Gaelic) as a variant of Ula.

Ula
Variants and diminutives: Udelle, Ulani, Ulla.
Meaning: 'wealth' (Old Norse); 'owner' (Germanic); 'sea jewel' (Irish Gaelic).

Ulani
Variants and diminutives: Lani, Ula.
Meaning: 'light-hearted', 'cheerful' or 'bright' (Hawaiian).

Ulima
Variants and diminutives: Ulema.
Meaning: 'wise' or 'learned' (Arabic). A female version of Ulim.

Ulrica
Variants and diminutives: Rica, Ula, Ulla, Ulli, Ullie, Ully, Ulrika, Ulrike.
Meaning: 'wolf' and 'ruler' (Germanic) as a female version of Ulric.
Notable namesakes: Ulrika Jonsson (British television personality).

Ultima
Variants and diminutives: Ulti, Ultie, Ulty.
Meaning: 'furthest' or 'last' (Latin). A female version of Ultimus.

Ulva
Variants and diminutives: Ulvi, Ulvie, Ulvy.
Meaning: 'she-wolf' (Old English).

Uma
Variants and diminutives: Ama, Amma.
Meaning: 'mother', 'light', 'peace of night' or 'desist' (Sanskrit); derived from the name of an ancient Indian creator goddess, also the shakti (female power) of Shiva, the Hindu god of destruction and personal destiny.
Notable namesakes: Uma Thurman (US actress).

Umay
Variants and diminutives: Umai.
Meaning: 'hopeful' (Turkish).

Umeko
Variants and diminutives: Ume, Umeyo.
Meaning: 'plum blossom' (Japanese).

Una
Variants and diminutives: Juno, Ona, Oona, Oonagh, Oonie, Unique, Unity.
Meaning: 'one' or 'together' (Latin); 'lamb' (Irish Gaelic).
Notable namesakes: a character in the poem *The Faerie Queene*, by English poet Edmund Spenser; Una Stubbs (British actress).

Undina
Variants and diminutives: Ondine, Undine.
Meaning: 'wave' or 'water', 'surge' or 'stream' (Latin).
Notable namesakes: Undine, a water nymph of Teutonic mythology, whose name has become a generic name for water nymphs, and the eponymous heroine of the story *Undine*, by German writer Friedrich von Fouqué, and of the play *Ondine*, by French writer Jean Giraudoux.

Unice
Variants and diminutives: Eunice.
Meaning: 'victorious' (Greek) as a variant of Eunice.

Unique
Variants and diminutives: Una, Unity.
Meaning: 'unparalleled' (Latin).

Unity
Variants and diminutives: Una, Unique.
Meaning: 'one' or 'together' (Latin).
Notable namesakes: Unity Mitford (British Nazi enthusiast and one of the celebrated Mitford sisters).

Urania
Variants and diminutives: Ourania.
Meaning: 'heavenly' (Greek). Also a female version of Uranus.
Notable namesakes: the goddess of astronomy, one of the Muses, as well as one of the Oceanides (water nymphs) and another name for Aphrodite, the goddess of love and beauty, in Greek mythology.

Urith
Variants and diminutives: Urice, Urit.
Meaning: 'light' or 'bright' (Hebrew). Also a female version of Uriah.
Notable namesakes: Saint Urith (Erth or Heiritha) of Chittlehampton.

Ursula
Variants and diminutives: Orsa, Orsel, Orsola, Sula, Ulla, Ulli, Urmi, Ursa, Ursala, Urse, Ursel, Ursie, Ursina, Ursine, Ursley, Ursola, Ursule, Ursulina, Ursuline, Ursi, Ursie, Ursy, Uschi, Urzula, Vorsila, Wuschi, Wuschie, Wuschy.
Meaning: 'little she-bear' (Latin). Also a female version of Ursell.
Notable namesakes: Ursa Major and Ursa Minor, constellations also respectively known as the Great Bear, Dipper or Plough and the Little Bear, Dipper or Plough; a moon goddess of Norse mythology equated with Saint Ursula, patron saint of girls, schoolgirls and the Ursuline order, a religious order of nuns dedicated to teaching founded by Saint Angela Merici; a character in William Shakespeare's play *Much Ado About Nothing*; the heroine of the novel *John Halifax, Gentleman,* by English writer Dinah Maria Craik; Ursula Brangwen, the heroine of *The Rainbow* and *Women in Love,* both novels by British writer D H Lawrence; Ursula Le Guin (US writer); Ursula Andress (Swiss actress).

Usha
Variants and diminutives: Ushi.
Meaning: 'dawn' or 'sunrise' (Hindi).

Utako
Variants and diminutives: Tako.
Meaning: 'poem' (Japanese).

Valda
Variants and diminutives: Velda.
Meaning: 'power' or 'rule' (Germanic) as a female version of Waldo.

Valentina
Variants and diminutives: Teena, Tina, Val, Vale, Valencia, Valentia, Valera, Valerie, Valida, Vallie.
Meaning: 'healthy' or 'vigorous' (Latin) as a female version of Valentine.

Valerie
Variants and diminutives: Lera, Lerka, Val, Valaree, Valaria, Valarie, Valarie, Valary, Vale, Valentina, Valentine, Valerey, Valeria, Valeriana, Valery, Valerye, Valka, Valli, Vallie, Vally, Valora, Valry, Valya, Wala, Waleria, .
Meaning: 'to be healthy' or 'to be vigorous' (Latin) as a female French version of Valerius.
Notable namesakes: Valeria Messalina, the promiscuous wife of Claudius I, Emperor of Rome; Saint Valeria.

Valeska
Variants and diminutives: Val.
Meaning: 'glorious' (Russian).

A B C D E F G H I J K L M N O P Q R S T U V W X Y Z

Valma

Variants and diminutives: Alma, Val, Velma, Vilma.
Meaning: uncertain; possibly 'may flower' (Celtic).

Valonia

Variants and diminutives: Val, Vallonia.
Meaning: 'acorn' (Greek); derived from a name for the unripe acorns and acorn cups of the *Quercus aegilops* species of oak tree, which are used for tanning, dyeing and ink-making.

Vanda

Variants and diminutives: Wanda.
Meaning: uncertain; possibly 'family' or 'wanderer' (Germanic) or derived from the name of a Germanic people, the Vandals, or 'wand' or 'shoot' (Old Norse) as a variant of Wanda; 'plait' (Congo and Mende – Africa).

Vanessa

Variants and diminutives: Essa, Ness, Nessa, Nessi, Nessie, Nessy, Van, Vana, Vania, Vanna, Vanni, Vannie, Vanny, Vanya, Venesa, Venessa.
Meaning: uncertain; possibly 'butterflies' (Greek); a name coined by the Irish writer Jonathan Swift by combining and reversing components of the name of one of his friends, Esther Vanhomrigh, for the eponymous heroine of his poem *Cadenus and Vanessa*.
Notable namesakes: the title of a novel by New Zealand-born British writer Hugh Walpole; Vanessa Bell (British artist and designer); Vanessa Redgrave (British actress).

Vania

Variants and diminutives: Ivana, Ivanna, Vanessa, Vanna, Vanya.
Meaning: 'God has favoured', 'God is gracious' or 'God is merciful' (Hebrew) as a diminutive of Ivanna (Ivana); possibly 'butterflies' (Greek) as a variant of Vanessa.

Vanna

Variants and diminutives: Ivana, Ivanna, Vanessa, Vania.
Meaning: 'God has favoured', 'God is gracious' or 'God is merciful' (Hebrew) as a diminutive of Ivanna (Ivana); possibly 'butterflies' (Greek) as a variant of Vanessa.

Vanora

Variants and diminutives: Vevay.
Meaning: 'white wave' (Celtic).

Varda

Variants and diminutives: Vardia, Vardice, Vardina, Vardis, Vardit, Vered.
Meaning: 'rose' (Hebrew and Arabic).

Vashti

Meaning: 'best' or 'lovely' (Persian).
Notable namesakes: a wife of King Ahasuerus in the Old Testament.

Veda

Meaning: 'knowledge' or 'I know' (Sanskrit).
Notable namesakes: a number of sacred ancient Hindu writings, such as the Rig-Veda.

Vela

Variants and diminutives: Vella.
Meaning: 'sail' (Latin); derived from the name of a constellation of the Southern Hemisphere.

Velda

Variants and diminutives: Valda.
Meaning: uncertain; possibly 'power' or 'rule' (Germanic) as a variant of Valda; possibly 'field' (Germanic).

Velika

Variants and diminutives: Lika, Veli.
Meaning: 'great' (Slavonic).

Velma

Variants and diminutives: Valma, Vilma, Wilhelmina, Willa, Wilma.
Meaning: uncertain; possibly 'will' and 'helmet' or 'protection' (Germanic) as a diminutive of Wilhelmina (William).

Velvet

Variants and diminutives: Velve, Velvi, Velvie, Velvy.

Meaning: 'hairy' (Old French).
Notable namesakes: a type of fabric; velvet glove, an expression indicating careful handling; velvet revolution, an expression denoting the peaceful overthrow of a ruling regime; velvet scoter, the common name of the *Melanitta fusca* species of sea duck; velvet shank, the common name of the *Flammulina velutipes* species of edible fungus; the Velvet Underground, a US rock group; Velvet Brown, the heroine of the novel *National Velvet,* by British writer Enid Bagnold.

Venetia

Variants and diminutives: Venda, Veneta, Venezia, Venita, Venus, Vinetia, Vinita.
Meaning: 'district of the Veneti' (Latin), the Veneti referring to the ancient people who established Venetia, today the Veneto (Venezia-Euganea) region of Italy, whose capital is Venice (Venezia).
Notable namesakes: the eponymous heroine of the novel *Venetia,* by British writer and politician Benjamin Disraeli.

Ventura

Meaning: 'good fortune' (Spanish).

Venus

Variants and diminutives: Venita, Vespera, Vin, Vinita, Vinnie, Vinny.
Meaning: 'beauty', 'charm' or 'love' (Latin); derived from the name of the goddess of love and beauty in Roman mythology.
Notable namesakes: a planet that is also known as the Morning or Evening Star (Vesper); Venusburg, a mountain in Germany; Venus's looking glass, the common name of the *Legousia hybrida* species of flowering plant; Venus's-hair, the common name of the *Adiantum capillus-veneris* species of maidenhair fern; Venus flytrap, the common name of the *Dionaea muscipula* species of insectivorous plant; Venus's flower basket, the common name of the *Euplectella* genus of deep-sea sponges; Venus's-girdle, the common name of the *Cestum veneris* species of ctenophore; Venus Williams (US tennis player).

Vera

Variants and diminutives: Verasha, Vere, Verena, Verene, Verina, Verine, Verinka, Verity, Verka, Verla, Veronica, Verusya, Viera, Wera, Wiera, Wiercia, Wierka.
Meaning: 'truthful' (Latin); 'faith' (Russian).
Notable namesakes: characters in the novels *Moths,* by the British writer Ouida, and *A Cigarette-maker's Romance,* by British writer Marion Crawford; Vera Fyodorovna Panova (Russian writer); Vera Lynn (British singer).

Verena

Variants and diminutives: Vera, Veradis, Vere, Verene, Verina, Verine, Verinka, Verita, Verity, Verla, Verna, Verochka, Veronica, Virna.
Meaning: uncertain; possibly 'truthful' (Latin) or 'faith' (Russian) as a variant of Vera; possibly 'a slave born in [his or] her master's house' or 'of spring' (Latin) or 'alder tree' (Old French) as a variant of Verna.
Notable namesakes: Saint Verena.

Verity

Variants and diminutives: Vera, Verena.
Meaning: 'truth' (Latin).

Verna

Variants and diminutives: Verena, Verona.
Meaning: 'a slave born in [his or] her master's house' or 'of spring' (Latin); 'alder tree' (Old French) as a female version of Vernon.

Verona

Variants and diminutives: Rona, Verna, Verone, Veronica.
Meaning: uncertain; possibly 'certainly' or 'indeed' (Latin) when derived from the name of the city in the Veneto region of Italy; possibly 'true image' (Latin) as a variant of Veronica.

Veronica

Variants and diminutives: Berenice, Berenike, Bernice, Nika, Ron, Roni, Ronie, Ronni, Ronnie, Ronny, Vera, Verenice, Verona, Verone,

Veronika, Veronike, Véronique, Veronka, Vonni, Vonnie, Vonny, Vron, Vronni, Vronnie, Vronny.
Meaning: 'true image' (Latin), referring to the cloth that, according to traditional Christian belief, was miraculously imprinted with the image of Christ's face after Saint Veronica offered it to him to wipe away his sweat on the road to Calgary.
Notable namesakes: Saint Veronica, patron saint of photographers; a genus of flowering plants; a matador's pass made in bullfighting; Veronica Lake (US actress).

Vespera

Variants and diminutives: Vespi, Vespie, Vespy.
Meaning: 'evening' or 'evening star' (Latin); derived from Vesper, the alternative name of the planet Venus when visible in the evening.
Notable namesakes: vesper, an old word for the evening and also the name of an evening prayer, hymn or service in Christian tradition.

Vesta

Variants and diminutives: Vessi, Vessie, Vessy, Star.
Meaning: uncertain; possibly 'goddess of the hearth' or 'keeper of the sacred flame' (Latin); derived from the name of the goddess of the hearth in Roman mythology, in whose temple in Rome the Vestal virgins tended a perpetual flame.
Notable namesakes: an asteroid; an alternative name for a match.

Vevila

Variants and diminutives: Vevi, Vila.
Meaning: 'harmonious' or 'together' (Celtic).

Victoria

Variants and diminutives: Nike, Tora, Tory, Vic, Vici, Vick, Vicki, Vickie, Vicky, Victoire, Victoriana, Victorina, Victorine, Vika, Viki, Vikie, Vikki, Vikkie, Vikky, Viktoria, Viktorie, Viktorija, Viktorka, Viky, Vita, Vitoria, Vittoria, Viqui.

Meaning: 'victory' (Latin).
Notable namesakes: the goddess of victory in Roman mythology; Saint Victoria; Victoria, Queen of the United Kingdom and Empress of India, from whose name the adjective Victorian, referring to her reign and various aspects of it, such as its artistic or design style (also dubbed Victoriana), is derived, and for whom a number of places and institutions are named, including a state and the Great Victoria Desert in Australia; the capital of British Columbia, Canada, as well as of the Seychelles; Victoria Island in the Canadian Arctic; Victoria Land in Antarctica; Mount Victoria in Papua New Guinea; a district of Hong Kong; Lake Victoria (Victoria Nyanza) in Africa; Victoria Falls (Mosi-oa-tunya), a waterfall on the Zambezi river in Africa; the Victoria and Albert Museum and Victoria Station in London; the Victoria Cross, a British decoration honouring conspicuous gallantry; a type of horse-drawn carriage; a genus of water lily; a variety of plum; and Victoria Day, a national holiday in Canada. Other notable Victorias include Victoria Holt, a pseudonym of the English novelist Eleanor Hibbert, Crown Princess Victoria of Sweden, Victoria Wood (British comedienne) and Victoria Beckham (British singer).

Victorine

Variants and diminutives: Tori, Vic, Vicki, Vickie, Vicky, Victoria, Victoriana, Victorina, Vikki, Vikkie, Vikky.
Meaning: 'victor' (Latin) as a female version of Victor.

Vida

Variants and diminutives: Davida.
Meaning: 'beloved' or 'friend' (Hebrew) as a diminutive of Davida (David).

Vina

Variants and diminutives: Davina, Lavina, Vinia.
Meaning: 'wine' (Latin); also a diminutive of any name ending in '-vina', such as Davina, meaning 'beloved' or friend' (Hebrew) as a female version of David.

Vincentia

Variants and diminutives: Centia, Vin, Vince, Vinnie, Vinny.

Meaning: 'conqueror' (Latin) as a female version of Vincent.

Viola

Variants and diminutives: Vi, Violet, Violetta, Violette.
Meaning: 'violet' (Latin); derived from the name of the genus of flowering plants that includes violets and pansies.
Notable namesakes: a type of violin derived from the viol family of stringed instruments that included the viola da braccia, the viola da gamba and the viola d'amore; viola clef, in musical notation, another name for the alto clef; a leading character in William Shakespeare's play *Twelfth Night*.

Violet

Variants and diminutives: Vi, Viola, Violante, Violeta, Violetta, Violette, Voleta, Voletta, Yolanda, Yolande, Yolane.
Meaning: 'little violet' (Old French) as a variant of Viola; derived from the common name of various species of the *Viola* genus of flowering plants.
Notable namesakes: a purple colour; shrinking violet, an expression used to describe a shy or modest person; Violet Hunt (British writer); Violette Leduc (French writer); Violet Elizabeth Bott, a character in the 'Just William' series of children's books by British writer Richmal Crompton.

Violetta

Variants and diminutives: Vi, Viola, Violet, Violeta, Violette, Voleta, Voletta.
Meaning: 'little violet' (Italian) as a variant of Viola.
Notable namesakes: the heroine of the opera *La Traviata*, by Italian composer Giuseppe Verdi.

Virginia

Variants and diminutives: Gina, Ginata, Ginger, Ginia, Ginney, Ginni, Ginnie, Ginny, Jinni, Jinnie, Jinny, Vegenia, Vergie, Vinnie, Vinny, Virgie, Virginie, Virgy, Wilikinia.
Meaning: 'virgin' or 'maiden' (Latin); derived from the Roman family name Verginius or Virginius.
Notable namesakes: a beautiful Roman whom her father killed rather than allowing her to be enslaved by Appius Claudius Crassus; Virgo, a constellation and sign of the zodiac; Saint Virginia; an alternative name for Queen Elizabeth I of England, 'the Virgin Queen', for whom the US state of Virginia was named, the state in turn giving its name to a number of Virginias, including Virginia Dare, the first child born to English settlers in Virginia, Virginia Beach, a city in Virginia, the vine known as Virginia creeper (*Parthenocissus quinquefolia*), a type of tobacco and the Virginia reel, a type of dance; Virginia stock, the common name of the *Malcomia maritima* species of flowering plant; Virginia deer, another name for the white-tailed deer, *Odocoileus virginianus*; the heroine of the novel *Paul et Virginie*, by French writer Jacques Henri Bernadin de Saint-Pierre; Virginia Woolf (British writer); Virginia McKenna (British actress); Virginia Wade (British tennis player); Virginia Bottomley (British politician).

Vita

Variants and diminutives: Victoria, Vida, Viva, Viviana, Vivien.
Meaning: 'life' (Latin); 'victory' (Latin) as a diminutive of Victoria.
Notable namesakes: Vita (Victoria) Sackville-West (British writer).

Viva

Variants and diminutives: Vita, Viv, Vivia, Viviana, Vivien.
Meaning: 'to live' (Latin).
Notable namesakes: an exclamation meaning 'Long live ...!'; an abbreviation of viva voce, a type of oral examination.

Vivia

Variants and diminutives: Vita, Viv, Viva, Viviana, Vivien.
Meaning: 'to live' (Latin) as a variant of Viva; 'living' (Latin) as a variant of Vivien.

Vivien

Variants and diminutives: Bibiana, Fithian, Vevay, Vita, Viv, Viva, Viveca, Vivevca, Vivi, Vivia, Vivian, Viviana, Viviane, Vivianne, Vivie, Vivien, Vivienne, Vivyan, Vyvyan.

Meaning: 'living' (Latin); derived fom the Roman family name Vivianus. Also a boy's name (generally Vivian or Vyvyan).
Notable namesakes: a name for the Lady of the Lake in the *Idylls of the King*, a cycle of Arthurian poems by English poet Alfred, Lord Tennyson; Vivien Leigh (British actress); Vivienne Westwood (British fashion designer).

Waikiki
Variants and diminutives: Kiki.
Meaning: 'spring' or 'flowing water' (Hawaiian).
Notable namesakes: a resort area in Hawaii.

Walburga
Variants and diminutives: Walpurga.
Meaning: 'power' and 'protection' or 'fortress' (Germanic and Old English).
Notable namesakes: Saint Walburga (or Walpurga), patron saint of famine alleviation, on the eve of whose feast day (1 May), called *Walpurgisnacht* or Walpurgis Night, according to German folklore, witches convene for a sabbath on the Brocken, in the Harz Mountains.

Walda
Variants and diminutives: Waldi, Waldie, Waldy.
Meaning: 'power' or 'rule' and 'people' or 'army' (Germanic) as a female version of Walter.

Wallis
Variants and diminutives: Wallace, Wallie, Wally.
Meaning: 'Celt', 'Breton', 'Welshman' or 'foreigner' (Old French); derived from an English family name. Also a boy's name.
Notable namesakes: Wallis and Futuna, island groups in the Pacific Ocean; Wallis Simpson (née Warfield), the Duchess of Windsor.

Wanda
Variants and diminutives: Vanda, Vandis, Vona, Vonda, Wanaka, Wandi, Wandie, Wandis, Wandy, Wandzia, Wanja, Wenda, Wendeline, Wendi, Wendy, Wendye.
Meaning: uncertain; possibly 'family' or 'wanderer' (Germanic) or derived from the name of a Germanic people, the Vandals; possibly 'wand' or 'shoot' (Old Norse).
Notable namesakes: the eponymous heroine of the novel *Wanda*, by British writer Ouida; the heroine of the British film *A Fish Called Wanda*.

Warrene
Variants and diminutives: Warnette, Waurene.
Meaning: 'game preserve', 'wasteland' or 'sandy soil' (Gaulish) or 'to protect' or 'to preserve' (Germanic) as a female version of Warren.

Welcome
Meaning: 'welcome' (Old English). Also a boy's name.

Wenda
Variants and diminutives: Vendelin, Wanda, Wendeline, Wendey, Wendi, Wendoline, Wendy.
Meaning: uncertain; possibly 'to change course' (Old Norse); possibly 'family' or 'wanderer' (Germanic) or derived from the name of a Germanic people, the Vandals, or 'wand' or 'shoot' (Old Norse) as a variant of Wanda; possibly 'fair' and 'ring' (Welsh) as a diminutive of Wendoline (Gwendolyn); possibly a variant of Wendy. Also a female version of Wendell.

Wendoline
Variants and diminutives: Gwendoline, Gwendolyn, Vendelin, Wenda, Wendelin, Wendeline, Wendey, Wendi, Wendie, Wendolin, Wendy.
Meaning: 'fair' and 'ring' (Welsh) as a variant of Gwendolyn.

Wendy
Variants and diminutives: Wenda, Wendey, Wendi, Wendie.
Meaning: uncertain; coined by the Scottish writer J M Barrie for the leading female character of his play

Peter Pan, having been inspired by Margaret Henley, a young girl who called him her 'friendy-wendy' or 'fwendy-wendy'.
Notable namesakes: Wendy house, a model house for children to play in named after Wendy's house in *Peter Pan,* the above-mentioned play; Wendy Craig and Wendy Hiller (British actresses).

Whitney
Variants and diminutives: Whitley, Whitnee, Whitni, Whitnie, Whitny, Witney.
Meaning: 'white' or 'White's' and 'island' (Old English); derived from an English family name, in turn derived from an English place name. Also a boy's name.
Notable namesakes: Whitney Houston (US singer).

Wilfreda
Variants and diminutives: Freda, Frida, Wilfrida.
Meaning: 'will' and 'peace' (Germanic) as a female version of Wilfred.

Wilhelmina
Variants and diminutives: Bill, Billi, Billie, Billy, Guglielma, Guilette, Guilla, Guillelmine, Guillema, Guillemette, Guillerma, Guillermina, Helma, Helmine, Ilma, Mimi, Min, Mina, Minchen, Minka, Minna, Minette, Mini, Minni, Minnie, Minny, Valma, Velma, Vilhelmina, Vilma, Vilna, Wileen, Wiletta, Wilette, Wilhelma, Wilhelmine, Willa, Willabelle, Willamae, Willamina, Willandra, Willene, Willeta, Willetta, Willette, Willi, Williamina, Willie, Willy, Wilma, Wilmena, Wilmet, Wilmette, Wylma.
Meaning: 'will' and 'helmet' or 'protection' (Germanic) as a female version of William.
Notable namesakes: Queen Wilhelmina I of The Netherlands.

Willa
Variants and diminutives: Wilhelmina, Willabelle, Willamae, Willamina, Willandra, Willlene, Willeta, Willetta, Willette, Willi, Williamina, Willow, Willy, Wilma.
Meaning: 'continuation' (Arabic); 'will' and 'helmet' or 'protection' (Germanic) as a female version of William.
Notable namesakes: Willa Cather (US writer).

Willow
Variants and diminutives: Willa, Wilda.
Meaning: 'twisted' (Greek); 'willow tree' (Old English); derived from the common name of the *Salix* genus of trees and shrubs.
Notable namesakes: Willow South, a city in the US state of Alaska; willowherb, the common name of the *Epilobium* genus of flowering plants; willow pattern, a decorative pattern incorporating a willow tree used for pottery and porcelain; willow grouse, the common name of the *Lagopus lagopus* species of grouse; willow warbler, the common name of the *Phylloscopus trochilis* species of warbler; willow tit, the common name of the *Parus montanus* species of tit.

Wilma
Variants and diminutives: Vilma, Vilna, Wilhelmina, Willa, Williamina, Wilmena, Wilmet, Wilmette, Wylma.
Meaning: 'will' and 'helmet' or 'protection' (Germanic) as a diminutive of Wilhelmina; 'will' and 'fame' (Germanic) as a female version of Wilmer.
Notable namesakes: Wilma Flintstone, a character in the US animated-cartoon television series *The Flintstones.*

Winema
Variants and diminutives: Nema, Win, Winnie, Winny.
Meaning: 'female chief' (Miwok – Native American).

Winifred
Variants and diminutives: Freda, Freddi, Freddie, Freddy, Fredi, Guinever, Gwenevere, Gwenfrewi, Gwinevere, Oona, Una, Usa, Vinette, Wenefreda, Win, Winefred, Winefride, Winie, Winifrin, Winn, Winnie, Winnifred, Winnifride, Winny, Wyn, Wynelle, Wynifred, Wynn, Wynne.
Meaning: 'reconciliation' (Welsh) and 'peace' (Old English); 'friend' and 'peace' (Old English) as a female version of Winfred.
Notable namesakes: Saint Winifred.

Winna

Variants and diminutives: Winn, Winni, Winnie,
Winny.
Meaning: 'relaxed' (Arabic).

Winona

Variants and diminutives: Wenona, Wenonah,
Wenonoah, Winnie, Winonah, Wynona.
Meaning: 'bliss' or 'joy' (Germanic); 'first-born
daughter' (Sioux – Native American).
Notable namesakes: Winona Ryder (US actress).

Xanthe

Variants and diminutives: Xantha, Xantho, Zanth,
Zantha, Zanthe.
Meaning: 'yellow' or 'bright' (Greek). A female version
of Xanthus.
Notable namesakes: one of the Oceanides (water
nymphs), as well as one of the Amazons of Greek
mythology; Xantho, one of the Nereides (sea nymphs)
of Greek mythology.

Xanthippe

Variants and diminutives:
Xantippe.
Meaning: 'yellow' and 'horse'
(Greek).
Notable namesakes: a
daughter of Dorus in Greek
mythology; the wife of the
Greek philosopher Socrates,
whose difficult behaviour
has resulted in her name
being used to denote a
nagging or quarrelsome woman.

Xaviera

Variants and diminutives: Javier, Xavier.
Meaning: 'new house' (Basque) or 'bright' or 'brilliant'
(Arabic) as a female version of Xavier.

Xenia

Variants and diminutives: Cena, Chimene, Xena,
Xene, Ximena, Xiomara, Zena, Zenia.
Meaning: 'hospitable' (Greek).
Notable namesakes: an alternative name of Athena,
the goddess of war and crafts in Greek mythology, as
well as of a nymph who fell in love with with the
shepherd Daphnis; a botanical process relating to the
influence of pollen.

Xylophila

Variants and diminutives: Phil, Phila, Philli, Phillie,
Philly, Xylo, Xylona, Zilo.
Meaning: 'wood' and 'lover' (Greek).

Yakira

Variants and diminutives: Kira, Yaki.
Meaning: 'precious' or 'beloved' (Hebrew). A female
version of Yakir.

Yarkona

Variants and diminutives: Kona.
Meaning: 'green' (Hebrew).
Notable namesakes: the name of a bird indigenous to
Israel.

Yarmilla

Variants and diminutives: Milla.
Meaning: 'market trader' (Slavonic).

Yasmin

Variants and diminutives: Jasmeen, Jasmin, Jasmine,

Yasiman, Yasmeen, Yasmin, Yasmina, Yasmine.
Meaning: 'jasmine flower' (Persian and Arabic).
Notable namesakes: the heroine of the play *Hassan*, by British writer James Elroy Flecker; Yasmin Le Bon (British model).

Yasu
Variants and diminutives: Yasuko, Yasuyo.
Meaning: 'calm' or 'peaceful' (Japanese).

Yedida
Variants and diminutives: Yedidah.
Meaning: 'beloved friend' (Hebrew).

Yehuda
Variants and diminutives: Judith, Yehudit, Yudif, Yudit, Yudita, Yuta.
Meaning: 'Jewish woman' (Hebrew) as a variant of Judith; 'praise' (Hebrew) as a female variant of Judah or Jude. Also a boy's name.

Yelena
Variants and diminutives: Helen, Helena.
Meaning: 'bright' (Greek) as a Russian version of Helena (Helen).

Yemina
Variants and diminutives: Mina.
Meaning: 'child of my right hand' or 'favourite child' (Hebrew) as a female version of Benjamin.

Yeshisha
Variants and diminutives: Shisha, Yeshi.
Meaning: 'old' (Hebrew)

Yigala
Variants and diminutives: Yigaala.
Meaning: 'God will redeem' (Hebrew) as a female version of Yigal.

Yoko
Meaning: 'across', 'ocean', 'female' or 'positive' (Japanese).
Notable namesakes: Yoko Ono (Japanese-born US artist and musician).

Yolande
Variants and diminutives: Eolanda, Eolande, Iolanda, Iolande, Iolanthe, Iolende, Jola, Jolan, Jolande, Jolanka, Jolanta, Joleicia, Jolenta, Joli, Olinda, Viola, Violet, Violante, Yola, Yolanda, Yolane, Yolanta, Yolanthe, Yoli.
Meaning: 'little violet' (Old French) as a variant of Violet, in turn a French variant of Viola; 'violet' or 'dawn cloud' (Greek) as a variant of Iolanthe.
Notable namesakes: the eponymous heroine of the opera *Yolanta*, by Russian composer Pyotr Ilyich Tchaikovsky.

Yovela
Variants and diminutives: Vela, Yovi.
Meaning: 'ram's horn', 'rejoicing' or 'celebration' (Hebrew).

Yseult
Variants and diminutives: Isaut, Iseult, Iseut, Isola, Isolda, Isolde, Isolt.
Meaning: 'ice' and 'rule' (Germanic) or 'lovely' (Welsh) as a French variant of Iseult (Isolde).

Yuki
Variants and diminutives: Yukie, Yukiko, Yukiyo.
Meaning: 'fortunate' or 'snow' (Japanese).
Notable namesakes: Yuki-onne, or 'Snow Maiden', a goddess who bestows a painless death in Japanese traditional belief.

Yulan
Meaning: 'gem' and 'plant' (Chinese); derived from the name of a Chinese magnolia, *Magnolia denudata*.

Yvette
Variants and diminutives: Ivetta, Yevette, Yve, Yvonne.
Meaning: 'yew' or 'small archer' (Germanic) or 'God has favoured', 'God is gracious' or 'God is merciful' (Hebrew) as a female version of Yves (Ivo and John).

Yvonne
Variants and diminutives: Evon, Evona, Evonne, Ivona, Ivone, Iwona, Iwonka, Yvone, Yvette.
Meaning: 'yew' or 'small archer' (Germanic) or 'God

has favoured', 'God is gracious' or 'God is merciful' (Hebrew) as a female version of Yves (Ivo and John).
Notable namesakes: Evonne Goolagong (Australian tennis player).

Zada
Variants and diminutives: Zada, Zaida, Zayda.
Meaning: 'fortunate' (Arabic).

Zahara
Variants and diminutives: Sahara, Zahra.
Meaning: 'flower' (Swahili – Africa) as a female version of Zahur; 'desert' (Arabic) as a variant of Sahara.

Zahira
Variants and diminutives: Sarah, Zaharita, Zaira, Zara.
Meaning: uncertain; possibly 'flower', 'splendour', 'eastern splendour' or 'dawn brightness' (Arabic) as a variant of Zara; possibly 'princess' (Hebrew) as a variant of Zara and Sarah.

Zaida
Variants and diminutives: Zadam, Zaidah, Zayda.
Meaning: 'growth', 'prosperity' or 'good luck' (Arabic).

Zalika
Variants and diminutives: Zuleika.
Meaning: 'well-born' (Swahili – African).

Zana
Variants and diminutives: Susannah, Zsa Zsa, Zuska, Zuza, Zuzana, Zuzanna, Zuzia, Zuzka, Zuzanka
Meaning: uncertain; possibly 'woman' (Persian); possibly 'alert' or 'vivacious' (Arabic); possibly 'lily' (Hebrew) as a diminutive of Susannah.

Notable namesakes: a goddess of beauty and courage in Balkan mythology.

Zandra
Variants and diminutives: Alexandra, Sandra.
Meaning: 'defender of men' or 'warrior' (Greek) as a diminutive of Alexandra, in turn a female version of Alexander.
Notable namesakes: Zandra Rhodes (British fashion designer).

Zara
Variants and diminutives: Sara, Sarah, Zahira, Zahirita, Zaira, Zarah.
Meaning: uncertain; possibly 'flower', 'splendour', 'eastern splendour' or 'dawn brightness' (Arabic); possibly 'princess' (Hebrew) as a variant of Sarah.
Notable namesakes: Mama Zara, a goddess of grain in Peruvian belief; a character – an African queen – in the play *The Mourning Bride*, by English playwright William Congreve; Zara Phillips, the daughter of Princess Anne of the United Kingdom and Mark Phillips.

Zarifa
Meaning: 'graceful' (Arabic).

Zarina
Meaning: 'golden' or 'golden vessel' (Persian).

Zariza
Variants and diminutives: Zeriza.
Meaning: 'hard-working' (Hebrew).

Zayit
Variants and diminutives: Zeta, Zetana.
Meaning: 'olive' (Hebrew). Also a boy's name.

Zaza
Variants and diminutives: Zazu.
Meaning: 'movement' (Hebrew).

Zea
Variants and diminutives: Zia.
Meaning: 'grain' (Latin).

Zehava
Variants and diminutives: Zehara, Zehari, Zehavi, Zehavit, Zehuva, Zohar, Zoheret.
Meaning: 'gold' or 'brilliant' (Hebrew).

Zehira
Meaning: 'protected' (Hebrew).

Zelda
Variants and diminutives: Griselda, Selda, Zelde.
Meaning: uncertain; possibly 'happiness' (Yiddish); possibly 'grey' and 'battle' (Germanic) as a diminutive of Griselda.
Notable namesakes: Zelda Sayre, the wife of US writer F Scott Fitzgerald.

Zelia
Variants and diminutives: Zele, Zelie, Zelina.
Meaning: 'zealous' (Hebrew).

Zelma
Variants and diminutives: Anselma, Selma.
Meaning: 'divine' and 'helmet' (Old German) or 'related to nobility' (Old French) as a diminutive of Anselma, in turn a female version of Anselm.

Zena
Variants and diminutives: Xena, Xenia, Zenia.
Meaning: uncertain; possibly 'woman' (Persian); possibly 'hospitable' (Greek) as a variant of Xenia.

Zenda
Meaning: 'sacred' (Persian).
Notable namesakes: the name of a castle in the novel *The Prisoner of Zenda*, by English writer Anthony Hope Hawkins.

Zenobia
Variants and diminutives: Zena, Zenaida, Zenda, Zenia, Zenna, Zenobie, Zinaida.
Meaning: 'power of Zeus' (Greek), referring to the supreme god of Greek mythology, whose name means 'shining', 'bright' or 'bright sky' (Greek).
Notable namesakes: a queen of Palmyra, the widow of Odaenathus, who was captured following the battle of Homs and taken to Rome by the Roman emperor Aurelian.

Zephira
Variants and diminutives: Zephyr.
Meaning: 'morning' (Hebrew); also 'the west wind' (Greek) as a female version of Zephyr.

Zeta
Variants and diminutives: Zayit, Zetana, Zetta, Zita.
Meaning: 'sixth' (Greek), referring to the name of the sixth letter of the Greek alphabet; possibly 'to seek' (Greek), 'girl' (Italian), 'little rose' (Spanish) or 'harvest', 'reap' or 'from Thera [or Therasia]' (Greek) as a variant of Zita.
Notable namesakes: in astronomy, a name for the sixth-brightest star of a constellation; Catherine Zeta Jones (Welsh actress).

Zevida
Variants and diminutives: Zevuda.
Meaning: 'gift' (Hebrew).

Zhen
Meaning: 'treasure' (Chinese).

Zia
Variants and diminutives: Zea.
Meaning: 'to shiver' or 'to tremble' (Hebrew). Also a boy's name.

Zigana
Meaning: 'Gypsy' (Hungarian).

Zilla
Variants and diminutives: Zila, Zillah, Zilli.
Meaning: 'shadow' or 'shade' (Hebrew).
Notable namesakes: Zillah, a wife of Lamech in the Old Testament.

Zilpah
Meaning: 'sprinkling' or 'dripping' (Hebrew).
Notable namesakes: the

mother of Asher and Gad by Jacob in the Old Testament.

Zina

Variants and diminutives: Zeena, Zinaida, Zinnia.
Meaning: 'mystical name' (Nsenga – Africa).

Zinnia

Variants and diminutives: Zeena, Zina.
Meaning: uncertain; derived from the name of the genus of flowering plants named for the German botanist Johann Gottfried Zinn.

Zipporah

Variants and diminutives: Cipora, Zippora.
Meaning: 'bird' (Hebrew).
Notable namesakes: a daughter of Jethro and wife of Moses in the Old Testament.

Zita

Variants and diminutives: Citha, Rosita, Sitha, Zeta.
Meaning: uncertain; possibly 'to seek' (Greek); possibly 'girl' (Italian); possibly 'little rose' (Spanish) as a diminutive of Rosita (Rosa); possibly 'harvest', 'reap' or 'from Thera [or Therasia]' (Greek) as a diminutive of Theresa.
Notable namesakes: Saint Zita, patron saint of the Italian town of Lucca, as well as of home-makers, servants, maids and other domestic workers, bakers and people who have lost their keys; the Empress Zita, wife of Karl Franz Josef, the last Habsburg emperor of Austria and king of Hungary.

Ziva

Variants and diminutives: Siva, Zivit.
Meaning: 'to shine radiantly' (Hebrew). A female version of Ziv.
Notable namesakes: a goddess of life in Slavic mythology.

Zizi

Variants and diminutives: Elizabeth.
Meaning: 'God is perfection', 'God is satisfaction',

'dedicated to God' or 'God's oath' (Hebrew) as a Hungarian diminutive of Elizabeth.
Notable namesakes: a creator goddess, also known as Zizia, in Teutonic mythology.

Zoë

Variants and diminutives: Eve, Vita, Zoe, Zoé, Zoey.
Meaning: 'life' (Greek).
Notable namesakes: an Aeon (angel) of Gnostic belief; Saint Zoë; an empress of Byzantium; Zoe Oldenbourg (Russian-born French writer); Zoë Wannamaker (British actress); Zoë Ball (British television and radio presenter).

Zohra

Variants and diminutives: Zarya, Zora, Zorah, Zorana, Zoreen, Zoreene, Zorene, Zorina, Zorine, Zorna.
Meaning: 'blooming' or 'dawning' (Arabic).

Zola

Variants and diminutives:
Meaning: uncertain; possibly derived from a French family name, a famous bearer of which was the French writer Emile Zola, in turn possibly derived from the German word for 'toll'. Also a boy's name.
Notable namesakes: Zola Budd, a controversial South African athlete.

Zorya

Variants and diminutives: Zarya, Zohra, Zora, Zorah, Zorana, Zoreen, Zoreene, Zorene, Zori, Zorie, Zorina, Zorine, Zorna, Zory.
Meaning: 'golden dawn' (Slavonic).
Notable namesakes: Zorya Utrennyaya, the goddess of dawn in Slavic mythology.

Zsa Zsa

Variants and diminutives: Susannah, Zana, Zuza.
Meaning: 'lily' (Hebrew) as a Hungarian diminutive of Susannah.
Notable namesakes: Zsa Zsa Gabor (Hungarian-born US actress).

Zuleika

Variants and diminutives: Zalika.

Meaning: 'radiant beauty' (Persian); 'lovely girl' (Arabic).

Notable namesakes: the wife (sometimes also called Rahil) of Potiphar in the Old Testament; the heroine of the poem *The Bride of Abydos*, by English poet George, Lord Byron; the eponymous heroine of the novel *Zuleika Dobson*, by English writer Max Beerbohm; the heroine of *The Emperor's Babe*, a novel in verse by British writer Bernadine Evaristo.

Zulema

Variants and diminutives: Salome, Suleima, Zuelia, Zuleika, Zuleima.

Meaning: 'peace' (Arabic); 'peace' or 'peace of Zion' (Hebrew) as a variant of Salome.

Credits and acknowledgements

The author would like to thank Emily Wood, Judith Millidge, Mark Akiwumi and Mike Haworth-Maden for their help in contributing to, and clarifying, some of the source material used in the writing of this book. Thanks, too, to John and Marianne Gibson for sharing their impressive knowledge of matters etymological and philological.

All images © stockbyte, except pp21&171,© D&S Books Ltd.

Bibliography

Ann, Martha, and Myers Imel, Dorothy, *Goddesses in World Mythology*, Oxford University Press, Oxford, 1993.

Benét, William Rose, *The Reader's Encyclopedia*, Guild Publishing, London, 1988.

Browder, Sue, *The New Age Baby Name Book*, Workman Publishing, New York, 1998.

Byars, Mel, *The Design Encyclopedia*, Laurence King Publishing, London, 1994.

Celtic Mythology, Geddes & Grosset, New Lanark, 1999.

Cottle, Basil, *The Penguin Dictionary of Surnames*, Penguin Books, London, 1978.

Crystal, David, *The Cambridge Encyclopedia of Language*, Cambridge University Press, Cambridge, 1987.

Fergusson, Rosalind, *Choose Your Baby's Name*, Penguin Books, London, 1987.

The Hutchinson Softback Encyclopedia, The Softback Preview, London, 1991.

Macleod, Iseabail, and Freedman, Terry, *The Wordsworth Dictionary of First Names*, Wordsworth Editions Ltd, Ware, 1995.

Nicholson, Louise, *The Best Baby Name Book*, Thorsons, London, 1990.

Read, Herbert (Consulting Editor), *The Thames and Hudson Dictionary of Art and Artists*, Thames and Hudson Ltd, London, 1994.

Wood, Emily, *The New Virgin Book of Baby Names*, Virgin Publishing Ltd, London, 2000.